The
Three
Edwards

A HISTORY OF THE PLANTAGENETS

The
Three
Edwards

By THOMAS B. COSTAIN

DOUBLEDAY & COMPANY, INC.
Garden City, New York

Contents

Book Three: EDWARD THE THIRD

Book One

EDWARD THE FIRST

CHAPTER ONE
A Proper King Is Crowned

1

THE Crusades were running down like an unwound clock. For nearly two hundred years men had been suffering and dying under the blistering sun of the desert without gaining any lasting results. Only the hold that saintly King Louis of France had on the hearts and minds of men had made another effort possible in this year of grace 1270; and the fact that he had again unfurled the flag with the gallant cross brings to the fore a young man who was to play a very great part in history.

Prince Edward, heir to the throne of England, had taken the cross at once. He was granted a subsidy by Parliament and on August 11 had sailed from Dover with a small band of zealous Englishmen. King Louis had taken his army to Africa earlier with the intention of striking into the Holy Land through Egypt. Edward's wife, the lovely Eleanor of Castile, had also gone ahead.

When the little English fleet arrived off Tunis, the prince learned that the great French king was dead. The blood burned fiercely in his veins when he was told that the son who had succeeded him had decided to abandon the crusade and was taking back to France the army his father had raised.

"By the blood of God!" cried Edward in a fine Plantagenet rage. "Though all my fellow soldiers and countrymen desert me, I will enter Acre with Fowin, the groom of my palfrey, and I will keep my word and my oath to the death!"

He was thirty-one years old; tall and long-legged, and with the handsome head of the Plantagenets, the golden hair, the blazing blue eyes, and the finely chiseled features. As would soon be made clear, he had all the good qualities of his family and few of their many bad ones; and he had something no Plantagenet had ever before possessed—a true sense of the responsibility of kingship, with a desire to rule justly and well when his turn came. He was going to make a great king, this Edward, perhaps England's greatest.

He found that, after all, he could depend on the aid of more than Fowin. Every man in the company responded when he announced his intention of going on. And on they went, a sorry little force of slightly more than a thousand men, a few knights, a few stout English bowmen, a few Frisians. Could anything have been more rash and foolhardy? But on the other hand nothing would have served so well to kindle again the guttering light of crusading zeal; if the spark, alas, had not been so close to total extinction.

It was particularly daring because all of the Near East had been roused to fighting pitch by the efforts of a far more dangerous leader than the chivalrous Saladin who had opposed Richard of the Lion-Heart. A former slave in Egypt named Bibars had risen from the ranks of the Mamelukes (a body of professional fighting men) and had made himself sultan. Bibars was cruel, unscrupulous, fiercely ambitious, and incredibly able. He meant to weld the Near East into an entity under his own control and to put an end for all time to these troublesome irruptions of knights in chain mail.

Nothing daunted, Edward and his gallant one thousand ("It is magnificent but it is not war," someone might have said on this occasion also) landed the following year, 1271, near Acre, a city still held by Christians but now under siege. So fiercely did the little force strike that the Mussulmen retreated and Edward marched triumphantly into the beleaguered city. The start of his desperate venture had been successful.

Knowing that he must strike quickly, for Bibars would soon be stretching out his steel-pointed claws to scoop him in, Edward carried the cross up the dusty road to Nazareth, which he captured. It was not a strategic victory, but there was a great moral advantage in having the home of Christ once more in Christian hands. A body of Saracens attacked them on the way back but were driven off. Edward then struck at the strong city of Haifa and won a second victory there. All this was indeed magnificent and it should have brought the laggard knights of Christendom to his aid. But the spirit had gone out of crusading, and the news that an English loon with long legs and a stout heart was striving to do with a thousand men what a hundred thousand had failed to do before him did not strike any spark.

On the evening of June 17 Edward sat alone in his tent, un-armed, wearing only a tunic, for the heat of the day had turned the desert into a furnace. He knew that a messenger was coming from the emir of Jaffa to propose terms of peace, and he knew also that he would have to accept them. Such reinforcements as had reached him had been pitifully small, and all about him the bearded sons of the Prophet were gathering, ready to strike.

He recognized the envoy who presented himself in the entrance of the royal pavilion, a plausible fellow who had already paid him four visits and was therefore above suspicion. It may have been that the offer to negotiate was no more than a ruse. At any rate, the turbaned visitor drew a knife from his belt and struck savagely at the unprepared prince. Edward took the blow on his arm and had succeeded in killing the assassin with the same knife before his attendants came to his assistance.

The knife had been poisoned and in a few days the prince's arm had swollen to a great size and the flesh had turned dark and gangrenous. His wife sat at his couch and wept bitterly. She had loved him from the day they had taken the marriage vows; Ed-ward, a tall youth with his blond locks clipped short below his ears, she the ten-year-old infanta with great dark eyes.

"Can I not be cured?" asked Edward when his surgeons grouped themselves about his couch and shook their heads and muttered.

Fortunately one of them thought so. When he proposed a he-roic operation the prince agreed but said that Eleanor must not remain in the room. It was a measure of her devotion that she had to be removed forcibly before the surgeon took a knife and cut away all the flesh from around the wound. The story that it was Eleanor herself who saved the prince by sucking the poison from the wound is not generally accepted, but there is no reason to think that she would have hesitated had the thought occurred to her, so completely did she love him. He did survive, fortunately, and in a very few days was able to sit up again.

Bibars could have crushed the little band of Englishmen, but he had gained respect for their fighting spirit and instead he pro-posed a truce to last for ten years, ten months, ten days, and ten minutes. Edward, thin and weak and discouraged, could do noth-ing but accept. Accordingly he signed the papers and on August 15 he went sadly on board his ship and set sail for Sicily. Another of the long series of crusades had come to an end; the smallest, the least important perhaps, but certainly the most daring and courageous.

2

While in Sicily, Edward received tragic intelligence from England. Three deaths were reported: that of his father, King Henry III; his uncle, Richard of Cornwall; and his first-born son, John, who had been left in England and had succumbed to one of the illnesses which kept infant mortality so high. Charles of Sicily was amazed that Edward's grief appeared greater for his father than for his promising young son.

"The lord who gave me these can give me other children," said Edward, "but a father can never be restored."

This was the highest encomium ever paid that unreliable, bickering old weathercock of a king, but it did not sound strange to those who understood the relationship between father and son. At home Henry had been a fond and indulgent parent and Edward had loved him deeply.

The new king did not return at once, for the message from England made it clear that he was under no compunction to hurry. Henry had been buried in the abbey-church of Westminster, close to the tomb of Edward the Confessor, and the nobility had sworn fealty to his successor at the foot of the high altar, the first time in English history that the reign of a new king had begun with the death of the incumbent. The people of England were ready to welcome him with open arms. They were proud of his military exploits and they spoke gratefully of his merits. He was even a learned man, they said. Did he not speak three languages, French, Latin, even English, each with "the silver tongue of oratory"? His reign, so ran the common report, would "shine with great luster."

The new king, accordingly, took his time about returning. He spent some months in Rome seeking papal punishment for the murder of his cousin, Henry of Almaine, by Guy, son of the dead Simon de Montfort.* He engaged in some spirited jousting in France and paid homage to the king of that country for the lands he still held there. He visited Gascony and chastised a disobedient underlord, one Gaston of Béarn. Finally, on August 2, 1274, he landed at Dover and was given a loud and warm welcome.

* See previous volume, *The Magnificent Century*.

A large part of the welcome was for Eleanor. The people of England had not taken to her when she first came from Spain as a girl bride. They knew that the old king, Edward's father, who was an absurd spendthrift, had depleted the royal treasury to give banquets for her and to have quarters fitted up for her in Windsor Castle in the Spanish habit, with costly tapestries, and carpets on the floors and with raised hearths and wardrobes and oriel windows. Moreover, on this first appearance, the infanta had brought a train of Spanish officials with her, little men of "hideous mien" who rode, not on horses like proper men, but on mules like monkeys!

This time they welcomed the mature and beautiful young woman who came ashore with the king. They cheered themselves hoarse when they saw the hungry affection with which both king and queen received the two surviving children of the three they had left behind; Eleanor, the oldest, who was developing into a rare beauty and who would always be the apple of her father's eye (he would even break off a match with the heir to the Spanish throne because he could not bear to have her go so far away), and the second son, who had been named Henry and who was a very sickly and wan little boy.

It was decided to hurry the coronation because Edward, back at last, had a world of things on his mind. Carpenters were set to work building frame kitchens at Westminster where food could be prepared for everyone, even the poorest apprentice in London. When the king arrived with a long train of barons and knights at the same time that King Alexander of Scotland put in an appearance with an equally long train of Scottish noblemen, it was decided to indulge jointly in an extraordinary act of generosity. The horses in both parties were turned loose while heralds announced that whoever caught one could keep it. The knights, it is said, grew hilarious watching while rich men, poor men, beggarmen, and thieves fought to get possession of the lordly steeds.

There was in Westminster a slab of marble called the King's Bench. As the first step in the ceremony, Edward was seated atop it on a white chair and proclaimed king. Then, accompanied by his glowing and lovely queen (for he had decided to set a precedent and have her crowned with him), he crossed from the palace to the abbey under a canopy carried by four of the most powerful noblemen in the kingdom. The old king had been an inveterate builder, and a good one (he would have been a much better architect than a king), and had spent his last days in turning the abbey

THE THREE EDWARDS

EDWARD I 1239 - 1307 reigned 1272 - 1307
married

1. ELEANOR, 1209, d. of Ferdinand III, King of Castile & Leon   2. MARGUERITE 1282 - 1318, d. of Philip III, King of France

Children of Edward I and Eleanor:

- EDWARD II of Carnarvon, Prince of Wales 1284 - 1327, r. 1307 - 1327, m. Isabella d. of Philip IV of France
- ELEANOR 1264 - 1298, m. Henry, Duke of Bar-le-Duc
- JOANNA of Acre 1272 - 1307, m.1 Gilbert de Clare, Earl of Gloucester 2. Ralph de Monthermer
- MARGARET 1275 - 1378, m. John, Duke of Brabant
- MARY 1278 - 1333 became a nun
- ELIZABETH 1282 - 1316, m. John, Count of Holland

Children of Edward I and Marguerite:

- THOMAS of Brotherton 1300 - 1338, m. Alice Hales
- EDMUND of Woodstock, Earl of Kent 1301 - 1330, m. Margaret of Liddell
- ELEANOR 1306 - 1311

Children of Edward II:

- EDWARD III 1312 - 1377, r. 1327 - 1377, m. Philippa, d. of Count of Hainault and Holland
- JOHN of Eltham 1316 - 1336
- ELEANOR of Woodstock 1318 - 1355, m. Raynald, Duke of Guelders
- JOAN of the Tower 1321 - 1362, m. David Bruce, King of Scotland

Child of Thomas of Brotherton:

- EDWARD m. Beatrice, d. of Earl of March

Child of Edmund of Woodstock:

- JOAN, the Fair Maid of Kent, m. Edward the Black Prince

Children of Edward III:

- EDWARD, Prince of Wales (the Black Prince) 1330 - 1376, m. Joan (the Fair Maid of Kent)
- LIONEL of Antwerp, Duke of Clarence 1338 - 1368, m.1 Elizabeth de Burgh 2. Violante Visconti
- JOHN of Gaunt, Duke of Lancaster 1340 - 1399, m.1 Blanche 2. Constance 3. Catherine
- EDMUND of Langley, 1st Duke of York 1341 - 1402, m.1 Isabel 2. Joan
- THOMAS of Woodstock 1355 - 1397, Earl of Buckingham, Duke of Gloucester later Earl of Essex m. Eleanor
- ISABELLA 1332 - 1379, m. Ingelram de Coucy
- JOANNA 1333 - 1358
- MARY 1344 - 1361, m. John, Duke of Brittany
- MARGARET 1346 - 1361, m. John, Earl of Hastings or Pembroke

Child of the Black Prince:

- RICHARD of Bordeaux

into an edifice of surpassing beauty. The original high altar had been extended and an apsidal chancel added. In the center of this new chancel, on earth which had been brought from the Holy Land for the purpose, a tomb of great magnificence had been raised for Edward the Confessor. Over this again a vast triforium was erected. It was in the dimly lit beauty of this new royal chapel that the returned crusader and his queen took their vows. Eleanor was in the customary white and gold, and her dusky eyes shone with content as she sat beside Edward on the falstool while Kilwardby, the Archbishop of Canterbury, preached to them.

There was a legend in Ireland that when a new king was seated on the *Lia Fail*, the coronation stone on the sacred hill of Tara, the stone remained silent if he was a true successor but groaned aloud if he was a pretender. The people who had come out from London on this fine morning to see the crowning were so well content with Edward that they might not have felt surprise if the marble of the King's Bench had suddenly acquired this capacity to discriminate and had cried aloud, "This is indeed a proper king!"

Although he had loitered on his way home, the new king's head had been filled with a great project which later would justify the motto *Pactum Serva* carved upon his tomb. The laws of England needed attention and he had brought in his train two men who could assist him in the work of amendment and codification which he saw was necessary. One was Francesco Accursi, the son of a famous Italian jurist, who learnedly occupied the chair of law at Bologna. He was destined for Oxford, where he would lecture on law and be available for advice on the major task which lay ahead. The second was a capable and bland young churchman named Robert Burnell, who had been of great assistance to Edward in the years before the prince went off to the Crusades. Edward was so convinced of the capacity of Burnell that he interrupted his departure in 1270 to ride at top speed to Canterbury when the death of Boniface of Savoy (an uncle of his mother's who had been foisted on the English people by royal pressure) left the archbishopric vacant. Edward was determined to have Burnell succeed the much-execrated Boniface. When he arrived, however, the monks had already gone into secret conference behind locked doors in the chapter house, so that, as they declared, they could achieve a spiritual communion in making their selection. The impatient prince thumped loudly on the door and, receiving no response, had it broken down. He then demanded of the indignant clerks that they select Burnell as the man best qualified for the exalted post.

There had been another occasion when the monks of Canterbury, filled with a sense of their own importance, had met secretly at midnight and selected their sub-prior Reginald and had then packed him off to Rome to get the papal consecration, thus precipitating the situation which resulted in the final selection of that greatest of archbishops, Stephen Langton. They listened to Edward in aggrieved silence and, as soon as he had withdrawn, they proceeded to elect their prior, Adam of Chillenden. But priors and sub-priors were not deemed of fit caliber for the archiepiscopal honors, and so again a pope, Gregory X, stepped in and selected a member of the Dominican order, Robert Kilwardby.

Long before the decision was reached, Edward was on his way to the Crusades. Burnell could not now be made archbishop, but the newly anointed king did the next best thing. On September 21, Edward appointed him chancellor, a post where he could be used to advantage in the mighty labor the king was planning.

CHAPTER TWO

The English Justinian—and the Queen
Who Had Many Handsome Children

1

EDWARD had not hurried on the way home from the Crusades, but he proceeded now to make up for his tardiness. Consider the schedule he followed. He landed at Dover on August 2, was crowned on Sunday, August 19; he proceeded at once to a reorganization of the civil machinery and on September 21 made Robert Burnell chancellor; on October 2 he appointed a commission with that brisk and efficient official at its head to review what had been done to the royal demesne during his absence, and on the first of November he was at Shrewsbury to discuss the adjustment of relations with Wales and to begin on what was his main function, the reform and codification of the laws of the land. This monumental labor was to continue throughout most of his reign, but the steps he initiated at the beginning were so carefully conceived and so ably conducted that on April 22 of the following year he felt free to summon a great Parliament at Westminster to convert his suggestions into the permanency of national law.

The laws of England had been in a sorry tangle since the coming of the Normans. William the Conqueror had retained much of the Anglo-Saxon machinery of justice, including the Hundredmoot and the Shire-moot, but the conflict between the grasping newcomers and the resentful English had led to feudal impositions. The despotism of the lords of the manor, with their tall grim castles, had reached its height in the reign of Stephen when each baron had his own dungeons, his own torture chamber, and his own gibbet. The diabolical practice of deciding guilt by a man's ability to carry a heated iron bar or to walk over red-hot plowshares had been hard to eradicate, as had another superstitious survival, the ordeal by water. The Normans had a preference for settling lawsuits by hiring champions to fight it out in the lists. The hatred between the newcomers and the downtrodden Saxons had imposed *presentment of Englishry* on the land, which meant proving the victim of murder to be English in order to escape the furious penalties exacted from whole townships in which a Norman had been assassinated.

The reforms of Henry II had tended to break the hold of feudalism by bringing justice under the supervision of the crown. His system of periodical assizes, presided over by itinerant judges, was not only revolutionary but so sound in practice that it has been continued to this day. The Great Charter had recognized the right of the individual, even against sovereign authority, but through the long years of his reign Henry III, Edward's father, had never ceased his stubborn efforts to disregard the limitations the Charter had placed on kingly power.

In setting about the arduous task of bringing order out of this tangle, the young king had the best advice. Henry de Bracton, a clear-thinking and able legal commentator, was not present in person (he had died six years before) but he was there in spirit. His books on English law, written during the previous reign, while a weak monarch sought to increase its perplexities still further, had been concise and convincing and had pointed the way to what Edward was striving to accomplish. With the king, of course, were Francesco Accursi and Robert Burnell. The latter might be termed the work horse of the combination. He it was who labored over the detail, who contrived and indexed and found ways to overcome difficulties, and who saw where compromise could be applied to vexed problems.

When Parliament met at Westminster, therefore, Edward had something tangible to lay before that body. It was a measure of fifty-one clauses and so broad in its applications that it has been described as practically a code in itself. It dealt not only with the clarification of common law but went into matters of governmental control. Most important of its many exactments was its affirmation of the Great Charter. The rights and privileges of the individual were to apply not only to men of noble birth but to all free men. The exact words of the Charter were employed, in fact, in denying the right to imprison or "amerce" the individual except by due process of law. The right of kings and their ministers to make irregular financial demands on the nation was denied. A redefining of wardships limited the power of guardians to profit from the estates of minors, not excepting the kings, who had battened on the heritage of widows and orphans. The highly practical measures of Henry II were confirmed and, where necessary, amended to suit new conditions.

Out of the reports laid before this first Parliament of his reign came the Statute of Westminster I, which embodied all of his recommendations. It would be followed by many other enactments over the years, each directed at some specific reform. In the end they would add up to a complete code, combining the best measures of the past with the new provisions that the spirit of the times made essential. In addition Edward would succeed in converting Parliament, which had been for two centuries a Normanized version of the Anglo-Saxon Witanagemot, into a House of Commons.

The strength of Edward was not in innovation but in his genius for adaptation and his appreciation of the need to define and codify. He would in the years ahead of him earn the title of the English Justinian.

Edward did not rest his case, nor indeed rest his labors, with the Statute of Westminster I. It was the first of many enactments, each carrying on to a further point the refinement and amendment of laws old and new. In 1285 he placed before Parliament a series of declarations that were embodied in the Statute of Westminster II, which is described in the *Annals of Osney* as follows: "He stirred up the ancient laws that had slumbered during the disturbances of the realm; some of which have been corrupted by abuses he recalled to their due form; some which were less evident and clear of interpretation he declared; some new ones, useful and honorable, he added."

The points covered had largely to do with land laws, with dower rights, and with advowson (the right to present to ecclesiastical offices). The holding of assizes at stated periods to permit of itinerant justices was remodeled to fit the changes in conditions since Henry II began the system. Manorial justice was sharply restricted. The second Westminster enactment deserves, in fact, to be ranked in importance with the first. The two, placed together, form an almost complete code bearing on the practice and extent of manorial jurisprudence.

A third enactment, called the Statute of Westminster, which was made law by parliamentary sanction the same year as the second from Westminster, moved backward in point of time to restate, define, and amend the old laws relating to popular action.

The obligations of the Hundred in regard to enforcement of justice and the defense of the realm were adjusted. The term "hundred" referred to divisions of land in a township (some variations being "ward" and "wapentake") and generally meant as much land as made up a hundred "hides," a hide in turn being as much land as could be tilled annually by a single plow. The Hue and Cry, a regulation by which all men were obligated to join in the pursuit and apprehension of offenders against the law, came under consideration and was amended, removing among other things all traces of the obnoxious *presentment of Englishry*.

It was on these amendments that Edward's reputation as a wise lawgiver rests.

2

While Edward labored thus to establish order in the land, his queen was equally active. She was finding some difficulty in settling down with her family. To begin with, she had no liking for the Tower of London as a home. This was not strange. It was too bleak, too grim, and too busy. The White Tower, which contained the royal apartments, was ninety feet high, with walls varying in thickness from twelve to fifteen feet. It had been built by a Norman architect, a monk of Bec named Gundulf, who was called the Weeper, and in accordance with Norman ideas he had been concerned only with its strength and durability. The White Tower was built for the ages, but it was square and graceless and cold. It developed also that Master Gundulf the Weeper had been guilty of a curious error: he had forgotten that the people who lived there would need to move about.

There was only one entrance to this towering block of masonry, a door so narrow that no more than one person could go through it at one time. Inside there was only a single well-stair, which began in the dark and damp vaults, where prisoners were kept, and continued on up to the floors above. Now the White Tower swarmed with people at all seasons and all hours. Not to mention the prisoners, who did not have a chance to get about, there were the king's guards, the workers in the Mint, the Jewel House, and the Wardrobe (the word "Wardrobe" included all the household departments as well as the household troops, the War Office, and the Admiralty), and the myriad clerks who served the officials of state in the Council Chamber and the Lesser Hall of the Justiciars as well as the members of the royal household with all their body servants and lackeys and grooms. The one entrance and the one well-stair with its hazardous stone steps were sadly inadequate for so many people. There was another serious drawback. The only fireplace in the Tower was in the state banqueting room on the second floor. The royal apartments were on the floor above, at the end of a dark passage from St. John's Chapel. The place was so lacking in comfort and coziness (a flagrant understatement) that the lovely queen from sunny Castile felt she must find a better home for her ailing children.

There were innumerable royal residences to choose from; so many, in fact, that a lifetime was hardly sufficient to get acquainted with all of them. It would be many years, for instance, before the devoted couple would perceive the charms of Leeds Castle, which stood on an island in the midst of a Kentish lake, and make it their favorite. But Eleanor's choice was limited by the fact that the king must not be many miles from London, and so it inevitably fell on Windsor Castle. It should have been a happy selection, for Windsor stood high and dry above a thickly wooded countryside, and it had come in for the serious attentions of Edward's father. The old king had seen that the King's House built by Henry I in the shadow of the round Norman keep had suffered too badly in the many sieges the castle had sustained. His instinct for building aroused, Henry III had constructed a new wall along a chalk range and inside the cover thus provided had raised a new King's House sixty feet long, a Queen's Chamber, a chapel of seventy feet, and a Great Hall of truly magnificent proportions. But, alas, his builders had been optimistic in their estimate of the strength of the chalk ridge. Gradually the handsome new walls began to creak and sag. Then one day the ramparts were seen to be heaving, and soon there was a loud crash; and down came all the walls, taking with them some of the pride of the builder king.

It was to the King's House of Henry I, therefore, that Edward's queen took her family. It had been renovated earlier and fitted up at great expense, as already noted, and so they were quite comfortable there. Although the queen was to continue bearing children with great regularity, she contrived to accompany her royal spouse on most of his journeyings at home and abroad. This meant there had to be a home in which to leave the children, and Windsor was selected.

There is a disagreement among authorities as to the number of children presented to Edward by his queen, some saying fifteen, others claiming a total of seventeen. On one point there is accord, however. Only four of the children were sons. Of the eleven or thirteen daughters, as the case may be, a number died in their infancy and nothing is known about them, not even their names. With those who lingered just long enough to acquire names, there has been little statistical recognition. Let us pick out one at random from the long list: Eleanor, Joanna, Margaret, Berengaria, Mary, Elizabeth, Alice, Blanche, Beatrice, Katherine; Berengaria let it be, the fifth (an unnamed one was born in the East), who was called after the sad princess from Navarre who married Richard the Lion-Heart and was so openly neglected all her life. Here is what is recorded of little Berengaria. She was born in 1276, the exact day not known, at Kennington, and died either that year or the next, being buried at Westminster beside two of her little brothers; so ends the story of her brief existence. It may have been that princesses given that rare and lovely name were destined to ill luck.

This much is well established, that all the royal children shared the Plantagenet beauty. Some of the daughters were blond and blue-eyed, some were cast in the duskier mold of Castile. Eleanor, the first, seems to have been the great beauty of the family. The second, Joanna, who was born at Acre and named after her maternal grandmother, was dark and of an imperious temper. She was left for several years at the court of Castile with her grandparents, who worshiped her, and she seems even at that tender age to have carried things off with a high hand. They could not fail to be bright, these children of a really great father and a vital and beautiful mother; all but one, and that story will have to be told later.

The first months at home were sad ones. The health of Prince Henry, the only son left after John's death, grew steadily worse. The king and queen did everything possible to save him. His wasted frame was kept wrapped in the skins of newly slaughtered sheep, in the hope that the animal heat would revive his energies. He was filled with all manner of queer medicinal mixtures. Wax replicas of his body were sent about to shrines to be burned in oil; a very strange superstition of that particular day. Nothing seemed to have any beneficial effect, and so finally they came to the last resort. A large number of poor widows were hired to supplement the efforts of the royal confessors by performing vigils ceaselessly for his recovery. Their mournful supplications, which filled the air at all hours, had no more effect than the weird efforts of the medical men. The heir to the throne, having been removed to Merton, passed away there.

Edward loved all his daughters devotedly, but he must have looked them over with an uneasy eye. Daughters made poor successors to a throne as contentious as that of England.

CHAPTER THREE

The English and the Welsh

1

To the English, Wales had always been a troublesome neighbor. To the Welsh, England was a constant threat to their liberty.

The Welsh were what was left (with additional population pockets in Cornwall and Devonshire) of the inhabitants of the island who had fought so bravely against the Romans, the natives who were called in Rome "the black singers." They were an imaginative race, poetic, high-strung, brave, and much given to singing and the harp. Back into their mountainous corner, their interests were limited, as were their opportunities for prosperity and abundance. They had faithful memories for the heroes of the past and they still believed that Arthur, the pendragon of glorious memory, would shake off his cerements someday and rise from the grave to lead them again to greatness.

They were in a fortunate position to carry on persistent warfare with the English. They could swoop through the passes in the hills and harry the countryside and then defy retaliation by retiring into the almost impassable land above which stood white-topped Snowdon. Although they were seldom united among themselves, the black singers could keep their wooded glens free of alien feet. This hit-and-run warfare had been going on for centuries when the Normans came over. William the Conqueror decided that something decisive must be done. He led one force into the mountains, getting as far as St. David's, and then decided that the risks outweighed the possible gains. As a second-best measure he decided to "contain" the mountaineers. The strip of country that bordered on the Welsh foothills, and through which all invading forces going in either direction had to pass, was converted into a feudal no man's land. The country was divided among three Norman leaders, Hugo the Wolf, William Fitz-Osborn, and

Roger de Montgomery. These palatine earls were given full control of their respective counties, in return for which they were to maintain armed troops in the field and assume the responsibility of holding the Welsh in check. This system had been in effect for nearly two hundred years when Edward came to the throne, and the earls had become known as Marcher Barons. Their control of the land had become so absolute that it was said "the king's writ did not run north of the Wye"; in other words, that they ruled in their own right and could wink at kingly powers. Political refugees were safe if they could get across the Wye.

A second move made by the resourceful Conqueror had been more successful. He had laid hands on southern Wales, which lacked the high barriers, and through the instrumentality of one Robert Fitz-Hamon had constructed a string of stone strongholds running from the Wye to the port of Milford Haven.

Edward fixed his piercing eye on Wales and he did not admire the prospect. His writ must run not only through the Marcher country but into the deepest fastnesses of the high Welsh hills. As a further stimulant, he was keenly conscious of the assistance Wales had given Simon de Montfort in the closing phases of his father's reign. That was a score to be wiped off the slate.

He made up his mind that the problem of Wales must now be settled once and for all.

2

At the start of his reign, however, Edward had not anticipated trouble because the ruler of the mountain country, Llewelyn ab Gruffydd, had made a most advantageous treaty with Henry III and was believed to be in a pacific mood. There was another reason which should have inclined the Welsh leader to peace. Some years before, when Simon de Montfort had raised the baronage against the feckless old king, the young Llewelyn had visited the commoner leader and had seen his daughter, Eleanor, who was called in the family the Demoiselle. Simon's wife was a sister of King Henry and had passed on to the Demoiselle a full share of the Plantagenet beauty. The Welsh prince had fallen instantaneously and completely in love with the girl and, when he left, it was with the understanding they would be married when peace in the country had been restored. Even after Simon's defeat and death and the confiscation of all the great estates and castles of the De Montforts, the infatuated Llewelyn still desired nothing better than to claim his promised bride. The Demoiselle had to fly to France with her mother after the battle of Evesham, and it was not until the mother's death that she was put on a ship to recross the Channel and join her lover.

Here was a chance for a state *coup* which could not be overlooked. Edward sent four vessels to lurk behind the Scilly Islands, with orders to seize the French vessel and carry off the Demoiselle. A brother who had accompanied her was sent to Corfe Castle as a prisoner, but the fair Eleanor was taken to Windsor Castle and kept there in semi-confinement for three years. During that time she was dangled before Llewelyn's eyes as a bribe for his good behavior.

Before the capture of the Demoiselle, however, a clash had been imminent. Hostilities blazed up all along the Marcher country, and the Welsh forces won successes at various points. Incensed by the defeat of an English army at Kidwelly, Edward decided on a major invasion and gathered a large force at Chester. Two other armies were to strike at the same time, one moving out from Shrewsbury under the command of Henry de Lacy and a second poised against South Wales under the Earl of Hereford. At the same moment an English fleet occupied the Menai Strait and cut off the Isle of Anglesey from all communication with Wales. Llewelyn depended on the food supplies which reached him from Anglesey and he now found himself at a desperate pass.

The outcome was easy to foresee. Edward was an aggressive general, striking hard and fast and often, and under the pressure he exerted along the Conway River the Welsh were forced back into the cover of the wooded hillsides surrounding Snowdon. Here they held out bravely. Edward did not sit down and wait for starvation to complete his triumph. While the Welsh tightened their belts and held on grimly, he proceeded to build several strong castles at strategic points and to strengthen those at Conway and Chester. In late autumn Llewelyn gave in and sent out word that he was prepared to make terms.

A treaty was signed at Conway on November 9 by which the Welsh prince gave up South Wales to the English and agreed to pay a fine of fifty thousand pounds. Anglesey was restored to him with the understanding that a yearly rental of one thousand marks was to be paid for it. The terms were hard, but later Edward agreed to remit the fine. This was generous because the Welsh prince, reduced to ruling a small part of the country around Snowdon, would have found it impossible to raise such an enormous sum.

The next year Llewelyn was summoned to meet the king at Worcester and to his delight found Eleanor de Montfort there with the royal family. She had remained constant to him through all the trials and delays, and they were married on October 13 at the door of the cathedral, a large number of the nobility of England having gathered to witness the ceremony. The happy couple, who found they were as much in love as ever, left at once for Wales. It seemed that at last the peace between the two countries had been established on a firm basis.

The Demoiselle (her girlhood name clung to her all through her life) was not destined to much married happiness. Two years later she died in childbirth, leaving a daughter who was given the name of Gwenllian.

After a few years of peace, Llewelyn decided on another effort to rid the country of the English. There had been continuous irritations. Archbishop Peckham was at odds with the Welsh because of some fumbling efforts to bring the churches in the two countries into closer harmony. The subordinate officials of the king were aggressive and greedy, and the Marcher barons as usual were looking for gains. And behind all this there was a prediction by the wizard Merlin which all Wales began to talk about. Someday, Merlin had declared, a Llewelyn would wear the crown of Brutus and reign over England as well as Wales. Was this the Llewelyn he had meant? Finally the prince's brother David, who had been allied with the English up to this time, came back and began secretly to urge Llewelyn to strike.

Accordingly Llewelyn struck. On the eve of Palm Sunday, 1282, when all should have been peace in the land, the Welshmen marched out to a wild piping and the roll of national songs sung by thousands of fine voices. At first, success perched on the banners of the Welsh leader. Had Merlin been right? Roger Clifford, one of the English leaders, was beaten and taken prisoner. Two mighty earls were sent to the rightabout. The English were building a bridge across the Menai Strait. In an excess of bravado three hundred English and Gascon soldiers crossed over before it was completed. The tide came in and cut them off, and the Welsh proceeded to wipe them out to a man.

Convinced that the full tide of success was running his way, Llewelyn committed the folly of taking his slender forces down into the open to face the might of Edward. In a relatively small skirmish near the upper waters of the Severn he was defeated and killed.

In view of the prediction of Merlin, Edward had the head of the fallen prince cut off and exposed on a pole above the Tower of London, crowned with ivy.

Gwenllian, the infant daughter of Llewelyn, was taken to England. When she grew old enough she took the vows at the convent of Sempringham. It may have been devotion on her part or the result of a desire on the part of the government at Westminster to have the Welsh royal line come to an end.

David, the turbulent brother, was still at large. He was finally trapped, through information supplied by some of his countrymen, in a boggy stretch of land near Snowdon and taken to Rhuddlan with his wife, two sons, and seven daughters. He had been at odds with Llewelyn most of his life and had fought on the king's side until the final campaign; and his role of double traitor seems to have roused a deep resentment in the English. He was taken to Shrewsbury and tried before a Parliament summoned for the purpose. There he was condemned to be hanged, drawn, and quartered as a traitor. Some authorities say that this method of execution was invented for his benefit. As a traitor to his knightly vows he was to be dragged at the heels of horses to the place of execution. Here he was to be hanged by the neck as a punishment for murders he had committed. He was to be cut down, however, before consciousness had left him and then, for profaning the week of the Lord's passion, his entrails were to be cut out. Finally, for plotting against the king's life, his head was to be chopped off and his body divided into four parts.

Whether or not the parliamentary judges were responsible for this dreadful method of execution, the gruesome spectacle seemed to find favor. For centuries thereafter it was used to dispose of men who had been convicted of treason. There would be a case, in fact, during the reign of Henry IV when official animosity against a convicted traitor, a man of low degree, would be so great that the various stages of the sentence would be carried out in different cities.

The head of the unfortunate David was elevated above the Tower of London beside that of his brother (of which little was left by that time). The cities of York and Winchester engaged in a dispute for possession of his right shoulder, and Winchester won. The three other quarters were awarded to York, Bristol, and Northampton.

David's qualities had not endeared him to his countrymen while he was alive, but the manner of his death made him a martyr in their eyes. The bards sang songs about him for centuries thereafter.

3

It became evident that Edward had something of his builder father in him when he turned his attention to the castles of England. He realized that they were ill planned and that something must be done about them. The Norman stronghold had been built for one purpose only, defense. It was a grim structure of high, thick walls surrounded by a moat. Inside there were no provisions for the comfort of the occupants. The sanitary arrangements were crude, in fact almost nonexistent; the bedchambers were little more than holes sunk into the walls and lacking light and ventilation. It had now become apparent that even for defense this type of castle was not the best. It lacked the means of interfering with besiegers. Archers who had to station themselves at narrow slits in the immensely thick walls had no chance of directing a deadly fire on attacking forces. By the latter part of the reign of Henry III a move was being made to have bastions at the corners of all defense walls so that a cross fire could be maintained by the archers.

Edward now began to build an entirely different type of castle. It was on what was called the "concentric" system, consisting of several lines of defense which had to be passed in turn. The great strongholds he raised in Wales—Caernarvon and Conway in particular—were mighty fortresses and so substantially raised that much of the masonry is still intact. In addition to being practical from a defense standpoint, they displayed a marked advance in the living quarters. Conway, which became a favorite with the royal family, was quite sumptuous, with a stately great hall and chambers with plastered walls and glass windows.

But even while Edward spent his time and thought on his castles, not to mention the great cost of them, the trend in the world at large was running the other way. Men were beginning to discover comfort and were no longer willing to exist in stately pig wallows. The manor house was being developed. Gradually the homes of the nobility would be built with an eye to ease and dignity in living. Where it was felt that more security was needed than a brick manor house could afford, a compromise was effected by raising the walls higher and giving them crenelated tops. In time it became necessary to have the royal assent to this method of fortifying a country house. The rapidity with which the tendency to live in fortified castles went out is best demonstrated by the number of permits to crenelate a manor house issued in consecutive reigns. There were 181 granted in the reign of Edward III, sixty by Richard II, eight by Henry IV, one by Henry V.

CHAPTER FOUR

A Prince Is Born

1

THE subjugation of Wales had been completed in 1282 with the deaths of Llewelyn and David, but peace between the English and the Welsh did not come by any means. Edward still found it necessary to spend most of his time in and about his new dominions and he devoted much of it to the completion of the great castles which were to hold the wild tribesmen under control.

Where Edward went, Eleanor went also. She was in Wales the next year, holding court at Rhuddlan Castle, and it was here that her daughter Elizabeth was born. A year later the tall fortress of Caernarvon was ready for occupancy. A grim reminder of the power of the conquerors, it stood on the sea, with one gate looking out over the Menai Strait and the other commanding a view of the white summit of Snowdon, where the bravest of the Welsh leaders still held out. As Eleanor was with child again, Edward took her to Caernarvon. The impending event was not considered of any greater importance than the many other accouchements. There was an heir to the throne, Prince Alfonso, named after the queen's brother in Castile. As several years had passed over his head, it was hoped that he would achieve the maturity denied his two older brothers.

At this point the story reaches debatable ground. Of recent years historians have been disposed to cast aside the best elements in the generally accepted legend of the birth of a fourth son in Caernarvon Castle who was to become king in his turn under the title of Edward II, the contention being that the early annals contain no mention of it and that it may, on that account, be an invention of some later writer. The legend, as it has been so often told, is set down for what it is worth.

The queen made her entrance into the castle through the east gate, a strong imposing structure. The natives of this part of Wales, who have not yielded in their adherence to the original story, still call this Queen Eleanor's Gate. It gave direct entry to the Eagle Tower, a lofty and menacing pile of masonry high enough and strong enough to awe (if such had been possible) the proud chieftains who still refused to accept the fetters of Saxon servitude. Rather high in the Eagle Tower is a suite of rooms which is pointed out today as the queen's; in one of them, a tiny chamber twelve feet by eight sunk into the thick stone walls, she gave birth to the new child. It must have been a cold and dismal room, because it contained no hearth; indeed there was little room in this far from regal niche for more than a bed. The grooms of the chamber had done their best to give a touch of cheer by hanging tapestries on the walls. The queen had brought many tapestries and wall hangings of gay colors from her native Castile, and it was her custom to have a supply of them carried in her train so she could enjoy that much alleviation of the bleak and dreary walls which always surrounded her. The child was a boy, a healthy specimen. He was placed in a cradle of oak, hung by rings to two upright posts, the whole of somewhat crude workmanship. This first couch of the royal infant has been kept and proudly displayed down through the centuries.

Edward had left his wife at Caernarvon and had returned to Rhuddlan, where matters of state demanded his presence. It was here that he received word of the birth of a son, and he was so pleased that he knighted the Welshman who brought the news and made him a grant of land. Even though the newborn infant would not be heir to the throne, it was well to have the succession doubly secured; and it is probable also that the continuous arrival of daughters had achieved a certain monotony for the royal father. It may have been concern for the state of health of his much-loved queen that caused Edward to depart in great haste for Caernarvon rather than the elation he felt over the arrival of another boy. He found Eleanor well and the new prince sleeping in abounding health in his plain cradle.

The legend has it that when the new son was three days old a number of Welsh chieftains came to Caernarvon to make their submissions to Edward. They begged him, if he would have peace in the land, to find for them a prince above reproach who would speak neither English nor French. The king was resourceful, as he was to prove innumerable times during his eventful reign. He listened to the plea of the tribesmen, and an ingenious plan took form in his mind. He accordingly left the reception chamber where the chieftains were assembled and, much pleased with himself, returned almost immediately with his newborn son in his arms. He held the infant out for their inspection. Here, he declared, was the prince they had asked for, the new Prince of Wales.

"He has been born a native of your country," he said. "His character is unimpeachable. He cannot speak a word of English or French. If it please you, the first words he utters shall be Welsh."

The chieftains, realizing they had been caught in a skillful trap, made the best of things. They knelt in turn and kissed the hand of the royal infant, swearing fealty to him.

Such is the legend. It is a pleasant one, the kind that, once heard, is never forgotten. It is one of the favorite stories of English history and the narrator hesitates to put it aside, to condemn it completely to the discard. It must be said, of course, that there are grounds for skepticism. It was not until 1301 that the prince, grown to man's estate, had bestowed upon him the title of Prince of Wales. This official step was taken when Parliament met in the city of Lincoln, and it is one of the strongest points advanced against acceptance of the old story.

But sometimes a small item, buried away in the records of the dark past, will obtrude itself into discussions of this kind. There is an entry in the royal household accounts of a date long after, when the small prince had grown to manhood and had taken his father's place as King of England, to be known as Edward II. Twenty shillings had been paid to one Mary of Caernarvon, his Welsh nurse.

Quite apparently he had been very fond of her and he remembered her well enough to have her come all the way to London to see him. This might indicate that the child born in the great castle had been more than just another royal infant, one of sixteen; that some significance had attached to him which made it advisable to keep a nurse of Welsh birth in attendance long enough for him to remember her after all these years. A trivial occurrence, perhaps; and yet it burns like a small candle in a darkly shuttered room.

Four months later Prince Alfonso died, and the healthy child who may or may not have been displayed proudly to the Welsh chiefs in Caernarvon Castle became heir to the throne of England.

CHAPTER FIVE

The Expulsion of the Jews

1

EDWARD's reputation carries several unfortunate blots. There were the Welsh and Scottish wars when the blood was hot in his veins and the urge to conquer led him into sanguinary injustices. No excuse can be made for his treatment of William Wallace. And there was the expulsion of the Jews from England.

The blame for this last injustice cannot be laid entirely on the shoulders of the tall young king. There had been a series of repressive measures initiated against the Jews by the church which led to civil restrictions in England during the reigns immediately preceding. They had been refused the right to lend on interest, although permission to engage in commerce was not withdrawn. A futile effort to afford them a means of subsistence was a regulation allowing them to buy farms and engage in agriculture. This had helped little, if at all. The Hebrew people of that day had no experience in the tilling of the soil and, to make matters worse, they were denied the right to hire help on the terms exercised by the feudal landlords. As a result the unfortunate people lived in a state of semi-starvation in the ghettos. Progressive centers continued to operate in provincial cities, notably Bristol and Exeter. Many of the more far-seeing became active, if not prosperous, in the wool trade.

The Jews had been very useful to the crown during the first century of the Norman period and they had enjoyed many special privileges. They had been allowed, of course, to practice usury and the prejudice against them was due to this almost as much as to the hostility of the church. The kings had been silent partners with the money-lenders in a sense. The usurers had been expected to contribute heavily to the royal coffers. Whenever the king was in financial difficulties, he turned to the Jews for generous donations. However, with the growth of the Templars to a position of financial predominance and an invasion of Italian money-lenders, who were acceptable to the church, the usefulness of the Jews to the crown ceased to be a factor.

One result of the earlier accumulation of wealth was that it became concentrated in the hands of a few. It was estimated that eighteen Jewish families controlled most of the wealth. How the rest subsisted is not entirely clear, except that they lived in the Jewish quarters in abject poverty.

These were the conditions which existed when Edward took the throne and he solved it finally by a formal decree of expulsion in 1290. There was a generally accepted story that Edward's mother, the highly unpopular Eleanor of Provence, had been the most bitter critic of the Jewish people and that she gave him no rest. Even after she retired into a nunnery, she continued to bombard him with her convictions on that score. This, no doubt, had its effect but the pressure came, in reality, from the people at large. There was a deep resentment of the luxury in which the wealthiest of the usurers lived and any excuse would start riots in the towns. The burning of synagogues was a favorite pastime of the mobs. The members of the nobility, who happened to fall into the clutches of the money-lenders, were the first to lead in the rioting. The influence of the church was always felt. The whispered insinuation of the king's mother played a part but it was no more than a final irritation which Edward had to bear.

The king's first move was made in Gascony. This was a fairly painless measure for the Jews. They swarmed back over the borders into France. But those in England suffered bitterly when the need came to pack up and leave the country. Edward strove to be fair in small matters. He passed a regulation allowing them to take their portable property with them. All houses and land were confiscated to the crown and any dismantling of the synagogues was prohibited.

An estimate sets the number of Jews who were thus compelled to leave the country at sixteen thousand. It is not hard to conceive of the sufferings to which they were subjected. The saddened people, burdened with their sorry belongings, were huddled in the harbors to await their turns to sail. The number of ships available to take them to the continent was hopelessly small. Those who had funds with which to bribe the captains got away first. It was the poor who were left in the city slums, subjected to persecution and every conceivable cruelty. Many were drowned in the course of the sailings to continental ports, because the captains paid no attention to safety measures. No efforts were made to rescue those who fell overboard.

Edward had offered to pay the passages of all who agreed to go to the Low Countries because it was believed they would find satisfactory employment there in the textile cities. Not more than a tenth took advantage of this offer. Some went to Spain and Portugal but the majority landed in French ports and drifted to Paris like metal filings to a magnet.

And so the children of Israel vanished from the life of England. Measures were adopted to remove all evidences of their stay. The synagogues were closed tight and permitted to fall into contemptuous ruin. The Hebrew schools were closed or renovated for other purposes. In London the high school in Fishmonger Lane became a center for commercial activities. The "badge of shame" which all members of the Jewish race had been compelled to wear, consisting of two fingers of yellow cloth sewn on the breasts of their garments, were no longer seen on the streets in cities and towns.

It was not until the year 1655 that the ban was revoked and they were allowed to become again residents of England.

2

The action of the English king had repercussions abroad. Sixteen years later the French king, Philip the Fair, followed Edward's example. This had the effect of driving the unfortunate people back into the Germanic countries. The action taken in Spain two centuries later could not be ascribed in any sense to the English precedent. That dreadful persecution was a part of the activities of the Inquisition.

The conditions in England, preceding the expulsion, had been reflected in France and Flanders but it had needed someone bold enough to set the example. There was a finality about expulsion which caused the other nations to draw back. Edward can, therefore, be charged with having started the refusal of the people of Europe to harbor any longer the people of the persecuted race.

CHAPTER SIX

The Plantagenets at Home

1

THE life of a king is not all fighting battles and sitting in council, and (if he happens to be a monarch of medieval days) the building of grim castles and the condemning of unfortunate men to be hanged, drawn, and quartered. He always had a home life, and from what can be learned of the relatively quiet hours he spent with his queen and children, a truer picture of the man himself can sometimes be obtained than by the study of his official actions.

Edward was a devoted husband and a fond father. If his eye had been disposed to rove a little when he was younger and the married beauties of his father's court had been prone to flaunt their willingness, he lost all interest in dalliance as soon as he and Eleanor began their life together. There would be no rifts in their marital happiness. Edward's father, Henry III, who so lacked the attributes of kingship, did leave behind one golden legacy, the love of family.

It has already been explained that Windsor Castle became the main home of this family of delicate sons and radiantly lovely daughters. After the death of the second son, the oldest daughter, Eleanor, became first in the line of accession. Edward even went to the length of having the members of the baronage swear fealty to her as his successor. It was recognized that the princess now needed an official home of her own, and at first she was given Maiden Hall, a retired angle of Westminster Palace. There was not much room there for an elaborate household, and the princess had to be content with "three men servants, three maids and three greyhounds." Later her retinue included "her own chamberlain, keeper of the hall, groom of the bedchamber, cook, salterer, shieldman and sumpterer, besides boys and damsels." Her younger sisters accompanied her on visits to shrines where they left alms of stated amounts. It is recorded that on such outings they had tiny bells sewn into the hems of their dresses, because it was held that there was efficacy in a delicate, tinkling sound, that it had magical powers for good. Even winter would not keep them off the roads. Together they would set out in a chariot of sorts drawn by five horses. If it was impossible to keep snug and warm in the vehicle (carriage-making was still a new craft), it was at least dry and reasonably comfortable. Princess Eleanor always saw to it that her favorite Rougement was taken along so she could desert the close interior and enjoy a gallop on the rare occasions when the sun came out.

When they grew older the princesses hunted with their parents and became accustomed to the spectacular characteristics of their tall father in the field. He was renowned for his horsemanship, preferring to ride strong and hard-to-manage mounts. Lithe and muscular himself, he could leap into the saddle by placing one hand lightly against the leather. His favorite was a bay named Bayard, but it was gray Lyard he called for when he rode into battle, the great horse of which it is written, "He ever charged forward." For the hunting field there was Ferrault, a shining blue-black jumper who "could leap over any chain, however high."

Falconry had become the favorite sport of the day. William the Conqueror had placed restrictions on hawking, just as he had laid down his vicious Forest Laws. In the previous reign the laws had been relaxed and interest in the sport had become widespread. When Edward rode out to hawk, he was likely to be accompanied by his queen and some of his daughters and many ladies of the court. Ladies became so adept at handling the wild birds that their male companions complained that they were turning falconry into a frivolous and effeminate pastime. With their smaller hands, women could quickly learn to manage the jesses, lunes, and tyrrits—straps, thongs, and rings—the bells to be balanced and also fastened to the birds' legs. They used the creance, a long thread to draw a bird back to its mistress's gloved fist, a quick action known as reclaiming the hawk. An important if indolent member of the retinue was always the cadge-boy. From his shoulders was suspended a wooden frame which held, before the start of the hunt, the birds to be used. Among them might be a "falcon gentle" with hooked and notched bill, or a "mewing" falcon just taken out of the mews or enclosure built especially for these birds when they were losing but one feather at a time instead of molting in the wholesale manner of other winged creatures. All the birds on the frame were females and were kept "hood-winked," the hoods made especially to fit their little heads and to cover their staring, intelligent eyes. Here were peregrines, fast-flying, swift-swooping; or the little merlin whose silhouette against the sky made an exquisite outline; the hobby was sometimes there, too, caught nesting in the southernmost part of England. It was larger than the merlin but not as long-winged as its sister flier, the kestrel. The short-winged, slow-flying goshawk was an especial favorite for the royal fist.

Once the hunters had reached a cleared space and released their birds, the cadge-boy, with nothing but an empty frame on his back, loafed about for tips. Thus came into general usage the word "cadge."

Sometimes Eleanor accompanied Edward to the hunt. Dogs from the royal kennels scurried before them through the woods, English and Italian "gaze" hounds (they hunted by sight rather than scent) with long bodies and noses, precursors of the whippet. There were heavy-set, honey-colored dogs, too, a breed brought to England by returning crusaders and similar in appearance to the modern boxer. Short, crooked-legged little fellows, said to have been bred first in Artois and Flanders, dotted the fields, a dog with a good nose, riotous and headstrong, with a musical bark that brought little underground animals from their nests and lairs. This is called the basset hound today.

But sometimes the king and his ladies rode out to enjoy the new beauty of the countryside which was being cleared and neatly planted. Often in the fields where the grass had sprouted thickly they would pass flocks of sheep particularly large and sturdy in conformation—the merino sheep from Spain. It was Edward's *chère reine* who had first suggested bringing these fine animals from her native Castile, and in time the Cotswold country of England would become noted for them.

The royal family seemed to be happiest on the wing. There was a constant visiting back and forth from one castle to another. Edward seems to have had an itching heel; he was known to change his place of residence as often as twice in three days. It should be stated that this was not always due to his roving spirit. A king's train was huge and capable of depleting the food supplies of a royal residence in no time at all.

Economy might be exercised within the household, but when Edward took his fair ladies on processionals he saw to it that the background was a fitting one. He spent large sums of money, for instance, on two royal barges to be used on the Thames. They were so commodious and elaborate that seventy-four bargemen were needed to operate them. It is recorded also that Ade, the king's goldsmith, was kept constantly employed in making plate against the time when the marriage of the princess would require a rich show.

Fashions in dress changed slowly through the Middle Ages. This may have been because the inventive faculty in man was at a standstill. He was beginning to build magnificent cathedrals, to paint pictures, to compose majestic sacred music, to write spirited poetry; but the flowing robes in which men arrayed themselves after escaping the intense discomfort of armor seemed good enough to be let alone. On the accession of Edward II there would be a sudden addiction to French styles and a complete swing over to oddity and extravagance in attire, but while the father was at the helm there was no more than a slow progress. The king himself was indifferent to dress. He shunned such rich and elaborate materials as cloth of gold, cloth of Tarsus, satins, silks, brocades, and trimmings of ermine and vare; he was content with the fine and substantial cloth made from English wool. His queen seems to have followed him in this, as in almost everything else. Perhaps it was because she was with him constantly on his travels, riding astride and finding it necessary to have warm clothes and to encase her slender feet in great, heavy riding boots. Perhaps one so naturally lovely did not feel the need of artificial aids to pulchritude. In any event, she had a preference for loose undergowns with sleeves that buttoned from elbow to wrist, and plain outer gowns lined with something in gay colors. The nonchalant attitude of the royal couple did not put any restrictions on the daughters, however, except that a certain economy was observed in the matter of materials. There is one record of the repairing of Christmas robes for the oldest daughter, one being so far gone that the tailor required seven days to make it presentable.

There were two tendencies of the day in the matter of costume which should be recorded. The first was the introduction of buttons. Used at first for decoration only, on books and purses and scabbards as well as clothes, the button began to prove its utility in holding clothing closer to the body, thereby providing a greater warmth and accentuating (where the ladies were concerned) the gentle curve of the figure. The button would become of increasing use as time moved along and would be largely responsible for the eccentricities and the fantastic developments of the succeeding reign.

The second had to do with color. In the warm and scented south the lord of the manor and the troubadour inclined to soft shades and poetic combinations, but in England it was still the day of the solid colors—stout reds, deep blues, and warm greens. The somber brown, which had been much in evidence before, was now left to the friar and the monk. White was not practical and black seems to have been little used. There was a vigor and stimulation about a gathering of any size in England as a result. When men in red and green danced at the Maypole with girls in blue, the eye of the beholder was filled with a beauty which sophisticated fashions could not attain.

The ladies, of course, were not entirely content to leave things at that. They experimented with head coverings and gradually evolved a round linen cap in place of the simple band about the hair. When the wimple, a hot and unattractive covering of linen or silk, was draped about these caps, the result was not felicitous or comfortable. Better far to have left the hair free to hang down the back.

2

Life in the castles might have its moments of picturesque grandeur, as when visiting royalty sat down in the great hall and the tables swarmed with the nobility and the rich churchmen. In the main it was a bare and very uncomfortable existence. Even in the King's House at Windsor, which Eleanor had bedecked with hangings and rugs, the rooms were cold in winter. So strong were the drafts that the tapestries would be blown about against the damp walls. The sleeping chambers were high up in the tall towers and were as small and unpretentious as the niche in the wall where Edward II was said to have been born.

There were always diversions, of course. During meals there was music from the minstrels' gallery, provided by the harp, the dulcimer, the jingling frame-drums (generally called timbrels), and the bladder-pipe, which was a small variety of bagpipe and consisted of a double clarinet with a bladder instead of a bag; even sometimes the portative organ, which had just been invented and was so minute that an itinerant musician could carry it about on his back.

Queen Eleanor had been raised in the court of her half brother, Alfonso of Castile, and so had acquired a taste for the arts and sciences. Alfonso, called *El Sabio* by his subjects, was both a scholar and a poet and he kept his court filled with learned men. It was not surprising, therefore, that Eleanor had an appetite for culture which did not find much satisfaction in the atmosphere of the English court. Even opportunities for reading were limited, the royal library consisting of three books, and these considered to be of such value that they could not be reached easily; they were locked up with the royal jewels. What were these three precious volumes?

A book of ancient chronicles, almost certainly in Latin.

A Latin work on agriculture.

A copy of fables in French called *Romaunt de Guillaume de Conquerant.*

The last named might have interested the members of the family had they been able to get it into their hands; but not very much, because it was made up of very foolish and incredible tales.

It is on record that both the king and queen played chess. One of the dignitaries of the Knights Templar in France presented Edward with a chessboard made of jasper and men of crystal. The king gave it in turn to Eleanor. The royal couple were inclined to the game, no doubt, by the commonly accepted but erroneous belief of that day that King Solomon had invented it. Chess was, of course, a far different game from the perfect diversion it was to become in later centuries. If the piece now called the queen bore that same name in those early days, Eleanor might have been disposed to demur because it could be moved one square only diagonally and was the weakest piece on the board.

There is a story that one day Edward was playing a game with one of his knights. Suddenly he sprang from his chair, impelled by a motive he could not later explain. As he moved away, a stone from the ceiling fell on the exact spot where he had been sitting. The safety of Edward was ascribed, of course, to divine intervention. If the incident occurred at Windsor, it might easily have been the work of the uncertain chalk ridge.

Eleanor strove to become a patroness of the arts and was willing to make personal grants, as large as forty shillings, for literary efforts such as translations from the Latin. An even more useful contribution to the cultural side of life in the country was her introduction of the fork. It has been assumed that this most useful of table articles was not known in England until a much later date, but in a list of the queen's plate there is mention of forks of crystal and of silver, with handles of ebony or ivory. A later item in the Record Commission includes forks among the domestic articles used by the king.

The king not only endeavored to keep pace with the cultural activities of his queen but was as amenable to household customs as the most humble of husbands. It was the rule on Easter Monday for the women in all large establishments to surround the master and hoist him, willy-nilly, in a chair and not let him down until he paid them a proper gratuity. This was popularly called "heaving." One year seven of the queen's high-placed young ladies took Edward in hand and "heaved" him in his chair amid much laughter and clapping of hands. The king took it with good grace and paid them the handsome sum of fourteen pounds for his release.

3

The histories of three of the princesses, Eleanor, Joanna, and Margaret, seem to run in a pattern. In an age when marriages, particularly in royal families, were arranged when the principals were little more than infants, these three daughters of England's greatest king seem to have found some belated happiness. When the queen died in 1290, Eleanor, as the oldest daughter, became the most important woman of her father's court. Here, that same year, she was to find sympathy and solace in a Frenchman of great charm, the Duke of Bar-le-Duc, a new and well-considered friend of Edward. He became a constant visitor to the court and they, Eleanor and the duke, had the opportunity of close association. In her babyhood Eleanor had been affianced to the future King Alfonso of Aragon, but they never met and destiny gathered him to his royal fathers. Three years passed and Eleanor happily married the Duke of Bar-le-Duc.

In April 1290 the fiery-spirited, sloe-eyed Joanna of Acre married England's most powerful peer, second to the king in importance, Gilbert de Clare, Earl of Gloucester. Joanna, too, had been given in betrothal at the age of five, to Prince Hartman, son of the king of the Romans. Edward seems to have arranged future marriages for his daughters with no idea of permitting their consummation but as perhaps a help toward some political expediency of the moment. Also, it is often plain that he could not part with his dearly loved daughters. Poor Prince Hartman went skating one winter's day. The story is that he accidentally fell into open reaches where the water was deep, and drowned.

Gilbert de Clare was not young when he married Joanna and took her to live at his country retreat in Clerkenwell, not far from the Tower, where the king and queen were again in residence. She left for her new home with great fanfare, laden with royal gifts. Among them were forty golden cups, many more golden clasps, "twenty zones of silk, wrought and trapped with silver to give away to whom she pleased." Hampers, coffers, baskets, and bags are listed without number. "One sumpter-horse carried her chapel apparatus, another her bed, a third her jewels, a fourth her chamber furniture, a fifth her *candles!* a sixth her pantry-stores and table linen, and a seventh her kitchen furniture."

Joanna was but twenty-three when the old Earl of Gloucester died. After being a widow a year, she secretly married a completely unknown squire in her late husband's retinue, Ralph de Monthermer. Through this marriage he became possessed in his own right of the earldoms of Gloucester and Hertford. The fact that a royal princess had dared to marry this obscure fellow became a *cause célèbre* which for a time separated her from the affection of her father. It proved to be a happy marriage, however, leading ultimately to a firm friendship between the new son-in-law and Edward.

Margaret, the fourth daughter of the king, married John of Brabant, an athletic young man, "stout, handsome, gracious and well-made," whom she had known during her childhood. The colorful splendor of their wedding celebration—the extravagant costumes, the king and his knights attired in full armor—creates an unforgettable picture. All London seems to have joined the knights with their ladies in marching and singing through the streets of the city and suburbs while more than five hundred minstrels, fools, harpers, violinists, and trumpeters, some English, some foreign, cavorted about the palace grounds. Margaret was a merry child of fifteen years, the duke a few years older. Everything seemed conducive to a happy union. Actually the marriage proved disastrous. Margaret soon found that she was to be but one of many women in her husband's life. In Brussels, where she eventually went to live, she was "doomed to the mortification of being perpetually surrounded with the bastard sons of her husband."

Of the two remaining royal princesses, Elizabeth, Edward's youngest daughter, married John, Count of Holland, a happy if uneventful union. Mary's life at four had been prearranged by her parents. She became a nun, veiled at the convent of Ambresbury in 1284, where the queen dowager, Edward's mother, Eleanor of Provence, had also taken the veil after the death of Henry III. Mary never forgot that she was a royal princess. She was seen everywhere and proved as much of a gadabout as her sisters. Life in the convent did not prohibit an active social existence outside, and she made demands regularly on the king for gifts of money and wine for her personal use. She died at fifty-four, the last survivor of the union of Edward and his first wife, Eleanor of Castile.

CHAPTER SEVEN

The Rebirth of Parliamentary Democracy

1

"IT was from me that he learned it!" cried Simon de Montfort when he issued from the town of Evesham with his small and tired army and found himself facing the converging forces of the then Prince Edward. The heir to the throne of England had indeed learned a great deal about generalship from this uncle who had defied the power of Henry III and had beaten the royalist troops at the earlier and spectacular battle of Lewes. And so Simon de Montfort knew that he would die on that tragic day and that his cause was lost.

Edward had also learned much from Simon which guided him when he became king. He remembered well a certain great day when his uncle had tried a memorable experiment. On March 8, 1265, a Parliament was assembling which would later be called the Great Parliament. At that historic gathering, common men for the first time sat down with the nobility and the bishops. Simon had summoned from two to four "good and loyal men" from each city and borough to attend and take part in the deliberations. What share they had in the discussions and to what extent their views weighed in the decisions reached are not known. Called "bran-dealers, soap-boilers and clowns" by those who resented this radical step, they nonetheless sat with their betters, if not in full equality, at least to face the same problems. A precedent had been set which would persist until the model for parliamentary rule had been fixed for all time.

Few particulars are known about this epochal gathering. It is unlikely that Simon de Montfort, who was a great man, looked at those common men sitting quietly in their plain cloaks and with their flat cloth caps on their knees and saw in them the forerunners of the elected members who would have the making of all law in their hands centuries later. But if he lacked that full vision, he must have had some part of it.

As a youth Edward had been such an admirer of this uncle he was destined to overthrow and kill at Evesham that the bond between them had once threatened to separate the prince from his somewhat less than admirable father, Henry III. He knew the thoughts which filled the mind of that great leader and innovator. And this may have been why he summoned a Parliament to meet at Shrewsbury in 1282 and included among those to appear two representatives from twenty towns and boroughs. Among the noblemen summoned were eleven earls, ninety-nine barons, and nineteen other men of note. No representatives of the clergy had been instructed to appear, perhaps because the session was being held at the edge of the Marcher country and within the shadow cast by the Welsh wars.

The names of some of the common members have been kept on the record. Henry de Waleys, the mayor of Shrewsbury, was one, as were Gregory Rokesley and one Philip Cessor. It is unfortunate that nothing is known of them beyond that. Waleys had seen the king two years before in connection with a royal loan; he was, in all probability, of some wealth and consequence. Among the others there must have been many of stout character, of vision, of courage, perhaps also some sly individuals who thought only of personal gain, a few even of mean attributes, human nature being what it is. Few, if any, could read or write. All had a share of the humility which alone made life tolerable for those of low degree.

It seems certain that Edward's move to give the commons representation was not yet a matter of settled policy with him. They were called at a moment of crisis when he felt the need of united support, their function to confer on war problems. It is a clear indication of his attitude that the men from the towns and boroughs were not summoned to take part in parliaments for a long time thereafter.

Then, after eleven years, he went back to the system of triple representation, the nobility, the clergy, and the commons. What had happened in the meantime to change his thinking? Had the vision which had come to Simon de Montfort returned to fill the mind of this able and courageous king? Or had he reached his final decision after observing the results obtained with the more restricted form of deliberative body? It is possible, of course, that the opposition of the higher orders had lessened. Whatever the reason, a Parliament met at Westminster on November 13, 1295, and included men elected to represent the commons, together with seven earls, forty-one barons, and two knights from each shire.

It was significant that the writ of summons began with a quotation from the Code of Justinian: "As the most righteous law, established by the provident circumspection of the sacred princes, exhorts and ordains that that which touches all shall be approved by all, it is very evident that common dangers must be met by measures concerted in common." Thus was a great truth laid down which was to continue as the guiding principle through the centuries while parliamentary procedure and power were being tested and corrected and finally brought to a working degree of perfection.

At this great gathering, in order to complete the representation, were the archbishops and bishops, attended (for consultation only) by their archdeacons and proctors.

This momentous gathering is generally referred to as the Model Parliament because it came so close to settling the form which parliamentary deliberations would finally assume. Edward's plan, to have the three bodies deliberate separately, was the forerunner of the separation finally effected into two houses, the House of Lords, in which the peers and the bishops sat, and the House of Commons.

It was a model Parliament in one other respect: it helped in the selection of Westminster as the one place of meeting. There had been a tendency to wander about in previous reigns, and often the barons had been summoned to Winchester, Northampton, or Oxford. Edward, being so continuously on the wing, had fallen into the habit of holding Parliament wherever he happened to be. There were sessions at Winchester, Northampton, Shrewsbury, Acton Burnell, Bury St. Edmunds, Clipstone in Sherwood Forest, Berwick, and Salisbury. This suited the king's convenience, but it was exasperating for the barons and bishops to be under the necessity of collecting their people and following the dusty-footed monarch all over the kingdom. The journey had to be made by those on horseback with trains of fifty or more servitors, knights, squires, valets, chirurgeons, confessors, grooms, men-at-arms, and archers. It is hard to conceive how the multitudes which constitute a parliament could be housed and fed in, say, Clipstone, where the king had a hunting lodge with the usual small houses about it, a chapel and a mill, and no towns within easy distance. Even Bury

St. Edmunds, which had been a royal town in Saxon times but was still relatively small, was hard pressed by the scores of cavalcades converging on it from every direction. What scrambling there must have been to provide food for so many hearty eaters and to find sleeping quarters for them all! Sometimes the deliberations had to be held in churches, inadequate castles, and even in large barns. If the energetic Edward found himself greeted with glum faces when he stalked in to Parliament to express his royal will, it may often have been the result not of dissent with his program but of the great discomforts the members were suffering. Twenty years of this dancing to the royal tune led to a general acceptance of Westminster as the place to meet.

2

The barons of England, who had forced King John to his knees and had been at odds, and sometimes at war, with Henry III all through the long reign of that exasperating monarch, were not entirely in accord with the forward-looking policies of Edward. They were inclined to hang back, to mutter their disagreement, even to adopt open measures of opposition. They were intensely jealous of their rights, and some of Edward's wise lawmaking seemed to them to tread too heavily on the iron-shod toes of feudal privilege. Nor did they favor the bringing of the bran-dealers and soap-boilers into the halls where the laws were made.

They said so openly at a meeting of Parliament which Edward called for February 25, 1297. He was at Salisbury at the time and accordingly the session was held in that ancient town. War with France had blazed up, owing in part to some hostilities between the sailors of the Cinque Ports (Hastings, Romney, Hythe, Dover, Sandwich, Winchelsea, and Rye) and the fishermen from Normandy. There was a wily and ambitious king on the French throne, Philip IV (all through this phase of history French kings were believed in England to be wily and ambitious), and he made this a pretext to seize Gascony, which was about all that was left to England of the immense possessions Eleanor of Aquitaine had brought with her when she became the wife of Henry II. Negotiations between the two monarchs came to naught and so Edward, needing money badly, took emergency measures to raise it. There were glum and hostile faces when Parliament opened. The two glummest and most hostile were those of the fifth Earl of Norfolk, who was hereditary marshal of England, and the Earl of Hereford, who held the post of constable. When Edward announced that he planned to lead an army into Flanders to fight things out with the French king and would send another army to recover Gascony, the meeting flared into opposition.

It was the marshal, Roger Bigod, who was most outspoken. When all the sons of the great William the Marshal died without issue in the middle years of the century, the post had gone to the son of Matilda, the oldest daughter, who married Hugh Bigod. The son of this marriage died in 1270 and his nephew, Roger, succeeded to the earldom and the baton of marshal. This was the member of the nobility who now took it on himself to oppose his will to that of the king.

He seems to have been lacking in the qualities of the fourth earl, who, although devoid of subtlety and the qualities of leadership, was brave and open in all his dealings. The nephew, who now faced Edward, had a degree of pride which verged on truculence. When Edward told his marshal that he was to go with the army to Gascony, Bigod flatly refused.

"With you, O King," he declared, "I will gladly go. As belongs to me by my hereditary right, I will go in the front of the host before your face."

Edward regarded the set expression of the marshal and the stiffness of his back and no doubt said to himself: "So! Now what have we here?"

Restraining himself from the peremptory response he would ordinarily have made, the king said, "But without me, you will of course go with the rest."

"I am not bound to go," asserted Bigod. "And go, I will not!"

This was too much for the hot Plantagenet temper which Edward had been holding in check. From his great height he looked down on the somewhat squatty figure of the marshal and his eyes began to blaze.

"By God, Sir Earl!" he cried. "You shall go or hang!"

"By God, Sir King!" declared the marshal. "I will neither go nor hang!"

This story is told because of the light it throws on certain phases of the character of the king. With any other of the Plantagenets, this episode would have exploded into violence at this point. Edward was in a white-hot rage but he was able, nonetheless, to handle the situation in a reasonable way. In the first place, he knew he was in no position to quarrel with the baronage, having the French war on his hands and rebellion flaring around his home frontiers. In addition, he knew himself on dangerous ground, having adopted means of raising money which broke the stipulations of the Great Charter.

The result was that Roger Bigod neither went to Gascony nor hanged. In concert with the constable and a number of other prominent barons he got together a party of fifteen hundred men who stood under arms until the issue was settled. This was close to open rebellion. Edward, however, did not fly into the rage which was so common to his grandfather, John of infamous memory, or John's father, Henry II. Instead he excused the two hereditary officers from performing the duties of their respective posts and appointed temporary substitutes.

At this point Edward made it clear that he had an appreciation of the need to retain the affection of his subjects. He went about it, moreover, with what would be called today a high degree of showmanship. On a platform in front of Westminster Hall he made a public appearance with his son and heir on one side of him and the Archbishop of Canterbury on the other. He proceeded to make an address aimed directly at the hearts of the people.

He had made mistakes, he acknowledged, and he begged his people to forgive him for whatever had been amiss. With tears in his eyes he went on to speak of the belligerence of the French king and what it meant. "I am going to meet danger on your behalf," he declared, "and I pray you, should I return, receive me as you do now, and I will give you back all that has been taken from you." He paused dramatically. "And if I do not return, crown my son as your king."

Archbishop Winchelsey, who had been bitterly debating with the king on what the clergy should pay toward the war, broke into tears at this stage. The young prince wept also, and this mood communicated itself to the great mass of people who had assembled to listen. With one accord the listeners raised their hands high in the air as proof of their complete loyalty.

The barons were not as easily convinced. As soon as Edward had crossed the Channel they drew up a list of grievances and under the leadership of Bigod and Bohun presented it to Prince Edward (then thirteen years of age), who had been appointed regent in his father's absence. It was demanded of the prince that he agree on behalf of his father to rescind every financial exaction to which they objected, including the imposition of forty shillings on wool, and to confirm the terms of the Great Charter and the Forest Charter. The prince, faced with a baronage in arms, agreed to the stipulations and signed in his father's name.

The document was then sent to Edward at Ghent, where his army was stationed. Instead of flying into a fury as his high-tempered forebears would have done, he gave the matter due consideration. It was clear to him, of course, that to assent to these demands would be to establish a new conception of taxation; that never again would a king of England be able legally to impose a tax without the consent of Parliament. Without undue delay he signed the document and returned it to England.

The personal pique of Roger Bigod had been the starting point of all of this, but back of his open disobedience had been the determination of the baronage to prevent kings from taxing them at will. A conclusion of the utmost importance had been reached.

But the king did not forget. When the French war was over, having proven as inconclusive as most wars, the king dealt with his difficult marshal. Bigod was deeply in debt and, as he had no children, he was persuaded to execute a will making the king his heir, in return for a settlement of the debts. That done, he found himself relieved of his post of marshal of England. He died, peacefully and in his own bed, a few years later. His landholdings were distributed among the king's children. The name of Bigod ceased to be included among the great families of England.

CHAPTER EIGHT

The Death of Queen Eleanor

1

TROUBLE was brewing in Scotland over the succession to the throne, and Edward was watching the progress of events with a shrewd eye, having a deep interest, as will be explained later. He had decided to have a few days' hunting in Sherwood Forest (a certain youth who would become known later as Robin Hood was thereabouts but not yet a thorn in the flesh of sheriffs) and he issued summonses for a meeting of Parliament later at Clipstone. The queen, who was often called Eleanor the Faithful, had gone north with him, but when he rode on to Clipstone she remained behind at Harby, a small village in Nottinghamshire, as a guest in the house of a gentleman of the court named Weston. She was seized almost immediately with a lingering fever. Master Leopardo, the queen's physician, did not consider it serious at first but, becoming alarmed finally, he sent hastily to Lincoln for certain medicines, including a special syrup. The report sent to the king was sufficiently alarming to bring him hurrying to her bedside. He left the Scottish situation still simmering and dismissed Parliament after no more than seven days of deliberation. When he reached Harby it was apparent that his beloved wife had not much longer to live. She died on November 28, in her forty-seventh year.

The king was so stricken with grief that he remained in seclusion for two days, eating and drinking little and turning a white and drawn face to such of his advisers as found it necessary to interrupt his vigil. He wrote, or dictated, a few notes, for one is still in existence addressed to the Abbot of Cluny, in which he says, "We cannot cease to love our consort, now that she is dead, whom we loved so dearly when alive." The body in the meantime was placed in a coffin filled with aromatic spices, and Edward emerged from his solitary mourning to accompany the cortege to Lincoln. The bier rested that first night at the Priory of St. Catherine close to that city, and it was probably then that the determination became fixed in the king's mind to express his grief in a memorable manner.

He recalled no doubt that twenty years before the coffin of Louis IX of France, known in history as Saint Louis, had been carried on the shoulders of his devoted followers from Paris to the burying grounds at St. Denis, the bearers being relieved at intervals so that all who so desired could have a share of the burden. Wherever the procession stopped, a cross forty feet high had been set up. This custom was to be followed in France on at least one other occasion, when the great French constable, Bertrand du Guesclin, died in 1380 before Châteauneuf-Randon in Languedoc. His coffin was carried all the way to Paris. So universal was the desire to honor that valiant warrior that everywhere men clamored for a chance to bear a share—knights, citizens, and field hands alike. Across the face of France went that amazing procession, and it was recorded that not one bearer but wept as he bore the weight on a bowed shoulder.

Feeling that his once beautiful and always loving consort was worthy of special remembrance, Edward decided to erect a stone cross of surpassing beauty at every place where her body rested for a night. Because she had been so well loved by the people of England, he decided also that the work must be entrusted to native hands; a wise decision, for the work of the stone carvers of England could not be surpassed.

The first of the Eleanor Crosses was set up on Swine Green opposite the priory in Lincoln. In addition to the cross, which was the work of one Richard de Stow, master mason, a tomb was built in the Angel Choir in Lincoln Cathedral to contain the viscera of the queen. The second cross was on St. Peter's Hill near the entrance to the town of Grantham. The third was at Stamford. The fourth was at Geddington, described as "one of the sweetest and quietest villages in England." This one differed from the others in that the platform for the cross was raised over a bubbling spring.

The fifth was at Hardingstone, about a mile from Northampton, the sixth at Stratford, the seventh at Dunstable where Icknield Way crossed Watling Street, the eighth at St. Albans. The ninth was at Waltham and the tenth at Cheapside in the outskirts of London. The eleventh, and last, was at the village called

Cheringe then but now known as Charing. It was the most elaborate and stately of all.

This sorrowful procession had lasted from December 4 until
December 14. All the noblemen and the bishops who had attended the Parliament at Clipstone were in the mourning train.

2

Time and the parliamentary forces in the civil war collaborated
to destroy most of these beautiful memorials. The stone used for
most of them could not resist exposure to the elements for much
more than two centuries, after which the beautifully carved figures
began to deteriorate. The Roundheads, as Cromwell's iron horsemen would be called in that bitter clash in the seventeenth century, are said to have destroyed the crosses at Lincoln, Grantham,
Stratford, Dunstable, St. Albans, Cheapside, and Charing.

Perhaps it was just as well that they thus passed out of existence, for the efforts made at restoration had not been successful.
One case of this may be recorded. The Cheapside Cross was handsomely designed by Michael of Canterbury, but it soon fell into
disrepair and an elaborate restoration was decided upon by one of
the mayors of the village, John Hatherly. The efforts were ill conceived and directed. Figures of kings, queens, and bishops were
added, all of them ludicrous in execution, as well as a Madonna
and a figure of the pagan goddess Diana. To complete the desecra-
tion, a conduit was laid from the Thames to the stone figure of
the huntress, so that a stream of water spouted from her mouth
continuously. The Parliament of 1643 ordered the destruction of
this monstrosity, and it is said that "drums beat, trumpets blew,
caps were thrown in the air and a great shout of joy arose from
the people" when, the impious Diana having been destroyed, the
top cross fell. The populace were said to have made knife handles
from pieces of the stone.

Edward would have been very much saddened had he known
that the memorials he raised to the memory of his beloved
Eleanor would fail to survive the ravages of time and the religious
rancors of civil war.

The cost of the Eleanor Crosses was estimated to have been in
the neighborhood of fifty thousand pounds, the equivalent of
many millions in present-day currency. The penny was still the

common coinage of England (all other denominations, such as shillings, marks, and pounds, being coins of account only), and one wonders what method was employed in paying such large amounts.

It must be added with some reluctance that the cost of the Crosses was assumed by the queen's executors. This would seem to indicate that she had been the possessor of great wealth in her own right, and moreover that the king, while inspired to this unusual gesture by his deep grief, was not above taking advantage of her wealth.

3

Foreign queens were not often popular with the people of England. Edward's mother, the fair and sophisticated Eleanor of Provence, was so heartily detested that her barge was stoned on one occasion when it bore her up the Thames from the Tower of London. John's consort, the very beautiful Isabella of Angoulême, was admired but not liked. Eleanor of Aquitaine, the wife of Henry II and the mother of Richard of the Lion-Heart, was considered a wicked woman and blamed, unjustly, for the death of the Fair Rosamonde. But Edward's queen was greatly loved in the country. She was not as brilliantly lovely as Isabella, nor to be compared for vivacity and charm with Eleanor of Aquitaine, who had been the toast of Europe. There were, however, a warmth and sweetness about her which won all hearts. Her endearing qualities may still be discerned from the statue in bronze on her tomb in Westminster Abbey. It was executed immediately after her death by a fine English sculptor, William Torell. Her delicate features are there shown in a gentle smile. The dusky softness of her long tresses can only be guessed at, but they form a pleasing background for her face.

It was not her beauty alone which appealed to the people. She was generous and thoughtful in the extreme, as witness her will. It contained bequests for all who had served her, even in the most menial capacities. Master Leopardo, who may have been too slow in sending to Lincoln for those drugs, was left twenty marks nonetheless. A leech sent by the King of Aragon received twelve and a half marks. The queen remembered her ladies-in-waiting with enough to serve as marriage portions. She did not forget her cooks and tailors and grooms. The nature of some of the bequests made it clear that she had revised her will a very short time before the end, which is an evidence of great thoughtfulness. One of the chronicles of the day had this to say of her: "To our nation she was a loving mother, the column and pillar of the whole nation."

Wax candles burned without dimming around her tomb in the abbey for more than three hundred years, a proof that the affections she had inspired were not soon forgotten.

CHAPTER NINE

A Vacant Throne in Scotland

1

It becomes necessary at this stage to consider the character of Edward not only in the light of his earlier record but also with regard to what follows. He had been a great king and he would continue to be great, but in a far different sense. The wise lawgiver, the just administrator give way now to the conqueror. A modern analysis might suggest that he had a split personality, but this would not be accurate, for the qualities that begin to come out strongly in him had always been there. While engaged in the heavy task of codifying the laws, he had been dealing with Wales. The precision and dispatch with which he concluded the Welsh campaigns had stamped him as a military leader of high mark, but in the settlements he made with the people of that country he had been decisive rather than admirable or just.

There have always been forces at work in the world which override justice. The sufferings that the defeated Saxons endured for two centuries after Hastings were gradually forgotten in the fusing of the two races. Who will say that the Indians of North America should have been allowed to keep that continent for themselves? Down through the ages empires have fallen, generally through the aggression of inferior races, but out of the resulting confusion good has come. It may have been that the English people, who were stirring and moving toward greater things, could not have endured forever a troublesome neighbor on their very doorstep; and this can be cited, perhaps, as in some measure a justification for Edward in the case of Wales.

But Scotland was a different matter. The Scottish people were troublesome neighbors also, and the border line between the two countries would inevitably have been the scene of continuous forays back and forth. But the trouble was far enough removed to make a solution possible that would fall short of absorption. The full blame for what happened cannot, however, be laid on the shoulders of Edward. The selfishness, pride, and treachery of many of the leading noblemen of Scotland made it impossible for them to agree among themselves. They invited Edward to come in and allowed him arbitrary powers. His culpability lay in his willingness to take full advantage of this and to wield the weapons thus placed in his hands with the thoroughness of a conqueror and, at times, the machiavellian skill of later-day diplomacy.

It has already been said that Edward was a thorough, if superior, Plantagenet; and the members of that gifted and dynamic family had always displayed the conquering strain. Edward was not the first king of England to cast covetous eyes on Scotland. It was unfortunate for his place in history that the great opportunity to act came in his day. It is hard to believe that the king who was so temperate and just in so many things could have allowed the hates engendered in war to lead to the butchery at Berwick and to the execution with such barbarity of the great Scottish leader, William Wallace. Otherwise his case might have rested on his work as a maker of forward-looking laws and as the foster father of the House of Commons, and he could have been acclaimed without any reservations as the best of English kings.

2

The waters of St. Tredwell's Loch, which always turned red when a death occurred in the royal family of Scotland, must have astonished the natives one autumn night in the year 1290 by the vivid color they assumed. The Maid of Norway had died, and her death was to involve the country in years of such sanguinary strife that many other waters would run red with blood.

The Maid of Norway was the granddaughter of the very pretty Princess Margaret of England, oldest daughter of Henry III, who had been married when eleven years of age to Alexander III of Scotland. This vivacious and dark-eyed child had been taken to Edinburgh by her strait-laced Scottish guardians and confined most strictly in the castle, to prevent her from seeing her husband, who was only ten years old. She was given nothing to eat but oaten bannocks and "paritch" and for recreation she could look out into the foggy skies and listen to a piper in the courtyard below. She was not released from this dismal life until an English army appeared at the border to demand her liberty. Later she was very happy with her husband, to whom she presented three children, two sons and one daughter, named Margaret also. The daughter in course of time married Eric II of Norway and died after giving birth to a third Margaret, who was called thereafter the Maid of Norway.

In the meantime the first Margaret had died and within two years both of her fine sons, Alexander and David, had passed away, leaving the succession to the infant princess in Norway. King Alexander, most reluctantly, for he had been very much in love with his English wife, married then a daughter of the French Count de Dreux, whose name was Joleta, in the hope of having more sons. Pending this development, it was agreed by the nobles of the country that the third Margaret should be considered the successor to the throne.

At this point Edward of England showed signs of possessing what was called in Scotland "the sign of the thread"; in other words, an instinct for bargaining. Seeing a way to bring England and Scotland together under one ruler, he negotiated with the King of Norway a marriage between the Maid and his son Edward, who had now reached the age of six and showed evidence of becoming a very handsome fellow indeed.

The hand of fate then intervened to give the situation a final ironic twist. Alexander of Scotland, still without children by his second marriage, came one night to Burntisland on his way to Kinghorn, where his wife was staying. It was dark and stormy and he was urged to delay his departure until morning. But the king was not one to be balked by inclement weather and, like Tam o' Shanter, he started out into the wild night. His horse missed its footing on the edge of a steep cliff and Alexander was killed in the fall.

He had been a good king and all Scotland mourned for him. As one chronicler put it:

> He honoured God and holy kirk,
> And medfull dedys he oysed to werk.

The people had every reason to mourn, for now all hope of a peaceful accession was centered in the small child in Norway. Arrangements were made to bring her at once to Scotland. A well-equipped ship was sent for her, fitted out with everything to please the heart of an infant queen—fine clothes and bonnets, soft mattresses, and sweetmeats and frails of dates and figs (a frail being a large basket), and all manner of toys, including perhaps a crown.

Playing cards had not yet been introduced into western Europe, but if they had it might have been said that now Edward of England had all the trumps in his hands. He arranged at once for a meeting at Salisbury to which commissioners from Scotland and Norway were summoned, to make the needful arrangements for the succession and marriage. Under the pretext that the rights of the youthful pair must be conserved, he demanded that Anthony Bek, Bishop of Durham, be made governor of Scotland in the interim. This was reluctantly agreed to, for the Scottish commissioners, having a trace of the same thread, knew a shrewd maneuver when they saw one.

When the ship returned from Norway and put in at the island of Orkney, the news was conveyed to the anxiously waiting people of Scotland that the little queen had succumbed to the hardships of sea travel while crossing the stormy waters between the two countries.

Almost immediately no fewer than thirteen claimants to the throne came forward. The land was threatened with civil war, and in desperation the lords of the northern kingdom appealed to Edward to act as arbitrator. This duty he undertook with readiness.

A mystery developed almost immediately in connection with the death of the Maid of Norway. It was whispered about that it was not the princess who had died, that in fact she had been spirited off the vessel before it sailed; how or why being left to the individual imagination. In 1301 a handsome young woman came to Norway from Leipzig and gave it out that she was the Princess Margaret. Her story was that she had been kidnaped by a woman named Ingeberg, the wife of Thor Hokansson, and sold into servitude. She bore sufficient resemblance to the deceased Maid to win her some adherents. Her story could not be substantiated in any way, however, and the law did not delay in dealing with the matter. The pretender was imprisoned and later burned at the stake as a witch. She became, to those who had believed in her, a legendary figure and for a long time she was revered as a saint.

3

The thirteen claimants were a contentious lot, although few of them had more than a shadowy case. There would have been fourteen if Alan Durward, Earl of Atholl, who had married a natural daughter of Alexander II, had not died a short time before. However, one Nicholas de Soules was there, having married another natural daughter of the same king, Ermengarde by name. The two Comyns of Badenoch were on hand, called the Black and the Red, and the first named was inclined to push his rights, which had to do with his descent from a Princess Devorguila. He occupied somewhat the same position as a favorite son in a presidential nomination race in America. He put himself forward but made it clear that, if necessary, he would retire and throw his support to the leading candidate, John de Baliol.

The decision lay in reality between two men, the already mentioned John de Baliol and Robert de Bruce of Annandale, although a third candidate, one John Hastings, was in the running briefly. Baliol was a grandson of Margaret, the eldest daughter of David, brother of William the Lion. Bruce was a son of the second daughter, Isabel, and based his claim on being of an earlier generation than Baliol. Hastings was the grandson of still a third daughter, Ada. Bruce had been acknowledged as his successor by Alexander II when it seemed unlikely that he would have an heir, but the subsequent arrival of a son, who became Alexander III, had nullified that preference. In any event, there was some doubt about the acknowledgment, nothing being on record to prove it had been made.

It seems to have been considered, with good reason, a rather poor choice. Baliol had the better claim from a legal standpoint but he did not appeal to popular sentiment. He lacked the qualities of leadership, being of a retiring character, if not actually timid. The pawky common people had nicknamed him *Toom Tabard*, which meant *Empty Jacket*, and suggests that he was held in rather low esteem.

Bruce was the stronger man of the two, but he was getting on in years, a circumstance that was offset by his having a solid male line of succession to offer. He had at the time a middle-aged son and a sixteen-year-old grandson, who would become Robert the Bruce, victor at Bannockburn and king and national hero of Scot-

land. A large group favored the Bruce claims, known as the party
of the Seven Earls, which indicates that the landed interests were
behind the lord of Annandale. This constituted a weakness as
well, for the Bruces and practically all of their supporters had a
strain of Norman blood in their veins. Bruce had extensive estates
in England and Ireland, as well as his lands in Carrick from which
he derived his earldom. The Scottish people wanted a king with
nothing but Celtic blood and undivided sympathies.

This was the issue which Edward was asked to arbitrate.

He summoned the lords of the north to attend him on May 10,
1291, at his castle of Norham, which stood at the border line between the two countries. There was not sufficient room in the tall
square structure at Norham for all the claimants and their friends
and their respective trains, and so the first meeting was held on
the haugh along the riverbank. The proceedings there were
opened by the chief justice of England, Roger de Brabazon, who
made it clear that the first step must be an acknowledgment of
Edward as the supreme and direct lord of Scotland. At this the
Scots became painfully aware that their feet were on alien soil and
that an alien voice was making a claim that struck at the very core
of their independence. They looked at one another in uneasy
amazement and finally they asked for time to discuss the point.
This was granted and they withdrew across the river to Scottish
soil, where their tongues were free to express what they felt. They
returned to the haugh on the English side with a demand for
thirty days' delay for consultation with the leaders of Church and
state at home.

When they arrived at the end of the thirty days, there were
only eight claimants in the party. The others, realizing the weakness of their cases or feeling an unwillingness to accept Edward's
terms, had remained at home. The two parties met in Norham
Church, and the Scottish spokesman, with a reluctance that
attested the bitterness of the struggle from which they had
emerged, announced their willingness to accept the overlordship
of the English monarch. The remaining claimants swore in turn
to abide by Edward's decision as that of the sovereign lord of the
land.

It was decided then to have the case debated before a body
made up of forty judges selected by Baliol, the same number from
the Bruce side, and twenty-four Englishmen appointed by Edward. The hearings before this body were protracted over a long
period of time, and it was not until the following year that a

meeting was held in the Dominican chapel close to the castle of Berwick. It was here announced that they had found in favor of John de Baliol.

The members of the board and the rival claimants then appeared before Edward in a magnificently staged reception in the great hall of the castle. The English king had summoned all of his leading barons and bishops to attend, and the flash of the jewels they wore was more noticeable than the touch of sunlight on steel. The atmosphere was one of friendliness, and Edward's smile was as warm for the Scots as for his English subjects.

Baliol was crowned at Scone on November 30, 1292. He appeared later at Newcastle to do homage to Edward as his liege lord. Here an incident occurred which caused a darkening of faces among the followers of the new king. Edward took the old seal of Scotland and broke it into four pieces, which were then deposited in a leather bag, to be placed finally in the treasury of England as proof of the significance of the ceremony. There was thoroughness in everything the English king did.

Thus a solution of the succession problem had been reached without any shedding of blood. But Scotland was not happy about it. The king of the Sassenach, the most determined ruler in all Europe, had placed his armored foot across their threshold. Even the nobles and the great chiefs, most of whom had landholdings in England, were apprehensive. Back at home the common people were openly antagonistic to the settlement. They would never place their confidence in, nor have any feeling of loyalty for, King Toom Tabard.

CHAPTER TEN

The Start of the Scottish Wars

1

KING John of Scotland soon found that he had paid too high a price for his crown.

Six months after his coronation, a citizen of Berwick, Roger Bartholomew by name, appealed to the English courts in a civil action having to do with shipping losses. Berwick was on the Scottish side of the border, but the plaintiff's determination to carry the case to Westminster was allowed. King John was summoned to appear in a case involving a wine bill of the late king and to serve in a Yorkshire court. Soon afterward one of the Scottish earls, Macduff of Fife, whose brother had been killed by Lord Abernethy, felt that the hearing of the case in the Scottish courts showed an edge of favoritism on the king's part for the defendant. Macduff took his case to Westminster, and King John was summoned to appear there. When he refused, he was judged guilty of contumacy and an order was issued for the seizure of three of his castles. Lacking the courage and will to stand his ground, John gave in and agreed to appear in person at the next meeting of the English Parliament. When he arrived in London, however, he found that his presence there was likely to have consequences of a much more serious nature. Edward was preparing for war with France, and it was made clear to the Scottish monarch that he would be expected, as a vassal king, to take troops to the continent in aid of the English.

The two kings quarreled bitterly. It was pointed out to Edward that the triple agreement reached at Salisbury before the death of the Maid of Norway had specifically denied the right to try Scottish actions at law in English courts. Edward brushed this aside and stood on the decision at Norham, where his suzerainty had been acknowledged without reservations. John complained that he was being forced to come into English courts with his hat in his hands, figuratively speaking, and that his demand to have a prosecutor appear for him had been denied, so that he had found it necessary to rise and take his place before the bar like any mercer or vintner. The result was that the empty-jacketed lord of the north, wrapping himself in such poor shreds of dignity as were left him, made a secret exit from London and rode hurriedly north to his own land.

The summoning of kings to appear before courts in other lands was not a new departure. The English kings, from the time they acquired possessions in France through marriage, had sworn fealty to the rulers of France, but only in respect to these holdings. A particular case was the summoning of John of England to answer for the murder of his nephew, Arthur, before the peers of France; a demand which that belligerent monarch ignored. The treatment of the new Scottish king was on an entirely different basis. Never before had a sovereign ruler been expected to plead before a foreign court in such purely internal matters as the Macduff case. Two explanations only could be seen for the course Edward was following. He may have been so deep in his preparations for the invasion of France that he left such matters in the hands of his high officials, who proceeded according to the letter of the law, or he may have been deliberately goading the new Scottish ruler into a refusal that would provide a pretext for an armed invasion of the northern country. The second explanation seems the likelier of the two. Certainly it was the view that the people of Scotland held.

While the question of the English king's right to try cases from Scotland in his courts was thus disturbing the relations between the two countries, there was continual trouble on the high seas. Scottish ships plying between Berwick and the continent were seized and their crews were imprisoned. No redress could be obtained, although the losses to the owners were ruinous.

When John returned from his humiliating experience at Westminster he found his country in an uproar. His compliance had been resented and the leaders were no longer prepared to leave matters of policy in his feeble hands. A board of twelve men was appointed to act as his advisers or, if need be, to control the policy of the state. It consisted of four earls, four barons, and four bishops.

The members of this board, with the Scottish Parliament to

back them up and the sentiment of the nation strongly with them, began to take vigorous action. A meeting of the Parliament was held at Scone, where a formal demand from Edward for troops to be sent to France was rejected. The Scottish leaders knew they were inviting armed retaliation, but the national ire had been raised to the point where the people were prepared to fight for their liberty. All English officeholders, including those appointed by Edward, were summarily dismissed and all lands held in fief by English subjects were declared confiscated.

The next step taken by the Scottish leaders was a bold one. They decided to seek an offensive and defensive alliance with France. The King of France at this time was a remarkable individual about whom much will be written later, Philip IV, known as Philip the Fair because he was acknowledged to be the handsomest man in Europe. There was something sphinx-like about this imposing monarch who sat silently on his throne and allowed his ministers, mostly lawyers of comparatively low degree, to make all announcements of policy. It was generally believed that he was slow of wit and lethargic of person (he became immensely corpulent in his middle years), but all the time he was king remarkable things were happening in France. It was to this impassive but inflexible king that the Scottish Parliament, realizing they had a death struggle on their hands, sent emissaries to propose an alliance against the extremely able and violently active English king. Philip the Fair listened and, according to custom, had almost nothing to say. He was shrewd enough to see, however, that he had little to lose and much to gain in the proposed alliance, and undoubtedly it was on his instructions that his legal advisers decided to take advantage of the chance to place a check on Edward. An agreement was reached between the two nations by which each promised aid to the other in case of English invasion. It was further arranged that a bride for King John's son and heir, Edward, would be found among the beautiful daughters and pulchritudinous nieces who surrounded the handsome monarch. A niece, Isabel de Valence, the daughter of the Count of Anjou, was the one selected.

The alliance with France proved fatal to the Scottish cause. As soon as he learned what had been done, Edward demanded that all the fortresses along the border be placed in his hands until the finish of the war with France. When this was refused, he decided to postpone action against the French until he had dealt with

what he termed the insurrection of the Scottish people. This decision was partly the result of a rash and unsuccessful invasion of
the northern shires of England undertaken by the Scots in
fulfillment of their promises to Philip the Fair. They sent an army
down into Cumberland led by the seven Scottish earls. The system of divided command which the Scots found necessary because
of the pride of the clan heads and their unwillingness to accept orders from one supreme commander, and which was destined to
lose them many battles, made this attack an abortive one. They
ravaged the countryside until they reached the fortified city of
Carlisle. Here they suffered a sharp reverse and found it necessary
to retreat to their own territory.

The only assistance lent them by France was a reopening of an
attack on English-held Gascony.

2

Edward lost no time in moving to the invasion of Scotland. He
raised an army of five thousand horse and thirty thousand foot
and shoved northward to the Tweed. The palatine Bishop of Durham had collected the armed levies of the north and with them
he crossed the Tweed near Norham while Edward was crossing at
the ford of Coldstream with the main part of the army.

Berwick was the first point of attack, lying on the other side of
the Tweed in Scottish territory. It was the great port of Scotland,
being the funnel through which the trade of the nation flowed. It
is sometimes claimed that Berwick was the richest seaport in the
whole island; at any rate, the customs receipts were one fourth of
the total revenue of all English ports. The Tweed had cut a deep
channel where the city perched on the north bank behind its
fortifications. The inhabitants of the city, with the arrogance of
their wealth and their vast trade alliances, believed themselves
safe from aggression. This opinion grew when the English fleet,
which sailed in to attack them from the sea, was repulsed with a
loss of many ships. William the Douglas, a stout fighting man,
commanded the garrison. The defenses consisted of a stockade
surrounded by a ditch. The stockade was not high and it was not
in good condition, and the ditch was not wide. Nevertheless,
when Edward moved up to the assault, the citizens lined the top

of the stockade and jeered at him, chanting a bit of doggerel at his expense:

> What meaneth King Edward, with his long shanks,
> To win Berwick and all our unthanks.

It seems rather trivial, but Edward was infuriated. It is probable that the name of Longshanks, which history elected to apply to him, dates from this episode. His legs were not unnaturally long. He stood six feet two in his prime, but when his tomb was opened long after his death it was found that he had been perfectly proportioned.

The confidence of the burghers was sadly misplaced. Enraged by the loss of his vessels and the taunts from the walls, Edward led the attacking party in person. The stockade was so low at one place that the king on his great stallion Bayard leaped over the ditch and then over the stockade. The foot soldiers followed in such numbers that the defenders were easily scattered.

The garrison of the castle surrendered on terms that permitted them to march out, but the poor citizens were less fortunate. The fighting rage in the English king had been increased by the death of his nephew, Richard of Cornwall, in the struggle, and he gave orders that all the men of the town were to be put to the sword. Sitting in the great hall where he had announced the result of the arbitration, Edward turned a deaf ear to all appeals to stop the slaughter. It was not until a procession of priests came into his presence, carrying the Host, that his mood changed. When the eyes of this strangely contradictory man rested on the Host, he burst into tears and gave orders that the carnage was to stop.

The number of the victims of the butchery of Berwick has been placed at different figures, but the lowest estimate is eight thousand, so it may be assumed that at least that number perished.

The Scottish people retaliated in kind. The Earl of Buchan, constable of Scotland, was leading a foray into the English territory in the west. When the news of Berwick reached these levies, they proceeded to sack the towns that fell into their hands with equal ferocity, and a mutual hatred was engendered which was to last for centuries.

Before proceeding deeper into Scottish territory, the English king set his troops the task of rebuilding the fortifications of Berwick, raising the walls higher and deepening the ditch. To set an example of industry, he himself wheeled out the first barrow, piled high with mortar and stones. He proceeded also to put the affairs of the city on a better basis, improving the laws and appointing capable men to administer them. The citizens, who hated him for his cruelty, were compelled to say later that he had done them a service in the model administration he gave them.

Before attacking Berwick, Edward had sent a summons to the new Scottish king and his lords to meet him at Newcastle. While still engaged in restoring the fortifications of the captured city, an answer was received in which John renounced his fealty and defied the invaders.

"The false fool!" cried Edward, the royal anger rousing again. "What folly is this? If he will not come to us, we will go to him."

So the English army, horse and foot, reinforced with Welsh bowmen and levies from Ireland, moved up from the Tweed. They crossed the Blackadder and the Lammermuir Hills and met the Scottish army, fresh from its invasion of Cumberland, and defeated it at Spottswood without any difficulty. The castle at Dunbar capitulated, and through the month of May the way to Edinburgh was cleared, Haddington, Roxburgh, and other towns falling to the invaders. On a day in early June, Edward came within sight of the capital city of Edinburgh.

That solid and admirable city, which the inhabitants themselves would later call *Auld Reekie,* was a mixture of splendor and wretchedness at this stage of its history. The castle, which topped an abruptly high hill, was not only a strong fortress but a residence of royal magnificence by the standards of the day. The city, clustering at the base of the hill, had been described some generations before as a small cluster of thatched and mean houses. David I had laid the groundwork for better things, however, by founding the Abbey of Holyrood on the edge of the town. A connecting link of houses began to grow along a spine of high land, and in time this new section, which was to be known as Canongate, became a prosperous commercial center. When the first Parliament was held in 1215 in Edinburgh during the reign of Alexander II, there was a High Street leading up to Castle Rock, on which clustered busy shops, and there was a section around Candlemakers Row where the artisans found employment. The peaked spires of churches, the swinging signboards of taverns, and the crenelated tops of manorial houses were beginning to lend dignity to the old town.

The English marched into Edinburgh without encountering opposition, but the castle held out for eight days. Edward moved on then to Stirling, where the castle had been deserted on his approach, and from there he progressed to Perth. At the latter place he received notice of King John's submission, that most spineless of rulers lacking the heart for protracted resistance. Edward received from him at Montrose the white rod, symbol of surrender, and promptly deposed him. Baliol was sent under armed guard to England and took no further part in the dramatic struggle between the two countries. At first he was a prisoner in the Tower of London, but the Pope interceded for him and he was allowed to go into exile on the continent. Here he lived in obscurity on his small French estates, not dying until 1315 and so knowing of the efforts of two brave leaders who rose after him to direct the resistance of the Scots.

After marching as far north as Elgin, receiving the submissions of the gentry everywhere, Edward returned to Berwick. He brought with him the Coronation Stone of Scone and the cross of *Halyrudhouse*, which was called the Black Rood. Nothing he could have done was more certain to create lasting enmity than his removal of the Coronation Stone. It remained an issue down through the centuries; and it is a sore point with the Scottish people at the present time, as witness the daring seizure of it, and its temporary removal to Scotland, in 1950.

At Berwick the English king received the submission of most of the Scottish leaders, the list filling thirty-five skins of parchment. This historic document was called the Ragman Roll for reasons not entirely clear, unless it was a term of contempt coined by the Scottish people. For an equally obscure reason the name became corrupted to the word "rigmarole," which has made a permanent place for itself in the English language.

Edward had needed less then twenty-one weeks to bring about the submission of the country.

CHAPTER ELEVEN

William Wallace

1

THE Scottish cause seemed hopeless. Their armies had dispersed and their leaders had sworn fealty to the conquering Edward. Their short-reigning and inglorious king had been deposed and was living abroad in exile. The Bruces, who were next in line for the succession, had thrown in with the English and were living on their English estates. Edward had placed his own garrisons in all the strong castles of Scotland and had appointed a group of hard-fisted officials to administer the country: John de Warenne as governor, Walter de Agmondesham as chancellor, William de Ormesby as justiciar, and Hugo de Cressingham as treasurer.

What the prostrate country north of the Tweed needed was a leader. When he came—and fortunately he appeared quickly—he was neither of the aristocracy nor of the people; he was from in between, the second son of a rather humble knight of Elderslie in Renfrew. His name was William Wallace and he was quite young when his rise to fame began; probably in his very early twenties, although there is much conjecture on this score, as there is indeed about almost everything that applies to the life of this remarkable man. He was, of course, a great fighting man and a born leader. The claymore (the dread two-edged broadsword of Scotland) became in his mighty hand a weapon to beat down antagonists and to shear through the strongest armor.

Years after his death an ancient lady, the widow of one of the lords of Erskine, who was living in the castle of Kinnoull, was visited by a later king of Scotland in search of information about Wallace. She had seen both Wallace and Bruce when she was a girl, she told the king. She affirmed without any hesitation that, although Robert the Bruce excelled most men in strength and skill with weapons, he was not to be compared with Wallace in either respect. In wrestling, she asserted, the knight from Elderslie could overcome several such as Bruce.

The answers she may have given to other questions have not been preserved, unfortunately, and so the chance to know Wallace as a man through the eyes of an acquaintance has been lost. Was he tall or short? Dark or fair? Was he handsome of mien? There is not a scrap of reliable evidence on any such points. It is believed, but largely because of his accomplishments, that he had the eye of a great leader; an eye that kindled in the threat of danger, that commanded loyalty, that shone like a beacon in the fury of battle; a *cler aspre eyn, lik dyamondis brycht.*

William Wallace has been a controversial figure for centuries. At first the long rhymed narrative of Henry the Minstrel, better known as Blind Harry (although now it is not even conceded that he was blind), was the chief source for the Wallace story. Blind Harry lived nearly two hundred years after the events of which he told. He made his living as a wandering minstrel, his stock in trade being a long narrative poem about Wallace, nearly twelve thousand lines in length, which he had written himself and committed to memory. For this epic effort he had drawn on the legends which were still in circulation in the country during his youth. Undoubtedly he had added to them and had depended on imagination whenever he deemed it necessary. The poem fortunately is still in existence, written in the Lothian dialect. Many editions of it have been printed. It has exceeded in sales all other publications in Scotland with the exception of the works of Bobby Burns and Sir Walter Scott. That Blind Harry lived the precarious life of a wandering minstrel is generally accepted, because in his old age he was granted a pension by James IV of eighteen shillings twice a year.

His version of the appearance of Wallace is summed up in one line, *Proportionyt lang and favr was his wesage.* He becomes rather more detailed as to the "wesage" by declaring, *Bowand bron haryt, on browis and brois lycht,* which means "wavy brown hair on brows and eyebrows light."

Historians and antiquarians are disposed to accept little of the old minstrel's story, knowing that so much of it is spurious; and that leaves them with the barest of bones from which to construct a figure of this heroic man. It is generally assumed that he was born at Elderslie near Ayr, that his father held his land of James the Steward, that his mother was a daughter of Sir Hugh Crawford, sheriff of Ayr. He had two brothers, Malcolm the elder, and

John the younger. William is supposed to have gone with his mother at some crisis to find protection in the household of a powerful relative at Kilspindie in the Carse of Gowrie and to have completed his education, such as it was, at the seminary attached to the cathedral of Dundee. Blind Harry's story that the boy stayed with an uncle in holy orders at Dunipace is not accepted now, which throws doubt on one of the most popular anecdotes: that he had one Latin verse dunned into his head by this uncle which went as follows:

> My son, I tell thee soothfastlie,
> No gift is like to libertie:
> Then never live in slaverie.

There were countless valiant souls in Scotland not content to live in "slaverie" after Edward left the country, convinced that he had stamped out all resistance. They began to manifest themselves in Galloway, Ross, Argyll, and Aberdeenshire. In the spring of the year following Edward's departure, a stout knight named Andrew de Moray led an outbreak which threatened to weaken the English hold on the north of Scotland.

Had the spirit of Wallace been less resolute, he might have been daunted by the strength with which the English held that part of the Upper Plain where so many hundreds of small streams feed the volume of the Clyde. A discerning eye on Tinto Top might see Dumbarton Castle and the castle at Ayr, swarming with English soldiery, and the town of Lanark, where one William de Heselrig held down all resistance with an iron hand. There was nothing here of the majestic aloofness and strength of the mountains in the highlands, nothing but sloping plain and moor and a few hills which were rounded and accessible; no country, this, for the only type of warfare open to patriotic Scots, the kind that later would be called "guerrilla." Nevertheless, Wallace soon became known as the daring leader of a small band of patriots who struck here and there at unexpected times, who appeared and disappeared and led the occupying forces a wild and unprofitable chase. His most spectacular feat was an attack with thirty men on the headquarters of Heselrig in Lanark, in which the English sheriff was killed. It was long believed that in retaliation the English destroyed the home of Wallace and killed his wife, whose maiden name was Marion Broadfute. Blind Harry was the sole authority for this anecdote. Wallace did kill William de Heselrig, but he did not possess a home and he was not married.

That Wallace quickly won a nationwide reputation is proof that he possessed a genius for warfare. He was not as favored as an earlier guerrilla fighter in the first stages of the French invasion of England to unseat the hated John, the colorful Willikin of the Weald. Willikin kept a large part of the French army in continuous alarm; but he had the dark, thick forests of the Weald into which he could disappear and from which he could emerge at the most unexpected times. Wallace was ringed about by the strongly held castles already mentioned and he operated in a country which was better suited to farming than to the strike-and-run-and-strike-again tactics of the guerrillas. As he lacked the thickets, deep gorges, and high wooded hills for concealment, it must have been that his safety was assured by the silent aid of the country folk. Even this would not have sufficed entirely, for the shepherd seldom left his sheep run and the farmer's feet were chained to his tilled fields. There were many wandering friars in the Lowlands, particularly the Culdees, the Allies of God, who had left the monastic life of their round bare towers for a secular addiction to the care of the sick and the poor. These lowly friars, moving about so quietly, may have supplied the eyes for the irregular troops fighting so successfully under Wallace.

Wallace, for some such reason, seemed to have a charmed life. The alien governors of the country angrily demanded that an end be made to the raids of *de Waleys*, and word of his activities reached even to the ears of Edward, stalemated in an abortive campaign against the French in Flanders. It followed that when a few of the Scottish nobility decided the time was ripe to organize the forces of revolt, they turned to William Wallace as one of the leaders.

2

The hills of Lanark were yellow with the mountain pansy and the tormentil when Wallace gathered his men about him and started north to answer the summons. At Perth he met Sir William Douglas, the first man of real consequence with whom he had come in contact. Sir William had commanded the garrison at Berwick and had been held a prisoner in irons for some time, gaining his release on taking an oath of obedience. It seems that oaths sworn under pressure were not regarded seriously, for here was the head of this great family, which through long centuries would be the proudest and most spectacular in all Scotland, in open rebellion again, his sword at his side and his heart filled with zeal for the cause. It was at a later date that the Black Douglas, as the head of the senior branch of the family was known, took as a motto:

> Let dog eat dog:
> What doth the lion care?

But Sir William had all the pride and the courage which were the distinguishing traits of the Douglases and had already earned for himself the sobriquet of The Hardy. The Douglas castle and estates were in Lanarkshire, so in a sense he and Wallace were neighbors, but it is doubtful if they had ever laid eyes on each other until they met on this occasion. They must have conceived a mutual respect, for they proceeded to work in concert with the best of results. They decided on an operation which appealed mightily to both of them; they would march on Scone, which lies close to Perth, and pay their respects to William de Ormesby, who was acting as justiciar of the country.

Scone was holy ground to all Scots. It was only a small village, but far back in history it had been the capital of the Picts. The legislative meetings which corresponded in Scotland to the English Parliament had met there on Moot Hill. The abbey still stood, despite Edward's threat to destroy it after carrying off the Coronation Stone. William de Ormesby may have thought that his presence at Scone would lend validity to his actions. In any event, he had set up his courts there and was making himself the persistent gadfly which stung most deeply the pride of the Scots and lightened their purses at the same time. His specialty seems to have been the levying of fines. If a man of any consequence refused to come to Scone and swear fealty to the English monarch, he was either outlawed or fined.

The combined forces of Wallace and Douglas marched to Scone but encountered no resistance there. The justiciar, considering himself too weak to oppose such a determined thrust, had gathered up his records and documents and taken flight.

This was the first substantial success for the insurgent forces, and all Scotland rejoiced at the freeing of Scone, even though the stone on which the head of the dying Columba had rested was no longer there. It proved a costly exploit for Douglas. The English king confiscated all of his estates in England and put his wife and children under arrest. Later Douglas himself became a prisoner and was sent back to Berwick, to the familiar cell he had occupied before and the same irons in which his wrists and ankles had been clamped. He died there within the year.

After the success at Scone, Wallace proceeded to sweep like a new broom of rebellion through the country as far north as the circuitous Tay. His forces had been augmented by many of the leaders of dissent, and this gave him a greater prominence in the eyes of the nation; but it would prove a weakness in the end. The Scottish leaders had absolute power in their own clans and they could not be brought to accept the theory of united command. They would fight in their own good time and wherever they saw fit, but they would accept orders from no one. The result of this pigheadedness was a defeat in which Wallace had no part.

Under prodding from the impatient Edward, the English officials in Scotland put together an army and marched unopposed through the Lowlands to a point beyond the Forth. The Scottish leaders could not agree on any plan of military action, and when the two armies met at Irvine no serious opposition was offered the English. The proud Scottish lords, who would not yield an inch in place or precedence to one another, yielded everything to the invaders. After the merest tiff, they laid down their arms and capitulated.

Wallace had played no part in this humiliating farce. While the noble lords were submitting themselves to whatever punishments might be devised for them, he was attacking the rear guard, succeeding to the extent of destroying the baggage of the enemy and most of the guard.

For a time after the farce at Irvine, Wallace continued to lead the only band in open resistance in the Lowlands, and word of his activities finally reached the royal ears. In the insistent notes which Edward dispatched to his lieutenants he began to refer to the knight of Elderslie as "the king's enemy." In the Highlands the fire had not been extinguished. Andrew de Moray, who alone seemed to share the military skill and the full fighting spark which animated the youthful Wallace, had a series of successes in the reduction of castles garrisoned by the English. One of the most colorful exploits of Wallace was chasing Anthony Bek, Bishop of Durham, from the house of Bishop Wishart in Glasgow.

The treasurer, Hugo de Cressingham, seems to have taken too

seriously the English triumph at Irvine. Believing that this absurd exhibition meant that the back of the resistance had been broken, he sent optimistic reports to Edward. This may have persuaded the king to devote his full personal attention to his French concerns. Toward the end of August he sailed again across the Channel, leaving the responsibility for subduing the recalcitrant Scots in the hands of the governor, the Earl of Surrey.

The treasurer had said in one of his letters to the king that "William Wallace holds himself against your peace." It would have been well for Edward had he given heed to this particular information. Wallace was indeed holding himself against the king's peace, and the hearts of all the common people of Scotland were with him.

CHAPTER TWELVE

The Miracle at Stirling Bridge

1

THE English leaders, fortunately for the Scottish cause, displayed a lack of energy in following up their success. Wallace took advantage of this breathing spell by gathering under his banner the common men of Scotland who had been left leaderless, and so he found himself for the first time with an army under his command. Moving rapidly, he laid siege to Dundee, at the same time sending a large part of his forces to a strong position near Cambuskenneth Abbey, where they threatened Stirling Castle, the gateway to the Highlands. This forced the English command to take action, and an army of fifty thousand foot and a thousand horse marched north under the command of the governor himself, John de Warenne, Earl of Surrey. Warenne was in the late sixties and had been fighting all his life. He had grown weary of warfare and he sat his saddle in bone-stiffened discomfort. He advanced to Stirling by slow stages.

What followed can only be described as a miracle. The military experience of Wallace was limited to his own guerrilla operations. The army he commanded consisted of forty thousand foot (at the most optimistic reckoning) and 180 horse, made up largely of the men who had lost their clan leaders at Irvine but who still wanted to fight. They were brave but they were not trained soldiers in any sense of the word. Their equipment was of the crudest nature. Few of them wore a habergeon, the shirt of iron rings which had been brought back to Scotland by crusaders, and they depended instead on tunics stuffed with wool, tow, or old cloth to soften the edge of a sword thrust. Their weapons were long spears or Lochaber axes. Only a few could be classed as *gall-oglauch*, the pick of the levies from hill and valley, who fought in the front rank when the clans went into battle. Their spirits were high enough, but how far would courage go in opposing the well-trained and well-armed English?

The most serious weakness, however, was the army's lack of organization. The best fighting force in the world would be helpless if it lacked authority behind it to supply arms and food and scouting facilities to keep an eye on enemy movements. Wallace lacked everything but men. The absurdity at Irvine had paralyzed the efforts of the high authorities who were supposed to direct the Scottish defense. No arms or food was forthcoming. The wild clansmen drew in their belts and subsisted on a few scraps of dried oatmeal. The few mounted men were quite inadequate to do the scouting thoroughly.

It is clear, however, that Wallace had been born with military genius. Never having heard the word strategy, perhaps, he selected nevertheless the ideal place for the test of strength. The plan of battle he followed showed him to be a master tactician as well. The strength of his army was concealed in the thickets at the base of the Ochils, a steep ridge of hills on the north of the Forth. That river, curling slowly through Stirling except when tidewater enhanced its flow, was crossed by one bridge only, a structure of wood which allowed no more than two horsemen to cross abreast. The Scots were in a position here to swoop down on the English, if they attempted to cross the river, and thus catch them on the Links in a bend of the river where the ground was too swampy for cavalry action. If the tide of battle went against the defenders, they had an easy line of retreat over the rocky Ochils behind them. Here, then, the followers of Wallace, as skillfully disposed as any army could be, watched and waited.

Warenne hugged the delusion that the Scots could be persuaded to give up the struggle and return to their homes. He made several efforts to persuade them and finally sent a pair of itinerant friars as emissaries to Wallace.

"Carry back this answer," said the Scottish commander. "We have not come for peace but to fight to liberate our country. Let them come on when they wish. They will find us ready to fight them to their beards!"

This precipitated a division of counsel in the English high command. Warenne was not an inspired general, but he was wise enough to distrust the situation. How could they tell how many wild clansmen were concealed at the base of the Ochils? It would take a full day for the English army to cross by that solitary bridge. Was it a wise operation to undertake in the face of a foe of unknown numbers? His inclination was to wait and see if a bet-ter way of crossing the tide-fed river presented itself. Some Scottish turncoats spoke of a ford farther up which could be used to turn the flank of the Scots. But Cressingham, the treasurer, had come with the English army and he was all for prompt measures. This ambitious and avaricious churchman, described in one of the chronicles as "handsome but too fat," was the evil genius of the English. His parsimony had handicapped the king's forces at the same time that his overbearing attitude had won him the hatred of the Scots. A time-server in his relations with the king, he was thoroughly distrusted by the other high-ranking officials. When a churchman charges soldiers with overcaution and even hints at cowardice, he puts them at a disadvantage.

"There is no use, Sir Earl," he said, "in drawing out this busi-ness any longer and wasting the king's revenues for nothing. Let us advance and carry out our duty as we are bound to do."

The decision reached was to cross the bridge and attack the Scots on the other side. It has already been stated that the men Edward had left behind to finish his work were not great soldiers. Nothing could make this clearer than the course they had decided upon. A single glance at the bridge spanning the Forth at one of its deepest parts should have been enough to make them change their minds. Why was the bridge standing?

Wallace had been first on the ground, and there had been plenty of time to destroy this convenient method of crossing the river. A half dozen strong-armed, broad-backed Highlanders, armed with their Lochaber axes—a long-handled type of ax with a hook on the back to yank and draw with—would have had the structure down in no time at all. But there it stood, unharmed, comfortable to cross, with a wide stretch of land left open on the other side, and no enemy in sight, even though the English felt that thousands of hostile eyes watched them from the thickets.

Successful strategy consists in fighting your battles at the time and place which offer the surest promise of a favorable issue. Wallace was a self-made soldier, with only brief experience in a small way to draw upon, but he was an instinctive master of strat-egy. He had decided, quite obviously, that this was the time and the place to offer battle to Governor Warenne and his large army. The bridge had been left intact as bait, to draw the attention of the enemy from the ford farther up the river where six men could cross abreast safely and where the terrain was not as favorable for defense. Fording a stream as variable and strong as the Forth was not an easy matter. How much simpler to take advantage of this bridge which the stupid Scots had neglected to destroy! Wallace had guessed right. He had gambled that the enemy would elect to use the bridge and had made his dispositions accordingly.

Warenne's tired bones kept him in bed beyond the time when the attack should have been made. Some of the English troops, impatient at the delay, crossed the bridge without raising as much as a derisive shout from the hidden Scots and then returned to their own side to wait for their ancient leader to waken. The sun was high when Warenne emerged. The bridge looked as secure as ever, the green haughs beyond were clear for a good mile, the thickets far back could not conceivably conceal any great number of Scots. The crossing began.

What followed was a supreme test of the generalship of Wallace. He had to choose unerringly the right moment to strike. If he launched his attack too soon, he would succeed only in destroying a small part of the enemy and the main English forces would be left intact. If he waited too long, the invaders would be able to establish a strong enough bridgehead to resist any attack and to enable the rest of the army to cross behind them.

Wallace showed that he had patience as well as judgment. From his high place of concealment he watched the first horsemen come over the bridge at a sedate jog trot to test the security of the structure. When it became evident that nothing had been done to weaken it, the pace became faster. After the horsemen, who spread out fanwise under the command of a capable officer, Sir Marmaduke de Thwenge, came the foot soldiers and the Welsh archers with extraordinarily long bows over their shoulders. Soon the lush green haugh was black with the human stream, and still no sound came from the cover where presumably the Scots were waiting. Or had they decamped during the night, fearing to face such a formidable host? How Wallace succeeded in keeping his excitable troops from any form of demonstration is hard to understand, save that it is known his hand was heavy in discipline and his displeasure swift and harsh.

The Scottish leader waited until eleven o'clock. By that time a very considerable part of the English army had crossed, but not enough to diminish his confidence that he could destroy them. He gave the long-awaited signal.

The wild battle cry of the men from the Highland glens split the air. From behind the semicircle of thicket along the base of the Ochils came thousands of figures leaping in a maddened fury, their robes drawn up around their waists to leave their brawny bare legs free, the chiefs with eagles' feathers in their bonnets, the common men with a sprig of thistle in theirs. They charged across the haughs, brandishing their deadly hooked axes and their long spears, still raising that high, keen cry which sent shivers down the spines of those who had never heard it before. There seemed to be no end to them. They poured forth from the scant cover like nondescript articles from a magician's chest; ten, twenty thousand, and perhaps more. The boggy ground did not delay them, for they were in their bare feet. It seemed a matter of minutes only, after the order was given, for them to make contact with the enemy.

Wallace had shrewdly grouped on his right the best trained of his men, who might reasonably be termed the *gall-oglauch* of the Scottish army. These troops struck the left flank of the English as they deployed from the bridge and went through them like a knife through a wheel of cheese. So instantly successful was this blow that they took control of the end of the bridge and no more of the English troops could get over. The efforts of those still on the swaying structure had to be devoted to resisting the pressure of the files pressing on behind them, a struggle which resulted in most of them being shoved against the Scottish spears or forced over into the rising waters of the river below. The English who had succeeded in crossing were then driven into a bend of the river to the right of the bridge, and here they were either cut down or shoved into the river, which was now salt with the incoming tide. Few, if any, managed to swim across!

Five thousand men died in less than that number of seconds. Many of the English leaders fell in the carnage, including Cressingham, who had ridden over with the van, intending no doubt to show what a churchman could do and perhaps conning over in his mind the self-laudatory note he would send the king. He was thrown from his horse in the first few moments of conflict and trampled to death. Later, discovering whose body it was, the Scots stripped off his skin and divided it among themselves as souvenirs.

The impotent Warenne sat his horse on the other bank and saw his best soldiers being hacked to pieces by the jubilant clansmen. Realizing that the battle was lost, he gave orders for the bridge to be burned, if possible, and for the army to retreat. His own departure was so precipitate that he rode straight through to Berwick. From that still desolate and sad city he continued on to York, where a letter reached him from the Prince of Wales, who was acting as regent in his father's absence. In this note he was admonished not to leave Scotland until the insurgents were beaten and destroyed.

A cautious general is content with victory and slow in the pursuit of a retreating foe; a great general strikes as hard and as boldly when his enemy is beaten as when the issue is still undecided. Wallace handled the pursuit of the beaten English in the latter tradition, a course made easier by the eagerness of his followers. The victors must have made use of the ford. They were, at any rate, soon hot on the heels of the retreating aliens.

And now the barons of the land, who had been too proud to fight under a commoner, or too sensitive to the possession of their personal estates, came out of retirement to join in the man hunt. Even James the Steward of Scotland and Malcolm, Earl of Lennox, who had been sitting in council with Warenne and promising him men in support of any action, emerged from the safe retreat into which they had skulked and took a hand in the chase.

The once proud English fled down the stony roads in a mad race for their lives. Their heels were seldom free of claymore or spear in the hands of the enraged hounds. They were tracked down in the forests, they were driven into the rivers and streams, the bracken became stained with their blood. Over it all the sun shone warmly as though with approval, and from every thicket the songs of the missel thrush and the sedge warbler seemed to rise higher because the land would now be free.

It had indeed been a miracle.

2

The activity of Wallace did not cease with the pursuit of Warenne's army. He recruited his forces, often by arbitrary methods such as hanging a few recalcitrant officials, and proceeded to reduce the towns which were still held by the English. The list of strongholds captured in a matter of weeks included Dundee, Edinburgh, Roxburgh, Stirling, and Berwick. Then he burned the English towns immediately south of the border and marched into England to harry Westmorland and Cumberland.

Some form of national organization was adopted, but there is nothing in the scanty records of the day to indicate what it was. Wallace was knighted and became officially known as guardian of the kingdom. Undoubtedly he either dictated the measures taken or had a decisive hand in them. That he assumed such a modest title is proof of his lack of ambition and the sincerity and depth of his patriotism. One factor in the situation remained unchanged: the nobility still held sullenly aloof. Accustomed to unchallenged authority in a personal realm, they could not thole any change which took away a jot of their hereditary power and privilege.

It seems more than probable that if the Scottish people could have formed themselves at this stage into a solid front against English aggression they would have defeated any further attempts to rob them of their independence.

Wallace has been charged with barbarous conduct in the chronicles of the day, most of which were written by English monks and reflect the English viewpoint. It is doubtful if he needs any defense. Wars are fought to be won, and they cannot be won by anything but violent measures. Faced by a foe who had fallen on Scotland with fire and sword, the new leader met the invaders with the same weapons. Wallace also burned and harried and left his dead behind him. He was a stern disciplinarian; but only a firm hand could hold together an army which in the first stages could best be described, perhaps, as tatterdemalion. For every story told of his cruelty, there is at least another which demonstrates his fairness and moderation.

A national or world crisis generally produces at least one great man. Scotland, in her hour of desperation, had found a truly remarkable leader in William Wallace.

CHAPTER THIRTEEN

Edward and the Horn-Owl

1

SURPRISE may be felt that Edward was absent from Scotland at such a critical moment, knowing the low caliber of at least some of his chief lieutenants. The truth was that he had another problem on his hands of at least equal importance. He and King Philip the Fair of France were engaged in what might reasonably be termed the first stages of the Hundred Years' War.

The French king has come down through the centuries as an enigma, because some of the very few flashes of him that history supplies make him appear stolid and slow, both of body and mind. It has been assumed that he depended on the clever lawyer chancellors he employed and that he gave little attention to affairs of state. Yet at all stages of his reign remarkable things were happening in France which made it clear that a ruthless intelligence was at work. Could his first chancellor, Pierre Flotte, a one-eyed jurist from Montpellier with a silver tongue, have been the master mind of the state? Was it Enguerrard de Marigny, a Norman squire, who had been a protégé of the queen? Or was it Guillaume de Nogaret, the best and least favorably known of the trio, who was so bold that he tried to make a prisoner of Pope Boniface VIII? Modern opinion seems to have veered to the belief that the power behind all the extraordinary things that happened was Philip the Fair himself.

In appearance he was what might be termed a super-Plantagenet, taller even than Edward of England. In any company he stood a full head above everyone else; and a most unusual head it was, of a pink and white complexion, with blond ringlets and handsome blue eyes. He was immensely strong and could crumple up almost any man with his great white hands. In character he showed some signs of his descent from his grandfather, that great and holy man, Louis IX, who is called St. Louis. One of his first acts on becoming king was to expel women from the court. Only three dishes were served at his table, and his guests had to drink water colored with wine. The deserts were always fruit grown on the royal estates. This may have been either asceticism or parsimony, and no one was sure which.

Once on a chilly day in Paris, with a mizzling rain falling, he was stopped by three soldiers who had some trivial complaint to make. The tall, silent king stood with the moisture falling on his white headpiece, his great feet sinking deep in the mud of the street, and listened attentively. This was what his saintly grandfather would have done, always having an ear for any subject, no matter how humble.

It was strange that he began his reign with the expulsion of women from the court, because in his household circle he was surrounded by them. He had two sisters, the princesses Blanche and Marguerite. Blanche was as lovely as he was handsome; gay, sparkling, slender, with a small foot and a trim ankle. This was the picture of her supplied to Edward by his brother Edmund, who was sent to Paris to make a report. Edward still grieved for his lost Eleanor but he was considering a second marriage, if only for reasons of state. The feminine fashions of the day were the least revealing of almost any period, and Edmund must have secured some of his information from gossipy sources. Authentic or not, the report he sent back depicted the fair Blanche as a veritable fairy-tale princess, and Edward decided that he wanted her for his second wife. The other sister, Marguerite, was slender and somewhat delicate of appearance, with a sweetness of mien rather than beauty.

Philip's own family consisted of three sons and one daughter, Isabella, who was a striking beauty and of whom much will be heard later. She resembled him and not her mother, Jeanne of Navarre, a plump woman with a high complexion, who made up in intelligence what she may have lacked in pulchritude.

In addition there were a great many nieces, most of them daughters of a brother, Charles of Valois, for all of whom husbands had to be found. Charles was a bothersome fellow, garrulous and lacking in judgment, who made a muddle of anything entrusted to him.

Such was Philip the Fair, and it may seem surprising that during the twenty-nine years of his reign many astonishing things came to pass. The feudal power of the French dukes, who had in their time ruled more of the country than the kings, was reduced, and new machinery for justice and legislation was evolved. The order of Templars was violently dissolved and all their immense wealth confiscated, the head of the order in France being summarily declared guilty of heinous offenses and burned at the stake. When Pope Boniface VIII, who was a strong advocate of the supreme power of the papacy, issued a bull, *Clericis laicos* (a papal bull was distinguishable by its lead seal), which forbade any king to levy taxes on the clergy without his consent, Philip's opposition forced its withdrawal. As a result of the hostility which followed, Nogaret went to Italy to arrest the Pope and take him back to France for trial and deposition. Only the illness of the Holy Father, who died soon after his room was violently entered by Nogaret at Anagni, prevented the plan from being carried out. Pope Clement, a Gascon by birth, was crowned at Lyons, and one of his first official acts was to appoint nine French cardinals. It was Clement who moved the papal court to Avignon, and thus began the seventy years of exile during which the papacy existed, in what was called a Babylonian captivity, in France. Nogaret may have been one of the blackest villains in history, but he would not have dared plan such a course had he lacked the backing of his king. Behind everything that went on was this ambitious, ruthless, dangerous king.

Nevertheless, the Bishop of Pamiers, Bernard Saisset, who was antagonistic to Philip, had this to say of him: "Our king resembles the horn-owl, the finest of birds and yet the most useless. He is the finest man in the world; but he only knows how to look at people fixedly without speaking." This opinion was widely accepted.

This was the French monarch with whom Edward found himself in almost continuous conflict.

2

One of the measures adopted by St. Louis to make sure that his people did not suffer from injustice under feudal law was the appointment of a corps of inspectors, known as inquisitor-reformers. These men were everywhere throughout the kingdom, attending the trials and listening to evidence, and reporting cases where any degree of unfairness could be charged. The greathearted king had, it is said, thousands of these inspectors at work to keep an eye on the dukes and counts and their bailiffs. In a world where police rule has so often been supreme, this practice in a faraway day is like a glimpse of Utopia.

Philip the Fair decided to have his own inquisitor-reformers, ostensibly for the same reason. He did not, however, content himself with the scope of his grandfather's plan. He used them for political purposes as well.

The English were still governing Aquitaine and Gascony, the sole remnants of the once great Plantagenet holdings in France. The inquisitor-reformers swarmed in these provinces, and anyone in trouble with the English authorities could appeal the case to the King of France. It reached a stage where the courts of Gascony were empty, although crime was rife in the land. Every malefactor or innocent man, as the case might be, cried out for French protection when laid by the heels. The inquisitors would take the prisoner away, and that would be the last heard of the case. The French courts were swamped, quite apparently, and it took a long time to bring a man to trial. Perhaps they did not make any effort to try them.

Finally the English bailiffs went about their work with large gags made of wood. When they took a prisoner, they pried his jaws open and clamped in one of the gags, saying, "Now, appeal your case to the King of France!"

The explanation was, of course, that the owl-like king had made up his mind to a drastic course of action. He was determined to make it impossible for the English to govern as much as a foot of French soil.

There was trouble between the two countries on the high seas also. The rivalry began when an English ship was seized in the Channel and a cargo taken which amounted to two hundred pounds' worth of wool. The owner demanded justice. When nothing came of the sharp protest lodged with those gimlet-eyed notaries of Philip the Fair, the merchant applied to Edward for letters of marque so he could seize a French merchantman which was lying conveniently in an English port. This request was granted and two hundred pounds' worth of wine was taken. A scream of protest rose from St. Malo, and in no time at all letters of marque were being issued right and left on both sides of the Channel. No merchant ships felt safe in venturing out from port. Cargoes were being seized with piratical thoroughness and in many cases the ships were destroyed. The two-hundred-pound limit was no longer regarded. There was no way of keeping an accounting of the gains and losses, and so it could not be told where the advantage lay.

Finally the shipowners of the two countries decided to fight it out among themselves. A fleet of two hundred English vessels, all privately owned but with towers built above their prows for offensive purposes, put out into the Channel. A fleet of two hundred and twenty-five French ships came out to meet them. A battle was fought off the coast of Brittany, with arrows blackening the sky and clouds of quicklime puffed out when the wind was right, and with maneuvering of ships to make boarding possible. The English won in the end. Most of the French ships disappeared. Some were sunk; some were captured and taken back to English ports. There was considerable loss of blood on both sides.

This episode came close to provoking war between the two countries. Furious protests reached Westminster from Paris, and Edward, in his role of Duke of Aquitaine, was summoned before Philip to answer for what had happened. Needless to state, the English king was too busy with other matters to obey.

But a more vital incitement to hostilities was the English alliance with Flanders. This alliance was the most natural arrangement in the world. The great Flemish cities—Ghent, Bruges, Courtrai, Lille, Ypres—had grown large and wealthy and powerful by their control of the cloth industry of Europe. The Flemish were master weavers, an industrious and practical people. To make the cloth they depended on England and Scotland for wool. This dependence worked both ways, for the English needed Flanders as a market for the loaded wool barges which came down the Thames to London. The alliance called for mutual support in case either country was attacked.

But France had always interfered in the affairs of the Flemish cities. When Guy de Dampierre, Count of Flanders, entered into an open alliance with England, Philip the Fair took the country over and imprisoned Count Guy in Paris. The Flemish cities were too wealthy and powerful and the citizens too stout of heart to remain under alien control, and in 1301 the weavers of Ghent rose in rebellion and massacred the French garrison. Philip sent an army to subdue the uprising under the command of Robert of Artois, who had won two battles and was regarded as invincible as well as the very pink of chivalry.

The confident Robert took his army up to the city of Courtrai (then a place of 200,000 population, which ranked it second to Paris) without any regard to the conditions he might expect to find there. Courtrai was well situated for defense, being surrounded by ditches and swampy land. The French commander had no belief in foot soldiers. He had a great array of mounted knights and a relatively small force of archers. He sent the archers in first and, when they seemed to have the advantage over the army of weavers, he was in such a hurry to finish the battle with his noble horsemen that he rode over the French archers without giving them time to get out of the way. When his knights came out in the open they floundered in the swampy ground and could neither advance nor retreat.

It was the practice of chivalry to take as many prisoners as possible and hold the captured knights for ransom, a very tidy way of making money. The armed weavers did not seem aware of any such rule. All they had ever wanted was to be left alone to make and sell their cloth and live in comfort and honor. Their idea seems to have been that battles were won by killing as many of the enemy as possible. They swarmed over the soft terrain where the knights were floundering in their heavy armor and proceeded to slaughter them all, including the invincible leader.

This victory has been called variously the Battle of the Bloody Marsh and the Battle of the Golden Spurs, the latter term rising from the fact that more than seven hundred pairs of gold spurs were taken from the heels of the victims and kept on display in an abbey of the city.

Although the English were under obligation to assist the Flemish cities and the French had their alliance with Scotland, neither country seemed disposed to take such matters seriously. When a plan for a truce between England and France was finally evolved, neither party to it had any hesitation in throwing allies to the wolves. The peace they made, however, was a patched-up affair which was not expected to work for any length of time. The issue between them was too deep to be settled over a council table. The French would never rest until the English had been expelled from the land. On the other hand, every Plantagenet king

dreamed still of the days of greatness when Plantagenets held
Normandy, Anjou, Brittany, Aquitaine, and Gascony. In the pact
they reached, moreover, there was a clause which would later give
the English kings a still more glittering objective, the conquest of
France.

CHAPTER FOURTEEN

The Defeat and Death of Wallace

1

EDWARD came back from the continent and proceeded at once to organize his forces for the reconquest of Scotland. He summoned Parliament to meet him at York on May 25 and included the Scottish noblemen. The order was a peremptory one; anyone who did not obey would be considered a traitor. None responded. This did not mean, however, that the nobility of the country had taken their places with Wallace. They still held aloof from the winner of that famous battle of Stirling Bridge. As Hemingburgh says in one of the chronicles of the day, "he was deemed base-born by the earls and the nobles."

There is much difference of opinion as to the size of the army the English king led into Scotland, some estimating it at more than eighty thousand, some convinced that he had no more than a tenth of that number, three thousand horse and four or five thousand foot soldiers, mostly archers. Although Edward had won an enviable reputation as a general he still held some belief in the theory which led to the defeat of French chivalry at the Battle of the Golden Spurs; he placed his reliance on cavalry and did not depend much on his foot soldiers.

Wallace, lacking the support of the nobility (not one earl was with him in the fatal battle which followed), had a much shrunken army to meet the threat. As at Stirling, the ranks were made up almost exclusively of recruits from the lowest orders; brave fellows, but hurriedly trained and poorly armed. A member of the Comyn family, John of that ilk and known as the Red, was in command of a handful of horsemen, considerably less than a thousand. Again the chief weapon was the spear, twelve feet in length and an excellent thing in repelling an attack of cavalry but of small use in hand-to-hand fighting.

Wallace's plans for the battle again demonstrated his skill as a strategist. He had laid waste the English countryside immediately below the border and had taken the precaution of sending a small force to attack the city of Carlisle, which Edward had selected as his chief base of supply. The Lowland counties, all the way from the border to the Forth, had been burned over, the inhabitants and livestock being moved behind the lines of defense at the Forth. Thus the English king had to move his forces up through bare fields and blackened hills which offered nothing in the way of food. A provision fleet had been sent by sea with instructions to join the army where the tidal waters of the Firth locked horns with the stout stream of the Forth. But Wallace and his small but determined army lay somewhere between.

By the time the English army reached Queensferry, where they hoped to receive supplies, they were close to the point of starvation. Edward, who was now in his sixtieth year and growing irascible with the passing of time, had to wait for several days before venturing farther inland to find and attack the Scots. Among his foot soldiers were many Welshmen armed with a new weapon, the importance of which had not yet been fully realized. It was a bow of unusual length which discharged arrows with sufficient force to pierce the thickest armor and could be used three times in the space required to wind and discharge a crossbow once. The Welsh are given credit for the conception of the deadly longbow, but the English took it over and improved it both in design and deadliness. In the following century the English yeomen would display such skill with this lethal weapon that the whole face of medieval warfare would be changed.

The presence of the Welsh, in spite of their powerful equipment, was not deemed an unmixed blessing. They are described as a cantankerous lot, which is not strange in view of past relations between the two races. There was a clash in camp in which eighteen priests were said to have been killed while trying to restore peace. The Welsh threatened to leave and join the Scots. Edward was reported indifferent to what might happen. "What do I care," he asked, "if my enemies join my enemies?" But, as things came about, it was a good thing for England that the Welsh did not leave.

It was at this point that a spy, alleged to be in the employ of two Scottish earls, March and Angus, was brought to the king. The army of Wallace, the spy reported, was no more than a few miles away, near the town of Falkirk, in readiness to strike as soon as hunger forced the English to retreat.

Edward was delighted with the news. "They need not follow me!" he cried. "I go to meet them. This very day."

The army set out at once and by nightfall was close to Linlithgow, where, as the crow flies, they were only a few miles from Falkirk. The troops settled themselves there for the night. It was now that an incident occurred which displayed the mettle of the English king. He was sleeping on the ground, wrapped in his robe stamped with the royal leopards, when his horse, which was tethered beside him, became restive and trampled on him. Two of his ribs were broken. To prevent any panic, the old king got to his feet, vaulted into his saddle without assistance, and gave orders to strike camp. It was still dark, a murky night without a glimpse of moon or stars. They went so slowly that they covered a few miles only; but when dawn broke, the cautious troops saw the bonnets and spear points of the enemy on a high ridge ahead.

It was to be a different battle from the miracle at Stirling, but Wallace had made the best possible plans for the test. The hillside where his forces waited was high and steep, but he had not stationed his men at the crest. Instead they were disposed for battle on a level spot about halfway up the slope. This arrangement may have been due to a desire to fight the battle there, which led Wallace to abstain from making his position so difficult that he would be drawn away from it by encircling movements on his flanks. As a further advantage, a moss stretched across part of the front, of sufficient softness to hamper, if not actually prevent, the free use of cavalry in attack.

In this position the Scottish leader had drawn up his men in three *schiltrons*, the forerunner of the British square. The *schiltron* was a hollow circular formation, with the spearmen in the front rank, where the length of their weapon was well suited to defense, and with reserves in the center to fill the gaps which would develop in the line. The Scottish archers were stationed between the *schiltrons* to hamper further the English attack. Little was expected of them, for archery had been neglected in Scotland and the bows they used were completely outdated by the deadly longbow of the Welsh. The cavalry, such as it was, was held in the rear as a reserve.

Although scholars fighting the battle over and over again with pen and ink have been inclined to criticize the Scottish dispositions, it has been acknowledged by military authorities that the brave Scot made the best use of the ground with the forces at his command. It has been pointed out that Wellington fought Waterloo on similar ground and with the same distribution of his regiments.

There seems to have been a dispute among the Scottish leaders before the battle began. Both Comyn the Red and Sir John Stewart, who had bluer blood in their veins than any of the others, contended that they outranked Wallace and should be in charge. How Wallace settled the matter is not known, but when the English attack came he was in command. He cried loudly to those about him as the horsemen under the marshal and constable of England came clashing and thundering up the hillside: "I have brought you to the ring! Dance the best you may!"

When Bigod and Bohun, the hereditary holders of those two eminent posts in the English army, came to the moss, they were checked temporarily (as the French Imperial Guard would be when they encountered the sunken road of Ohain at Waterloo) and had to divert their forces to right and left, for the moss was wide and dank and a much better aid to Wallace than his blue-blooded lieutenants. This took much of the sting and the force from the first blow of the cavalry. The *schiltrons* stood firm, the spear points as lethal as bayonets, the spirit of the men who formed the lines undaunted and leal. But the cavalry under that man of pride, Comyn the Red, melted away at the first sign of attack. They never came back. For the rest of that bitter day the brunt of the heavy, steel-mounted attack was borne by the ill-equipped foot soldiers in their woolen tunics. Sir John Stewart, who commanded the archers, fought with real valor, dismounting to join his clansmen and Lowland clerks and peasants, and dying in the struggle.

The battle continued, and for a time it seemed that the stout defense of the *schiltrons* must prevail. At this critical stage of the struggle it must have occurred to Edward that the pattern of the battle of Hastings was being repeated. He decided to do as William the Conqueror had done on that fateful day. He fell back on the archers. Whether the Welsh had any great part in what followed is uncertain, but the credit undoubtedly goes to the mighty longbow. The shafts, launched up over the rising ground, fell in the *schiltrons* like hail. What chance had those stouthearted Scots with no protection save shirts stuffed with wool? The only hope would have been to scatter the bowmen, but the circles could not be broken up and the Scottish cavalry had gone with the wind—

and with Comyn the Red. The ranks began to break. Edward, sitting cramped in his saddle and suffering agonies with his broken ribs, was still the best captain in Christendom. He saw his chance and sent a strong body of cavalry to swing far wide of the moss and attack the Scots from the rear.

The sudden appearance of this body completed the rout. The Scottish ranks broke. It was fortunate that Wallace had given consideration to the consequences of failure. The land behind the hillside at Falkirk was heavily wooded, and so the pursuit of the beaten Scots was very much hampered. Wallace himself is said to have encountered and killed Sir Brian de Jay, the master of the English Templars who thundered after him into a wooded thicket at Callandar.

Ten thousand Scots were killed in this battle and the back of the defense against invasion was, for the second time, broken. The gallant gentlemen who had refused to fight under Wallace the Base-born now emerged to blacken his name and debate the soundness of his judgment. This gave them personal satisfaction, no doubt, but availed the country nothing. Though he had been defeated, the strategic policy of Wallace still stood between the victorious king and the complete subjugation of the land. Wherever he took his troops, Edward found nothing but wasted country and burned towns. His provisions had not reached him, and his men went for long stretches of time without food. In the end he had to withdraw his army to Carlisle.

2

The next six years were devoted to consolidating the conquest of Scotland. It was not an easy task that confronted the English king. The Scots were as stubborn as they were brave, and the land itself offered cover to those who still fought against submission. Wallace, no longer regarded as their leader after the failure at Falkirk, was still among the most active of the die-hards.

It is known that he paid a visit to France with a train of five followers to beg assistance from Philip the Fair under the terms of the treaty between the two countries. Philip, who had become quite obese and more taciturn than ever, if possible, promptly made him a prisoner and offered to send him over to England. Edward thanked the French king and asked him to keep the Scot in close custody. Philip, however, had a change of heart. Perhaps he grew to admire the grave and doughty Wallace, or it may have been that he saw more advantage for himself in adopting a different attitude. Whatever the reason, he released Wallace and even gave him a letter to the Pope in which he craved the pontifical favor for the bearer. It is unlikely that the Scot went to Rome, although Blind Harry declares that he did.

He returned in time to witness what seemed the final collapse of the Scottish defense. Stirling Castle, which had been holding out valiantly, fell into English hands. Comyn the Red and most of the barons laid down their arms and threw themselves on the king's mercy. Wallace found himself almost alone in his refusal to submit.

The obduracy of this lone figure had ruffled the feelings of the English king beyond the point of endurance. Edward let it be known that nothing less than the immediate elimination of Wallace would suffice. The records mention many instances of grants paid to cover the cost of raids undertaken for the sole purpose of his capture. The remittance of punishments which had been meted out to various titleholders was promised if they would aid in the capture of the fugitive.

And now one John de Menteith takes the center of the stage. He was a younger son of Walter Stewart, Earl of Menteith, and had fought against the English in the earliest stages of the struggle. Later he was said to have been a "gossip" of Wallace's, which could be construed as meaning that he was in the confidence of the latter. In 1304 he was back in favor with Edward and was made sheriff of Dumbarton, an important post. The story is that he entered into an agreement with Aymer de Valence, who was in command of the English army, to capture Wallace, then in hiding not far away. They worked, apparently, with a servant of Wallace's named Jack Short, who held a grudge against his master. The latter brought the word to Menteith that the fugitive was near Glasgow at a place called Robroyston and offered to lead the way to him.

There is a strange lack of detail about the story of the capture of Wallace. The only explanation that fits the few facts known is that he was in a tavern and that Menteith identified him to the English troops who had been summoned. It is said that he "turned the loaf" (or, in Scottish terms, *whummled the bannock*) as a signal. This brings up a picture of Menteith eating in the tavern and keeping a close watch on the door. As soon as he saw Wallace enter, he carelessly picked up the loaf and turned it end to end. Wallace had not expected to find any but friends and was not prepared to defend himself. The mighty claymore remained in its scabbard as the English swarmed about him and pinioned his arms.

He was loaded with irons and taken at once to London. One report has it that Menteith himself took his prisoner to the English capital; another, that he made the journey in the train of the king. The latter explanation seems unlikely and has only one scrap of evidence to support it. For centuries thereafter the arch over the gateway into Carlisle Castle was pointed out as the spot where Wallace spent a long cold night chained in an open cart, there being no room for him inside.

The general belief in Menteith's guilt was substantiated by the honors which Edward proceeded to heap on him. Among other favors, he was made sheriff of Dumbarton for life. As a final evidence of the king's gratitude, he was given the earldom of Lennox.

The wheels of justice, so called, moved with lightning speed in disposing of the Scottish patriot. The day after his arrival in London, August 22, 1305, he was taken to the great hall at Westminster. A scaffold had been erected at one end and he was placed there, wearing a laurel wreath, a form of mockery typical of the period. Charges were made against him of being a traitor to the king (he had sworn allegiance only to the King of Scotland and so could not be a traitor to Edward), of sedition, homicides, depredations, fires, and felonies.

As he had been declared an outlaw, he was not allowed to make any answer in his own defense. This arbitrary regulation was one that might have been amended in the code so well compiled by the English Justinian (one's admiration for the great Edward sinks to its lowest point at this moment), but it would have made no difference. The fate of Wallace had already been determined and the trial was no more than a formality. He was found guilty by the five judges who sat on the case and was condemned to die by the now familiar method; he was to be hanged, drawn, and quartered.

The sentence was carried out with not so much as an hour's delay. Wallace was taken from Westminster to the Tower and then through streets crowded with avid watchers to Smithfield, being dragged the whole distance on a hurdle at the heels of the horses. The gallows at Smithfield had been raised high so that the multitude which assembled could see the body turn at the end of the hempen rope. He was cut down before dead and was then mutilated in the manner prescribed by law. His head was struck from his lifeless trunk and was hoist on a spear point above London Bridge.

Edward was one of the very few men in London who did not see Wallace die.

The body was cut into quarters and distributed for display in Stirling, Perth, Newcastle, and Berwick. They might at least have sent his head to Scotland, where his sightless eyes would have been turned to the land for which he had done so much.

CHAPTER FIFTEEN

Edward Takes a Second Wife

1

> And Laban had two daughters: the name of the elder was
> Leah, and the name of the younger was Rachel.
> Leah was tender eyed; but Rachel was beautiful and well
> favored.
> And Jacob loved Rachel; and said, I will serve thee seven
> years for Rachel thy younger daughter.

IT is not likely that Edward had ever heard the story of Jacob and
his two wives, Leah and Rachel, and the double apprenticeship he
had to serve. Copies of the Vulgate were few and far between in
the land. One was not included in the three volumes which made
up the royal library, but there may have been a copy, securely
chained, in the chapel at Westminster. The king was not a
scholar and his knowledge of Latin was scanty at best.

If he had known the story, he would have recognized the pattern which began to develop out of the frantic letters he received
from his brother, Edmund of Lancaster, in Paris. A truce had
been signed between the two countries, by which Edward was to
marry the engaging and beautiful Blanche and his son and heir
was to marry Isabella, the daughter of Philip, who was showing
promise of becoming as lovely as her aunt. Edward was so set on
Blanche as his second wife that he agreed on his part to give Gascony to Philip! This was an incredible deal, for the Plantagenets
were not only acquisitive but bitterly retentive and they had never
been known to give anything away willingly. Gascony was one of
the gems in the Plantagenet crown, and to give it away was such a
prodigal gesture that Edward's advisers must have thought him
temporarily bereft of his senses.

Edmund's uneasiness can be easily understood, therefore, when he found it necessary to report to Edward that Philip was becoming evasive in the matter of the agreement. Gascony had already been turned over to France, but the king's brother was dismayed to find the French court buzzing with other plans for the marriage of the self-willed Blanche. Rodolphus, Duke of Austria, had asked for her hand, and it was freely said that Blanche favored the Austrian match, in the expectation that Rodolphus would someday become the Holy Roman emperor.

Deeply apologetic over what he considered his failure as a diplomat, Edmund finally sent on to Edward an amended treaty of marriage in which the name of the younger sister, Marguerite, was inserted in place of Blanche. This change was probably not the fault of Philip. The truth of the matter was that the fair Blanche had put her foot down. She had no intention of marrying an old husband, even if he did happen to be the great Edward of England.

Edward discovered thus that elderly kings, like beggars, cannot be choosers. It was a blow to his pride that Blanche would have none of him, and it was a long and bitter time before he brought himself to the point of taking the younger sister instead. The matter had to be referred to the Pope finally, who settled it by laying an injunction on Philip to return the provinces that Edward had relinquished and on Edward to accept Marguerite as his wife, with a portion of fifteen thousand pounds left to her by her father, Philip the Hardy. Edward decided to make the best of a bad bargain, and agreed.

The younger sister traveled to England in great state with a long train, including three ladies of the bedchamber and four maids of honor, all of noble blood. Philip was not known to show much affection under any circumstances, but he seems to have been fond of his little sister May, as she was called at the French court. He did not make any trouble over the matter of that truly regal dower she was taking out of the kingdom.

The wedding took place at Canterbury on September 8, 1299. The very young bride was endowed with her marriage portion at the door of the cathedral, as was the custom.

2

The story up to this point had followed the same lines as Jacob's romance. Marguerite was probably no better favored than the tender-eyed Leah of the Bible episode while Edward's fancy had been fixed on Blanche as firmly as Jacob's had been on Rachel. But the outcome was much happier. Unlike Leah, who became scrawny and sallow and bitter of tongue with the years, Marguerite matured into an attractive and very sweet woman. Her nose was a mite too long for real beauty, but her eyes were large and bright; and the truth of the matter was that Edward became well content with his child bride. Marguerite seems to have loved her elderly bridegroom devotedly, and so the marriage was an almost immediate success. Perhaps the fact that Blanche's husband never became anything more important than King of Bohemia, which was rather humble compared to the throne of England, was not unwelcome news to the kingly Jacob. When the beautiful Blanche died in 1305, he expressed himself as deeply sorrowful because "she was the sister of his beloved consort, Queen Marguerite."

Edward had to leave for more campaigning in Scotland a week after the wedding, leaving his bride in the royal apartments in the Tower of London and enjoining his officers in charge that "no petitioners from the city should presume to approach, lest the person of the queen be endangered by the contagion being brought from the infected air of the city." The contagion was smallpox, which was raging in that most unsanitary of towns. The younger Edward, one feels, might have expressed some concern for the welfare of the citizens, who could not take refuge in the Tower, and perhaps have enjoined the officers to do something about holding the plague in check.

The next year the new queen went to Scotland with Edward, who was well content to have her thus fall into the familiar habit of his beloved Eleanor. She did not stay long in that war-torn land, for her accouchement was near. She traveled back to Yorkshire and to Cawood Castle, a truly amazing pile of medieval masonry. Here a prince was born who was named Thomas and from whom the Howards, the top-ranking family in the English peerage, would stem.

The next year the queen was at Woodstock and gave birth to a second son, who was given the name of Edmund after the perplexed negotiator of the marriage bond. Fortunately the sons of the somewhat frail Marguerite were born with a better heritage of health than the three sickly little sons that Eleanor had first brought into the world. Thomas and Edmund seem to have been stout lads and had no difficulty in surviving the usual ills of infancy.

Edward became quite uxorious, as elderly husbands so often do. He even developed a greater interest in music because his Marguerite was fond of it. The young queen had brought a minstrel with her from France who was known as Guy of the Psaltery. Edward enjoyed the fine programs that Master Guy provided and settled on him a yearly stipend of twenty-eight shillings. He also allotted three horses for the minstrel's use when the royal family went on their travels. The royal liking for music was shown in other directions, as witness an item in the royal household accounts: "To Melioro, the harper of Sir John Mautravers, for playing on the harp while the king was bled, 20s."

The queen bore one more child, a daughter who was named Eleanor, after the first wife; there did not seem to be any jealousy or pettiness in the king's new consort. The little princess, sad to relate, died in a few days.

Memories of Queen Marguerite have to do largely with her continual intercessions on behalf of people who fell into the king's displeasure. The Rolls carry many such references as "we pardon him solely at the request of our dearest consort." It was due to her that a ban laid on the city of Winchester, because a hostage from France had been allowed to escape, was lifted. Edward was getting very testy and he had not only taken the city's charter away but had imprisoned the mayor in the Marshalsea and had fined him three hundred marks, a great fortune in those days. Marguerite pleaded with the king until his displeasure was removed from both the city and its unfortunate mayor.

There can be no doubt that she did much to alleviate the king's burdens during his last years. Her affection for him was very real, for after his death she wrote, "When Edward died, all men died for me."

CHAPTER SIXTEEN

The Prince of Wales and Brother Perrot

1

EDWARD was not entirely pleased with the way his son was growing up. The prince was entirely normal in a physical sense. From the time he outgrew his Welsh cradle he had been a healthy, rosy boy. He lengthened out fast and seemed likely to approach his tall father in stature. He was not dissolute and he was liked by those about him. But there was something missing in him; he was not princely; in fact, it was becoming clear that he had a common streak which showed in his tastes. He did not take to books and reading. He did not care for swordplay. He was like a blunt weapon when he should instead have been capable of taking a steel-like edge.

At the age of five he had been given a household of his own, and the men at the head of it had not been chosen with the necessary care. It was a large household at King's Langley; seven knights, nine sergeants, as well as minstrels, hunters, grooms and cooks, and of course the upper echelon of administrators, magisters, and tutors. It cost the state in excess of two thousand pounds yearly. In one year this hearty circle consumed 239 casks of wine, not to mention ale and beer. The household seemed inclined to practical jokes, in which the prince himself took an active part. He went about on his travels (they usually visited as many as fifty places in the course of a year) with Genoese fiddlers to provide music and a tame lion. There was always a great deal of gambling going on with dice, and the young Edward did not seem too adept at it. He was always in debt. A rowdy and raucous household, in fact. The great-grandfather of the prince, King John of infamous memory, had a curious tendency to clown at the most inappropriate, even solemn, times; perhaps this accounted for the noisy antics of the prince and his liking for low company.

Perhaps he should have been a farmer instead of heir to a great throne. He was much more interested in horses and cattle and in a camel kept in the royal stables (how it came to be there, or why, was a mystery) than he was in the not too persistent efforts of Master Walter Reynolds to teach him Latin. He was happier helping to plant turnips than in discussing the strategy of a campaign; a fact that caused people to recall that he had been born on St. Mark's Day, when long processions were held with crosses swathed in black and prayers were said for good weather and fine harvests.

In one respect only did the young prince run true to form. Like most youths of royal blood, he was interested in his wardrobe. As it happened, the world was seeing a sudden revolution in men's apparel. The ladies, perhaps because they were preached at from the pulpit and partly because husbands had not yet been educated to spending money to clothe their wives, continued wearing modest long robes which seldom allowed as much as the tip of a toe to show and fitted snugly up under the chin. But suddenly the young men of blue blood and wealth began to support an extravaganza of fashion. The first indications of it seem to have come from France, where even in those days the tailors were an enterprising and imaginative lot. The first step was the introduction of the *cote-hardie*, a close-fitting garment like a waistcoat which fell some distance below the waist but exposed to view the masculine leg in tight-fitting hose. With this foppish fashion, as it was called in conservative circles, went a positive frenzy for fantastic color schemes. The *cote-hardie* could be parti-colored, red on one side and perhaps tan on the other. The shades would be reversed for the hose. Sometimes greater extremes were reached with diagonal and vertical bars of contrasting colors. In these garments the young men of fashion strutted about like animated chessboards. Their shoes, moreover, had such long toes that they curled up in front. This queer fashion was carried to such extremes in later years that the tips had to be tied to the ankles with silken cords. Their hoods were supplied with long tassels which had to be tied around the neck and became known as *liripipes*.

Young Edward was tall and straight and his legs were well turned, so he became a leader in this rather silly revolution.

The king did everything possible to train the boy along the right lines. When the prince was thirteen years old, as we have already said, the father had to take an army to the continent to strike a blow for his Flemish allies, and before leaving he appointed his son regent. It happened to be a troubled time, one crisis following another. Warenne got himself thoroughly beaten by Wallace at Stirling Bridge; the barons became incensed with the king's attitude in levying taxes without parliamentary sanction and insisted on a confirmation of the Great Charter and the Forest Charter. A *Confirmatio cartarum* was laid before the youthful regent, and on the advice of the chief officers of the crown he signed it in his father's name; an act which Edward confirmed later. The boy, in fact, seems to have behaved with proper decorum and even a trace of dignity.

The king began to devote a great deal of time to the education of the young Edward in all matters of statecraft and personal conduct. In one year he addressed no fewer than seven hundred letters to his heir, full of sage advice and often couched in terms of sharp reproof.

Almost from the time he was born there was much speculation as to his matrimonial future. First a marriage arrangement was made by which he would wed the Maid of Norway, but this eminently satisfactory plan became null when the little princess died before reaching Scotland. Then Edward conceived the idea that his son should marry the daughter of Guy de Dampierre, hereditary ruler of Flanders, whose name was Philippa, although she seems to have been called the little Philippine. The King of France put a stop to that by swooping down on the Flemish cities and taking Guy and his daughter prisoners. The father was imprisoned for most of his life and the little Philippine became a member of the French royal household. Finally it was settled that the heir to the English throne was to marry Isabella of France, Philip's daughter, who was called Isabella the Fair.

King Edward had ever reason to know that the Capetian family tree had sprouted something strange and fearsome in Philip the Fair. That the daughter of this cruel and capricious monarch might take after him in character as well as in looks should have given Edward reason to pause and wonder. Would the lovely and sophisticated Isabella be a suitable mate for his undeniably naïve son?

The king made two great mistakes in his efforts to map the future life of his long-legged heir. This was the first.

2

From the time Henry II married Eleanor of Aquitaine and so became ruler of all the western provinces of France, the princes of the Plantagenet line had spent most of their time abroad. Richard of the Lion-Heart was seldom in England, not even when he became king. Edward would have followed this example if the troubles in which his father had involved himself with the barons in England had not made it necessary for him to stay at home and fight the king's battles. Both of these high-spirited and brave princes had preferred to live in the south, making the old Roman city of Bordeaux their headquarters but being much of the time in Gascony. Life was gracious and comfortable in that great city on the Garonne, with its soft airs and golden sunlight beating down so warmly on the leaves of the plane trees; with its wealth and culture. It was pleasant to sit on the open terrace of a low, white stone palace and look out over the lands of the triangle where the grapes grew; much more desirable, in fact, than to be housed in a tall, frowning, mysterious hotel in malodorous Paris or in a grimly frowning Norman castle in foggy London. There was another reason: the companionship they found in the knights and cadets of Gascony who had the minstrel strain in them but were nonetheless longheaded, shrewd, and gallant.

One of these old retainers of Edward's, a certain Arnold de Gaveston, put in an appearance in London in a destitute condition, having escaped from a French prison. He was accompanied by a son called Piers or Perrot. In striving to provide for this unfortunate old comrade-in-arms Edward took the boy into his household as a squire. The boy behaved himself so well that the king decided he would be a suitable companion for his own son. It seemed to the king that the handsome and accomplished Gascon youth would introduce a better note into the oafish household at King's Langley, where they were still emptying five casks of wine weekly and keeping the dice rolling on the trestle table both above and below the salt. So Piers de Gaveston was sent to live there as a comrade for the prince; and this was the second of the two grave errors of which the king was guilty.

With the first glance that passed between them, Piers de Gaveston gained a complete ascendancy over the young prince. He was one of the figures who appears frequently in history and who can only be described perfectly by a modern word, incandescent. A prime example of this was a long-legged and decorative young man named George Villiers who would come along in the reign of James I and be given the title of Duke of Buckingham. A room seemed to light up when men of this caliber entered. They were always handsome and filled with amusing talk. The youthful Gascon had these qualities. He was, moreover, adept at games and the use of weapons.

There were two serious flaws in his character which began to show as soon as he was certain of his hold on the heir to the throne of England. He was greedy for wealth and honors, and his pride was like tinder. Nothing was too much for him to ask. At the least hint of opposition he would flare up into tempers, even at the expense of the most important men in the realm. There was one occasion when the boisterous train of the prince, headed by young Edward himself and Gaveston, invaded the preserves of Bishop Langton, the king's treasurer. After pulling down the palings, they proceeded to wreak havoc among the deer and smaller game. Langton was not one to accept such treatment in silence, prince or no prince. He had been one of the king's most respected councilors for many years and stood high in the royal regard. He went to the king and told his story, with the result that the prince was sent to Windsor Castle with none of his personal household to wait upon him. Here he was kept in disgrace for six months. He was not allowed to see "Brother Perrot" or Gilbert de Clare, who had borne a part also in the household revels.

In 1306, when the heir to the throne had reached the age of twenty-two and had been given the title of Prince of Wales, he went with his father on a final campaign in Scotland, or at least what they hoped would be the last. He did not distinguish himself particularly, except in the ferocity with which his troops were urged on to ravage the countryside. At the close of the season's fighting he sat in the Parliament at Carlisle, where arrangements were discussed for his marriage to Isabella of France. Edward had never expressed any interest before in matrimonial arrangements, but the reports of the beauty of the French princess had made him favorable to and even eager for the match.

It was during these discussions that the full extent of the favorite's hold on his affections became evident for the first time. There had been a great deal of talk about them, and it was being said openly that there was an immoral side to the tie. The king must have heard something of this, for he was keeping too close a watch on his son to have missed it; but if so, he had kept the knowledge to himself.

At Carlisle, however, the prince made a demand which caused his father to fall into one of his blackest rages. He wanted the province of Ponthieu in France to be given to Brother Perrot. Ponthieu contained the busy city of Abbeville at the mouth of the Somme. It had belonged to the queen, Edward's mother, and on her death it had remained among the royal possessions. The demand of the prince was a monstrously foolish one. The fief was strategically situated on the Channel and was of the first importance to the English king; it would have taken all the armed might of France to wrest it from him.

The curious part of the story is that his old enemy, Bishop Langton, was selected by the prince as mediator in the matter. The bishop, most unwillingly, conveyed the request to his sovereign and was the victim of the first stages of the royal indignation. When young Edward was summoned into the cabinet, he was seized by his father and dragged by the hair (so it is said) about the room.

"Thou wouldst give away lands!" cried the king. "Thou who hast never won a rod!"

It was on the young Gascon that the punishment fell. He was banished to his first home in Gascony.

It is not recorded whether Gaveston was compelled to obey the rules imposed on those sentenced to banishment. This was what they had to do: proceed at once to the nearest seaport and embark on the first ship leaving for the continent; and, in cases where a vessel was not immediately available, to strip each day to shirt and drawers and wade out into the water until it reached the chin, as an earnest of their intention to obey the sentence.

The haughty Gascon would have found this daily ritual a humiliation hard to bear. However, as Dover was designated as his port of departure, he probably experienced no delay in getting off.

CHAPTER SEVENTEEN

Last Stages of an Eventful Reign

THE concluding years in the life of Edward were not happy ones. He had retained most of his teeth and his eyes were filled with the same fire while his hair which had once been the color of straw was now a snowy white; but the aches of old age and many campaigns were in his bones. His temper had become shorter. He was having trouble with Robert de Winchelsey, the Archbishop of Canterbury, with his barons, with his son, and with Scotland.

Archbishop Winchelsey is less well known than he should be, considering the controversial part he played through the latter half of the reign. He had been a rather handsome man and a speaker of considerable power, but by the time he was chosen to succeed Peckham he had become corpulent and coarse of feature. His manner was open, friendly, and even jovial. He was a man of real piety and his personal life was above reproach. A spare trencherman, he refused to eat anything but the plainest food and had the best dishes given to the poor, much to the indignation of his servants, who thought they should be considered first. The archbishop never spoke to women.

This was an age when the Church struggled to maintain the supremacy of Rome over temporal power. The Pope, Boniface VIII, the most violent contender for that principle, had fallen foul of the taciturn but volcanic Philip the Fair and had issued a bull, *Clericis laicos*, in which the clergy were forbidden under pain of excommunication to give any part of their revenues to temporal rulers without papal consent. This was aimed at Edward as much as at France, for he had been exacting heavy subsidies from the churchmen of England.

What stand would Winchelsey take in this delicate position?

He soon made it clear. At a convocation in St. Paul's he delivered a sermon in which he said, "We have two lords over us, the king and the Pope, and though we owe obedience to both we owe greater obedience to the spiritual than to the temporal lord."

The other bishops, who knew the temper of their temporal lord and had made a point of meeting his demands, sat in silent dismay. Edward was enraged beyond measure when he heard what had happened, and from that time on there was continuous trouble between them. At first Winchelsey refused to allow any subsidies at all. When Edward demanded a fifth of all church revenue, the archbishop compromised with an offer of a tenth. Finally the latter agreed to allow each bishop to make his own decision but flatly refused to give as much as a shilling of the Canterbury revenues. This dispute went on for years. The other bishops resented the uncompromising attitude of the primate because of the difficulties in which it involved them, and Winchelsey found himself with few friends, except among the common people, who saw a successor to the martyred Thomas à Becket in the militant but tactless archbishop. There were minor troubles as well. Winchelsey took the part of the prince in some of his disputes with his father. He never missed a chance to trample on the toes of the Archbishop of York, denying him the right to carry his episcopal cross in front of him on his visits to Canterbury territory.

Then the situation changed. Boniface died, partly as a result of the French king's attempt to have him kidnaped and carried into France. In 1305 the choice fell on a Gascon, Bertrand de Goth, who was Archbishop of Bordeaux and who took the name of Clement V. His selection, without any doubt, had been due to French influence and gold. His first two acts of any moment were evidence of this. Instead of going at once to Rome, he had his coronation at Lyons and then returned to Bordeaux. Here he filled the cardinalate with Frenchmen. Winchelsey found himself without papal support in his struggle with the king. Edward had at an earlier stage ordered the sheriffs to confiscate the lay fees in the province of Canterbury, with the result that the archbishop had found it necessary to subsist on charity. Even his horses had been seized and he had been forced to travel on foot, which was particularly trying to one of his increasing corpulence. Two of Winchelsey's most active enemies, Bishop Langton of Lichfield, who acted as treasurer, and the Earl of Lincoln, were sent to Lyons to represent Edward at the new Pope's coronation, and they took full advantage of the opportunity to poison Clement's mind against the archbishop; which, under the circumstances, was not a difficult thing to do. The new Pope lost no time in acting. On February 12 he suspended the archbishop from all his functions and summoned him to appear before the curia within two months. During Winchelsey's last visit to London, Archbishop Greenfield of York came down and triumphantly paraded the streets of the city with his cross carried erect in front of him.

The primate's first move on receiving the summons from the Pope was to see Edward and beg for his aid. The king received him in what contemporary writers called his *torve* mood. He displayed no trace of cordiality. His eyes were hot with anger, his words incisive and unfriendly. He proceeded to go over the archbishop's record in full detail, stressing every move he had made to oppose the royal will. The archbishop is reported to have broken down and wept copiously.

Early historians gave a different reason for the bitter anger of the king. It was said he produced a letter which Winchelsey had written to one of the two earls Bigod and Bohun at the time they set themselves up in opposition to the king's will. It was no less than a proposal to remove the king and put the young prince on the throne in his place. There was no documentary proof of this, and the story has since been ignored as too impossible to believe. If the primate had been indiscreet enough to broach such a suggestion, he would not have been so foolhardy as to put it in writing. The king's reaction also would have been much more drastic. A charge of treason would have been laid against Winchelsey without any doubt.

The situation was taking on a dramatic resemblance to that which led to the murder of Thomas à Becket. Edward made it clear that he could no longer abide the presence of the primate in the kingdom and that he had no intention of interceding for him with the Pope. The upshot was that Winchelsey, pale and shaken from this exhibition of royal wrath, left London and made preparations to obey the papal summons.

The primate crossed the waters to Bordeaux, where the Pope was still holding his court. He refused Winchelsey an audience in curt and unfriendly manner. This reception, coming on top of everything else, affected the archbishop so adversely that he suffered a stroke.

If the quick communications of modern days had been possible then, there would have been much holding of breaths in ecclesiastical palaces and state chancelleries, for at this point the parallel

with the Becket case became startlingly close. If the old archbishop had died, there would have been a general belief that he
had been persecuted to death by his unfriendly king and the
indifferent pontiff. The wave of horror which swept the Christian
world when Becket was murdered in Canterbury Cathedral would
not have been equaled, but the indignation would have been deep
and lasting. Edward was so complex in character that it is impossible to say what his reaction might have been in that event. Fortunately for the king, the primate did not die: it was Edward
himself who heard the call to another life while Winchelsey
continued to await the Pope's pleasure. It seems that the archbishop had told his followers that he had had a vision of the
king's death and so he was prepared for it. He recovered from the
effects of the stroke rather quickly when the confirmation of his
vision was received.

2

The trouble Edward was having with the barons was not concerned with anything they were doing at this time; it went back to
the sharp encounters of the past. When he gave instructions to
the delegation being sent to attend the coronation of Pope Clement at Lyons, he asked them to discuss with the pontiff a matter
which "lay deep in his heart." He still felt the humiliation of
being compelled to agree to the *Confirmatio cartarum.* He had
only agreed, he declared, because of the dire straits he was in at
the time, and he still felt that the barons had taken advantage of
his position. What he desired, in short, was to be relieved of the
oath he had taken at the time. It did not prove a hard matter to
arrange. The Gascon-born Pope granted him the absolution at
once.

This was a familiar situation to anyone whose memory went
back to the previous reign. Henry III, that weathercock king, had
on many occasions broken the restrictions placed upon him by the
Great Charter and, on being brought to heel by the barons, had
abjectly sworn oaths to sin no more. The ink would hardly be dry
on his signature when messengers would be on their way to Rome
to ask for absolution of his vows. This was always granted him
and so he had no hesitation about breaking his oath whenever it
seemed advantageous to do so.

This was outrageous behavior, but in a weak and fickle king it came to be accepted. But here was Edward preparing to follow in the same path, and that was a different matter. Edward was a strong king and not one from whom such shabby tactics were expected.

Did it mean that a belief in autocratic rule was so deeply rooted in all kings that even Edward, the most enlightened monarch of his day, was no different from any others in this respect? Did it mean that, when he was improving and codifying the laws, he was acting with a reservation, a secret conviction that he himself would be above any of the restrictions established? Or did it mean that he had outlived that fine phase of his life and now lacked the clear sense of kingly responsibility with which he had begun his reign?

The last explanation seems the most likely. He was old and short-tempered and resentful of anything that stood in his way. He was seeing the past in a different light, remembering the rebuffs and losses he had sustained and thinking less of the triumphs and satisfactions. Certainly the refusal of the Scots to lay down their arms and acknowledge themselves conquered was a contributing factor.

3

Edward's dissatisfaction with his heir had been increasing with the years. The prince had grown into a reasonable facsimile of his father, being tall and of a handsome and sometimes impressive appearance; but there the resemblance seems to have stopped. His physical strength was great, but he did not enjoy using it in martial exercises. He was not then, and never would be, a soldier. Instead he liked to employ his great muscles in manual ways. He could shoe a horse, and enjoyed doing so, and he could thatch a house. Horses, in fact, were a passion with him, and his household records are full of information about his interest in breeding them. From the Earl Warenne, the loser at Stirling Bridge, he purchased a fine stud, and from one of his sisters he secured a white greyhound of which he became very fond. These interests were commendable enough in their way and, if he had been lucky enough to have been born the son of a country gentleman of no great prominence, he might have gone through life without attracting any unfavorable notice. It was his great misfortune that he had been born a prince, and with bad appetites that developed inordinately because of the power that came into his hands.

The king strove to instill in him a love of order and a capacity for attention to administrative detail, against the day when the complexities of the justiciary and the chancellery at Westminster would demand his attention. This does not appear to have been in any degree successful. Edward II remained to the end of his days incapable of any such concentration.

The greatest of the old king's worries was the vulgarity of his son's tastes and the low-grade associations into which they plunged him. There is a wardrobe item, dated 1298, of a payment of two shillings to Maude Makejoy for dancing before the prince in King's Hall at Ipswich. This is the only reference available to this particular episode, but it is not difficult to reconstruct the scene: the royal youth of fourteen, already tall and stout of limb, dressed no doubt in parti-colored hose and with the richest of materials on his back, lolling in his seat and laughing in loud approval of the sinuous twistings and stampings of Madame Maude, and calling to one of the familiars of the household to drop a suitable reward into the probably not too clean palm of the lady; with, in all probability, his tutors seated in the idle circle, grinning and slapping their spindly thighs. This seems the only explanation to account for the listing of such a minor item in the household accounts. The official who gave the money to the dancer would not expect to be paid for it by the prince and would take this method of making certain of reimbursement.

There is a record also of compensation paid to one of the court fools because he had been made the butt of some particularly painful horseplay on the part of the prince.

The king seems to have been most particularly distressed by the freedom of talk indulged in by his son. Edward was not one of the strong and silent young men. He liked to talk. In fact, he seems to have been a bit of a babbler and would speak freely of anything he had heard, even though it might be in the nature of a secret of state. Undoubtedly it reached the stage where interested parties, even the envoys of foreign states, made a point of learning the gossip of the princely household.

On the credit side of the ledger there were instances where he showed flashes of nobler impulses. He was generous and sometimes kind. It must be added, however, that such intervals were brief and could not be construed as an indication of the real character of this most frivolous of all the Plantagenets.

The members of this kingly family seem to have been subject to a rule of rotation. Henry III was the son of John, the worst of kings, and the father of the best, Edward I. The unfortunate prince with whom these brief references are concerned was an outward copy of his father but with no solidity or fineness of character. Nonetheless, he in turn was to beget the great conqueror king, Edward III. What is known of the youth and the formative years of Edward II leaves a feeling of pity for this princeling to whom dignity was burdensome and who had no inner reserves of power to draw upon when faced with the grave responsibilities of kingship. His father seems to have sensed this, for he alternated firmness with kindly understanding in his efforts to train his successor.

Perhaps Queen Eleanor was partly to blame. She was so completely the wife that she had little time left for the care of her children. Edward, it is evident, was left without much motherly attention while the devoted queen accompanied her beloved husband on his state processionals and his incessant campaigns.

CHAPTER EIGHTEEN

Robert the Bruce

1

THE family of the Bruces, second choice in that arbitration for a crown, had never been reconciled to the selection of John de Baliol as King of Scotland. The grandfather had died in 1295 and had been followed by his son, the Earl of Carrick, in 1304, leaving the grandson, who is known in history as Robert the Bruce, to continue the family pretensions.

The Earl of Carrick had been a romantic figure. He contracted a marriage with the widowed Countess of Carrick when she was a royal ward, without the king's consent. The story ran that he was hunting on her estates and she saw him there for the first time, falling in love with him so completely and violently that she instructed her men to abduct him. They were man and wife when they appeared again in the public eye. Though some skeptics declared this was all a ruse to cover up the fact that Bruce had married her with no regard to the royal wardship, it seems to have been a love match. At any rate, they brought into the world five sons, four of whom were destined to die violently in the struggle for Scottish freedom, and five daughters, all of whom married husbands of high lineage.

The Earl of Carrick was so little reconciled to the decision in favor of Baliol that he made an excuse to go to Norway when Baliol summoned his first Parliament. After that ineffective monarch ran foul of Edward's power and was sent into exile, Carrick demanded the reversion of the crown. But Edward had other plans. He was reported to have responded in verse:

> Have I nought ellys to do nowe
> But wyn a kynryck to gyve yhowe?

After that the second Bruce seems to have receded into a purely minor part and died quietly, and unhappily, on his English estates.

The grandson in the meantime had been turning his coat with a regularity that made his career a difficult one to follow. At one stage he would be superintending the English efforts to breach the stout walls of Stirling Castle with the machines King Edward had brought up from England, called by such expressive names as the *Tout-de-Monde*, the *Parson*, and the *Lup-de-Guerre*. At another he would be sharing the guardianship of Scotland with Comyn the Red in open defiance of the English king. He was forgiven several times and taken back into the king's peace. Edward, in fact, showed a degree of patience with him that is hard to reconcile with his harsh treatment of others.

Then things began to clarify for the sole guardian of the Bruce holdings and claims. Wallace, who had stood by Baliol, had been executed. Baliol himself was falling into blindness in exile at Castle Gaillard in Normandy and had lost interest in Scottish affairs. Comyn the Red, who now took on himself the Baliol claims because of a distant relationship, was a ruffler and a hothead. Robert the Bruce, no longer content to play small parts in the sanguinary drama, stalked to center stage and assumed the leading role.

Robert the Bruce had not intended to declare himself as early as this. It was known that Edward had only a short time to live, and Bruce was wise enough to realize it would be the better part of valor to wait for the death of that stout warrior before unfurling the Scottish royal flag. But an incident forced his hand.

On the tenth day of February, 1306, he went to Dumfries and there met John Comyn the Red in the Franciscan monastery. Dumfries stood on the north bank of the Nith and, despite the fact that it was a peaceful and prosperous town of wide and friendly streets, it had become the scene of much fighting and bitterness between the adherents of Scotland's many monarchial parties. The town had been originally of Baliol sympathies because the Princess Devorguila, mother of John de Baliol, had built its stone bridge of nine tall spans. Why Bruce and Comyn met there has never been satisfactorily explained, although it is believed they came by appointment to discuss the situation. There was no love lost between them certainly. At an earlier meeting in Selkirk Forest, the Red had leaped upon the younger Bruce and threatened to kill him. The same trace of black blood showed itself at once, although this time it was Bruce who attacked the other. It was in front of the high altar that this occurred, and Bruce's passion ran so high that his dagger struck deep into the Comyn's side. And so the man who had thought himself entitled to command at the battle of Falkirk and had left Wallace to face the attack while he rode off ingloriously with the Scottish cavalry, fell to the stone floor.

There is a legend that Bruce came out of the monastery very pale of face and agitated of spirit to join his friends who had waited outside.

"I sank my dagger in the Comyn's side," he said. "I think he is dead."

"Then I shall go back and make sure," declared one of his men, drawing his own dirk, which was one of the long and heavy variety used by the men of the Highlands.

Comyn was still alive, and so the follower of Bruce stabbed him again and thus made certain of his death.

The same legend has it that, before going to meet Comyn the Red, Bruce had received from a friend in England twelve pennies and a pair of spurs as a warning of treachery. It is a good story, and although it smacks of minstrelsy and invention, it is worth the telling.

The die was cast. There would be no forgiveness after this, even if Bruce had sought it; and at last he saw the light and was prepared to fight now in spite of everything. He proceeded to act with creditable dispatch. He went to Scone, where he was met by that brave churchman, Bishop Wishart of Glasgow, and given absolution and the coronation robes. It was an illustrious company which assembled there to declare their support to the new leader. In addition to Wishart there were the bishops of St. Andrews and Moray; the earls of Lennox, Atholl, and Errol; young Sir James Douglas, a nephew of the king; a considerable smattering of the gentry bearing such names as Barclay, Fraser, Boyd, and Fleming; the four brothers of Bruce—Edward, Nigel, Thomas, and Alexander—and last but certainly not least Isabella, Countess of Buchan.

It was, in fact, an imposing representation of the nobility of Scotland. What a different reading it might have given to history if all these blue-blooded Scots had assembled on the hilltop near Falkirk and ranged themselves behind the leader with the heavy claymore, William Wallace!

The right spirit certainly was displayed by the Countess Buchan.

She was a daughter of Duncan, Earl of Fife, but her husband was a Comyn (popularly called Patrick-with-the-Beard) and on that account a bitter enemy of the Bruce. She stole away from home, ordering the fastest horse in the stables to be saddled for her use. Arriving at Scone before the ceremony, she announced that, as her brother, the present Earl of Fife, was away, she had come to place the crown on the head of the new king in his stead. This honor was conceded to her.

2

Edward had been so certain that the conquest of Scotland was complete that he had set himself to the task of establishing administrative machinery for that country after the order of things in England. For the purpose he had summoned to Carlisle a small group of barons and bishops, English as well as Scottish. The outcome was a division of the northern country into judicial districts over which justices and sheriffs were appointed. Edward signed the necessary papers and threw down his pen, convinced that he had completed his task.

Almost immediately, however, the word reached him that new fires of rebellion were blazing on the hillsides in the north and that Robert Bruce had been crowned at Scone. He swore a mighty oath that this time there would be no compromise. Aymer de Valence, a relation of Edward's in descent from the second marriage of the beautiful widow of King John, was his lieutenant in Scotland. Orders were sent him that all who had taken up arms must be killed or made prisoners and executed. In the meantime an army was assembled in England and was started north under the nominal command of Prince Edward. To prepare him for his responsibilities, the young prince was knighted at Westminster. In turn, then, the prince knighted two hundred and seventy young gentlemen who were to have their baptism of fire with him.

Conferring knighthood had developed into a complicated and rather beautiful ceremony since the beginning when the accolade, a tap on the shoulder with a sword, had sufficed. It began the previous evening when the candidate was shaved and then taken to a special chamber where a bath was prepared with scented water and a covering of linen and rich cloths. While he bathed, two old knights talked to him solemnly about the duties of the order. Later still he was led to the chapel, where he stood throughout the night, keeping watch over his armor and saying prayers and meditating. At break of day he bathed again, confessed, heard mass, and offered a taper with a piece of money stuck in the white tallow. With his future squire riding before him and carrying the sword and the gold spurs which were to be attached to his heels, he made his way to the great hall. Here he knelt on one knee and was given the accolade. The knight who performed the ceremony would say a few words, not the usually accepted phrase, "I dub thee knight" (this came in later, when the ceremony had been much simplified), but some felicitous message such as, "Be thou a brave and gentle knight, faithful to thy God, thy liege lord, and thy lady fair." Finally there would be feasting and drinking and telling of stories and listening to the minstrels. At one time the candidate was supposed to confer his spurs on the cook of the establishment as a fee, but this was never general, nor did it survive long, for gold spurs were not easily come by and a cook, after all, was only a cook.

In order that all this shaving and scrubbing and standing vigil could be carried on with two hundred and seventy candidates at one time, very special arrangements had been made. Some of the trees in the Temple Gardens were cut down to make room for the tents of this great mob of embryonic knights and their squires and servants. Some stood watch over their armor in Temple Church, but most of them performed this essential part of the ritual at Westminster Abbey. The next day the young men, their faces glowing from the unusual attention of two baths in a few hours, their eyes shining with the proper exultation, were led up one by one for the official tap on the shoulder. The crush was so great in the abbey that two men were suffocated in front of the high altar. There could not have been any room left in the great church for the sanctuary seekers who infested it ordinarily, lurking in the shadows, begging furtively for food, and under no circumstances venturing outside. Perhaps they had been herded together and shut up in the crypt until the ceremony was over.

It seems certain that the king, who could more accurately be called longheaded than long-legged, had planned this brilliant ceremony for a double purpose: to present his tall son to the people of England in the most favorable light, and to impress on the idle mind of that young man a fitting sense of the important part he would soon be called upon to play.

After the ceremony of knighthood was over, there was a feast for all who had taken part, a truly gargantuan meal, with great haunches of venison and roasts of beef and mutton and scores of casks filled with the best wines from Bordeaux. Near the end of the feasting and drinking, two swans under folds of gold network were placed on the table before the king. He swore "by the gracious God of all and the two swans" that he would avenge the death of Comyn the Red and not rest himself until he had killed Robert the Bruce. It was then the turn of Prince Edward, and he proceeded to swear, also over the brace of swans, that he would never rest more than one night in the same place until the land, meaning Scotland, had been conquered. It will be observed that both father and son were more sensible in the nature of their vows than most kings on the point of riding out to war. It had been the usual thing for them to swear never to bathe, never to have a haircut nor to have a beard trimmed until their objectives had been attained; with the result that it was often impossible to tell a mighty king or a bombastic knight from the *shrewels* that scared crows away from the grain fields.

One of the candidates who was awarded his spurs on this busy day was a dark young man whose family had played an active and not always admirable part in the Marcher country. His name was Roger de Mortimer and his bright dark eye was destined to win the favor of a certain beautiful lady far, far above him. Included in the number also was a handsome young fellow named Hugh le Despenser, junior. These two were to play spectacular parts in the painful story of Edward II. It would have been better for both of them, and certainly for poor Prince Edward, if they had overslept that morning and never had the opportunity of being knighted, and so have been prevented from getting into things at all; for both of them, after periods of strutting and imposing their wills on others and earning the hatred of everyone, would die the painful death reserved for traitors, while Edward, largely because of their activities, would suffer a still more ignominious end.

3

Aymer de Valence was not a brilliant soldier but he was crafty. When he reached the neighborhood of Perth and found the Bruce ready to meet him with an army hastily assembled but filled with new fire and zeal, he declined the invitation to fight a pitched battle. Later in the day, when the Scots had dropped back to Methven and were unprepared, he attacked them suddenly and won a complete victory.

Bruce retreated into the hills but, realizing that his cause was a lost one for the time being, he finally found refuge with the small force still faithful to him in the western isles. The rest of his men, who had returned to their homes, were not so lucky. Many were captured and either hanged or beheaded as the old king had ordered. Nigel Bruce was captured in Kildrummy Castle and taken to Berwick, where he was hanged. Thomas and Alexander were defeated in an effort to land a force at Lockryan and were sentenced by Edward himself to be dragged at the tails of horses to the gallows and there executed. Sir Simon Fraser was sent to London to provide a spectacle for the citizens. Here he was executed in what had now come to be the accepted way; he was hanged first, then drawn and quartered and his head cut off to be placed in the noble company of what little was left of Wallace's head rotting on London Bridge.

Edward seems to have had an ingenious turn for devising punishments. When he learned that the Countess of Buchan had been captured, he had her sent to Berwick and ordered that a cage be constructed there in which she was to be confined "at his pleasure." The cage was built in one of the high turrets of Berwick Castle, in the shape of a crown, in view of the nature of her offense. It was of strong latticework, crossbarred and strengthened with iron. Here the brave countess, refusing to express any contrition, was kept, as one chronicle phrased it, "like a wild beast" and was an object of curiosity to all visitors at the castle. Two women, both English and so not likely to feel sympathy for her, were selected to keep a watch on her and supply her needs.

The king's original purpose may have been to hang the cage outside the turret where all who passed could look up and see the prisoner. It was found that the weather was too severe for this, what with the heavy rains and the bitter cold of the winters. A compromise was made by which the cage was suspended outside only when the day was fine.

Here the brave lady remained for four years, as Edward II continued her punishment after his father's death. Her husband, who was called Comyn the Black because of his beard, made no effort to get her free. He was so determined to avenge the murder of Comyn the Red that he took up arms on the English side. He never forgave his wife, and it was not until his death in 1313 that she was freed from the less rigorous confinement in a monastery to which she had been sent after her release from the cage.

There is a legend that in the next century Louis XI took a leaf from the English king's book and punished Cardinal Balue for an act of treason by putting him in an open cage elevated on the tower of one of the royal castles. Here the cardinal, who had once been entrusted with most of that sly king's dirty work, was kept for eleven years, through rain and sleet and frost, a supply of food and a bottle of wine being lowered to him on the end of a rope once a week.

Robert the Bruce had struck too soon and it had been costly, in lives, in possessions, and in prestige. But he would come back. The next spring would see him land again on the west coast, with small forces but with high hopes. The days of indecision, of time-serving, were over. From this time onward he would have one thought only, one purpose in life, to break, no matter at what cost, the chains that Edward had riveted on Scotland.

CHAPTER NINETEEN

The Death of Edward

1

It is unfortunate that the war-making years of Edward came in the late period of his reign rather than early. He is remembered, not so much as the fair and thoughtful king who won the love of his subjects by his genuine interest in their welfare, but rather as the conqueror who concealed all traces of the well-doer while he carried fire and sword into the lands he was determined to subdue. And yet the good king manifested himself in even the most sanguinary interludes.

The winter which followed the discomfiture and flight of Robert the Bruce was a period when the face of the furious warrior receded and the able and discriminating Edward appeared instead. He began looking into domestic affairs and decided, among other things, that his people were being charged too much for food. Accordingly he drew up and issued an order: the best soles were to cost no more than threepence a dozen, pickled herrings were to be available at twenty for a penny. Small items, these, but significant of the workings of the royal mind; no detail was too casual for his attention.

Edward had always been intensely fond and proud of his pretty fair-haired daughters, and now only three of them were left: Margaret, Mary, and Elizabeth. It was with the greatest gratification that the old king learned of the birth of a daughter on May 4 in the once royal city of Winchester. He was so delighted with this gift from his young French consort that he gave forty shillings to the low-born messenger who brought him the news. It was at his request that the child was named Eleanor after his first wife and his well-loved oldest daughter, both long since dead. Queen Marguerite lacked all wifely pettiness and was quite content to let him have his way. The child was christened in great state, in a coverlet of cloth of gold, and then displayed in a cradle, covered with ermine and wrapped snugly in a counterpane of cloth of gold. She was, it is believed, a wonderfully pretty child, as fair as any of the dozen or more little blond princesses born into this family.

The royal nursery for the second family of the king was at Northampton. The following month the new daughter had to be conveyed there from Winchester. Edward took the most practical interest in the arrangements for the journey. A special litter of green cloth, lined with crimson silk, was provided for the infant, and a gilded cradle. The litter was slung on silken cords between two horses, and so the royal infant rode in as much comfort as possible. It was a very slow trip, for the king had admonished those in charge to take the utmost care of his daughter; in fact, it consumed sixteen days to cover the ninety-odd miles between the two cities. To be doubly sure, the old king sent many letters to the keeper of the Princess Eleanor, one Adeline de Venise, giving instructions about all the precautions he deemed necessary.

The little Eleanor was only four days old when the king, sick and weary as he was and immersed in state detail, began to negotiate for her marriage. He wrote first to the widowed Duchess of Burgundy, proposing a match with her son Robert, who was to succeed to that ancient title in course of time. Letters went back and forth between the two parents, and it was finally agreed that England would provide a dowry of ten thousand marks and five thousand more for the bride's attire. On these terms the marriage would take place when the two infants had reached a suitable age.

This, perhaps, was the real Edward; the affectionate father, the keen administrator, the careful custodian of the interests of all his people. But the other Edward was due to return and to keep possession of the royal mind and mood until the rapidly approaching end of this tempestuous life. Word reached him that nothing he had done to enforce peace in Scotland had been effective. Undaunted by the heads of their slaughtered leaders turned northward with sightless eyes from the tops of castles and bridges, not in any sense deterred by the thought of the brave and high-spirited Countess of Buchan subsisting in cramped discomfort in her crossbarred cage, save to entertain a smoldering determination to set her free; fearing nothing, the Scots were stirring again.

Robert Bruce had emerged from somewhere in the islands off Scotland's stormy west coast and had made a successful landing. With him was Sir James Douglas, the second member of what was to become a truly historic partnership, Robert the Bruce and the Black Douglas. They had few men with them and so they faced the most frightening odds, for the glens of the north as well as the hills and mosses of the Lowlands swarmed with the English and their sympathizers. The desperate pair performed remarkable exploits which have been told and retold until every proper Scot can recite them word for word. Aymer de Valence was still in charge of affairs in the north country. After being defeated in a defile called the Steps of Trool, he came back to Carlisle, which Edward had reached by painful stages in a horse litter. The acerbic tongue of the sick monarch sent him promptly to the right-about, but only to meet Bruce and Douglas again and to lose a quite brisk skirmish at Loudoun Hill.

This was too much for Edward. By God's good grace, was he alone capable of commanding the army he was assembling for the final thrust into Scotland? It was to be the largest and best-trained force that England had ever seen. It should not be difficult for his fumbling and not too alert fourth cousin to accomplish the complete subjection of the stubborn Scots. But De Valence was doing nothing of any merit, so the tired king reconciled himself to another summer in the field. He presented his horse litter to the cathedral at Carlisle and slowly and painfully climbed into the saddle.

2

The word that the king was growing weaker had reached all parts of England. It came to the anxious ears of the queen, who was staying with her young family at Northampton, and to the nuns at Ambresbury, where the sixth daughter of the king, the Princess Mary, had taken the veil. The princess had not been forgotten; in fact, she lived a busy life. She paid regular visits to her royal father and received presents from him, of money, special foods, even horses. Although she wore nothing but the black serge robe of the Benedictines, she had luxurious quarters. At night she slept in a wide bed with hangings of satin and tapestry and she had her own pantry and her own staff of servants. She was, moreover, a great traveler and was probably as often on the road as at her post in the convent.

The princess and the new queen had become the closest of friends and they decided to make a pilgrimage together to the shrines of St. Thomas at Canterbury and Dover, hoping they could avert the threat to the king's life by prayerful intercessions. It was a long train which set out for the purpose, and a long journey lay ahead of them, more than a hundred miles. The queen took her two young sons with her but left her infant daughter, about whose safety the king had been so solicitous, in the comfort and warmth of her ermine-draped cradle. They were not alone in their efforts to stay the hand of death. At all the shrines in England the subjects of Edward were praying for his recovery.

In the meantime the still impatient though desperately ill king was making small progress with his army. In the first two days he spent in the saddle he covered no more than four miles. Realizing that this rate of progress would never get his forces into contact with the enemy, he had a second litter improvised and rode in it, in great discomfort, the third day. His pain was so severe, however, that the train had to proceed at a snail's pace, and by the end of the third day they had done no better than reach Burgh-by-Sands. From here they could see the water of the Solway Firth, beyond which lay Scotland.

The king was now so weak that he could go no farther. He allowed himself to be carried from the litter to a bed, and there he prepared himself for death. Although he prayed earnestly for the welfare of his soul and composed messages of farewell for the members of his family, he remained the warrior king to the end. His spirit was as indomitable as ever, as was evident from the orders he gave his son.

One hundred English knights were to go to the Crusades, under oath to remain a full year. They were to take his heart with them.

Piers de Gaveston was not to be recalled to England without the consent of Parliament.

His final injunction was, "Wrap my bones in a hammock and have them carried before the army, so I may still lead the way to victory!"

He died on July 7, two days after his devoted wife and daughter had started far in the south on their long pilgrimage of intercession for him.

Ten days after his death an inventory was made of the possessions the old king had carried with him. They consisted for the most part of holy relics: a purse containing a thorn from the crown of Christ, a sliver of wood from the holy cross, one of the nails from the cross, a bone from the arm of St. Osith, one from the head of St. Lawrence, a fragment of the sponge which was lifted to Christ on the cross—more than a hundred relics in all. No monarch could have been more devout, nor more assiduous as a collector.

His sixty-eight years had been years of storm and stress, filled with the rattle of arms, the thunder of cavalry, the dip and toss of transport ships, the bitter clash of wills; but the good he did would never end, while the hatred aroused by his ambition would subside in the course of time, and so the scales inclined heavily in his favor when his record came to be weighed. It must still be said that he was a great king.

Many years after, when the independence of Scotland had finally been achieved, Robert the Bruce paid a great compliment to the memory of Edward I. "I am more afraid," he declared, "of the bones of the father dead, than of the living son; and, by all the saints, it was more difficult to get half a foot of land from the old king than a whole kingdom from the son!"

Book Two

EDWARD THE SECOND

CHAPTER ONE

The New King Makes Many Mistakes

1

EDWARD was twenty-three when he looked on the dead face of his father and realized that he was now Edward II and King of England. The thought failed to sober or inspire him. He proceeded, in fact, to disregard all the commands of the dying warrior, his first act being the recall of Piers de Gaveston. He never turned a hand to organize the party of one hundred knights who were to take his father's heart to the Holy Land. The vehement demand made by the dying monarch that his bones should be carried in front of the army was disregarded. Instead the young king escorted the bier to York, from where it was sent on to London for burial later in Westminster Abbey.

Edward then returned to Carlisle, where the army of invasion awaited his orders. He had little stomach for this military heritage that had come into his hands, being in no sense a soldier, but he must at least make a gesture, so he led the army into Ayr; the word "led" being purely rhetorical, for the second Edward, unlike his martial father, who had ridden his steed Bayard over the walls of Berwick and through the moss at Falkirk, preferred to direct his army from the rear. They reached Cumnock and camped there for several weeks, receiving the vows of fealty of some of the Scottish noblemen and considering what to do next. The decision was to do nothing. In spite of the commands left by the old king, the army retired to Carlisle on the supposition that any activities among the Scots were local and sporadic.

Immediately a bonnet appeared from behind every bush. As soon as the back of the somewhat less than soldierly new king had been turned, Bruce was at work in the Highlands, leading many successful forays. The Black Douglas, commanding in the south, recaptured his castle in Douglasdale by a ruse which delighted every Scottish heart. Leading his men by a secret footpath, he came to a dark shaw which overlooked the gray-towered castle. Here they waited while a small party went forward in wagons filled with fodder. The garrison, being in need of supplies, threw open the gates. When the wagons came to a stop in the gateway, the drivers drew their pikes and long dirks from under the hay and held the space open while the Douglas and his men charged through the green bracken and took the castle with little difficulty.

In London the new king piled mistake on mistake. Here his lost friend awaited him, Brother Perrot in a coat of rich material from the East and a plume in his hat, and his mind filled with all the latest quips and anecdotes. The reunion was most affectionate and the king conferred on Gaveston the earldom of Cornwall; a most injudicious act, for this title had always been reserved for members of the royal family and it carried with it, moreover, an interest in the tin mines of Cornwall, those great stannaries from which came the close-packed bundles conveyed every day down the tin trail to the markets of Europe. Then he betrothed the gay jackanapes from Gascony to a member of the royal family, his niece, Margaret of Gloucester. Margaret was the daughter of his giddy and willful sister, Joanna of Acre. At first the girl seemed willing enough, for Master Perrot was handsome and high of spirits. Later the marriage would become a source of much trouble.

The new broom, wielded in the reckless hands of the young king, disposed of all the high officers of state. It swept his old critic, Bishop Langton, right out of the treasury and into the Tower of London. As a successor to Langton, Edward offered his baronage another bitter pill to swallow in the person of Walter Reynolds, a man of low station and mean attributes, who will be remembered as one of his wine-bibbing mentors.

2

Of all the kings of England, Edward II was one of the least fitted for the post and certainly one of the most poorly trained. He never grew up, but at no time did he show the enthusiasms and the touch of ideality which the perennial juvenile will often display. His concern seems to have been with his personal interests and pleasures and he had no conception of what it meant to be a king. If anyone had said to him that a king, after all, was no

more than the representative of the ruling class, he would have
thrown back his handsome head and laughed loudly. Nevertheless, the nobility still held to this conviction. "By God, Sir
King," Roger Bigod had said to Edward I, "I will neither go nor
hang!" The first Edward had realized the need to curb the power
of the feudal families and had been far-seeing enough to broaden
the base of representation in Parliament by the introduction of
commoners. The baronage still remained the dominant force in
Parliament, of course, and it would take centuries of experiment
and growth before the Commons could assume control. In the
meantime only as strong a ruler as Edward I could hold his barons
in check. The second Edward lacked the qualities which would
have enabled him to follow in his father's footsteps. He seemed to
hold the old belief that a king could do no wrong, and it amused
him to see Piers de Gaveston strutting about and taunting the nobility. He and his gossip would show the haughty earls and barons
who was now the master in England!

The favorite went so far as to give offense to the one man who
of all others should have been exempt from his insults. Thomas of
Lancaster was a first cousin of the king, being the son of Prince
Edmund, a brother of Edward I. He was hereditary high steward
of England and the holder of five earldoms, including Lancaster,
Leicester, and Derby. He entertained on a lavish scale. In that
connection it is interesting to quote some figures from the accounts of his cofferers. In one year they paid out 3,405 pounds for
food. In addition it was found necessary to lay down 369 pipes of
red wine and two of white. White wine was reserved for invalids
and children. Ladies liked the stout red wine as well as did their
menfolk, particularly if it was well spiced and mulled. These were
enormous expenditures for those days. Lancaster's great castle at
Pontefract must have been filled with guests at all seasons, and
the accommodations of its eight towers must have been strained
to provide sleeping quarters.

Lancaster was a man of overweening ambition but entirely lacking in the qualities which must go with the achievement of high
objectives; an insensitive, coarse, violent fellow, lethargic in person
and dull of wit. Because of his rank, however, he was the most
powerful man in the kingdom and certainly should never have
been selected by the upstart Gascon as a butt for his jests.

Royal families are no different from others in certain human respects. They have their divisions and feuds, they seethe with jealousies, they indulge in gossip and innuendo. The faults of the

head of the family are well known to all the collateral branches, the brothers and uncles and cousins. Cousin Lancaster was the leader of the opposition where Edward II was concerned. He knew all about that young man's record and thought poorly of him from every standpoint.

When Edward announced after his coronation that he now desired to begin the business of administration, there was a tendency among the nobility, many of whom had found Gaveston amusing, to regard this as a happy omen. They were even willing to make financial grants, despite the fact that Edward had depleted the treasury to get funds for his favorite. Two of the barons stood out, Cousin Lancaster and Hugh le Despenser.

"Wait and see," grumbled the holder of five earldoms, whose feelings were still raw from the antics of Master Piers.

He was right. The country would soon discover that the reins of government had passed into the most careless and incompetent of hands.

CHAPTER TWO
The Marriage of Edward

1

The short reign of Edward II—1307-27—was an unfruitful period, a time of military defeat and constitutional inertia. But it reads like a play or a novel because of the conflicts which arose between the leading figures on the stage, Edward himself and his favorites, his beautiful but false queen, Isabella the Fair, and her paramour, and that glum exponent of discontent, Cousin Lancaster. The story of these people is a series of climaxes, all violent and unhappy; but, it must be added, engrossing and exciting.

The story begins with an almost incredible error of judgment on the part of the king. When he had completed arrangements for his marriage to Isabella of France by agreeing to wed her at Boulogne, he faced the need of appointing a regent to act in his absence as custodian of the Great Seal and to exercise power in certain contingencies. It had been the invariable rule to appoint a member of the royal family when a suitable one existed, generally the queen or the heir to the throne. The logical selection, therefore, was Cousin Lancaster. Partly to express his dislike of that consistently hostile prince, and partly to pay a tribute to his favorite, Edward selected Gaveston for that highest of honors!

2

In the cathedral of Boulogne, the illustrious company was literally carried away by the beauty of the contracting parties. Edward was tall, well formed, handsome. Isabella, although only thirteen years of age, was incomparably beautiful; as fair as her father had been but with nothing of the cold perfection of feature which so often accompanies golden hair. There was a piquancy of feature and a sparkle generally about her. Later it would be realized that she was as hard, as flawless, and as sharp-edged as a diamond; but in her first blooming none of this showed. She was magnificently attired in blue and gold. The crown on her head, sparkling with precious stones, was only one of two which her father, generous for once, had given her. The other was packed away with a large assortment of gold and silver articles. Her ladies-in-waiting had been babbling about the contents of the chests in which her clothes were kept. Ah, what gowns of velvet with gold embroidery, of sunny cloth from the East, of rich materials from the looms of Flanders! Never had a bride been so richly endowed.

The company was a distinguished one. Philip the Fair in rose cloth, a huge figure of a man with his once fair complexion turned florid in a face as round as a wheel of country cheese; the kings of the Romans, of Sicily, of Navarre, and their queens; the Archduke of Austria; Charles of Valois and his tribe of marriageable daughters; Louis of Evreux; the Duke of Brabant; the dowager Queen Marguerite of England, proud of the success she had made of her marriage with the first Edward; and an immense assemblage of princes and princesses and counts and lords.

The bride and groom were seeing each other for the first time, but there was no evidence of an instant attraction between them. To Edward the bride was a very pretty girl, not far removed from the doll stage. To Isabella, her bridegroom wore a question mark as well as a fine satin jacket and a handsomely jeweled cloak. She had been told many strange things about him. But they might have reached a stage of marital happiness if each had striven to please the other. Edward was careless and casual and more interested still in his gossip and playfellow, Brother Perrot, and Isabella was quick to take offense and to show it.

The fault was more on Edward's side. Throughout the period of festivities, both in France and in England, he behaved like a country loon and gave the nobility of France a chance to look down their very superior noses at him. Isabella never lost a chance to complain to her father, to write him letters, to raise her pretty voice of spiteful reproach.

The match, which looked so brilliant as the handsome young couple stood together at the altar, was doomed to failure.

When they landed at Dover on February 7, Gaveston met them in such an imitation of oriental splendor and so much jewelry on his person that he quite eclipsed the king. The English nobility observed the scene with smoldering anger. The feeling against

Gaveston was growing as the word circulated that Edward had already depleted the treasury by many thousands of pounds given to his favorite. It was even said that a fund of thirty-two thousand pounds, which had been set aside for the expense of a new crusade, had already vanished into the jeweled pockets of Master Piers.

When the Gascon appeared, the king left the side of his bride, crying, "Brother! Brother!" and clasped him in his arms. The bride watched this effusive welcome with an eye that had ceased to be girlish and had lost all of its dewy quality.

Worse was to follow. King Philip had given many costly presents to his son-in-law in the way of rings and gold chains. The next day Master Piers put in an appearance wearing some of them on his person. It was a good thing that Philip had not crossed the Channel with the rest of the party, for he had already demonstrated one violent way of dealing with such matters. A few years before, Queen Marguerite of England had sent costly presents to the wives of two of Philip's sons. When a pair of young gallants turned up at court later wearing the gifts openly, that far from gentle king had acted with sudden ferocity. Not only were the two courtiers flayed alive on a public square by the royal executioner, but the foolish daughters-in-law were sent to prison, where one of them died. If Brother Perrot had been a subject of the French king, he would have been given short shrift.

The outcome of this absurd folly was that some of the English nobility, with Cousin Lancaster as spokesman no doubt, went to Edward and told him that unless he banished Gaveston from court they would absent themselves from the coronation. Edward, taken seriously aback, assured them that he would arrange matters to their satisfaction.

3

Isabella had become instantly popular with the people of England. The first glimpse of her fresh beauty when she landed with the king at Dover had started talk spreading about the country. Her arrival in London for the coronation was a triumph. The citizens, as usual, had prepared a rousing welcome. The streets were covered with flags and bunting, and there were tall temporary structures here and there representing castles and fairy bowers. The conduits ran wine and everyone could fill a cup; and most as-

suredly everyone did. The mayor and the aldermen rode first in
the procession which had been formed to greet the king and his
new bride, and after them came the members of all the guilds,
more than thirty separate organizations; four solid miles of shining faces and bright new liveries.

The lord mayor handed over the golden key of the city. "Your
humble citizens, O King," he declared, "prostrate themselves at
your feet and surrender to you themselves and all that they have."
It was the old formula which had been observed with each royal
visit since London Town had secured its charters. But it had a rit-
ualistic flavor which pleased everyone, particularly after the brief
glance the good burghers and their wives had obtained of the
sparklingly lovely queen.

If Isabella felt that London was small and dirty and lacking in
the distinction of Paris (and no doubt she did), she did not allow
it to show. She bowed and smiled and raised her hand in a continuous greeting. She took an open interest in everything that was
shown her and everything told her about the points of historic importance: the streets over which the fair Saxon princess Matilda
rode to the hearings at Lambeth to decide whether or not she
might wed King Henry I; the exact spot where the spirit of St.
Thomas of Canterbury had been seen before the masonry of the
wharf at the Tower of London had toppled and fallen into the
river at the raising of his shining cross; the clock at St. Paul's
where the arm of an angel pointed to the hours and the still more
amazing one at Westminster which showed the tides as well as
the time; London Bridge, so massive and impressive with its rows
of stalls and shops, its homes and its church, the great weight of
which had caused the collapse of four of the stone piers not more
than a quarter of a century before. Perhaps she shuddered in-
wardly when her eyes were directed to the Tower of London,
standing so high and grim above the rest of the city, and learned
that this would be her home.

The popularity which the queen won on that first day did not
abate for many years. The foolish conduct of the king won a sympathy for her which was generally felt. Through all the shifts and
troubles of the next few years, London was consistently loyal to
the beautiful queen. Isabella was discerning enough to realize the
value of the city's support. To cast forward into the future, when
her first child was born, a fine healthy boy who was destined to
become Edward III and to be known as the conqueror king, she
sent a letter to the citizens.

Isabella, by the grace of God, Queen of England, Lady of Ireland, and Duchess of Aquitaine, to our well-beloved the Mayor, and Aldermen, and the Commonality of London, greeting. Forasmuch as we believe that you would willingly hear good tidings of us, we do make known to you that our Lord in His grace has delivered us of a son, on the 13th day of November with safety to ourselves, and to the child. May our Lord preserve you. Given at Wyndesore, on the day above-named.

It could not have been done with a surer touch. Three days were given over to rejoicing in the city, so general was the enthusiasm felt at this happy event. Once again tuns of wine were set up in the streets at which all could drink to the royal child and to the health of the beautiful queen.

4

In spite of the hostility of the barons, Brother Perrot was at the coronation on February 25. In the procession to the abbey, Lancaster carried *Curtana*, the sword of mercy, and his brother Henry bore the rod and dove. Immediately behind them, strutting in sheer magnificence like the Grand Cham, was Piers de Gaveston, carrying St. Edward's crown! There was talk of stopping the procession and ejecting the favorite, even of killing him on the spot, but better counsel prevailed.

This was no more than the first unpleasantness, the worst episode of many which marred the day. It developed that the Gascon had been given full charge of the coronation arrangements and had been seriously lax about them. Seats had not been provided for all who were entitled to them. The abbey was so unnecessarily crowded that one knight, Sir John Bakewell, was trampled underfoot and suffocated. The ceremony, which should have been completed by noon, was not over until three o'clock. The royal party and the guests emerged from the abbey in a state of exhaustion. The banquet, which should have been ready hours before, was still in the making. Early dusk had fallen when the guests were summoned to their places. The food was badly cooked. The service was exasperatingly slow. In his first chance to show what he could do, the king's companion had failed utterly.

The young queen was greatly disturbed by this farcical note. Her remonstrances had no effect on her royal husband, so she took to voicing her dissatisfaction in further letters to her father. Philip, running true to form, saw a chance in this to create dissension in the neighboring kingdom and set about creating an opposition party. Cousin Lancaster was chosen to head the dissentients, and it was largely through his efforts that a meeting of the council was held. Struggling hard to save his favorite, Edward could do no more than get postponements. Finally, however, the barons got together on April 28 in a very dangerous mood.

The meeting was almost unanimous against the king and Gaveston. The only one who stood out, in fact, was the nobleman named Hugh le Despenser, who had served Edward I long and faithfully but who was sufficiently political-minded to see a chance here to win the favor of the new king. His voice was drowned out in the loud chorus of baronial demands; and later, when Parliament met at Northampton, he was dismissed from the council for his stand.

The king was compelled to bow his head to the storm. It was decided that Gaveston was to be stripped of all offices and honors and sent away. For good measure, the bishops declared that he would be excommunicated if he ever attempted to return to England.

The king had given in, but between them this fine pair saw a way out of the difficulty. Gaveston was sent from England, but only as far as Ireland, where he was to serve as the king's lieutenant at a fine salary. Edward rode to Bristol with him and stood sorrowfully at the docks while the vessel containing the Gascon and his company (a large one, needless to state) warped its way out into the Channel.

Queen Isabella wrote to her father, "I am the most wretched of wives." Once she wrote that Piers de Gaveston was the cause of all her troubles, adding that the king had become "an entire stranger to my bed." King Philip responded by continuing his intrigue with the leading barons, particularly with the Earl of Lancaster, who was always ready for any course of action directed against the king.

5

The favorite remained in Ireland for a year and seems to have conducted himself rather well. At any rate, he put down native disaffection and established a degree of peace in the part of the country lying about Dublin and known as the Pale. But Ireland, he felt, was not a proper setting for his brilliant gifts and he even went to the extent of addressing letters to the King of France, begging his assistance in having the ban raised. He wrote to the Pope, beseeching to be freed from the ban of the Church. He had no success with that man of few words but violent deeds, Philip the Once Fair, but the Pope looked on his plea with leniency and removed the ban of excommunication.

Brother Perrot returned to England at once with an almost regal train. With him were Irish malcontents, a few Englishmen, and a great many foreigners, including some needy Gascons. They landed at Milford Haven and made their way like conquering heroes to Chester, where the prodigal (as he was sometimes called) was received with affection and pleasure by King Edward. Things had been going a little better in the country. Baronial nerves had recovered to some extent as a result of a year's relief from the presence of Gaveston. For one reason or another the council was persuaded to look with leniency on the case of the homecomer. A Parliament was held at Stamford on July 27, 1309, and an active minority headed by the Earl of Gloucester worked hard for him. Gloucester was his brother-in-law, still a minor and a young man of some instability. Gloucester's sister was not too happy in her marriage with the vain Gascon, but the brother nevertheless used all the influence he could bring to bear and finally succeeded in getting a favorable vote. It was agreed that Gaveston could remain and the earldom of Cornwall was restored to him.

This was a great victory, and if the insolent alien had possessed any common sense at all he might have settled down to a peaceful life on his share of the immense Clare holdings which had come to him with his wife. But Gaveston was a vainglorious winner as well as a poor loser. He must make a public display of his victory. He loved tournaments and, to do him justice, he had a sure seat in the saddle and a deft hand with the lance. It happened that the king had arranged to hold a tilting at Wallingford, and Gaveston decided to make this the scene of his public vindication.

The old Roman town of Wallingford, standing in the flat valley of the Thames about halfway between Reading and Oxford, was in a holiday mood for the tournament. Flags flew from the high turrets of the castle and pennants fluttered from the pavilions of the knights. Spectators had been coming for days, and now the common people were beginning to arrive, barefooted, with their shoes slung over their backs to save the soles but quite proud nevertheless in their new *courtepys* (which they called court-pies), a garment which aped the knightly tabard but was made of inferior cloth.

This was one of the brilliant events of the reign. The men in the stands, having doffed their riding cloaks, were as gay as peacocks, from their liripiped and plumed hats, topper-shaped and made of beaver, to the upturned tips of their toes. The *cote-hardie*, which was relatively new, was already giving way to a garment called the doublet, which was so attractive and at the same time so practical that it would continue in use for centuries. It was a sleeveless coat (later it would be fitted with puffed and slashed sleeves), fitting the chest rather snugly and going only to the waist.

The ladies, still drab and overly modest in their long kirtles and tunics and robes, were beginning to assert themselves a little against their popinjay husbands. Audacious things were being done with their headdresses, making them still higher and rather like windmills, and they were wearing their hair in long braids tied with gay ribbons.

Piers de Gaveston showed unusual restraint in arriving before the king and queen and riding direct to the tilt house, a temporary structure with a sloping roof and blinds on the sides. He was followed by many knights and squires, however, and his shining armor was of the best; from the continent, forsooth, and fitted with the latest articulations for shoulders, elbows, and knees. He did not wear the *cyclas*, a loose surcoat, because it was an English invention and therefore not fashionable. Undoubtedly he expressed some umbrage that he was classed with the challengers instead of the champions, and when he came out for action there was little or no applause. The nobility scowled and Queen Isabella went suddenly quiet and seemed to lose all pleasure in the tilting.

Gaveston gave the nobility more cause for mortification by outshining and outpointing them in the jousting. He had many gifts, this insolent Gascon, and one was his great skill with weapons. At the close of the tilting, however, he proceeded to throw away all the favor he had won for himself by his prowess. His tongue began to wag and he gave free rein to a gift he had for finding nicknames. He tossed his quips about with an airy unconcern for consequences.

Cousin Lancaster he called *The Fiddler* because that man of dull wit had arrayed himself in a rather outlandish attempt to follow the latest fashions.

His own brother-in-law, Gloucester, was loudly libeled as *Filz à puteyne*, the whore's son, an allusion to willful Princess Joanna, who had run away and married a man not even a knight when her elderly first husband died.

The Earl of Pembroke, Aymer de Valence, who had a prominent nose and a dark complexion, became *Joseph the Jew*.

The Earl of Lincoln, who was heavy of build, was dubbed *M'sieur Boele Crevée* or *Burst-belly*.

Finally he spoke of the Earl of Warwick, who had the unfortunate habit of foaming at the mouth, as *The Mad Hound*.

"Let him call me hound!" cried Warwick in a black rage and probably lending point to the witticism. "Someday the hound will destroy him!"

6

While Edward was thus allowing his insolvent favorite to undermine him with all classes of people from Cousin Lancaster down to the lowest kitchen knave, the situation in Scotland drifted into a curious and costly impasse. Robert the Bruce was king, but he was still a king without a country. The people of Scotland had been won over to him, with the exception of the adherents of the Comyn family, but all the great fortresses were in English hands. There was no possibility of establishing peace and order in the land until the forts had been reduced and the English expelled. The Bruce proceeded to this task with great determination.

It thus became necessary for the English king to maintain strong garrisons in the Scottish fortresses, which meant that supplies had to be sent in by sea at very heavy expense. Scotland was costing Edward so much, in fact, that the royal treasury remained empty. Edward was caught in a cleft stick as far as the war was concerned. The English nobility had no stomach for further fighting and would protest against taking the field, but at the same time their pride had been touched by the turn of events. They did not want Scotland lost. The new king could not please them, no matter what policy he pursued.

Edward's desire to protect Gaveston led him into all manner of subterfuges to keep Parliament from meeting. This cost him the taxes which otherwise would have been voted. The royal pockets were empty. The situation became so acute that there was no money to pay the expenses of the royal household. The queen had no income until a special arrangement was made for revenue to be paid her from estates in Ponthieu. She resented this impoverishment most bitterly.

In order to save Gaveston, Edward made an extraordinary concession. He agreed to the selection of a commission which would take over the administration of the kingdom. The members became known as Ordainers because of the nature of the oath they took "to make such ordinances as should be to the honor and advantage of Holy Church, to the honor of the king, and to his advantage and that of his people." The commission consisted of twenty-one members, none of them commoners, and prominent among them were all the enemies of the favorite. Archbishop Winchelsey had been summoned back to assume his duties at Canterbury and was a member. He had ceased to favor the king and was again disposed against the granting of Church funds for state purposes.

Knowing his peril to be great, Gaveston left the court. When Edward went to Berwick to make a pretense of beginning active measures against the Scots, Gaveston went with him. He remained in the north for the better part of a year.

CHAPTER THREE

The Death of the Favorite

1

WHILE the king played at war-making in the north and so avoided the need of facing his angry baronage, the feeling against him and his favorite grew steadily. The queen still kept up a show of loyalty to her husband, which added to the sympathy felt for her everywhere. She may have poured out her indignation in letters to her father or in the talks she had with the leaders of the Ordainers, but nothing was allowed to show on the surface.

In February 1311, the Earl of Lincoln died. He will be remembered as the full-bodied baron who had been given the nickname of *Burst-belly* by the effervescent Gaveston, a fact which he himself never forgot nor forgave. Nevertheless, he had been made regent while Edward went off to his ineffectual campaigning in the north. Cousin Lancaster was married to Lincoln's daughter, an only child, and so succeeded to all the estates and added the earldoms of Lincoln and Salisbury to his already formidable list of titles. He stepped also into the late earl's shoes as regent of the kingdom.

Lancaster went north at once, ostensibly to pay homage for his new properties, but in reality to convince the king that he must delay no longer in returning to face the Ordainers. Edward received him with civility. When Gaveston joined them, the regent, who resented having been called *The Fiddler* and who knew that even his friends now called him that behind his back, drew himself up haughtily and had nothing to say, not even condescending to return the insolent alien's gesture of greeting. Edward was furious, but there was nothing to be done about it. Lancaster had all of the barons and bishops and most of the commoners behind him. The king was standing alone. He grumblingly promised to return.

It was six months before he kept his promise. First he rode

across country to the most remote part of the North Sea coast where the towering castle of Bamborough stood on the top of an almost perpendicular rock one hundred and fifty feet in height. There was only one possible approach to the black keep in its circle of high walls, a steep and winding road cut through the rocks on the southeast. The waters of the North Sea at high tide broke loudly on the rocky base of Bamborough. Remembering perhaps how an earlier owner of this grim rock sentinel, Robert de Mowbray, had held William Rufus at bay, Edward was sure that here was the perfect sanctuary for his friend.

It was late in August when the king faced the Ordainers at Westminster. They had a long list of grievances and demands to lay before him, and the chastened monarch agreed to all of them readily enough, save a clause which banished Gaveston from the kingdom for all time. When Edward stood out angrily, the barons gave him a choice: send the Gascon away or face civil war. It did not take long for him to make up his mind.

What armed forces he had were in Scotland, holding out in the strong fortresses of that country. They could not be summoned to his aid without leaving Bruce a free hand. It was doubtful, in any case, if they could get out, with a hostile nation hemming them in. On the other hand, the barons were united and ready.

For the third time Gaveston was sent into exile, with Flanders his only chance of sanctuary, even Gascony having been closed to him. He went unwillingly and as openly antagonistic to the nobility as ever. The Ordainers then proceeded to find and dismiss all the relatives and friends of the Gascon for whom places had been found in the royal household and the administrative offices. Edward was not consulted about this housecleaning and he resented it bitterly.

"Am I an idiot," he cried, "that they won't let me look to my own household?"

Gaveston was like the proverbial bad penny. He left for Flanders in October. Apparently he did not like that prosperous but sober country, for the next month there were rumors in England that he had returned in disguise. These stories began to take on substance as the bad penny became bolder. He was seen in the west at many points, flaunting his identity and his prosperity openly. Before Christmas, which Edward was spending with the queen at Windsor, he paid an open visit to the royal castle. When Isabella protested against this folly, the troublemaker treated her with contempt. He was, he declared, the good friend and loyal servant of the king. What booted it if others, even the queen herself, were not pleased?

The country seethed with indignation, and in London the trained bands marched to protest the recklaw attitude of the favorite and to voice sympathy for their much-loved Isabella. Edward paid no attention to public opinion. He had finally made up his mind that the friend of his boyhood would remain with him in spite of everything. He even issued a writ announcing the return of Gaveston and lauding his action as an evidence of loyalty. Soon thereafter he restored all the estates of the favorite.

A state of war developed immediately. The old archbishop, who had once been the stoutest supporter of Edward while his father was alive, now went over to the other side. He excommunicated Gaveston for breaking his oath by returning. The barons began to arm their adherents and to gather at strategic points. Lancaster was chosen general of the people's army. Edward had no course left but to return to the north, hoping to stalemate the barons again by leaving them unopposed. Although the queen was heavy with child, he took her with him and wrote to Philip of France to explain the situation. "She is in good health," he set down, "and will (God propitious) be fruitful."

Isabella accompanied him without protest, although she must have realized the seriousness of the situation. There is nothing on record to let any light into the working of her mind at this stage. It seems likely, however, that she still entertained the hope that the king would see reason and strive to correct the errors of the past. It is certain that she had no real love for him. Her heart may have fluttered slightly when she first saw her tall and blond bridegroom at Boulogne, but lasting attachments are seldom formed at the age of thirteen. Before she had reached a stage where a permanent romantic interest might be found, the eccentric behavior of the king had alienated any hint of tenderness between them. As for Edward, it was only too clear that he had never felt any affection for his young bride.

It may be accepted, in spite of the breach between them, that the queen was still ready at this point to do everything to assist in settling the trouble.

The royal party went first to York and then to Newcastle, where Master Piers became very ill. The king was so alarmed that he summoned the best man of medicine in the north, one William de Bromtoft, to attend his friend. When Gaveston recovered, Edward paid the physician the sum of two pounds, a truly royal fee.

As soon as the Gascon was well enough to travel, the king took him on a boat for Scarborough, leaving the queen behind with the people of her household at Tynemouth Castle. The royal lady was both hurt and angry at this desertion, which made it only too clear that he cared nothing for her comfort or safety. She protested tearfully at being left, but the king had only one thought in his mind, to get his friend to a place of safety before the baying hounds of the baronage closed in about them. As it was, the army of Lancaster entered the day after the departure of the royal fugitive.

In view of what would happen later, history has blackened the character of the queen. But she was not wholly bad. While she stayed at Tynemouth Castle, alone and ill, this story is told in the form of a brief item in the household books:

October 9. To little Thomeline, the Scotch orphan boy, to whom the queen, being moved to charity by his miseries, gave food and raiment to the amount of six- and six-pence.

Little Thomeline made a good impression on the queen, apparently, for she decided a permanent home must be found for him. Here is a later item from the household books:

To the same orphan, on his being sent to London to dwell with Agnes, the wife of Jean, the queen's French organist; for his education, for necessaries bought him, and for curing his maladies, fifty-two shillings and eight-pence.

There were many homeless children all through the northern counties of England and the Lowlands of Scotland as a result of the continuous warfare, the never-ceasing raids and burnings. The orphan in question was perhaps one of thousands. Lucky little Thomeline that he caught the eye of the queen!

2

Edward had chosen Scarborough as their sanctuary ahead of Bamborough for several reasons. Bamborough, like an eyrie on its impregnable rock, offered no manner of escape. Beyond it, less than twenty miles, lay Berwick and the Scottish border. It was a *cul-de-sac* and there was little chance of getting a boat there if a quick departure became necessary. Scarborough, on the other hand, was an active shipping port with boats plying both north and south. A peninsula of the general shape of a blacksmith's hammer ran out into the sea, cutting the harbor in two. On the highest point on this rocky arm of the land stood the old Norman castle which had been built in the time of William the Conqueror. It lacked the isolation of Bamborough, but it was well fortified and could be held indefinitely by an adequate garrison. Edward, who still believed he had friends who would rally to his banner, considered Scarborough the best base of operations. He was guided also by the knowledge that the baronial army had been behind him at Newcastle by a very few hours. A wily fox will often double on its tracks when the hounds come too close.

So the king and the fully recovered Gascon arrived at Scarborough and took possession of the castle. The trip had taken longer than they had expected, and reports reached them that the forces of Lancaster were marching down the coastal roads. The garrison was not large and it was of dubious loyalty, and so Edward was sure they could not hold out long. To go farther by water was out of the question, for that would take them to London, the very heart and soul of the antiroyalist cause. Edward decided that the only course open to him under these circumstances was to leave his friend in sanctuary at Scarborough and strike across country to York. Here he hoped to rally forces and return to the aid of his friend. He was sadly disillusioned to find that the royal city of the north had already welcomed the barons and that sentiment in his favor was slight indeed. Hearing that Lancaster had sent the earls of Pembroke and Warenne to take Scarborough, the king proposed to his opponents that Gaveston be brought to him so that an understanding for the future might be reached. This was agreed to. In the meantime, after two days' resistance, Gaveston had given himself up on promises that he would see the king and that he would have a fair and legal trial.

It developed that most of the barons were against the proposed meeting between king and favorite, feeling certain from experience that no good would come of it. But the Earl of Pembroke had given his word and, like Brutus, he was an honorable man. It had been arranged that Parliament was to meet at Wallingford in August, and so the earl proceeded in that direction with his prisoner. Gaveston had surrendered on May 19, and it was nearly a month later that Pembroke and his armed escort passed through Northampton and came to the Cherwell. He crossed that pleasantly meandering river with the intention of following it to its junction with the Thames. At twilight on June 19 they came to Deddington, where the earl left his prisoner under guard in a house in town while he went to spend the night at a nearby castle.

The stage was now set for tragedy. The violent Earl of Warwick, still smoldering from the favorite's impudence to him, came to Deddington with a number of other magnates. That so many of the baronial leaders were in the party makes it clear that this was not a matter of chance, that Warwick and his friends had been waiting for just such an opportunity as this. Learning where Gaveston was being held, they roused him out of his bed and took him forcibly from the town. They first ransacked his belongings and found evidence to fan the flames of their grim resolution. One of the acquisitive Gascon's weaknesses was a passion for fine jewelry, and it was now revealed that he had employed his hold over the king to get his hands on many of the crown jewels. In addition he had in his possession much gold and silver plate from the royal table and a great many necklaces and rings and chains which had been presented to Edward at various times by the queen and other members of the royal family.

The feeling against Gaveston was so violent that the barons could not wait to have him tried by a proper court; and yet it was not so much because of his interference in state matters as it was resentment over smaller things: his wealth, his insolence, his disregard of their rights and privileges, the names he had coined for each of them. What followed the forcible removal of the Gascon is not very clear. One version has it that he was taken to Warwick Castle and that Lancaster and several other noblemen arrived soon after. A consultation was held and it was decided to put him to death without more ado. He was taken to Blacklow Hill the next night and beheaded there. According to another version, the judging occurred on the hillside at Blacklow and the evidence against the prisoner was discussed at some length. He was charged with having an evil influence over the king, and it was even claimed that he had practiced sorcery to gain it. In support of this charge it was advanced that he was the son of a witch who had been burned at the stake in Guienne for sorcery. This, unfortunately for Gaveston, was true.

There is no evidence to prove either version right, but it seems certain that all of the barons who had taken part in the decision were present at his death. There was clearly a desire for anonymity in everything they did: in their choice of so late an hour and so isolated a spot as Blacklow Hill, in their reliance on the moon and the stars for light. There was surreptitiousness in the manner in which they sat closely together on the damp sod, knee to knee, hats drawn down low.

How did the once gay Gascon behave during these grim proceedings? Did he strive to prove himself innocent? Did he let his high temper flare in a reiteration of his contempt for them? Or did he lose his courage and beg abjectly for mercy? Nothing is known of his attitude.

The sentence was carried out at once. There had been such haste about everything, it may be taken for granted that the proper equipment for an execution had not been provided. No doubt a battle-ax in the steady hands of a man-at-arms was the means of carrying out the sentence. The stump of a tree may have served as the block.

3

One of the charges brought against Gaveston had been that during the time he was entrusted with the custody of the Great Seal of England he had stamped a large assortment of charters and papers which he could fill in later according to his fancy. This was a particularly heinous offense. The Great Seal was an essential part of the machinery of government. No charter, no declaration, no letter of appointment, no official decision was legal unless it carried the imprint of the Great Seal. For that reason the Seal was never supposed to leave the possession of the king. If affairs of state took him overseas, it was necessary to appoint a regent and to entrust the Seal to him until the monarch returned. There was, in fact, an official at the chancellery called the Keeper of the Seal whose chief duty seemed to be to stamp all the documents prepared and then get the instrument back into the king's hands late in the day. If this symbol of royal power was lost or mislaid, a state of paralysis set in at Westminster. Documents would pile up in the chancellery and the justiciary which could not be sent out, royal officials would gnaw their fingernails in perplexity and whisper together in white-faced groups; a truly Gilbertian state of affairs.

To avoid this dire possibility, a small seal was kept as a substi-

tute. Once, when Edward II was going to France to do homage
for the duchy of Aquitaine, he was asked to hide the Great Seal in
some very secret place, and the small seal was brought out for the
use of the master of the rolls while he was away. It was during this
visit that a fire broke out in the middle of the night at the castle
at Pontoise, where the king and queen were staying. They had a
narrow escape, getting out at the last possible moment in their
nightgowns. When word of this reached Westminster there was
much shaking of heads. Does anyone know where the Seal is? they
asked one another. No one did. It had been a narrow escape indeed.

On another occasion, when Edward was going to Scotland, he
gave the Seal, carefully locked in its velvet purse, to Richard
Camel, his chamberlain, with instructions to deliver it without
delay to the queen. The queen was to give it in turn to Lady
Elizabeth de Montibus, her lady of the bedchamber, who would
place it in a casket, lock the same, and give the key to the queen.
In the morning the queen would give the key to the Lady Elizabeth, who would unlock the casket while her royal mistress
watched. The queen would then deliver the purse into the hands
of the Keeper of the Seal. He in turn would take it to the Exchequer, summon the superintendents who had put their seals on it,
have them break the seals and produce the Great Seal. After the
day's work had been done, the same procedure would be followed.

The Great Seal had been in the keeping of Gaveston on many
occasions, but he did not believe in such tiresome precautions. He
carried it about as openly as a drummer with his stick.

That it had been entrusted to him was one of the kingly lapses
which the barons found hardest to condone. It was a symbol of
power almost on a par with the crown, for without it business
came to a halt.

Three centuries later, when James II was running away from his
Dutch son-in-law, William of Orange, he paused long enough to
scoop up the Great Seal. As he crossed the Thames, he tossed it
into the water with an ill temper which expressed the thought,
"Now, how will you run your country?"

4

King Edward was prostrated with grief and rage when he heard
of the execution of Gaveston. He wept openly and shouted

threats of retaliation. After a time he gained sufficient control of himself to take the body for burial to King's Langley, where they had lived as boyhood friends. Later he established a chantry where prayers were to be said perpetually for Gaveston's soul.

The favorite's death proved a great boon for the king at a time when the whole country seemed against him. The bad faith of the leaders in thus illegally committing the Gascon to the block divided the baronial strength in two. The Earl of Pembroke, who was a man of high honor, as already stated, would not forgive Lancaster and Warwick for breaking the pledge he had given the Gascon. With the Earl of Warenne he went over to the king's party and almost immediately the complexion of things changed. With Gaveston out of the way, public sentiment turned back to the king. Cousin Lancaster found himself the leader of a minority party instead of dictator of the country.

And then an event occurred which has been the prime resolver of troubles throughout the ages, the most certain method of solving marital difficulties, healer of wounds, the patcher of family solidarity. At Windsor, where the disconsolate king had gone to be with the queen, Isabella took to her bed on the twelfth of November and at forty-five minutes after four the following morning was delivered of a child. It was a boy, a healthy, handsome specimen, whose first cries had a lustiness which seemed to promise that he had no intention of yielding to the infantile weaknesses which had carried off so many royal heirs. The next King of England had been born. No one had any doubts of that: not the queen, who was now eighteen and close to the peak of her great beauty; not the father, who became so intensely proud of his son that, for the time being at least, he forgot the fate of his favorite and was happy beyond measure; not the holders of hereditary posts at court, nor the French noblemen who had been sent over in anticipation of the happy event; and most certainly not the good citizens of London, who received the news by the queen's own hand and celebrated feverishly for three days.

The Count of Evreux, who was Isabella's uncle, went at once to Edward and suggested that the infant be named Louis after the heir to the French throne and as a compliment to the queen's father. But for once Edward had no hesitation in saying no. The newborn infant would be King of England and he must bear the fine English name of Edward.

The arrival of this healthy little stranger seems to have brought the royal parents together at last. For a time Isabella exercised a wifely influence over her spouse and Edward seemed content to have it so.

CHAPTER FOUR

The Great Scandal of the Middle Ages

1

THE view from Ludgate, high on its hill, was across the Fleet River and the substantial bridge which had been built to bear the heavy traffic from the west. Between the Fleet and the Old Roman Wall was a sour little piece of swampy land which had been given to the Dominicans. Undemanding and gentle, they had drained the land and turned it into a habitable quarter after all. On the other side of the Fleet the land was quite different; it was fair and very dry and, where it followed the long arch of the Thames, it was dotted with many noble houses.

The largest and busiest of these was like a small town in itself. Behind a gray stone wall could be seen the crowded roofs and domes of many buildings, including a round structure which obviously was a church and an elaborate chapel on the bank. This establishment had long since overflowed the walls, and there was an open stretch of fifteen acres where the ground had been trampled to the consistency of hard clay by military games and the exercising of horses. Beyond this was a row of utility buildings on the site of what is now Fleet Street. There were several smithies, with sparks flying from the chimneys and out of the open doors while knights in white robes with the red cross on the shoulder (the cut of the robe far removed from the popular tabard) waited for their horses to be shod. Beyond there was a squatty structure which seemed to be devoted to the storing of exotic supplies—spices, pepper, salt, and herbs—a long grain house, a windmill, and a row of stables which were regular beehives of activity.

Over the front entrance in the wall, barred, strong, severe, floated the *beauséant*. It consisted of two bars, the upper one black to denote death to their enemies, the lower white, denoting love and peace for mankind. On the banner was the legend *Non*

nobis, non nobis, Domine, sed nomini, tuo da gloriam. This was
the banner of the Order of the Knights Templar.

The Order of the Knights Templar had been founded to protect the pilgrims who walked to the Holy Land during the period
of the Crusades; a noble endeavor which attracted only the
bravest and least selfish of men. Consisting of nine knights only at
first, it grew rapidly. It was an ascetic order. The uniform was
white, in token of chastity. The good knights existed on two
meals a day and had meat only three times a week. They spoke
rarely and used signs at table to indicate their wants. They went
to bed immediately after compline and slept in their shirts and
breeches, and with lights beside the beds, to be ready in case of
emergency. They seldom bathed. They forswore communication
with the rest of the world. No letters could be received and none
sent except by the express permission of the Master. Being men of
wealth for the most part, they turned all their possessions into the
common fund and respected the orders of the Grand Master as
they would the commands of heaven. They had done a magnificent work over the years.

But the Crusades were over now and the Templars had been
driven from the Holy Land. Even their fabulous Castle Pilgrim, a
seemingly impregnable fortress near Acre, with springs and orchards and fields of grain inside its walls, had been taken. Their
reason for being had come to an end.

Over the years, however, the Templars had become wealthy, by
donation and legacy. When their fighting days seemed at an end,
they turned their attention to the utilization of their possessions;
with so much success that they had become the bankers of civili-
zation. It was no wonder that they were rich. They owned nearly
ten thousand manor houses and estates scattered over the face of
Europe. They paid no taxes, they were not subject to the laws of
state or Church, and although usury was illegal they were allowed
to charge interest, disguised as rents, on loans. In England they
had custody of the crown jewels. Taxes were collected and paid
through them, a percentage staying in the hands of the order.
Pensions were paid through the Temple. They provided facilities
for the transfer of funds from one country to another. A pilgrim
could deposit funds in London and draw on the order in Jerusa-
lem. They issued letters of credit which were honored everywhere.
They loaned money to kings, to members of the nobility, and to
the great merchants, and were always allowed to charge interest.
Money and prized possessions were deposited in the Temple, and

the owners could call at intervals to reassure themselves that the stuff was still there. In other words, they had on their own initiative developed an international organization which operated as the banks do today.

Kings looked with envy on the great stores of wealth which time and these exceptional opportunities had made possible. When Edward I had completed his conquest of Wales, he faced arrears for the pay of his troops. His pockets empty, he went with one Sir Robert Waleran to the Temple on the pretext of wanting to see his mother's jewels, which were being kept there. While waiting, he broke open one of the coffers (how he could do this in such a well-conducted and closely defended establishment was never explained) and carried off gold bullion and jewels to the value of fifty thousand pounds. This relieved him of his immediate difficulties and he was afterward able to compound his indebtedness to the order.

It was said that when Edward II first became king he decided to follow the nefarious example of his father. He went to the Temple and took forcible possession of great stores of silver and gold belonging to the Bishop of Chester. The story went that he turned it all over to Piers Gaveston. It was even hinted that the Gascon went with the king and aided in the robbery.

The knights were still ready for any demand on their services. If another crusade had been launched, the Templars in their white robes, with their long beards and short hair, would have responded in full force. But the crusading fever no longer boiled in human veins, and so gradually a change had come about. The knights were not now stinted at the table and their waistlines were broadening. Each member was allowed to have three horses, where one had done for two men at the start, and a squire as well. It was whispered about that instead of the coarse clothing of drugget and sacking, which had once sufficed, the knights now wore silken underclothing and appeared at the evening meal in sable-lined cloaks over velvet doublets. Whether or not this was true, it was certain that they cut a noble appearance in public. They rode mettlesome Arabian steeds, and their stirrups were of gold. Their swords had gold and jeweled hilts.

Inevitably the order became the target of criticism. Strange rumors began to circulate, actuated by envy and tipped with malice. In the beginning the Templars had established secrecy in their proceedings and rites. The meetings of the chapters were held at midnight behind locked doors. For the reception of new members, sessions were held at dawn and no one was allowed to speak afterward of what happened. Sitting over their small fires at night, with the window shutters barred against the devil, people talked of these midnight rites of the Templars and shuddered as they tried to conjure up the nature of them. It was a common topic in the taverns. The story most often told, and most eagerly believed, was that the Templars had turned away from the true religion and had become devil worshipers. They knelt before an idol in the form of a black cat which was called Baphomet. Still more revolting things were hinted at, and mothers called their children in from play when they saw a white-robed knight approaching.

In England the order was held in better repute than elsewhere, although some of the stories got into circulation. Children were warned about "the Templar's kiss," which meant death. There was a popular saying in England, "to drink like a Templar."

In spite of these indications of a gradual weakening of discipline in the order, the fact remains that the Grand Masters often showed the iron fist in dealing with misdemeanors. Commenting on the white and black bars on their banner, someone said, "The Templars were wholly white to the Christians they served but black and terrible to members who became miscreants." Here is a case in point. There is a narrow stair leading to the triforium of their church in London, and looking out on it is a penitential cell, four feet six inches by two feet six inches, in which no one can either stand up or lie down. In this torture chamber Walter de Bachelor, Grand Preceptor of Ireland, was kept until he starved to death for disobeying the Grand Master. He had one consolation only: through some bars in the cell he could listen to mass in the church.

They could be impervious to pity where their own members were concerned. Geoffrey de Magnaville died while under a ban of excommunication. His body was soldered in lead and hung up on a tree in the orchard. It was not taken down until evidence was found that he had expressed contrition before dying. He now lies in the Temple Church.

2

It has already been told how Philip the Fair tried to kidnap Pope Boniface VIII. When Boniface died in 1305 because of his rough handling at Anagni he was succeeded by a frail old man,

Benedict XI, who lived for a short time only. It was believed that he had been poisoned, and the cardinals, cowering at Perugia in fear and trembling, took the better part of a year to select a successor. Owing to the influence and gold of France, the Pope finally selected was a Gascon, Bertrand de Goth, the Archbishop of Bordeaux. The story is related that he was given the post on six conditions, imposed by Philip, and that the sixth was sealed. He was not to know the nature of it until the time came for Philip to demand of him its fulfillment. It is hard to believe that even for the exalted glory of the pontificate a man would accept such conditions, but the events which followed lent some trace of substance to the story.

In 1304 one Florian of Béziers, who was under sentence of death, received a pardon for issuing a revelation of the iniquities of the order. An apostate Templar named Nosso de Florentin, who had been condemned to life imprisonment for impiety, made a statement of the abominations he had seen while a member of the order. They charged jointly that on initiation each new member was required to spit on the cross and that on Good Fridays the cross was trampled underfoot. At all the midnight sessions there was worship of Baphomet (which was believed to indicate an inclination toward Mohammedanism) and that evil spirits in the guise of beautiful and seductive women were introduced into the chapters. After these major accusations, the informers descended to absurdities such as the smearing of idols with the fat from roasted children and a liking for standing in circles and tossing the bodies of newborn children from one to another until they died. It was even stated that at each meeting of the general chapter one of the priors would disappear and never be heard of again, which was accepted as evidence of human sacrifice.

Philip decided that the time had come to proceed against the order and he laid out his plan of campaign with fascistic ingenuity and lack of all scruples. First he gave it out that he believed all the orders which had grown out of the Crusades—the Templars, the Hospitalers of St. John, and the Teutonic Knights—should be merged into one organization to be called the Order of the Knights; with headquarters, of course, in France. In response to an invitation to discuss the plan, Jacques de Molay, the Grand Master, came to France, prepared to oppose it, bringing with him sixty knights and so much of the accumulated wealth held at Cyprus that twelve horses were needed to transport it. This was deposited in the Temple in Paris.

In the meantime Philip and his machiavellian minister, Guillaume de Nogaret (one of the blackest and most villainous intriguers of all time), had introduced twelve spies into the order with definite instructions as to what they were to report. The French king then went to Clement V and informed him that the Templars must be abolished. It is said that Clement, who had been a compliant tool in most matters, hesitated at this. If he did, the crowned instrument of evil may have reminded him of the sixth, and still sealed, condition.

With all the evidence needed and the chief fly already in the parlor, the trap was sprung. Philip went to the Grand Inquisitor, Guillaume of Paris, who had authority to act without the knowledge or consent of the Pope, and secretly denounced the Templars as guilty of heresy. On September 14, 1307, writs were sent to the royal seneschals in every town of France which owned a Templar chapter, with orders to prepare for a nationwide *coup*. On the night of October 13 they were to surround the chapter houses, arrest all the knights, seize the archives, and take possession of all property. The utmost secrecy was enjoined. Not a hint of the royal purpose must leak out.

The plan was carried out without a hitch, and by midnight on the date set every Templar in France was under arrest. Jacques de Molay was in the toils with all of his attendant knights. The way had been prepared for one of the most diabolical and ghoulish betrayals in all history.

This was on a Friday. On the Saturday morning the bewildered knights were brought into courts all over France and formally charged with a catalogue of crimes which shocked the world. Needless to state, they pleaded their innocence. On the Sunday, complaisant preachers talked in the open to the populace, rehearsing the whole list of startling but absurd charges.

The authorities proceeded then to extract confessions by torture. The officers of the king, under the direction of the admirable Nogaret, applied the instruments. If a prisoner resisted their efforts, he was turned over to the agents of the Grand Inquisitor, who were experts at loosening tongues. Of one hundred and forty knights put to the torture in Paris, thirty-six died, protesting their innocence to the end. Many lost the use of their feet from the torture of fire. Their legs were fastened in an iron frame, the soles of their feet greased over; they were placed before the fire and a screen was drawn backward and forward to regulate the heat. Victims of this roasting operation often went raving mad. There were other "most revolting and indecent torments such as can only be made public in a dead language." Forged letters purporting to come from Grand Master de Molay were shown to the prisoners exhorting them to confess themselves guilty. Many Templars finally confessed whatever was required of them.

The results were completely satisfactory from the standpoint of the king. Of the prisoners in Paris, 138 confessed, including the Grand Master, who, being old and frail, could not stand the agonies inflicted on him. At a public appearance Jacques de Molay confessed to denying the divinity of Christ and spitting on the cross. He swore to his innocence on all other charges.

A new Archbishop of Sens had been appointed, a creature of the king's named Philip de Martigny. His authority extended over Paris, and one of his first acts was to drag before the Provincial Council of Sens all Templars who had made confessions and then revoked them. They were accused of being relapsed heretics and were condemned to death by fire. The next morning fifty-four Templars were led to execution into the open country at daybreak near the Porte St. Antoine des Champs at Paris and were fastened to stakes rounded by fagots and charcoal. They persisted in their innocence and burned to death in a most cruel manner in slow fires. They met their fate with great fortitude.

Meanwhile hundreds of other Templars were dragged from Paris dungeons before the Archbishop of Sens and his council. Neither the agony of torture nor fear of death could force confessions from some of them, and these were condemned to perpetual imprisonment as *unreconciled heretics.* Those who made the required confessions of guilt and continued to repeat them received absolution, were reconciled to the Church and set free.

Later still, 113 more were condemned as relapsed heretics and burned at stakes in Paris. Others were burned in Lorraine, Normandy, Carcassonne; twenty-nine others were burned by the Archbishop of Rheims at Senlis. One dead Templar who had been the treasurer of the Temple in Paris was dragged from his grave and his moldering corpse burned as a heretic.

But Philip the Unfair realized that the order could not be abolished without the co-operation of the other monarchs. Not consulting Pope Clement, who was still highly distressed and unwilling to proceed to the final extremity, he wrote to the kings of England, Aragon, Castile, Portugal, and Germany, demanding that they follow his lead. To the great credit of his son-in-law, he found Edward of England not prepared to do anything without

making a thorough investigation, even though the arch instigator
sent a special agent, one Bernard Pelletin, to coerce him. Edward
even wrote to the other kings, questioning the wisdom of following the French course. The Spanish kings showed reluctance and
Portugal refused flatly to take any action.

In the meantime the tom-toms of incitement were being beaten
frantically in all parts of France. New charges were constantly
being added to the shocking catalogue. It was now said that the
Templars had confessed to worshiping an idol covered with animal skin and with carbuncles for eyes, and of burning the bodies
of diseased members and mixing their ashes into a powder to be
given to new members.

The Pope now took an active part in the conspiracy. In 1308 he
issued a bull demanding the arrest of all Templars. This had the
expected effect. Action was taken in England, as will be explained
later, in the Spanish countries, and in Cyprus. Some of the
knights defended themselves in their strong castles of Monzon
and Castellat, but both were finally reduced. In October of 1311 a
Grand Council was summoned by the Pope at Vienne, where
Philip took his seat at the right hand of the Pope. The latter came
out into the open in a sermon which condemned the order
officially. In a second bull, *Ad providam*, published in May 1312,
the properties of the order, except in a limited number of countries where the prosecution had been light, were assigned to the
Knights of St. John. This decision was the first reverse Philip had
experienced; he wanted all the property himself. However, there
were methods of circumventing the papal order which he pursued
later.

3

The final act of the great tragedy had the old and feeble Grand
Master as main character. Up to this point Jacques de Molay had
played an inglorious part because of his inability to withstand torture. He had confessed to some of the indictment and had later
reiterated his avowals at public hearings.

Philip, shaken by the decision to transfer the property to the
Knights of St. John, decided on a dramatic step. As the Grand
Master had never failed to shrink into weakness when threatened
with the fires of recantation, it was believed that he would do so
again. Accordingly he was summoned from his cell to appear on a

scaffold in front of Notre Dame. With him were Gaufrid de Charney, the master of Normandy, Hugh de Peralt, the vicar-general, and Guy, the son of the dauphin of Auvergne. There was a large gathering to witness the final humiliation of the heads of the order.

The four knights, loaded with chains, were brought to the scaffold by the provost of Paris. The Bishop of Alba read their confessions aloud and the papal legate called upon the prisoners to confirm their depositions. Hugh de Peralt and one other, Gaufrid de Charney, assented. But when the name of Jacques de Molay was called, the Grand Master, whose hair had turned white in prison and whose face was thin and pallid, stepped to the front of the platform and raised his chained arms to heaven.

"I do confess my guilt," he cried, "which consists in having, to my shame and dishonor, suffered myself, through the pain of torture and the fear of death, to give utterance to falsehoods, imputing scandalous sins and iniquities to an illustrious order which hath nobly served the cause of Christianity. I disdain to seek a wretched and disgraceful existence by engrafting another lie upon the original falsehood." He was interrupted by the provost and his officers, and the platform was hurriedly cleared.

Philip moved then with fierce determination and dispatch. He did not consult the officials of the Church or the Inquisitor. The next day the Grand Master and his younger companion were taken to what was called "the little island" in the Seine which lay between the king's gardens and the convent of St. Augustine. Here they were bound to stakes over small fires of charcoal and slowly burned to death.

The horrified spectators heard the voice of the Grand Master cry out from the flames: "We die innocent. The decree which condemns us is an unjust decree, but in heaven there is an august tribunal to which the weak never appeal in vain. To that tribunal I summon the Roman pontiff within forty days."

The witnesses shuddered when the tortured voice continued: "Oh, Philip, I pardon thee in vain, for thy life is condemned. At the tribunal of God, within a year, I await thee."

All that is left to tell is that Clement V, that weak and ambitious man, died of dysentery early the next year and that Philip the Fair expired a few months after.

The summary execution of the Grand Master and his companion did not provoke the officials of the Church to any protest.

The only action came from the Augustinians, who objected to the trespass on their land!

4

For a short while, and to his honor, Edward II forbade the infliction of torture upon Templars in his dominions. He really believed in their piety and the decency of their morals, but, being a weak character, he was speedily overcome by the influence of the Pope, who wrote him in June 1310 upbraiding him for not submitting the Templars "to the discipline of the rack."

Influenced by admonitions of the Pope and solicitations of the clergy, Edward on August 26 sent orders to the constable of the Tower, John de Cromwell, to deliver all Templars in his custody, at the request of the inquisitors, to the sheriffs of London, so that the inquisitors might proceed more conveniently and effectually. On the same day Edward directed the sheriffs who received the prisoners from the Tower to place them in care of jailers, appointed by the inquisitors, who would confine them in prisons in various parts of London at such places as they and the bishops considered most expedient. They were to do with "the bodies of the Templars whatever should seem fitting in accordance with ecclesiastical law."

On September 21, 1310, the ecclesiastical council in London met and had further inquisitions and depositions taken against the Templars. These were read aloud, and immediately disputes arose touching on various alterations observable in them. Now began further questioning of the Templars to try to extract the "truth," and if "by straitenings and confinement they would confess nothing further, then the torture was to be applied." But it was provided that the examination by torture should be conducted without the *"perpetual mutilation or disabling of any limb, and without a violent effusion of blood."*

The inquisitors and bishops of London and Chichester were to notify the Archbishop of Canterbury of the results of the torture, that he might again convene the assembly for purposes of passing sentence, either of absolution or condemnation.

On October 6 the king sent fresh instructions to the constable of the Tower and to the sheriffs. Apparently the Templars were shuttled back and forth to various prisons at the will of the inquisitors. At this time it is recorded that many of the jailers actually showed reluctance in carrying out orders and were often merciful and considerate of the unhappy Templars.

Orders were also sent to the constable of the Castle of Lincoln, the mayor and the bailiffs of the city, where many Templars were being held. On December 12, 1310, by command of the king, they were taken to London and placed in solitary confinement in different prisons and even in private houses, where soon came orders to load them down with fetters and chains.

In some way the Templars had heard reports of the fate of their brothers in France and that they were promised freedom if they swore to untruths. They refused the offer. They continued to declare that everything that had been done in their chapters in respect of absolution, reception of brethren, and other matters, was honorable and honest and might well and lawfully be done. After such affirmations the Templars were sent back to their dungeons loaded with more chains. During April 1311 seventy-two witnesses against the Templars were examined in the chapter house of the Holy Trinity in London. Nearly all were monks—Carmelites, Augustinians, Dominicans, and Minorites. The evidence was *entirely hearsay*.

The final outcome of all this examining and torturing, this shuffling of prisoners from one dungeon to another, was that the order was dissolved and all property of the order was confiscated. There were no executions, no rising of flames about the writhing bodies of innocent men. The knights were permitted to drift into civil life.

In view of the nature of the evidence, this seems drastic and unwarranted; but, knowing what had happened to their brothers in France, the English Templars counted themselves fortunate.

CHAPTER FIVE

Bannockburn

1

A FIRST visit to Stirling Castle is an experience never to be forgotten. The deep interest aroused is not supplied by the castle itself. It is large and old, but it is not the stark gaunt structure which stood so high on the edge of the precipice of rock in the days of Wallace and Bruce. Some of the original foundations may still be there.

It is the view from the battlements which fills the eye and causes the imagination of the visitor to soar. A glance to the south, across the battlefield of Bannockburn, provides a picture of the Lowlands. To the east is flat country traversed by the Forth, which winds and curls and winds again on its way to empty itself into the Firth. Then the eye turns to the north, where the range of the Ochils extends above the river and recalls memories of the crafty battle that Wallace fought there. North and west of the Ochils are the mighty Grampians, from which the initiate can identify the peaks of Ben Lomond, Ben Nevis, and Ben A'an standing up in aloof grandeur against the sky. There is a wildness, a sense of mystery and of violence in the mountains of the north, like a key to Scottish history. Lying between north and south, Stirling is the door to the Highlands and the scene of many of the most dramatic episodes in Scottish history.

No castle in Scotland, certainly, has been more frequently and more insistently besieged. When Robert the Bruce moved his force down to the Torwood, his ragged and often shoeless men singing their favorite marching song, *Hey, Tuttie Taitie*, Stirling had been continuously beleaguered for more than ten years. Sometimes the garrison was Scottish and it was the English who vainly strove to force their way up the one steep and winding approach. Sometimes the stronghold was held by the English, while the

Scots blocked the roads and tried by devious means to gain an entrance.

There is a reason why the indolent English king was compelled in 1314 to assemble the strongest army of the day and advance to fight the Scots at Bannockburn, which lies three miles south of the castle. Robert the Bruce and his valiant lieutenants, his sole remaining brother Edward, his friend the Black Douglas, Sir Robert Keith the marshal, and the hard-fighting Randolph, Earl of Moray, had all been so insistently at work that only three castles of any strength remained in the hands of the English: Edinburgh, Stirling, and Roxborough. In 1313 the Black Douglas took Roxborough and Randolph captured Edinburgh by a daring climb up the steep rock. That left Stirling; and it fell to the lot of Edward Bruce, the most daring and ingenious of them all, to lay siege to the granite towers on the precipitous hill.

The constable of Stirling was an English nobleman named Mowbray. After a long period of feints and attacks, the two leaders got together and made a compact. Mowbray agreed to lay down his arms and surrender if he were not relieved by the English king before midsummer of 1314.

Robert the Bruce was not pleased with his reckless brother when he heard of the agreement. He thought the situation over and gave his head a dubious shake.

"That was unwisly doyn, perfay," he is reported to have said, the curious turn of phrase being the work of one of the bards who have handed down accounts of the incident.

The king went on to say that now there must be a truce around Stirling while Edward of England had a year in which to gather a mighty army for the relief of the castle.

But his brother was convinced of the wisdom of what he had done. Was there any possibility of carrying the great stone pile during the time allowed in the truce? He doubted it, having already striven desperately and unsuccessfully to crack this hardest of nuts. If the English king did not march north to the relief, then the castle fell into their hands without another blow being struck. If, on the other hand, Edward did come, they had a double opportunity: to defeat the English army and have Stirling turned over to them. And, he added, must they not fight the son of the dread old king sooner or later? Why not now?

2

Robert Bruce had been right. The English king considered the
situation at Stirling Castle a national challenge. The stronghold
must not be allowed to fall. The test of strength which had been
pending since the death of Edward I could no longer be postponed. It was decided that the strength of England must be mus-
tered for an attack in force.

Edward, who had become more dynastic-minded since the birth
of his son, sent the Earl of Pembroke to take charge of the defense of the northern counties until such time as the royal army
moved up to the attack. A writ was dispatched to no fewer than
ninety-three barons to meet the king at Newcastle with all their
men-at-arms and feudal retainers. At the same time he commanded Edward de Burgh, the Earl of Ulster, to cross the water
with an Irish force numbering four thousand, including archers,
the Gascons to come out in force, and a supply fleet under the
command of John of Argyll to operate along the east coast.

The first summons was not successful and Edward sent out a
second and more urgent demand. This time he was more specific,
asking twenty-one thousand foot soldiers from the northern counties and Wales. Believing now that his preparations would prove
adequate, the king traveled to Berwick to take command. Here he
suffered a very great disappointment. Four of the powerful earls
did not put in an appearance—Cousin Lancaster, Warenne, Warwick, and Arundel—although they sent troops. Edward found it
necessary, therefore, to issue a third writ, in which he said, "You
are to exasperate, and hurry up, and compel your men to come."

The upshot was the assembling, finally, of an imposing army.
Never before had such a well-equipped force of such size marched
to the north to try conclusions with the Scots. The chronicles of
the day, which tend to exaggerate everything, fixed the English
strength at one hundred thousand, but more recent calculations
reduce this figure to something between twenty and forty thousand. Twenty-five thousand is probably close to the actual figure,
and this would include the cavalry and the archers from Ireland
and Wales. A larger force could not have operated on the narrow
front beyond the Burn of Bannock, where Robert the Bruce
waited with his army. This much may be set down as true, however: the army was splendidly equipped and caused a wave of awe

and fear to spread through the Lowlands as it progressed northward. The train of carts following the army was twenty miles long!

The earliest reports estimated the Scottish army at thirty thousand, but this is absurdly high. Modern calculators have reduced the figure to something in the neighborhood of seven thousand, including a body of five hundred horse. The horse troops were light compared with the English cavalry, which consisted of knights armed to the teeth on huge Flemish chargers and numbered two thousand. One fact is clear: that the disparity was great, and that Scotland's only hope lay in the spirit of her sons and the skill of her king in selecting where he would stand and fight.

There was a moment when even the stout heart of the Scottish king almost failed him. It was early on the morning of Sunday, June 23, 1314. The Scot pipers and drums had roused the army early and mass had been celebrated. A light ration of bread and water was issued, for it was the vigil of St. John. Two of the Scottish leaders, the Black Douglas and Sir Robert Keith, who was the marshal of Scotland and had charge of the scanty cavalry, had ridden out before dawn to catch a first glimpse of the English. These two stout campaigners gazed with awe when the mist rose and the early sun shone on the burnished arms of the invaders. It was their lot to see first the approach of "proud Edward's power, chains and slavery." The cavalry was in the van; and two thousand mounted men with polished shields and helmets, with pennons flying and trumpets sounding, can look as formidable as the army which someday will ride to Armageddon. Behind the horsemen came files of foot soldiers stretching back as far as the eye could see, marching steadily with swaying of shields.

The Black Douglas looked black indeed when he returned with Keith to tell what they had seen. Robert the Bruce was seated on a pony, because it was more sure-footed on such rough and marshy ground, and he was wearing a gold crown over his helmet, to identify him to his men. It would identify him also to the enemy and so can be classed as jactance, an open flouting of the foe, as though he said, I am Robert the Bruce, crowned at Scone, and if I fall the flag of Scotland will fall; and make what ye may of it, bold knights of the Sassenach!

He listened to their story of the overwhelming might of Edward while he studied the thin ranks of his own men and their nondescript weapons. After sober reflection he advised them to say little, to let it be accepted that the English, while numerous, were disorganized, a plausible story after the rapid march of the invaders by the inland route through Lauderdale.

When a general has a defensive action on his hands he knows moments of serious doubt while watching the enemy advance. Has he overlooked any possibilities? Has he forgotten anything? Are his troop dispositions sound? The Bruce remained where he was for some time, gazing about him with anxious eyes. He studied the ground sloping away in front of him, up which the English must fight their way. It was narrow, with the junction of the Burn of Bannock at the Forth on his left and the heavily wooded Gillies Hill and Coxet Hill on his right; much too narrow for the operations of a large army. The only stretch of open ground was the Carse, which lay between the river and the burn, and even this was studded with stunted trees and underbrush and the yellow of the sod was interspersed like shot silk with the green of the swampy mosses. In front of his permanent line, which faced the Carse, he had dug a row of pits and filled them with pointed stakes and iron rods known as calthrops. His position, in fact, was stronger than the one Wallace had chosen at Falkirk. But what of the archers who had won at Falkirk for the English? Douglas and Keith had said nothing of them, having seen only the chivalry of the Sassenach in their steel harness and the foot soldiers with shields and spears. Had the English forgotten the lesson of Falkirk?

The Scottish army lay hidden back of the lines, but two corps were out in front, one covering St. Ninian's Church and village in the center, the other at the point where the burn turned sharply northward to empty into the Forth. Even the camp followers had been thought of; they had a place of concealment on Gillies Hill from which they could make their escape if the battle went ill; a thoughtful move, for an army in the exultation of victory will wipe out the fleeing camp followers as a playful gesture.

Had he left anything undone? He did not think so.

The English arrived at Bannockburn late in the afternoon following a twenty-mile tramp over heavy roads. They were tired and hungry, but Edward, basing his course on the precepts of his father, who always struck early and hard, decided to attack the two Scottish divisions which were in sight. A regiment of cavalry was sent forward to advance by the Carse Road. At first Scot commander Randolph did not see the approaching army, earning the reproof from his king, "a rose from your chaplet has fallen," but he started briskly to work then and routed the Englishmen.

The English vanguard, commanded by the earls of Gloucester and Hereford, made an urgent advance in the hope of seizing the entry to the flat lands of the Carse, a strategic necessity. They found themselves opposed by a strong corps commanded by a knight on a gray pony and with a high crown fitted over his helmet.

"The king!" ran the word through the English ranks.

Perceiving that what they had thought was no more than a scouting party was in reality a formidable force led by the great Bruce himself, the English hesitated. Before they could retire, however, there happened one of the incidents which are told and retold in the annals of chivalry. One of the English knights, Sir Henry de Bohun, rode out into the open with his lance at rest and shouted a challenge to the Scottish king. Robert the Bruce lacked a lance but he seemed content with the battle-ax he was carrying, and so accepted the challenge by advancing from his own ranks. Bohun charged furiously, but almost at the point of contact the king's knee drew the pony to one side and the iron-clad challenger thundered past. Rising in his stirrups, Bruce had a second's time in which to deal a blow with his battle-ax. It landed squarely on the head of the charging knight and almost split his skull in two.

Returning to his party, the Scottish king was upbraided for having risked his life in this way. Bruce made no direct response but looked ruefully at the shaft of his ax.

"I have broken it," he said.

The shadows of night were falling by the time the English vanguard, very much chagrined by the defeat and death of their champion, had galloped back in a disorderly retreat.

3

At the break of dawn, in the far-distant region where the great spirits reside, St. Magnus must have been at work burnishing his spiritual armor; for, according to the word that later spread over all of Scotland, he had work to do that day.

The Scots had spent the night in prayer. The Abbot of In-chaffray had said mass and the foot soldiers were still on their knees when King Edward, arrayed in shining chain mail and jeweled tabard, and full of confidence in an easy victory, rode along his lines.

"They kneel," he remarked to those about him.

"Ay, Sir King," said Sir Reginald de Umfraville, who had been fighting Scots for ten grim years, "but to God. Not to us."

The English attack had been badly conceived. Because of the narrow front on which they must operate, the army had been divided into three main "battles," each of three lines. The first, made up of cavalry in the lead and foot soldiers behind, went across the Carse and up the sloping ground, behind the crest of which the Scots had been assembled in a dense adaptation of Wallace's *schiltrons.* The existence of the pits had not been suspected, and a toll of the horsemen was taken before the first of the attack came into contact with the hedge of Scottish spears. Their efforts to break through the clustering pike points was of no avail. In the meantime the second "battle" had followed up the hill. They could not get close enough to take a hand in the fighting and could do no more than halt and wait, conscious of the fact that the third "battle" had been ordered forward on their heels and would soon be on the hillside also. The attack, in fact, had been so clumsily contrived that the arrows of the English archers, massed on their right, were falling as thick on the attacking lines as among the Scots.

There was worse to follow. The lesson of Falkirk had been so faultily remembered that the archery division had not been provided with any form of protection. Robert Bruce, who was in personal command of the reserves behind the lines, saw at once the great opportunity which had thus been thrown his way. He ordered Keith to take his handful of cavalry around the left of the line and attack the English bowmen.

It was not an easy task, but Keith and his gallant five hundred accomplished it. They made their way around Milton Bog and came out against the flank of the archery corps. Great battles have often been won by a charge of cavalry in small numbers, delivered at exactly the right time and the right place. This was one, for in a matter of minutes Keith's horsemen, shouting a keening battle cry of "*On them!*" had thrown the bowmen into utter confusion and had slain large numbers.

Bruce, seeing victory in his grasp, led his reserves, who had been chafing for a share in the fighting, through the gaps between the *schiltrons* and fell on the fatigued first "battle" with claymore and pike. The first English line fell back on the second and forced a retreat into the laboring ranks of the third. It was utter confusion then on the slopes, which were already slippery with blood. Nothing much was left now of the bowmen who might have won the day for the English if the knights had been assigned to protect them up the slope to the point where they could riddle the Scottish ranks with steel-tipped death. Perhaps the gallant knights had refused to play pap-nurse to greasy varlets; this had been known to happen. Whatever the reason, the bowmen had no chance to display their worth on this tragic field.

The whole English line began to waver. Thousands of men who had not yet struck a blow fell into a panic and tried to break through the ranks of fresh troops coming to their aid.

And then the miracle happened which might be termed the Coup of the Camp Followers. The men and women of menial role who had been relegated to a place of safety back of Gillies Hill had been able to watch the course of the battle below them. It was clear to them now that the day was going very well indeed. Some unidentified and mute but not inglorious Wallace conceived a way to have a part in victory. The command was given and all of them—drivers, cooks, nurses, knaves—began to strip the leaves from branches. They used broken pike handles and broomsticks and even crutches and attached to them old clouts and the petticoats of the women and the tails of their plaid cloaks. Waving these improvised flags, they went charging through the underbrush, shouting at the tops of their voices.

To the panic-stricken English this could mean only one thing: that reinforcements had arrived for the Scots who were so eager to take a hand in the fighting that they had not chosen the slower course around the foot of the hill but had come charging over the crest. The faltering English line broke at this. Gilbert of Gloucester tried to rally the troops but was killed. Clifford fell into one of the pits and was killed before he could extricate himself. Twenty-seven other barons fell in the pandemonium.

Edward and his closest advisers had watched the confusion into which the army had fallen with bitter wonder and dismay. When the retreat from the hillside turned into a rout, Aymer de Valence, Earl of Pembroke, who knew a defeat when he saw one, having figured in many in his time, seized the reins of the king's horse. It was time for Edward to leave. Surrounded by the five hundred picked horsemen who served as the royal guard, they rode at a furious gallop around the left of the Scottish lines and cut north in the direction of Stirling Castle. One of the knights with the king was a Gascon named Giles de Argentine, who stayed with the beaten monarch until they shook off a fierce attack by Edward Bruce. "It is not my custom to fly," he said then. Wheeling about, he rode straight for the Scottish lines, crying, "An Argentine! An Argentine!" In a very few minutes he had begun a flight to wherever it is that brave soldiers are transported.

On other occasions Edward had not shown much courage in battle, but now, perhaps in desperation, he showed some of the Plantagenet mettle. They encountered more pursuers and an effort was made to drag him from his horse. He beat the enemy off. With a mace, which became a lethal weapon in his strong hands, he cut his way through to safety.

At Stirling Castle the royal party was refused admittance. It was pointed out that, inasmuch as the effort to relieve the fortress had failed, the castle must now capitulate. They did not want the king stepping into that kind of trap. Accordingly Edward and his morose followers rode sixty miles to Dunbar, where they made their escape by sea.

What part did St. Magnus play in the victory? All Scotland was thrilled with a story that late in the morning he appeared from the clouds above Aberdeen in a coat of shining mail and on a great white horse. He rode down the streets of the granite city, crying out in a mighty voice that Robert the Bruce had that day defeated Edward of England on the field of Bannockburn.

4

The pursuit of the English was conducted briskly but not to the exclusion of looting. The equipment of the beaten army had not only been ample but luxurious. An estimate places the loot taken from the field at two hundred thousand pounds, but this seems as exaggerated as the figures given of the size of the armies. It was considerable enough, however, to compensate the people of Scotland for the losses they had sustained in the twenty years of warfare. In addition to what had been left on the field there were many hundred knights captured, and the Scots saw that each of them paid a heavy ransom.

Scotland had been a poor country to begin with; and the continual burning of the countryside and the destruction of their herds and flocks had brought the people close to starvation. Bannockburn paid most of it back.

There were exchanges, of course. The Earl of Hereford had been taken prisoner on the field and the Scots demanded for him fifteen prisoners held by the English. These included the wife and daughter of Robert the Bruce and the venerable Bishop of Glasgow.

When Robert Burns sat himself down to write his famous war song, *Scots wha hae*, he intended to set it to the air of the Bruce marching song, *Hey, Tuttie Taitie*. His publishers did not approve the idea, thinking the air lacking in distinction and grandeur. It was for a time sung to that measure, nonetheless, with great success. A new setting has been used ever since for this famous epic.

5

The Scottish victory at Bannockburn did not bring peace. The Scots, having driven the last of the Sassenachs across the border, save for the city of Berwick, were willing and anxious to discuss terms. The English, humiliated and angered beyond measure, were not so disposed; they proceeded to take the military command out of the feeble hands of Edward and entrusted the army to Cousin Lancaster, who, as it soon developed, was no better. Realizing that the end to the long struggle was not yet in sight, Robert strove to make the English realize the cost of war by striking fiercely at the border counties. As a further measure he sent troops into Ireland in an effort to divert the attention of the foe. Edward Bruce was put in command, and it was announced that the King of Scotland intended to raise his resourceful and ever daring younger brother to the Irish throne. Roger de Mortimer, who has been mentioned as one of the young knights who won his spurs during the wholesale knighting of adolescent Englishmen by Edward I, was in command in Dublin at the time.

The resourcefulness and daring of Edward Bruce were not equal to the task. He established his rule over Ulster and remained there until 1318, when he sallied out to attack a large English force in a particularly foolhardy mood and was defeated and killed. In the meantime the mercenary Mortimer had also departed, leaving behind him personal debts contracted during his term of office amounting to one thousand pounds, "whereof he payde not one smulkin." A smulkin was a pleasantly characteristic Irish word for a brass farthing. This act of high-handed unconcern for everything but his own interests was the first in a career which would be marked by an insolence greater even than the open mockery of Gaveston and an avarice beyond all measure.

Bruce became doubly anxious for peace when he realized that a touch of leprosy which he had acquired in his wanderings was beginning to tighten its grip on his system and to rob him of power in his limbs. The *mickle ail*, it was called in Scotland, where it was widely prevalent. Every town had been obliged to provide some kind of leper hospital, which had its own churchyard, chapel, and ecclesiastics, even though the building itself might be no more than a frame shack on the edge of a wind-swept moor. It was highly ironic that the great fighting king, after struggling so long and enduring so much hardship, should thus be barred from the peace and comfort for which he had longed.

Realizing that his days were numbered, King Robert appealed to the Pope to bring about peace between the two countries. In 1320 he directed a message in the name of the barons of Scotland to Pope John XXII. It was a well-reasoned presentation and contained one clause which tells in a heart-felt way the plight of the northern kingdom.

Admonish and entreat the king of the English, for whom that which he possesses ought to suffice, seeing that of old England used to be ample for seven kings or more, to leave in peace us Scots dwelling in this little Scotland, beyond which there is no human abode, and desiring nothing but our own.

It was unfortunate for Scotland that John XXII was Pope at this period. He was an appointee of Philip the Unfair and had been elevated to the papacy at Avignon through the efforts of that monarch; after, it may be added, a stalemate of two years. He proved to be a heavy-handed pontiff, as witness his course when a second pope was raised to the Vatican in Rome through German influence. This was a Minorite friar named Pietro Rainalducci de Corbara, who was given the title of Nicholas V. When the German influence declined, leaving Nicholas alone, he sought to make his peace with Avignon and was brought into the presence of John with a halter around his neck. A sentence of perpetual imprisonment was passed on him and he died in a prison cell in Avignon.

John disregarded the Scottish appeal. In fact, he went to the other extreme and in 1323 laid all Scotland under an interdict.

CHAPTER SIX

After Bannockburn

1

IN 1315, the year after Bannockburn, England experienced heavy and continuous rains. There was something strange and fearsome about them. They were not of the steady, mizzling variety nor the pleasant rains which blew up suddenly and as suddenly passed, leaving the air cool and the earth sweet. Instead they came in the wake of sullen gray-black clouds from the northeast which closed off all view of the sky and of the sun by day and the moon and the stars by night. The lashing downpour turned the ground into quagmires, and the continuous drip from the trees and underbrush and from the eaves of the houses drove people finally into a state of despair.

Everything was going wrong since the old king died and this foolish, feckless son had taken his place. The national pride had been humbled at Bannockburn and now a divine hand was showing its disapproval: so ran the story throughout the country.

The crops rotted in the fields and the fruit on the trees did not ripen. Lucky the husbandman who had cut and stored his hay early, for his stock at least would have something to eat. The inevitable sequel followed: the rivers grew swollen and overflowed their banks. Even the smallest brooks and becks became angry and vehement. Whole villages were inundated. The toftman whose home had been destroyed or carried away found small comfort in the wreckage deposited by the hostile waters on his land.

Finally the rain stopped and the waters receded, becoming gentle again. Somehow the people of England lived through the dismal winter that followed. But in the spring it was the same again, and the untilled and unplanted fields became soggy and rank. There was a serious famine in 1315. A plague carried off the cattle, and it became commonplace to find on the highways and under the trees the bodies of the homeless who had died of starvation. None of this could be laid at Edward's door, and there may have been some slight consolation for the unhappy and hungry people in the lack of bread at times on the royal table. In their minds, however, there were bitterness and a sense of dissatisfaction. Would not a good king, an energetic king, have been able to do something for his people?

During the Whitsuntide festival the king and queen kept court at Westminster. One evening they were dining in public in the great banqueting hall; a foolish thing to do, for the sight of ladies and gentlemen in fine silks and furs regaling themselves with meat and wine is certain to rouse resentment among people who are gaunt and ill from hunger. In the midst of the meal a woman on horseback and wearing a mask guided her mount in through the wide-open door and rode up to the head table. Without a word she delivered a sealed letter into the hands of the king.

Edward, suspecting nothing, had it opened and read aloud, discovering to his anger that it contained an indictment of his conduct as king. The woman who had tarried outside the hall was unmasked and brought in again to the royal presence. She had no hesitation in naming the knight who had entrusted the missive to her: the scion of a good house and known for his bravery and sobriety. When apprehended, the knight said "he had taken this method of apprizing the king of the complaints of his subjects."

In the meantime things seemed to be going wrong in every way. The Scottish raiders ranged as far south as Furness, a part of Lancashire which includes the Lake District. They came close to getting their hands on the wealth of Furness Abbey, one of the richest in England. Whatever the rains and the floods had left, the Scots burned behind them. Philip the Fair lived long enough to learn of his son-in-law's failure at Bannockburn and then turned away from life, perhaps to answer the summons issued from the flames by the dying Grand Master of the Templars. Llewelyn Bren, dispossessed by the heirs of the Earl of Gloucester and brushed aside scornfully when he complained to Edward, rose in rebellion with his six sons and seized all of Glamorganshire. The son of a tanner named John Drydras, although sometimes spoken of as John of Powderham, took advantage of the general discontent to announce himself as the real son of Edward I and to declare the ruling king a changeling. The man was an impostor, for he had no kind of proof whatever, save long legs and blond hair, but for a time people listened to him and wondered. In the end, of course, they took Master Drydras and hanged him with the usual extremes of cruelty. The queen bore another son at the royal castle of Eltham, a healthy specimen who was given the name of John and who would live a rather uneventful and not long life as a bachelor. Edward was so pleased that he gave one hundred pounds (an absurd extravagance at such a time) to Sir Eubulo de Montibus, the bearer of the good tidings. The queen increased her popularity with the people by pleading for the life of one Robert de Messager, who had been convicted of speaking "irreverent and indecent words" about the king.

2

It happened that before Bannockburn the Earl of Lancaster had displayed his lack of patriotism in a rather extraordinary way. He did not accompany the royal army and he did not send any of his men. Instead he assembled quite a considerable army at his castle of Pontefract in the openly expressed belief that if Edward were successful against the Scots he would return with his victorious army and compel the barons to give up the concessions they had won from him. This sorry pretense paid him golden dividends. Edward returned a fugitive to face an angry Parliament at York; and there was Lancaster with his fresh troops to make sure of the king's submission. It was said that the earl had stood on the battlements of Pontefract as the defeated Edward passed and had jeered at him.

The recalcitrant barons contented themselves at York with demanding the dismissal of the king's chief officers. Archbishop Reynolds, who had been filling the role of chancellor as well, had to surrender the Great Seal to John de Sandale. This mediocre individual did nothing outstandingly right in his term of four years, nor anything particularly wrong. He was guilty of one error of common decency in using his position to get delicacies for his table in the middle of the famine. Two purchasers were sent out to all parts of the country to take the best poultry they could get their hands on, with letters patent under the Great Seal to compel compliance. While England starved, the good chancellor lived, literally, off the fat of the land.

Walter of Norwich took Sandale's place as treasurer. Most of the sheriffs were dismissed also and replaced by nominees of the barons; to be more exact, the selections of the great Earl of Lancaster.

A general Parliament was held next year from January to March, and here the work begun at York was followed to the logical conclusion with great thoroughness. Hugh le Despenser, who had been standing very high in the king's favor, was dismissed from the council, and the same fate was meted out to Walter Langton. Lancaster was appointed commander-in-chief against the Scots. When Edward accepted these conditions, a reasonable grant was made to him. It was stipulated, however, that the ordinances must be observed and that the expenditure of the money thus obtained should be governed by the Ordainers. The prime humiliation was the setting of an allowance of ten pounds a day for the upkeep of the royal household.

Lancaster followed up his advantage the next year when a special session of Parliament was held at Lincoln. Here he was appointed head of the council to govern all the acts of the king.

Edward's cousin had won a complete victory. The king was now under his thumb. Lancaster had made himself the power behind the throne.

But his use of this authority soon made it clear that he was a man of most limited capacity. None of the steps he took to alleviate the distress of the nation during the famine had any usefulness. He objected to everything without having alternatives to suggest. He seldom attended the meetings of Parliament or council and, when he did, was invariably many days late, causing endless delays. In fact, he was like the critic who has bullied the administration for years from the opposition bench and then makes a sorry failure of it when he gets into power himself.

It was whispered also that he had accepted a bribe of forty thousand pounds to hamper English operations against Scotland. This charge can be set aside as pure invention. Where would the poverty-stricken King of Scotland get such an enormous sum for such a purpose? It was very clear that Lancaster's failure in the Scottish campaign was not deliberate but had been due to his utter lack of military capacity.

To make matters worse, he found himself involved at this time in a private war. He had married Alice, the handsome twelve-year-old daughter of Henry de Lacy, and through her had inherited the earldoms of Lincoln and Salisbury. It was not a happy marriage. They had no children, and the good earl indulged himself in one illicit romance after another. About the time he began to realize that holding the reins of power was not an unmixed advantage, the lady ran away from their castle at Caneford in Dorset. There was one trait in Lancaster's character that everyone knew: he would pursue a personal grudge with unrelenting bitterness to the end of his days. His wife's defection roused him to unusual fury and he accused the Earl of Warenne of carrying her off. Warenne denied this but he did acknowledge that he had assisted the lady in making her escape. Lancaster refused to believe him and proceeded to burn the Warenne lands. He even seized the earl's castle at Knaresborough.

It turned out later that Warenne had told the truth. The lady disappeared from sight, but when Lancaster died she emerged from hiding and married the man she had loved all the time. He was a landless squire, lame moreover, named Ebulo le Strange. It is not likely that the runaway countess lived happily ever after. The path of one who stooped low enough to marry a mere squire was almost certain to be a thorny one.

3

During this unsettled period Queen Isabella seems to have become reconciled to the role she was fated to play. She certainly felt no depth of affection for Edward, but on the surface at least she was a dutiful wife. She occasionally wrote to her brother, who had succeeded to the French throne, but in none of the letters is there a reference to how she felt. There is this on which to base an opinion: after the birth of the second son, John of Eltham, she brought two daughters into the world. Eleanor, the first, was born at Woodstock in 1318. The second, named Joanna, was born in the Tower of London in 1321, a gloomy place for what should have been a joyous and festive event, and one little to the taste of the beautiful mother.

At the same time it was no secret that she looked with favor on the Earl of Lancaster. He was, in the first place, her own cousin through his mother of Artois. He had taken it on himself to rid the country of the hated Gaveston, and that endeared him to the queen, although she may have been politic enough to dissemble her feelings. Undoubtedly she considered the ambitious earl an instrument to keep her husband in order, for Isabella had no illusions about the character of the man she had married.

In spite of her political views the beautiful queen was, if not a model wife, an obedient and useful consort during the years which followed Bannockburn and saw the ripening of the feud between the king and his cousin. There had never been a hint that she took any illicit interest in other men. She might have glanced slyly out of the corner of a starry eye at stout London aldermen and swished her scented wiliecoats at court receptions, but this was no more than the habitual exercise in mass subjugation in which beautiful women indulge, and it was never done for the sole benefit of one candidate for favors. In view of Edward's shortcomings as a husband, this is much to her credit. She was striving, quite clearly, to make the best of a quite bad bargain.

Eleanor, the first of the two princesses, resembled her parents in looks only. She was gentle in disposition and manner and with the patience to accept with grace the adversities of an unkind life. That she was gentle was made clear by the equanimity with which she accepted the failures of two efforts made by her father to secure brilliant marriages for her. The first was with Alfonso X, the young King of Castile, the second with Prince John, heir to the throne of France. Both efforts failed through dower disputes, and so the little Eleanor lost the opportunity to wear a queenly crown.

It was made clear that she was unusually pretty when Raynald II, Earl of Gueldres and Zutphen, provinces in the Netherlands, came to England on a visit. This is taking a plunge some years ahead of our story. A strong and stocky Low Countryman, Raynald was generally known as *Reynaldus de Fusco-Capite*, which meant Raynald the Black-Haired; and, as it was later learned, he was not an admirable character in many respects. In fact, he had headed an opposition party to the rule of his somewhat wander-witted father and had taken over the government himself. The poor old man was confined to prison for six years until he died.

Raynald had recently become a widower. Not more than one glance at the quiet, blue-eyed princess was needed to bring him to the point of an avowal. He asked, begged, beseeched, and finally demanded the fair Eleanor as his wife. So determinedly did he press his suit that the match was finally arranged.

It is fortunate that a record was kept of the wardrobe and appointments of the little princess, for it offers a detailed view of the elaborate sham with which the bareness, discomfort, and ugliness of life, even for rulers and their families, were hidden under a pretense of elegance.

She was going to the land where the finest and richest of cloth was woven, the land of great industrial cities and immense trading fleets. It behooved the English, therefore, to see that she did them credit. Her bridal trousseau (the word meant no more than "bundle" at that time, but there does not seem to have been any other in use to convey the exact meaning) was large and varied and beautiful. Never before had such clothes been made, at least not for an English princess. The materials represented the weaving artistry of the whole known world. There were samite and baudequin and the richest velvets and brocades from the East. There were silks from far Cathay which held imprisoned the ardent rays of a distant sun and were called variously Kiss-me and Fairy's Eye and Beyond-the-sea. There were substantial materials which were still startlingly attractive, called Camelot (an English make) and Camocas and Turkey cloth. The materials from Turkey were in a great variety of shades, including deep reds and greens, bewitching blues, and less determinate shades such as pansy, canary, and summer gray.

Consider, first, her wedding gown. It was made of Spanish cloth of gold, a perfect match for her hair, and was embroidered in colors with some, at least, of the divine skill which went into the modeling of the tiny snowflake. To wear over this dazzling robe there was a short mantle of crimson velvet, also decorated by skilled though sometimes tired fingers. Her veil was of the finest lace, as delicate as the pattern on a frosted pane and so fragile that it would be little short of sacrilege to stretch it on the frames of the tall hairdresses which ladies were beginning to wear.

There were dozens of other costumes for less ceremonial use: a mantle with hood made of blue Brussels cloth and trimmed with ermine, completely suited to displaying the fair English charm of the bride; a surtunic of cloth of gold on which hunting scenes with stags and dogs had been embroidered; a pair of pelisses of green cloth with strings of golden beads, for use in autumnal days before the cold of winter made it necessary for princesses to conceal their charms under heavy cloaks equipped with the device to hold clothes together and insure warmth which the French would improve later and call the *toute-autour*. And there were, of course, an infinite variety of caps and gloves and shoes. In the matter of shoes there were many pairs of the finest Cordovan leather which had been brought into use in England in the days of the fair Eleanor of Castile.

But it was in other directions that the most affectionate ingenuity had been called upon to make certain the little princess (she was under fifteen at that time) would properly impress the rich and observant burghers of the Low Countries. There was, in particular, her chariot. It was not one of the ugly whirlicotes which were coming into use in both England and France and were little more than chairs on wheels. Eleanor was to have for her own use, on ceremonial occasions and when the weather was fine, a very special coach, painted most gaily with the coats of arms of both countries. It was lined inside with purple velvet on which gold stars glistened. A degree even of comfort for the occupant had been attained. There were silken curtains at the side windows, cushions for her feet, and supports to grasp when the roads were rough and the coach rocked and swayed like a ship at sea.

Even more special and feminine was the bed which had been made for her. It was covered with green velvet in which the lions of England had been combined in a design with the crowned lions of Gueldres. There were voluminous curtains of Tripoli silk on the sides, for protection from night drafts and staff curiosity. This latter was a point of some moment, for of privacy in royal apartments there was none. Rising in the morning and retiring at night were events shared with the ladies and gentlemen in waiting, of whom there were many. Each had special and sometimes hereditary duties, such as holding the chemise of their lady or coming forward at the right moment with the kingly boots. Even after retirement a number of male aides slept in an adjoining room, two or three to a bed, with swords drawn and ready in case an attempt were made at assassination. In an equally accessible closet were a bevy of ladies, for visits to the oratory or the bishop's throne during the night could not be undertaken unaccompanied.

It was quite probable, of course, that Eleanor found she was expected to share the ancestral bed of the earls of Gueldres.

Life on the continent was more sumptuous than in England, but it had been seen to that the delicate palate of little Eleanor was protected. There is in the Wardrobe Roll of the year a long list of the items contained in her larder for the journey, including cloves, ginger, cinnamon, saffron, dates, figs, raisins from Corinth, and many pounds of white loaf sugar, particularly the much-prized variety from Cyprus.

As has been said before, a glimpse at the wedding plans for Princess Eleanor at this point involves a view of the future. The king, her father, was dead when her betrothal took place, and her mother was being held in Castle Rising, for reasons which will be reached later. The affection and perception shown in preparing the girl for her venture alone into a strange country was due, therefore, to the admirable wife, Philippa of Hainaut, who had been found for the older son of the family.

The princess did not go alone exactly. Her train was large enough to fill many vessels when she sailed from Sandwich for the port of Helvoet-sluys in May 1332. With her were William Zouch of Mortimer, Sir Constantine Mortimer, who was to act as her household steward, Robert Tong, her treasurer, eight knights and as many ladies-in-waiting, one hundred and thirty-six men servants, including minstrels, squires, and pages, and a host of women servants.

4

The marriage of the Princess Eleanor was not a happy one, although it started well. Her husband, proud of the eminent birth of his lovely bride, brought her to his palace in the city of Nimeguen, where she was enthusiastically received by his subjects. In course of time, largely through English influence, he was elevated to the rank of duke. This gave him the right to issue coinage and to control forests and added greatly to the pride of the new duke, who proceeded to institute hereditary offices such as marshal, chamberlain, cup-bearer, and steward. He purchased or conquered adjacent lands and added many fortresses to his holdings. He was, in fact, a capable ruler, strengthening the dikes, making better use of wastelands and turf bogs, and dividing common lands and forests among the poorer people. These enlightened measures not only brought immigrants in large numbers but added to the ducal revenues.

He had four daughters by his first marriage, and so it was an event for wide and boisterous rejoicing when the little Eleanor gave birth to a son. The child was named Raynald and, when a second son arrived two years later, he was called Edward after the English kings.

Raynald would have been better suited, perhaps, with a wife of vivacious ways or even one of unpredictable character who would match his tempers and provide zest to the daily life of the huge ducal palace. The sweetness and social timidity of his fair English wife (the result, it was believed, of her unhappy life at home) seemed to pall on him. Two years after the arrival of his second son, Duke Raynald had his consort moved to a separate house in a part of the city far from the palace. The reason he gave was that she had contracted leprosy. As she was allowed to take her sons with her, this was a most transparent excuse. No examination of her condition had been made by the court physicians, and so the duke's subjects waited until the real reason came out. Raynald was taking steps to obtain a divorce. He had already selected a livelier woman to take the fair Eleanor's place.

Eleanor, who had accepted her dismissal with gentle resignation at first, was stirred to action at this point. She arrayed herself in no more than a single garment of the flimsiest material and over this threw a warm mantle. Taking her two young sons with her, she came to the palace on a day when Raynald had summoned all his nobles for consultation.

"I am your mistress and lady," she said proudly to the guards at the gates and the well-fed custodians of the duke's dignity who strove to stop her in the halls.

So, without being announced, she came through the door and into the company of her husband and the attendant nobles. Leading her small sons by the hand, she walked forward until she stood by the chair at the head of the table where Raynald sat.

Some accounts of what followed say that she threw off her cloak and displayed her slender figure in its single garment "as far as delicacy permitted." Others assert she revealed herself in complete nudity to prove that she was in perfect health. At first thought it is hard to believe that one of her gentleness of spirit could be guilty of such an act. Sometimes, however, the most timid of mortals, when pressed to an extremity, will go farther, in a sudden revulsion of feeling, than the boldest. Let it be assumed, therefore, that the modest Eleanor did not scruple to show enough of her fair white body to the assembled company to prove that she was without disease or contamination.

What is more, she made a speech. "My beloved lord," she is reported to have said, warmly wrapped again in her cloak, "here am I, earnestly seeking a diligent examination in reference to the corporeal taint of which I am frivolously accused. Let it be seen whether I am subject to any loathsomeness or impurity." The hand of a monkish writer of chronicles can be seen in that use of words.

She had made it abundantly clear that she was in perfect condition. Not all the reports of all the doctors in Christendom, not all the wisdom of the East could have proved her case so well. The presence of her sons beside her, both in the best of health, was additional proof if such had been needed.

The duke took her back and the application for divorce was dropped.

The task of the narrator would be a pleasant one if it were possible to end the story with the simple statement that the fair Eleanor lived thereafter in peace and happiness. Unfortunately there were still great trials ahead of her. Raynald died in 1343 as the result of a fall from a horse. The older of the sons succeeded him as Raynald III at the age of ten years. It is said that the boy's mother, suddenly displaying decision and a soundness of judgment equal to any occasion, aided in an orderly administration of the now extensive duchy "in integrity and peace."

The son proved to be of a turbulent disposition and, when old enough to assume control of office, soon had himself in all kinds of trouble. The younger son, Edward, was cast in an identical mold and they quarreled bitterly. The mother strove to keep the peace between them and was rewarded, according to the records, by the seizure of all her possessions, even of her dower rights.

The Low Countries were divided at this period into two parties, the one composed of the older and more aristocratic families, who owed their wealth to great landholdings and to control of shipping, the other made up of the newer magnates who had reached prosperity through the success of the Dutch and Flemish people in manufacture and commerce. Although the Netherlands were divided into many sections, all quite independent, the feud between the two parties had spread into all of them. At first the parties were called the Cods and the Hooks. The Cods (Kabbeljaw) were the municipal factions, and it was supposed they took their name from the light blue and scaly-looking Bavarian coat of arms, while the Hooks were the nobility, capable of catching and controlling the Cods. The two parties had affiliated bodies in all the Dutch and Flemish provinces, although they bore different names in each. In Gueldres they were known as the Bronkhorst and the Hekeren, from great families which supported them.

Well: the two sons of Eleanor began to quarrel violently and perhaps it was inevitable that they should each lead one of the two factions. The younger son, Edward, was the more warlike and aggressive, and he not only succeeded in defeating his brother in open conflict but managed to take him prisoner. Raynald, the older, had of course become duke on his father's death, but he was so corpulent that the people had been somewhat scornful of him and had nicknamed him *Crassus* (the Fat). Edward, who seemed to have an ingenious turn for cruelty, in which he took after his great-grandfather of that name, put poor Crassus in a cell in the castle of Nieuwkerk in which the doors and windows were always open; but such was the girth of the older brother that he could not squeeze his way through any of them.

This provided Duke Edward with a ready answer when he was charged with a lack of proper feeling. "My brother is not a prisoner. He may leave when he so wills."

"But, Your Grace, he is too broad to get through the doors!"

"Am I to blame, then, that my brother is a gormandizer?"

In the meantime Edward enjoyed ten years of turbulent rule. He was finally killed in battle with his neighbors, the Brabançons. Raynald had been well fed in his cell which bore out the truth that "stone walls do not a prison make," not, at least, when narrow doors will suffice. On the death of Edward he was released and restored to his dukedom. But alas, poor Crassus! He was now huge and a far from inspiring sight; and he had lost all capacity to cope with administrative troubles. Perhaps it was just as well, for the good of the realm, that he died within a year.

Through all this trouble the poor mother of these ignoble sons had lived in poverty, finding it necessary to accept aid from the monks of a monastery at Harderwyck which she had established in her days of power and wealth. She seems to have been too proud to ask help of her English kin. Some funds were provided for her after both sons had passed into the shades, and she died in comparative comfort in 1335 in a Cistercian convent near Malines.

CHAPTER SEVEN

The New Favorite

1

EDWARD's weakness of character was most clearly manifested in his inability to stay long without someone to lean on, to share his interests, his occupations, his hobbies, his likes and dislikes. When he found such a friend, he lavished affection on him and was happy only when in his company. He went much farther, unfortunately: he lavished wealth and power on his favorites as well. Nothing was too good for them, even if the demands of the favorite went beyond the bounds of reason or infringed illegally the rights of others or even ran counter to the constitution. For Gaveston, he had been ready to sacrifice everything: the good will of the people over whom he ruled, the relationship with his wife, even his hold on the crown of England.

After Gaveston's violent death, he lived a more normal existence. This was due in some degree to the birth of his son and the improved understanding, or perhaps compromise, with the queen. This state of affairs lasted longer than might have been expected; for several years, in fact.

One of the prominent barons of the day was Hugh le Despenser, Earl of Winchester, who held extensive lands in the Marcher country. He had stood on the king's side at all stages of the continuous hostilities between the ruler and the dissenting group headed by the Earl of Lancaster. He had even voted for the return of Gaveston from exile and the restoration of his titles and lands. By so doing he had won the enmity of the baronial party, who considered him a deserter, and had been expelled from the council. After Gaveston's death he slipped quietly and inevitably into a favored position with the unstable king, and it was generally believed that he was urging the king to seek revenge on those who had played a part in the death of the Gascon. His course, in the opinion of those who knew him well, was dictated by avarice. It was his insatiable desire for land and money which led him to seek the ear of the king and not a liking for power in itself. He seems to have been endowed with some of the obvious characteristics of gentility; he was courteous, urbane, and easy in his dealings with friend and foe. In addition, he was a man of parts, a clever diplomat and a good soldier.

His son, Hugh le Despenser the younger, had married Eleanor, the oldest of the three daughters of Gilbert de Clare, Earl of Gloucester and the wealthiest peer in England. He might well have been content with such prospects, but he shared the traits of his father to such a remarkable degree that he was never satisfied. He was clever and ingratiating and handsome in face and figure. In spite of all these advantages he was ruled by such a passion for wealth that he was blind to the risks he took to obtain more and more possessions.

At first the son had taken the opposite course from his father, aligning himself with the party of Lancaster. This might readily have been a matter of deliberate policy. Centuries later, when the Stuarts in exile were making warlike efforts to regain the throne, it was not unusual for families to divide their allegiance. A landowner with two sons would send one to serve under the Pretender and the other would remain at home or even enlist in the government forces, thus making sure that, no matter which way things went, one of the two could retain the family property. One can imagine the wily Despenser, with a calculating glint in his cool gray eye, taking the younger aside and whispering in his ear: "Good son, I have committed myself to the king. But suppose that the barons win? Can we take the risk of having all our lands confiscated? Nay, my son, you must see to that by throwing in your lot with this pestilential Lancaster and his crew."

Whether or not it was a matter of pure self-interest, the well-favored son of the family allied himself so strongly with the baronial faction that Lancaster, whose judgment in such matters was always faulty, was convinced the younger Despenser had earned the ill will of Edward. After Gaveston's death he was made chamberlain of the royal household, a post which the Gascon had held, in the belief that the appointment would be obnoxious to the king. This brought the young man into constant contact with Edward, and the result was far different from the one that the inveterate fumbler, Cousin Lancaster, had expected.

The new chamberlain went about his duties with suavity and

confidence, creating an atmosphere of cheerfulness and ease. On the surface, at least, he no longer took an active part in the troubled politics of the realm.

The young Earl of Gloucester, Despenser's brother-in-law, was killed at Bannockburn, and there was inevitably a furious race among the husbands of the three sisters, to whom the immense Clare holdings would revert. The husbands of the two younger sisters, Hugh of Audley and Roger d'Amory, believed that Despenser had bested them in the division by taking nearly the whole of Glamorgan. Their hostility grew when he claimed, and even began to use, the title of Earl of Gloucester. It has been an accepted theory that the ill feeling in the family was the reason for Despenser's desertion from the baronial cause and his devotion thereafter to the interests of the king. This does not seem a realistic explanation. The barons still had the whip hand, and no one with an eye to the main chance would have changed his coat to attach himself to the waning fortunes of the incumbent of the throne.

It is more likely that Lancaster had been wrong in assuming a dislike for Despenser on the part of the king or that, at least, he was slow in detecting a change of sentiment on Edward's part. Propinquity and the easy manner and personal charm of the new chamberlain were certain to have this effect. The king began to show a predilection for his amiable and plausible aide, a fondness for his company. The queen, who was watching her spouse with suspicious care, detected this at once. The enmity, even hatred, which Isabella displayed later for the two Despensers was not a sudden manifestation of feeling. It had been building up, without a doubt, from the time her observant eye had first detected the familiar symptoms in her royal husband.

Gradually there was a swing toward Edward on the part of many of the barons, and the time came when that astute pair, the acquisitive Despensers, might ally themselves together on the royal side with reasonable safety. The incompetence of the Earl of Lancaster had disillusioned the barons, and many of them still shared with Pembroke the antagonism which had grown out of the way the latter's promise to Gaveston had been disregarded. Technically Cousin Lancaster was still chief of the council and could dictate to Edward on points of state policy, but actually he had withdrawn from active participation and, like Achilles, was sulking in his tent. The Despensers were shrewd observers of the political scene. They realized that the pendulum was swinging back. If Edward had shrewd guidance, he could at this juncture regain all the power and privilege he had lost. Father and son, in thorough accord, shoulder to shoulder, moved into the breach.

It was soon realized by all that the younger Despenser had taken the place of Gaveston, and the feeling against him ran high. The son seemed to be possessed of the same false confidence which had sent the Gascon to his death. Certainly he paid no heed to the growing enmity of the barons and used his influence over the king to get more and more land. Although he had received the largest share of the Clare estates, he was not satisfied and kept demanding that the earldom be granted him officially. Without warning he seized Newport, which belonged to Audley, his brother-in-law. He whispered in Edward's ear that the Mortimer family was becoming too powerful in the Marcher country and should be restrained.

Father and son had built a close barricade around the king, excluding almost everyone from intimacy with him, even the queen. They were like a pair of blue-blooded Uriah Heeps, getting their hands on everything, suggesting all manner of legal twists to take power and property from others, begging for this, demanding that. The king was either unable to stand out against this insidious influence or was happy to lavish his favors on them. It was not quite the same as when Gaveston had been the recipient of the king's bounty, for the Despensers were of noble blood and had wide connections. It could not be charged, therefore, that they were greedy outsiders, one of the most serious complaints against the Gascon, nor did this new team of sycophants do anything to enrage the barons personally as Gaveston had done. But if they did not rub their hands together in the accepted manner of stage villains (on the contrary, they were invariably courteous and obliging), they inspired a sense of fear and insecurity in the baronage.

Lancaster, acting for once with some acumen, saw his chance to regain the confidence of his fellow barons. He came out strongly for action against the new favorites, and the nobility almost to a man rallied behind him: the aggrieved brothers-in-law of the younger Despenser; the Mortimers, who had always been a tough and hard-bitten lot; the earls of Hereford, Warenne, and Arundel. Without waiting for parliamentary action, the neighbors in the Marcher country invaded the lands of the favorites and burned their houses. They were led by the Mortimers, who had adopted a special uniform, green with a yellow sleeve on the right arm. In a few nights of pillaging they practically destroyed all the properties the younger Despenser held through his wife and did damage amounting to hundreds of thousands. In addition they had ravaged sixty-three manors belonging to the elder Despenser, which he claimed represented a loss to him of forty-six thousand pounds; an indication of the enormous wealth he had been able to accumulate through the influence of the king. The elder's detailed statement of losses provides an interesting light on the life of a great baronial establishment of the day. He was robbed by his neighbors of twenty-eight thousand sheep, one thousand oxen, twelve hundred cows with their calves, five hundred and sixty horses, two thousand hogs and, from his larders, "six hundred bacons, eighty carcasses of beef and six hundred muttons." It paid well to stand in the favor of Edward!

The king, in a panic, issued a writ forbidding any attack on the Despensers. But writs were of small avail against a whole ruling class in arms, so in May 1321 Edward had to call Parliament to deal with the situation. The barons attended in force, wearing a white favor on the arm as a sign of their unanimity. This led to the session's being called the Parliament of the White Bands. The one thing on which the magnates were in agreement was the need to be rid of the leeches. Charges were brought against the Despensers and a decree was passed condemning them to exile and the forfeiture of much of their property, all the ill-gained part, at least.

The elder Despenser was sensible enough to bow his head to the storm. He accepted the decree of banishment by going abroad. The son, however, was of tougher mettle. He left in a fury of dissent. Where he set himself up is not on record, but it is possible that he had found a refuge in Bristol Channel, perhaps on Lundy Island, the centuries-long home of pirates. At any rate, he suddenly appeared with an armed vessel and seized two merchant ships coming in to port and robbed them of their cargoes.

The king, regarding this act of piracy, perhaps, as an amusing piece of horseplay, had begun to plan and conspire to get them back, almost as soon as he had affixed the royal seal to the decree of banishment. The Gaveston story was to be repeated, apparently, over and over.

2

During the month of October 1321, Queen Isabella decided to make a pilgrimage to the shrine of St. Thomas at Canterbury. Leeds Castle, which had been given to her as part of her dower, was selected to break the journey, and the queen sent her marshal ahead to announce her coming.

One of the lesser barons, Bartholomew Badlesmere, had been made castellan of Leeds but was away at the time. Having been put in that post since the rise of Lancaster to his position of dominance, Badlesmere had left instructions to his wife not to admit anyone who did not carry the necessary order. Had he paused to consider the character of his wife, he would have qualified his instructions to cover a situation of this kind. Every word in the English language which applies to women of violent disposition—harridan, virago, beldame—could be used to describe his far from fair lady. She was, as well, a bitter partisan by association and had, it was soon made clear, no regard at all for the royal family.

She met the queen's official on the lowered drawbridge and with an angry wave of her hand bade him begone.

"The queen," she declared, "must seek some other lodging. I will not admit anyone without an order from my lord."

The marshal, most rudely taken aback by the attitude of the castellan's wife, demanded if she knew that he was there on behalf of Isabella of England. That the queen, moreover, owned this castle and would not consider seeking lodging elsewhere. None of this had any effect on iron willed Lady Badlesmere. She reiterated what she had said. How was she to know if this demand for admittance came from the queen? In any event, let the queen go where she listed: she would not spend the night at Leeds.

While this argument was in progress, the royal party put in an appearance at the outer barbican. The madwoman screeched an order to her archers, who had assembled along the battlements, and the queen was greeted, not by the usual obsequious compliments and the strewing of flowers along the drawbridge, but by a volley of arrows. Six of her party were killed or wounded. Isabella of England, in a state of mind beggaring description, turned her horse and fled.

There had been some trouble earlier between the queen and this furious beldame. This added a still more violent tincture to the report of the extraordinary incident which reached the ears of the king. Badlesmere himself added fuel to the flames of the royal wrath by writing an explanation, couched in impudent terms, in which he excused the action of his wife in closing the castle to the queen. Edward spluttered with a degree of anger he had seldom felt before and decided to take action at once to avenge the affront.

The Ordainers, in whose hands rested all authority, seemed little disturbed over the incident. Lancaster, with his gift for doing the wrong thing, chose to be stiffly hostile. The queen's indignation mounted with each day and hour, so Edward finally decided to take the punishment of the Badlesmeres on his own shoulders. He made an announcement accordingly that, inasmuch as his beloved consort had been treated with violence and contempt, a general muster of all persons between the ages of sixteen and sixty was called to attend the king in an expedition against Leeds Castle.

It was London which responded with the greatest good will to this summons. The queen was still the darling of the citizens, and the trained bands turned out in force to avenge the injury which had been done her. They kept pace with the mounted knights in their eagerness to have a hand in the punishment of the castellan and his wife. Badlesmere himself, after having defended his wife's folly, had been very careful not to join her in the castle. He had, in fact, gone in great haste to Stowe Park, which was the seat of the Bishop of Lincoln, his nephew, which seemed a reasonably safe place. The belligerent chatelaine expected that Lancaster would come to her support and she defied the royal forces when they appeared before the castle. She did not fully understand that dilatory gentleman. Lancaster had come to see that he was on the wrong side of things in this instance and he had no intention of involving himself. The virago of Leeds was left to face alone the storm she had raised.

The attack launched against the castle was a spirited one, and in a matter of a few days the garrison surrendered. The punishment was first vented on the garrison, who had been guilty only of obeying orders; the usual procedure in these chivalrous days. The seneschal, one Walter Colepepper, was taken up to the battlements and there hanged with eleven of his men. Lady Badlesmere was taken to the Tower of London. It has been said that she thus became the first woman prisoner to be lodged in the White Tower. This is not correct, for an unfortunate and lovely lady, a daughter of Robert Fitz-Walter and best known as Maud the Fair, was kept in the Tower by King John and was killed there finally by a poisoned egg sent to her by that worthy king.

Lady Badlesmere was promised a hempen ending, which would have pleased the people of London who had followed her through the streets, jeering and storming at her and calling her Jezebel. But after a long imprisonment she was released. Her husband was not to fare so well.

The capture of Leeds Castle was Edward's first successful military exploit. It seems to have gone to his head. He returned to London with the forces which had rallied to his support, which included no fewer than six earls, in a mood to assert himself and reclaim the royal prerogatives which had slipped from his hands. Nothing could have been more fortunate for him than this incident provided by the Badlesmere woman. The baronial strength had been so sharply split that Edward could have found parliamentary support for almost any steps he might dictate. The queen, moreover, was showing how much she resembled her implacable father. The hanging of a few minions had not satisfied her, and she was now urging the king to take action against the barons, even Lancaster, who had been responsible in a sense for the humiliation she had suffered. The time was indeed ripe to come to grips, to toss aside the ordinances, to defy the Ordainers, to break the power of Lancaster.

Unfortunately Edward's first thought seems to have been to take advantage of his new popularity to bring the Despensers back. On December 10 he appeared at a convocation of the clergy and won from the bishops an opinion that the banishing of the precious pair had been illegal. With this backing he summoned the Despensers to return.

The familiar pattern was being repeated. If there had been a grain of sense in the king's head, he would have seen that the end must also be the same.

CHAPTER EIGHT

The King in the Saddle

1

EDWARD realized that he must cross the Severn if he expected to break up the noisy rebellion the Marcher barons had started along the borders of Wales. When he reached Shrewsbury and rode along the peninsula, it seemed to him that he was unlikely to accomplish his objective. There were armed men in large numbers on the other side, wearing the green and yellow. Mortimer again! That obnoxious fellow, who had blocked the way at Bridgnorth, had kept pace along the other side of the river and was prepared, obviously, to dispute any attempt to pass over.

It is probable that the king had always disliked Mortimer of Wigmore. As a minor and an orphan, Mortimer had been put under the guardianship of Piers de Gaveston, an arrangement that promised to be most profitable to Brother Perrot. By some legal wriggling the guardianship had been broken, much to Edward's annoyance. Mortimer was almost the complete antithesis of the slothful, careless king. He was brisk, fiery, keen, and acquisitive. He had, moreover, a dark kind of good looks, accentuated by a lively black eye, which made him popular with the other sex. He had, as might be expected, married an heiress, one of the most eligible in the kingdom, Joan de Genville. His wife's holdings included much land in Shropshire, the town and castle of Ludlow, and a generous share of County Meath in Ireland. In passing, one might conjecture that in this period of history some disability may have attended these amassers of unusual wealth which made it possible to beget handsome daughters but no sons. All the great estates at one time or other fell into the possession of heiresses, some of whom allowed themselves to be trapped into matrimony by handsome but unscrupulous young men such as Mortimer.

Mortimer had not been particularly active against Edward but he had been made one of the Ordainers and had been on the commission to reform the royal household. His active resistance had started with the rise in favor of the Despensers. He hated them both, the mealymouthed father and the pushing son. Their greed, as it happened, had prompted them to separate Mortimer from some lands he regarded as his own, and that was something he could not forgive. And so here was Roger de Mortimer and his uncle of Chirk with a solid little army on the other side of the Severn, prepared seriously to block the king's progress.

To Edward's great surprise, however, he found that they were no longer in a fighting mood. Lancaster, as usual, had failed to keep his promises. It had been agreed that he would bring his strength down from the north to support the Marcher barons in their resistance to the king, but instead he was dawdling around his castle of Pontefract and showing no inclination to help. The king was allowed to cross the river, therefore, and on the other side he was met by an angry and disappointed pair with an offer to lay down their arms. All they demanded was a safe-conduct.

Ever since the capture of Leeds, Edward had been riding on the crest of a wave. Everything had been going right for him, but this was, clearly, the best stroke of all. He packed his two prisoners off to London, to be incarcerated in the Tower pending the disposition of their case. He was carrying in his pocket a petition from the common people who had endured the harshness and tyranny of the Mortimers and were asking that no grace be shown them. In spite of the letters of safe-conduct, it was not in Edward's mind to be lenient. He appointed a commission to try them, but when a sentence of death for treason was pronounced on the pair, he seemed to relent. The sentence, at any rate, was commuted to life imprisonment in the Tower.

As it turned out, this was an evil mischance for the king. Mortimer in the Tower could be more harmful than Mortimer ruffling it on the borders of Wales.

With the capture and disposal of the Mortimers, the resistance in the west collapsed. The king took the castles of all the other dissenting barons and then spent Christmas at Cirencester in a mood of deep satisfaction. He enjoyed the jests of the Lord of Misrule and the other mumming antics of yuletide. He dipped a gold mug in the wassail bowl with no thought but to enjoy himself again as in the old days at King's Langley.

On February 11 he issued a writ for the recall of the Despensers.

2

All that remained for Edward to do now was to deal with Cousin Lancaster.

The latter found himself in a desperate dilemma because of his inability to make up his mind. Several courses had been open to him, but he had taken none. He could have moved down to support the Marcher barons, as he had promised to do before they took up arms, in which case the king would have found himself between two arms of a pincer. He could have disbanded his troops and announced his intention of supporting the king. He could have run away, either to Scotland or the continent. He could have gone into hiding. The castle of Pontefract stood on a high hill covering eight acres and had many secret subterranean chambers in the rock beneath it. Here he could have remained until the storm blew over, as the Jacobite leaders did later in caves in the Highland glens. But he did none of these things. He sat around and waited while everything went wrong. And then suddenly he found himself alone in arms against the king, who was hurrying north with a victorious army to deal with him.

Still the earl did nothing. Perhaps he believed himself above any form of personal punishment, being of royal blood and first cousin to the king. If so, he was sadly mistaken. The king had conceived as great a hate for him as he had for the king, and it would be a sad day for Cousin Lancaster if he fell into Edward's hands. It may have been that he did not believe the king could take advantage of the situation; this fumbling and stupid king who never before had done anything right. Perhaps, having a firm belief in his own military capacity, he was certain he could beat Edward if it came to a clash at arms.

Whatever the reason, he sat at Pontefract while the king captured Berkeley Castle and began his march to the north. He heard the news of the capture of Kenilworth and Tutbury and of the death of Roger d'Amory. He knew the Mortimers were realizing the extent of their mistake in trusting themselves to the king's mercy. Finally, he was well aware that Sir Andrew Harclay, who was in command of royal troops to check Scottish raids, had thrown himself across his, Lancaster's, line of retreat. His main supporter, the Earl of Hereford, joined him at Pontefract, full of alarm and convinced that nothing could save them.

Then Lancaster did the worst thing possible. He made a half-hearted effort to prevent Edward from crossing the Trent, thereby stamping himself as a traitor. Then he turned with such troops as were left him and ran for it.

Harclay took prompt measures at this point. He brought his troops down to intercept the runaway earls and defeated them easily at Boroughbridge in Yorkshire. Hereford was killed while crossing the bridge. A soldier hidden under the bridge thrust a lance into him through a crevice in the boarding. Lancaster was taken prisoner. He was turned over at once to the king.

3

It was on March 6, 1322, that Lancaster fell into the hands of Harclay. Six days later he was tried at his own castle at Pontefract on charges of treason. It could not properly be called a trial; rather, it was a formal hearing conducted before the king and a group of prominent peers, with the verdict decided upon in advance.

It is unfortunate that little was recorded of the event, for it is one of the most dramatic in English history. Lancaster, as the eldest son of Edmund Crouchback, was cousin to the king and the second man in the kingdom. He had taken full advantage of his rank to oppose Edward at every step during the latter's fifteen years on the throne, constituting himself the leader of all discontent. Finally he had, with the backing of the baronage, assumed the role of virtual dictator. Legally he still exercised the powers granted him in July 1316 by the Parliament meeting at Lincoln.

And yet here he stood, with head bent and face pale, at one end of the great hall in his own castle while the king, who had always seemed to him an oaf and a weakling, sat at the other end with the crown on his head. It was a warm day, with a bright sun (how often this happens when someone faces the violent death prescribed by law!), but the thoughts in Lancaster's mind would have been better tuned to dismal clouds and raw winds. He had always believed he should have been the king. He had been compelled to watch the sad performance of Edward II on the throne which might have been his save for the accident of parentage which had brought Edward I into the world ahead of Edmund Crouchback. It is doubtful that he felt regrets for the course he had followed as he heard himself denounced as a traitor. He had never seen him-

self as others had, as an indecisive man of little capacity who had
been actuated by personal spite rather than by patriotic impulses.
But he must have been filled with a despairing realization of the
folly which had brought him to this sorry pass.

Edward, being of shallow character, was prone to quick and
angry reactions rather than to the harboring of deep hatreds; but
for this cousin who had balked him at every turn, who had been
guilty of the cruel dispatch of Gaveston, who had stood on the
battlements above the hall, where they were now convened, to
jeer at him as he passed in his moment of most bitter humiliation,
for this man there was in him no inclination to mercy.

Seated about the king were many of the greatest peers of England: Edmund Plantagenet, Earl of Kent and the king's half
brother; John de Dreux, Duke of Brittany; the earls of Pembroke,
Surrey, Arundel, Atholl, Angus; Lord Hugh Spencer (meaning the
elder Despenser, who had lost no time in rushing home), and
Lord Robert de Malmesthorp, chief justice.

A formidable list, and not one face in the group with any hint
of friendliness for this overweening man who had been brought,
without his armor on his back or his sword by his side, to stand
trial before them.

The voice of Lancaster was not raised during the proceedings.
He was informed that inasmuch as his traitorous actions were
known to all and had already convicted him he would not be
asked to plead, nor would he be allowed to speak in his own defense. The hearing must have been brief, consisting of the reading
of a long statement in lieu of a legal indictment.

"With banners displayed," ran the statement, "as in open war,
in a hostile manner . . . resisted and hindered our sovereign lord
the king, his soldiers and faithful subjects, for three whole days so
that they could not pass over the bridge of Burton-upon-Trent
. . . and there feloniously slew some of the king's men."

Later in the statement there was a reference to the train of incidents which weighed heavily on the mind of the king: when he
and Brother Perrot had played the hares before the baronial
hounds, with Lancaster sounding the horn to harry them out of
Newcastle-upon-Tyne and to lead finally to the tragedy of Blacklow Hill. "When our said lord the king had got together provisions, horses and armor, jewels and several other goods and moveables of great value and in large quantities; which goods and
moveables the said Earl Thomas, with horse and arms, and a great
power of armed men, took, despoiled and carried off."

The most damaging piece of evidence was proof found on the slain Earl of Hereford of an effort made to form a confederacy with Robert the Bruce. Lancaster had been corresponding with the Scottish king earlier, using the nom de plume *King Arthur*, an indication, clearly, of the high vaulting nature of his inner ambitions. It will be recalled also that the country had seethed at one stage with rumors that Lancaster was actually in the pay of the Scottish king. The communication found on Hereford's body contained a direct invitation to come into England with an army, offering in recompense the good offices of Lancaster in getting for Scotland "a good peace."

The prisoner listened while the statement was read, if not with penitence or fear, at least with a conviction of the conclusion to be reached. The king, who is not reported to have taken any part in the proceedings, may not have followed it with equal concentration. It is more likely his mind was filled with the memories which had hardened his resolution: the voice of his friend Gaveston raised in defense of his life, the derisive laughter which had reached him from the battlements of the castle, the letters to the archenemy of the kings of England, signed so vaingloriously *King Arthur*.

Finally the droning voice of the clerk intoned the words of summation:

"Wherefore our sovereign lord the king, having duly weighed the great enormities and offences of the said Thomas, earl of Lancaster, and his notorious ingratitude, has no manner of reason to show any mercy on him, in reference to pardoning those crimes. . . . Nevertheless, because the said earl Thomas is most highly and most nobly descended, our sovereign lord the king, having due regard to his high birth and quality, of his own mere good pleasure, remits the execution of two of the punishments, as aforesaid, viz. That the said Thomas shall not be drawn and hanged; but only that execution be done upon the said earl, by beheading him."

The aides who had been captured with Lancaster, not having high birth and quality, were not so well treated. They were condemned to die with all the refinements reserved for traitors. They were hanged, drawn, and quartered.

The sun was still high in the heavens and the air pleasant when Cousin Lancaster was taken to St. Thomas' Hill, which lies some distance from the town, although it could be seen from the

eight tall towers at Pontefract. He made the journey on the back
of a small gray pony. As he passed through the town he was
pelted with stones and offal by the people in the streets, many of
whom were his dependents.

"King Arthur!" they cried in mockery. "Where are your knights
to help you now?"

The earl was beginning to lose the fortitude he had shown in
the great hall. His hand was unsteady and he swayed in his seat.

"King of heaven!" he cried. "Grant me thy mercy, for the king
of earth has forsaken me!"

If it seems strange that he was taken such a distance and to a
hillside, when the courtyard of the castle would have been a more
suitable place for the execution, it may be considered that this is
what had happened to Gaveston. Was it the king's purpose to recall to the mind of the condemned man the part he had played in
that never forgotten nor forgiven episode?

The block was ready when they reached St. Thomas' Hill. Lancaster knelt beside it in such a position that he faced the east. He
was rudely instructed to look instead toward the north, "In the direction of your friends, the Scots!" It was in that direction that his
head fell.

4

With the death of Lancaster the baronial opposition fell to
pieces. Edward, behaving more like a true Plantagenet every day,
took full advantage of his success. It was given out that the two
Mortimers and Audley, the sole surviving brother-in-law of the
younger Despenser, would be confined in prison for the balance of
their days. Bartholomew Badlesmere, the repentant husband of
the harridan of Leeds, was yanked out of Stowe Park and hanged.
Other executions took place, about thirty in all. A great silence
fell over the ranks of the dissenters.

A Parliament was assembled at York with both Despensers in
attendance, the younger having given up piracy with avidity to
obey the writ summoning him home. With much high-sounding
talk and many promises of good government, the ordinances were
abolished and the Council of Ordainers was dissolved. "A skele-
ton, with pap!" said the man in the tavern, the friar on his barefooted rounds, the villein with sweaty hand on the plow handle;
meaning that fair words had been used to disguise an evil meas-

ure. The expression was often thus reversed from its usual form, when it meant a good deed performed with a grumbling mien.

Edward made another abortive invasion of Scotland, failing to capture Berwick, was nearly captured himself, and brought the Scottish forces back on his heels over the border, like hornets with a sting in the edge of the claymore. An English mother was sitting one night on the battlements of a castle, singing a lullaby to her child, *Do not fret ye, little pet ye, the Black Douglas shall not get ye.* "Don't be too sure of that," said a voice behind her. It was the Black Douglas, who had led his men in a wild climb up the walls. He captured the castle but spared the lives of the garrison.

It seemed useless to go on with this costly war of reprisal, so on May 30, 1323, Edward made a truce for thirteen years with Robert the Bruce.

Queen Isabella's anger over her lack of welcome at Leeds Castle had cooled before Lancaster was executed. She did not hear of his death until some time later. Although nothing is on record about her reactions, it may be taken for granted that she was shocked and greatly disturbed by it. But things were happening all the time to shock and disturb her. When she gave birth in the Tower to her last child, the daughter who was named Joanna, the apartment in which she lay was so badly in need of repair that the rains came through the ceiling and kept the bed clothing damp. The royal lady, as might have been expected, was furious that the royal suite could have been so neglected. Edward became angry in turn and had the constable of the Tower, one John de Cromwell, discharged from his post. He did not, however, lay any of the blame where it rightly belonged, on the shoulders of the Despensers, who were back in harness and making such a sorry mess of public affairs that there was not enough money in the treasury to pay for a new roof.

The Despensers were poor administrators. They were fattening their own purses while the financial condition of the kingdom went from bad to worse. The younger, with the daring of a rope walker crossing a chasm, undertook changes in the queen's own household with a view to economy. He succeeded to the extent of discharging all her French servants and packing them back to France, and then taking from her the revenue of her dower properties and allowing her in exchange a pension which she complained was unfair and completely inadequate for her needs; which was not surprising, for the amount paid was only twenty

shillings a day. She complained to Edward, not once but many
times, but he was now riding high and full of satisfaction at having his beloved Despensers back with him. He paid little attention
to her.

Isabella realized then that the old days, the evil days, had returned, although it was now the younger Despenser who controlled her husband instead of the impudent Gascon. There was
no longer a Cousin Lancaster to lend an ear to her complaints.
Public opinion about him was turning rapidly in his favor. It was
reported that miracles were happening at his tomb (this story became so persistent that Edward had the entrance sealed up), and
the people of the north country, who had not taken him to their
hearts while he was alive, were spreading a prophecy that grass
would never grow again where the battle of Boroughbridge had
been fought. There was even a movement on foot to have him
canonized. Still he *was* dead and could no longer support the
queen in her grievances against her insensitive and infatuated husband. She turned then to her third brother, Charles the Fair (another physically handsome specimen), who was now King of
France, her two older brothers having died without male issue,
thus reviving the talk about the curse laid on the family by the
dying Grand Master of the Templars. In one of her letters to this
brother she declared she had become no better than a servant in
the royal household. In another she spoke of Edward as "a gripple
miser," a strange epithet to apply to one who had been a spendthrift all his life. What she meant, of course, was that he behaved
like a miser to her and lavished everything on the demanding
Despensers.

Four years of this sort of thing followed. There was no longer a
baronial party to spearhead a movement against the king and the
new favorites, but feeling against him in the country began to run
high. The younger Despenser was hated then almost as universally
as Gaveston had been. He was blamed for the bad times which
had gripped the country: the lack of food, the lack of work, the
stagnation in trade. To make matters worse, Edward used no tact
in his dealings with prominent men in the country.

The discontent grew deep. The coals were ready, the fire laid:
all that was needed was a spark to ignite the blaze.

CHAPTER NINE

The Royal Triangle

1

THE center of the stage must now be given to one of the most unpleasant of villains: Roger de Mortimer, eighth Baron of Wigmore, lying in the Tower of London under a sentence of life imprisonment.

He has already appeared for brief intervals and never in the most favorable light. A determined, ambitious, and cruel young man, whose energy and drive had made him the real leader of the Marcher barons and whose marriage to an heiress had raised his fortune and influence considerably; a handsome fellow, obviously, with ease of deportment, and without a scruple.

It had been customary for prisoners of consequence in the Tower to live in some degree of state. When John Baliol, the stickit King of Scotland, was immured there, he was allowed to take with him a large retinue, including even huntsmen to look after his horses, greyhounds, and beagles. Altogether he cost the crown seventeen shillings a day. Later his staff was reduced to two squires, three pages, two grooms of the chamber, one barber, one tailor, one laundress, one butler, and one pantler. One half crown a day was saved this way.

In later years, when prominent prisoners were allowed the services of no more than one or two servants, it would be cited as evidence of extreme severity.

It is apparent, therefore, that Mortimer and his sixty-five-year-old uncle were kept in unusually rigorous confinement. They must have shared one cell, a "lofty and narrow chamber," with little light, airless in summer and clammily cold in winter. It is not likely that a servant of any kind attended them, and for food they had to be content with what the jailers brought, which would be very plain fare indeed. Here they remained for over two years, by which time the uncle, Mortimer of Chirk, died.

But Roger de Mortimer was not the kind of man to remain forever in confinement, not when he had willing friends on the outside and high-placed friends within. It is not recorded when or where he first saw Queen Isabella, but it is agreed that it must have been while he was in the Tower. This may seem to be stretching the probabilities, but after a close consideration it appears distinctly possible. The queen came to the Tower for her accouchement and remained there for some time after the birth of her daughter. The Tower held relatively few prisoners in these days and the queen would hear much about the bold young baron who was existing under the same roof. A building which serves the double purpose of royal residence and prison inevitably rings with rumor and gossip. Isabella would have all manner of stories poured into her ears by her ladies; how handsome the prisoner was, what his habits were, what he said to his jailers. All such small talk would be repeated and added to and commented on at considerable length.

It must be remembered also how limited the facilities of the Tower were, with its one entrance and one stairway. Mortimer was often summoned for hearings, and it may be taken for granted that word got around. Avid eyes would watch from around turns in the dark corridors as he was escorted to and from the one stairway shaft. It is quite conceivable that on such occasions one pair would belong to Isabella, for a queen can be just as curious as a lady-in-waiting or a domestic. And life in the Tower was sometimes as dull for her as for any of the others.

There is a certain amount of attraction about a prisoner, particularly if he has been in captivity a sufficient time for his hair to grow long and his cheeks pale and his eyes to have the look of desperation which close confinement breeds; most particularly when he is handsome to begin with and has a reputation for bravery in the field and a way with women.

Yes, it is highly probable that the queen saw the prisoner. It is well within the bounds of probability, in fact, that communications passed between them. One glance might have been enough to plant a romantic interest in the receptive mind of the queen. She was ripe for romance. Although the mother of four children, she had no true wifely feeling for her husband. He had awakened contempt in her almost from the first; and love does not go with contempt. She was about twenty-six years of age when the opportunity came to see Mortimer, and if a little beyond the peak of her beauty she was still a woman of loveliness and charm. Mortimer would most certainly have grasped at any indication of interest on the part of the queen.

There is room for speculation also in the manner of his escape from the Tower; for escape he did, most boldly. It would have been impossible for him to get out of that "lofty and narrow chamber" and over the high walls unless he had help from inside. The rather circumstantial reports of the escape which have been handed down make it clear he had such assistance. Gerard de Alspaye, the sublieutenant of the Tower, was won over to his aid and was chiefly instrumental in hatching the plan and carrying it through. Why would a man in a comfortable minor position risk his post, his life even, to let an important prisoner loose? Mortimer's estates had been seized and he was not in a position to pay a large enough bribe. It is almost certain that the sublieutenant would not take this risk unless he knew he had the support of someone of high rank.

It is not difficult to believe that the queen, her emotions aroused by the fine dark eyes of the prisoner, had communicated with him, had in fact made occasion to see him. It is easy enough, too, when served by loyal gentlemen and ladies-in-waiting, to have a cell door opened and a corridor kept clear and thus to receive a guest when the silence of night has settled over the dark Tower. It would be risky but possible to carry on a liaison under the eyes of the court. It is easy to imagine also that the sublieutenant could have been won over if pressure of the right kind had been brought to bear on him.

On the night of August 1 it was customary for the garrison and the prison guards to celebrate the feast of St. Peter and Vincula with much eating and drinking. Alspaye saw to it that the supplies for the occasion were drugged. When all of the company had fallen into a stupor, the sublieutenant accompanied Mortimer out through a hole which had been dug in the wall of his cell (undoubtedly with tools supplied by Alspaye) and into a passage which led to the roof of the royal kitchens. This took them to an inner ward, where a rope ladder was produced.

A complete silence had settled over the Tower. In the kitchen they had found the cook and his staff, after partaking of the feast, lying in sodden slumber amidst their ovens and pans. If there were sentries on the walls, they had crumpled against the stone of the battlements and were snoring loudly to the stars.

One highly romantic version of the escape has it that the queen came out from the shadows of the ward, wrapped in a cloak and hood for concealment. There was a last embrace, a few whispered words of reassurance and warning, and then she helped Mortimer to climb the wall by holding the rope ladder firm in her own fair hands. The prisoner is asserted to have called down when he reached the top, "Now, Fortune, be my guide!"

It is extremely doubtful that she would have shown so little discretion. If she were the baron's accomplice, she undoubtedly had enough sense to remain in her bed, reassured by the lack of sound from the battlements and the absence of any peremptory challenges from the sentries.

Accompanied by Alspaye, the escaped prisoner reached the river, where an open boat was waiting. They were ferried across the Thames and on the opposite side found seven of Mortimer's men ready for them with horses. They rode through the night, pausing only to change horses, until they reached the coast of Hampshire. Here another boat waited, and it was given out that they were going to the Isle of Wight. In reality they were conveyed to a large merchant ship hovering off the coast which belonged to a London merchant by the name of Ralf Botton. The ship took them to a port in Normandy. Mortimer, still accompanied by the sublieutenant, made his way direct to Paris and the French court. It was learned later that Adam of Orleton, Bishop of Hereford, had arranged all the outside details with great skill and foresight.

The king was in Lancaster when the word of Mortimer's escape reached him. He fell into a fury of activity and, believing the fugitive would make for his own possessions, he directed the hue and cry into Wales. It was some time before the truth came out, and then the harassed king had matters on his mind which seemed of even more importance than the escape of an important prisoner. The absence of Alspaye placed the guilt of complicity on his shoulders, but no whisper involved the queen.

That Isabella had taken some hand in the escape and that the most lurid of clandestine romances in the royal annals of England had begun while Mortimer was a prisoner became something more than conjecture as a result of what happened after the fugitive reached the court of Charles IV, the last of Isabella's three brothers.

2

Queen Isabella visited Paris the next year. There was a great rush to see her as she rode through the streets of the French capital with her train; this queen of surpassing beauty who had left France many years before and had lived such a stormy life with her English spouse. She rode astride (the sidesaddle would not be used for another century or more), and her black velvet skirts were very full and so long that no more than the tips of her riding boots of white checkered leather could be seen. Her hair was unplaited and held in cases of gold fretwork on each side of her head. They cheered her proudly and said among themselves what a lout this Edward of England must be to neglect so fair a creature.

When she first went to England as a bride she had been aware that the clothing of the English was strangely different. To her girlish eyes the people had looked dowdy and old-fashioned. She had known, of course, that Paris established the mode, but it had never occurred to her that a country as close as England could lag so far behind. In her first years as queen she had managed to keep pace with things in the world of style but inevitably had lost contact. When she managed to convince her husband that she should go back to France as a peacemaker, she immediately took steps to have her wardrobe thoroughly overhauled. Tailors came from Paris at considerable expense to see that she had clothes of the very latest style and design.

And so she was richly and fashionably clad when she appeared at her brother's court. It is contended in some chronicles of the time that it was then that she first laid eyes on Roger Mortimer. The latter had been cordially received by the king after his escape and was on hand to be presented with the knights of France. The queen and the fugitive were said to have fallen deeply, completely, overwhelmingly in love at the first glance.

But the events leading up to her visit to France seem to refute this supposition. In the first place, Charles the Fair would not have received a political refugee with favor unless he had been properly prepared in advance; by letters from the queen herself, it is alleged. As soon as the Englishman put in an appearance, a situation developed which was not understood at the time but was recognized later as the first step in a well-laid plan. Charles had begun immediately to contend that Edward must come to France to do homage for Aquitaine and Ponthieu, on pain of having them seized. Edward was advised by the Despensers that it would be unwise for him to leave the kingdom. What they really meant was that it would be unwise from their standpoint; for Edward, under alien influences, might be persuaded to dispense with them. He blithely accepted their word for it and sent over his cousin Pembroke to discuss matters. Pembroke died almost as soon as he arrived and then the king sent Edmund of Kent, his half brother, to take his place. Edmund was a dull young man with no head for diplomacy whatever and he accomplished nothing. Then Isabella came forward with a suggestion: she would go to France and get her brother's consent to a delay. Secretly the king may have been glad to be rid of her for a time. Her hostility to the Despensers had been causing continual scenes. He had been growing weary of the light of indignation in her eyes, the angry tapping of her small foot, the bitterness of her tongue. Let her go and perhaps she would be in a better mood when she returned. So Edward put no obstacles in the way and Parliament gave its consent.

Her arrival in France brought the situation at home into the open for the first time. The queen did not hesitate to say that Edward was abnormal and preferred his favorites to her. Although she had borne him four children, she did not feel that she had had any real married life. There was no desire on her part to return unless Edward rid himself of the Despensers. She even declared openly that unless he did so she could not go back. Her life would be in danger from Nephew Hugh, the king's fond name for the younger of the pair, who was bitterly antagonistic to her.

All this seems to have been according to plan. But Isabella was foolish enough to throw caution to the winds where Roger Mortimer was concerned. Stories began to spread about them. It was whispered that, although Isabella had her rooms with the French royal family and Mortimer was living somewhere quite modestly with only one squire and one cook, they had reached an adulterous relationship. The whispers grew in volume until they could be heard clear across the Channel.

In the meantime the queen had succeeded in getting her brother to agree to a truce between the two countries and to delay any advance of French forces into Gascony until Edward could come over to pay homage. On the heels of this arrangement she wrote to her husband and suggested that if he still did not wish to come he could confer the title of Duke of Aquitaine on their oldest son and send the boy over in his place. This should have been as unmistakable as the cry of *Weather ahead* from the lookout at sea. But Edward had been finding life peaceful, and the Despensers were more convinced than ever that it would be a mistake for him to trust himself into alien hands. And so, in September of that year young Prince Edward, quite happy and bedazzled with his fine new title, departed for France to join his royal mother. This was an important step in the plan.

Prince Edward did homage for the provinces held in France, and Charles, in his turn, withdrew the forces he had sent against Gascony. There was now apparently nothing to hold the queen and the heir apparent from returning home.

But they did not return. There were many reasons. They were in a position abroad to make demands on the king and to insist on the dismissal of the Despensers as the price of their return. The country was sadly in need of better government, and nothing could be done if they came humbly back. There was, moreover, the relationship which had developed between Isabella and her "gentle Mortimer," as she had fallen into the habit of calling him. She had now no desire to return and resume her place beside the king. When a woman of passionate nature has existed in a loveless marriage and has reached the late twenties before yielding to a clandestine impulse, it may be taken for granted that she will not be guided by anything but the dictates of her love. Isabella seems to have taken few precautions and to have worn her heart quite openly on her sleeve.

The behavior of the queen was so indiscreet that Walter Stapledon, Bishop of Exeter, who had been one of the advisers sent over with the young prince, decided that steps must be taken. He was a sound and courageous man and did not hesitate to reproach her. Isabella gave him no satisfaction. Mortimer, she declared, was a brave knight and an amusing companion; what harm could there be in a preference for his company? Stapledon felt the time had come when the king in England should know the whole truth. He made a surreptitious departure from the French court and succeeded in getting across the Channel, despite the fact that the queen had warned Mortimer to prevent him from leaving. The bishop's report to the king was that the queen's infatuation for Mortimer was the real cause of the delay. He intimated also that other plans were being considered, even an intention to land an army of invasion. Edward instituted at once a watch on all English ports. Mail was delayed and examined and arrivals from France were questioned and sometimes held in custody.

King Edward has been praised for the way he handled the situation, particularly in the matter of the letters he sent to his wife, to his son, and to the King of France, which are termed manly and touching. The truth of the matter is that he behaved with his usual lack of acumen and decision. It must have been clear to him that an invasion was impending and that he must take immediate steps to prevent it. His father would have ordered an instant return on pain of losing all rights and properties and would have demanded of the King of France that he cease to harbor them if he desired peace to continue between the two countries. Edward showed his pique by taking the poor wife of Mortimer into custody with all her children and treating them with severity, when he might have packed them off to join their fugitive husband and father. Their presence would have served as a dampener at least on the open philandering of Isabella and Mortimer. Certainly steps were necessary to collect an army to defend the realm. Instead the king entered into long, repetitious correspondence.

His letters have an appealing quality, it is true, but they are lacking in vigor and incisiveness, and in two respects they reveal the weakness of character which he had so often displayed. First, they go to great lengths to answer Isabella's expressed fear of violence at the hands of the younger Despenser, Nephew Hugh. He seems more concerned to defend the Despensers than anything else. In writing Isabella, he says, "He has always procured from us all the honor he could for you, nor to you has either evil or villainy been done since you entered into our companionship." To Prince Edward he describes Hugh as "our dear and faithful nephew." To Isabella's brother, the king, he states, "Never in the slightest instance has evil been done to her by him, and since she has departed from us and come to you what has compelled her to send to our dear and trusting nephew letters of such great and special amity?" He goes on to charge that she has "spoken falsehoods of our nephew." There is continually, in these letters, an insistence on the blamelessness of his favorites and the fairness of his dear Nephew Hugh.

The other great lack in his missives is that he neglects to say the only thing that could conceivably heal the breach. He does not write one sentence to indicate a willingness on his part to change the conditions to which they must return. Far from promising to get rid of the obnoxious Despensers or to limit their power, he depicts them as perfect servants who have been sinned against though never themselves sinning. He makes it clear they are to remain, the elder Despenser, who had reached the years of senility, the younger, and even the worthless individual they had foisted on him as chancellor, Robert de Baldock, Archdeacon of Middlesex, who had no qualifications for the part save a willingness in all things to pander to the desires of Nephew Hugh. While the king hunted and hawked and amused himself with horseplay and raucous humors, the Despensers and their tool Baldock had brought the country to a sorry pass; but he shows no recognition of this nor any intent to improve things. Did he know that his military summonses were being disregarded, that the taxes were not being collected, that laws were not being enforced, that the courts were filled with untried cases, that bandits and highway robbers infested the country with nothing being done about it, that the Despensers seemed interested only in their own enrichment? If he was aware of such things, there is no indication in his letters of any intent to correct the abuses.

There are no promises of any kind in what he writes. Come back on my terms and I will forgive you. That is all he holds out.

Finally Edward sent copies of the letters he had addressed to Charles of France and to the Pope, and this brought results. The pontiff, in the indignation caused by the adulterous conduct of the queen, demanded of the French king that he send Isabella and her son out of the kingdom under penalty of excommunication. Charles was deeply disturbed at this and intimated to his sister that the time had come for her to leave.

In dealing with this situation in his *Chronicles*, Jean Froissart gives the melodramatic version. He says that the queen's cousin, Robert of Artois, who was now her only real friend at the French court, came to her in the middle of the night with word that Charles intended to turn them all over to Edward. He advised strongly that she start at once for Burgundy, where she would be out of reach of both kings and would be kindly received and protected.

The result was that the queen, the prince, gentle Mortimer, and all others who had been received into the conspiratorial circle, including Edward's ambassadors and his half brother, Edmund of Kent, departed from France without delay and made their way to the Low Countries.

3

When Isabella, her son, and her long train of followers came into the Netherlands on the invitation of Sir John of Hainaut, they saw that they were in a different world; a land of low and monotonous plains under heavy skies and, all about them, behind high strong walls, splendid and prosperous cities in which people had found that industry yielded dividends in rich living and content. Perhaps their greatest surprise came when they reached the city of Valenciennes and stopped before the castle of Count William of Hainaut. The exterior looked strong and capable of standing siege, but within it was designed for a colorful and realistic kind of life. Immediately inside the great gate was a courtyard and opposite it an entrance of folded oak, with a bronze head of some fabulous creature serving as a knocker, which gave onto a room of singular cheerfulness.

This room served in place of that strange monstrosity in Norman castles, the great hall. It lacked the high arched ceilings and so achieved warmth under its low galleries. There were six tall windows to give light. The floor, miracle of miracles, had not a single rush malodorous with age, but was of paving stones, scrubbed every day and so kept white and aseptic. There was a glow about the whole apartment, owing largely to its red hangings and the glazing of the windows.

It was in this unusual apartment that the tired queen and her companions made the acquaintance of William, Count of Hainaut, the older brother of Sir John, who had escorted them on their way. Standing behind the count in a row were his four daughters, who might best be described as a muster of young peacocks, so bright were the colors they presented, their flaxen hair, their apple-red cheeks, their dresses of green, and their red shoes. Prince Edward was just entering his teens, which is a period of susceptibility, and his first impression must have been that never before had he seen girls so different but so attractive for that very reason. Margaret, Philippa, Joanna, and Isbel! How could a youth of his years resist falling in love, not with one, but with all four?

This was exactly what he was expected to do. After the meal served them, a truly gigantic one with haunches of meat, fish swimming in sauces, and a succession of sweet dishes of strange but enticing tastes, he was told so by his mother. The count, it seemed, loved each of his little towheaded daughters equally. He would certainly be happy to have one of them marry the future King of England, but when the time came he would expect it to be the oldest of the four. Was it Margaret who pleased Edward most? No, it was not Margaret. There was another who had brighter cheeks than her sisters and was just a bit more plump. Philippa? Yes, it was Philippa. He was advised to keep any such preference to himself and to allow it to seem that his admiration was equally divided. Besides, there was the Parliament in England to be considered. It would be most unwise to let it be known that he had made up his mind before the consent of that body had been obtained.

It was known both to mother and son that King Edward had started negotiations for a marriage of the prince with the infanta Eleanor of Aragon, a most distinguished and desirable alliance. Isabella was aware, however, that if she could win the support of Count William it would be possible to get together a force for the invasion of England. What better inducement could she offer than a brilliant match for one of his four daughters? She had made it clear to the count by correspondence before leaving France that such was her thought. An understanding was reached between them that the marriage would be arranged after her return to England.

So Prince Edward remained a fortnight in Hainaut in the pleasant company of the four gay, chattering daughters of the house. He managed to keep a neutral attitude, although he had long talks with the slightly plumper Philippa and found his secret preference growing more certain with each hour. He may have conveyed a hint to her of his feelings in the matter.

In the meantime Queen Isabella was conducting a campaign for armed support. The impression had been widely spread throughout the Low Countries, largely by the efforts of young Sir John, who undoubtedly had fallen in love with her, that she was a fair lady in great distress and that all chivalrous knights should rally to her support. Her conduct was exemplary. Mortimer stayed in the background and was accepted as no more than a member of her English entourage. She even attired herself in dresses of seeming modesty, taking little advantage of a sudden turn in feminine styles which had been under way in Paris. Her dresses conformed to the new fashion in having tight bodices and buttoned sleeves and very full skirts which swayed like slow waves on a quiet sea, but they were made of subdued materials and lacked the rich embroideries in pearls and thread of gold. She thus created the impression of an exile who could not afford the best apparel of the moment but could look beautiful in the plainest of wear.

As the weeks passed, the train which followed her on the recruiting journeys she undertook grew larger, like the lengthening tail of a comet. She managed to inject a great deal of gaiety into it, as had Eleanor of Aquitaine when she took a company of well-born ladies to fight in the crusade led by her first husband, the King of France, wearing such dazzling uniforms that the brave knights were more interested in the lady crusaders than in fighting the paynim.

Knights joined the English queen from all parts of the Low Countries—Holland, Friesland, Brabant, Gueldres, as well as Hainaut—most of them youths eager for a chance to show their mettle. There were recruits from Germany as well and from as far away as Bohemia. It was a large and gallant company, 2,757 strong, which Isabella and Sir John of Hainaut finally led to Dort, where a fleet was assembled to take them across the water to England. Sir John was in command, with Roger Mortimer in charge of the English contingent.

They had a stormy passage and on September 24, 1326, landed with some difficulty on a strip of beach between Orford and Harwich. There was not a house in sight and only a few natives who scuttled for cover at the first glimpse of them. The young knights set to work to make an abode in which their beautiful lady could spend her first night back on the soil of England. For the purpose they used some bits of wreckage found on the beach and four carpets. The queen thanked them with bright smiles in spite of her weariness.

The next morning, with banners flying, they started their march inland. Isabella rode in front with Sir John of Hainaut beside her. She was in the gayest of moods. Mortimer rode well back in the ranks; she was striving to conduct the adventure with the utmost decorum.

CHAPTER TEN

The Fall of the King

1

EDWARD was in the Tower of London when the news reached him of the landing of the queen and Prince Edward on the coast of Suffolk with an army of foreign knights and mercenaries. With him were the two Despensers, the wife of Nephew Hugh, who was a niece of the king, and Baldock, the chancellor. The news seemed to have dumfounded him. He had not expected that things would come to this, despite the reports which had reached him from the continent. He looked at those about him with an almost blank stare, as though asking what was to be done now.

Even a king as disorganized and unready as Edward has sources of information. Spies on the continent had sent word of Isabella's activities and of the favorable impression she was making. It had been clear she was planning an invasion, but Edward's only move at first was to write more letters. These were addressed to the Pope and the King of France and begged assistance in the crisis which threatened him. Later he talked to the members of the council and the leaders of Parliament. They did not display any willingness to aid in raising an army. During August he paid visits to a number of cities, hoping to enlist the nobility but finding the same lack of interest. If he had announced his intention of banishing the Despensers for all time, he would have had a far different reception. But if he thought of any such concession, he set his mind stubbornly against it. He had not broken the power of the baronial opposition and sent his cousin to the block to give in at the first hint of more trouble. Had he taken action at once, he could have brought in an army of mercenaries himself, but it was seemingly impossible for him to act with promptitude. Even when the reports from abroad became more disturbing daily, he

made no effort to establish concentrations of armed men along
the coast to resist a landing.

And now on this warm day of September 27, with his few
remaining adherents about him, sticking like limpets to the only
rock in sight, he received the news that the queen had landed. He
had been hoping against hope that she would decide at the last
minute against taking such a great risk, but it had come to pass
and he must meet the threat without an army back of him and
small chance to raise one.

There was still one course open to him. He could send the
Despensers into permanent exile, demand the seal from Baldock
and discharge that worthless official, and then ride out to meet his
wife and son to discuss terms. But he had one vice so strongly
bred in him that it had become almost a virtue: he would not give
up his worthless friends even to save his crown or his life.

He had passed his forty-second birthday and the years seemed,
on the surface, to have treated him well. Because of his ceaseless
addiction to the chase, his tall frame had not broadened percep-
tibly. There was a cheerful ruddiness in his cheeks. Nor did age
show in his face; instead he looked carefree and blandly uncon-
cerned. Had all the worries and defeats and heartbreaks of his ill-
spent life passed him by lightly? There was even a hint of
boyishness about him still, as though he had not in reality grown
up; and a look in his eyes as though he realized this and wondered
about it.

But the passing of the years was suggested in one respect: there
was a definite trace of carelessness in his dress. The days were long
since gone when he and Brother Perrot had strutted about in the
very latest clothes from Paris, the multicolored tunics and tabards
in red and yellow or blue and gold, and the smartly fitted hose in
checkered designs; yes, those days were gone and would never
come back. Nor would Brother Perrot.

An observant eye would have noted a suspicion of bagginess at
the knees, and his plain gray coat, ending just below his waist (in
Paris they were now being worn much longer), showed unmistakable wrinkles.

The first moments of panic passed and he became somewhat
optimistic. What were the people of England going to think of
the "she-wolf of France" landing on English soil with foreign
troops? Were they not certain to ask themselves what promises
she had made to her Low Country volunteers? Was it not clear
that she had guaranteed rich English estates to them as William

the Conqueror had done with his Normans? Under the circumstances he believed that no Englishman would join the she-wolf and that deluded young cub of a son and—here the Plantagenet violence showed in his face—that murderous thief, that black traitor, Mortimer. If only he could win London over!

If he could win the support of the great city! If the apprentices would bring their weapons out from where they slept under the counters so he could make the trained bands the nucleus of an army! If he could use great London Town as a base!

Despite the bad conditions which prevailed throughout the country after twenty years of misrule, London had gone on growing in population and wealth. The stretch of river front which ran from Ludgate Hill to Westminster was being rapidly filled with the London houses of the great nobles. But they, the nobility, did not constitute London. The real London lay in the city, that close huddle of small parishes where the tradesmen had organized themselves into guilds on such a broad basis that each guild had its own hall, its own church, its own streets, its own laws and regulations, its own ceremonial uniform. Some had their own patron saint, as for instance St. Crispin, to whom the shoemakers bowed.

It had all started in London with the weavers. Then the goldsmiths had followed suit, then the saddlers, the fishmongers, the bakers, the cordwainers, the lorimers, even the law clerks. In France the law clerks were called the Basoche and were so powerful that most lawyers graduated from their ranks. The worthy burghers deserved the prosperity which had followed the careful cultivation of their respective fields. Proverbs 22:29 tells the story in a few words: *Seest thou a man diligent in his business: He shall stand before kings.* There was an anecdote that was often repeated with great pride when they met in their halls. It came from the Welsh *Red Book of Hergest* and was in dialogue form.

"Open the door."
"I will not open it."
"Wherefore not?"
"The knife is in the meat, and the drink is in the horn, and there is revelry in Arthur's Hall, and none may enter therein but the son of a king of a privileged country, *or a craftsman bringing his craft.*"

In addition to the guilds and the wealth they produced, London was the great port of the islands. The wool and tin, which constituted the greatest part of the country's exports, came down the river to be shipped overseas from London. It was no wonder that London could lend the most effective support to king or popular leader or general of an army. It was not as fully recognized then as it became later that in all civil conflict the side which London took became the winning side. The kings of the red rose, Charles I, the exiled Stuarts, would all learn the strength and stubbornness of London.

It was not surprising, therefore, that Edward entertained the hope that London could be won over, even though he expressed it with a dubious frown. He knew how partial London had always been to Isabella.

The first step he took in this crisis was to issue a proclamation that all who had taken part in the invasion would be treated as traitors, save the queen and his son Edward. A price of one thousand pounds was set on the head of "the black traitor" Mortimer. Then he summoned to the Tower a party made up of the mayor, the aldermen, and the heads of the guilds. It was in his mind clearly that he would have one advantage in his dealings with them. Hamo de Chigwell, who was serving his sixth term as mayor, had always been favorably disposed to him.

The king raised the point of the dangers which might be expected from the presence of foreign troops and asked, Would it be a case of the Norman invasion over again? This did not carry as much weight as he had hoped. The Flemish people were the natural allies of London because they bought practically all of England's wool. They had always been found honest and fair in their dealings.

The result was a compromise. The citizens agreed that no foreign force would be allowed to enter the city, but they stipulated also that no London troops would be permitted to serve more than a mile from the city walls. In reality, this was a defeat for Edward, who needed active support.

The king made up his mind to retire into the west, where he believed the sentiment of the people was more favorable to him. Leaving the Tower and his second son, John of Eltham, in the hands of the wife of the younger Despenser, he betook himself to Bristol.

The Londoners dropped the mask of neutrality at once. Bishop Stapledon of Exeter, the stout prelate who had come back from Paris to warn Edward of the queen's designs and of her conduct, had remained in the city. He was seized by the mobs and beheaded. His body was buried under a pile of rubbish and his head was sent on to Gloucester, where it was presented to Isabella as evidence that, in spite of everything, the heart of London was still with her. Lady Despenser, alarmed by the rioting in the streets, surrendered the Tower to the mobs.

2

Queen Isabella had shown great courage in bringing her small army across the North Sea. The baronial strength had been crushed before she left England and there was no evidence that it had been reviving. She had been in correspondence with some of the barons and could count on the aid of a few. Would there be enough to give her the strength to meet the king's army?

She was not left long in doubt. The landing had been made on the domain of Thomas of Brotherton, half brother to the king and her own blood cousin. He greeted her with bells ringing and bonfires blazing. The common people turned out in cheering mobs to welcome back the injured wife and queen. Women strewed her path with flowers.

Henry of Lancaster, called Wryneck, came galloping down from the north with a body of men. He was the brother of Thomas, who had been so summarily disposed of, and had succeeded to the huge family estates. Burning with the desire for vengeance, which he had been compelled to suppress for four years, he threw in his lot with the invaders. The army grew with every mile as baron after baron appeared to join them. Three bishops came as well, Ely, Lincoln, and Hereford. By the time the invaders reached Wallingford, the queen's confidence had grown so great that she issued a declaration, setting forth the mistakes the king had made and the iniquities of the favorites, and incidentally putting an offer of two thousand pounds on the head of the younger Despenser, twice the amount that Edward had offered for Mortimer.

When they reached Oxford, the Bishop of Hereford preached an incendiary sermon from 2 Kings 4:19, *My head, my head acheth*. It may be in order to pause here and have something to say about this bitter and savage churchman. He has already been mentioned, Adam of Orleton, as having aided Mortimer in his escape from the Tower. If Mortimer is the villain of this story, the bishop must be considered as second in that category. He had been advising Isabella from the beginning, it is believed, and it was always the violent course he proposed. In his sermon on the Bible story of Elisha and the woman whose son had died, he drew this conclusion, "When the head of a kingdom becometh sick and diseased, it must of necessity be taken off." It was evidence of the high feeling in the land that the sermon was received with approval.

In the meantime, the king, finding that no one came to join him, had been retreating toward the west. It was his intention, if his fortunes took no better turn, to hide among the Welsh people who had always displayed affection for him. He paused at Gloucester to summon all loyal men to his banner, getting no response whatever. Then he spent a day in the Forest of Dean, where in the shadow of the great oaks he could commune with his inner being and take stock of his resources. The result was a temporary gain in resolution and the sending of the elder Despenser to Bristol in the hope that he could hold that strong city in the king's interest.

But Bristol was filled with fervor for the cause of the queen and, when the invading army arrived before the gates, they surrendered the castle and everything in it, including the senior Despenser. Isabella's two young daughters had been sent to Bristol for safety, and the queen had an affectionate reunion with them. After embracing them, Isabella turned to sterner matters. Despenser, clad in his armor, was brought before her. The doddering old man realized that there was no hint of mercy in her handsome eyes. He had still enough courage to say to her, "Ah, Madame, God grant us an upright judge and a just sentence." His sentence may not have been just, but it was exceptionally speedy. He was immediately taken out and hanged in his armor.

It is said the two young princesses were allowed to look at what was happening from a window of the castle and were frightened almost into hysterics by the sight of the steel-clad figure turning slowly at the end of a stout rope.

The king's party continued to dwindle until he was left with no one but the younger Despenser and Chancellor Baldock and, of course, some servants. They took ship for Lundy Island, to which supplies had been sent; an indication that it probably had been Lundy where Nephew Hugh had served his brief second exile in piratical operations. The winds made it impossible for them to reach this notorious isle and they had to put back to land. Edward is next heard of at Caerphilly Castle, where he again endeavored, with no response, to set up his standard and summon all loyal men to his aid. By November 10 he was at Neath Abbey and still seemed to have some small remnants of hope left, for he again sent out commissions of array. From Neath, where his standard had flapped in the wind as dismally and as unnoticed as everywhere else, he sent a company with the old Abbot of Neath to start negotiations in his behalf with the queen. It is not likely that they secured an audience with her; at any rate, nothing came of it.

There are stories told of some adventures the king was supposed to have had on his wanderings. Leaving Caerphilly at night in the disguise of a peasant, he is said to have reached a farmhouse where he was put to work at digging. He proved so clumsy with the spade that his identity was discovered and he escaped with considerable difficulty. This anecdote, a favorite one, can be discarded. He had some of his company still with him at Caerphilly, and his handling of a spade would have deceived the most critical eye. Edward, in fact, was skilled with tools and was always happy when working on the land.

On November 16 the king was captured with the sorry remnants of his following and conducted to the castle of Llantrissant. Nephew Hugh and Baldock were taken to Bristol and surrendered into the hands of the queen.

3

Through the earlier stages of the history of these violent days it has not been difficult to regard Isabella with some favor. Considered the most beautiful princess in Europe, she had been married for reasons of state and for nearly twenty years had been subject to her husband's abnormalities and eccentricities. But now a different Isabella appears. She shows that she is indeed her father's daughter, that implacable monarch who trampled the Templar order into dust like a flesh-and-blood golem. Flushed with her success, she proceeded to give full rein to a lust for power as well as an appetite for revenge. Later she would display other serious flaws of character and, moreover, would demonstrate an inability to wield the responsibility she was so determined to possess.

With victory in her hands and her husband safely locked up in Llantrissant, Isabella collected her people about her and led her army to London. It was a triumphal procession. All the young knights-errant from the Low Countries were with her, including

Sir John of Hainaut. Mortimer was more in evidence than before, and Adam of Orleton was also much in the fore. The head of Walter Stapledon was still in the queen's possession, but she had a praiseworthy object in keeping it: she wanted it honorably buried in his own cathedral with the rest of his body, which had been rescued from under a pile of rubbish in London.

There was one participant in the first stages of this triumphant journey who did not display the enthusiasm of the others, Hugh le Despenser the younger. The marshal of the queen's forces saw to it that the captive favorite rode on the back of a small and mean specimen of a horse. In every town and village they reached, trumpets sounded and heralds called attention to the passing through of this once powerful man perched on his mangy steed; a form of derision to which Despenser paid little heed. He was refusing food and drink. As a result he grew steadily weaker, and when they reached Hereford it was feared he had not much longer to live. Not to be cheated of their revenge in this way, they quickly placed him on trial before Sir William Trussell, a member of the justiciary. He was charged with many offenses, among others that of urging the execution of Thomas of Lancaster, of conspiring against the queen, and of mismanagement of the affairs of the realm. He was even blamed for the defeat at Bannockburn and for the steps taken to conceal miracles at the tomb of Lancaster. Trussell, who was to gain for himself a reputation of unnecessary severity on the bench, sentenced the deposed favorite in the following terms:

Hugh, all the good people of the kingdom, great and small, rich and poor, by common assent do award that you are found as a thief and therefore shall be hanged, and are found as a traitor, and therefore shall be drawn and quartered; and for that you have been outlawed by the king and by common consent, and returned to the court without warrant, you shall be beheaded; and for that you abetted and procured discord between king and queen, and others of the realm, you shall be embowelled and your bowels burned; and so go to your judgment, attainted, wicked traitor.

Accordingly the unfortunate man was attired in a black gown with his escutcheon upside down and a crown of nettles on his brow. He was dragged to the place of execution, a gallows fifty feet high, and here all the grim and savage ritual was carried out.

It is said that he died patiently, but it may have been that his weakened condition brought about a loss of consciousness. The queen was present.

Before leaving the younger Despenser at the almost unanimous verdict which his acquisitiveness had made inevitable, it should in fairness be pointed out that he had striven during his days of power to make improvements in the administrative departments. There was nothing of the standstill conservative officeholder in him. Realizing that Westminster functioned with leaden slowness and muddle-headedness, he undertook to improve procedure with changes which were called radical. This admirable effort accomplished no more than to increase the enmity of his ill-wishers.

Robert Baldock would have been executed at the same time, but on account of his priesthood he was sent on to London instead, to be held in the palace of Adam of Orleton for punishment later. Perhaps by design the word of his arrival was spread through London. He was so unpopular that the citizens stormed the palace and dragged him out. So sorely was he abused that when he was taken to Newgate Prison he died almost immediately of his injuries. The feeling against Baldock seems to have been due to the perversion of justice he had permitted in the courts.

The people of London did not wait for the usual ceremonial of entry at Temple Bar when it became known that Isabella and her troops were nearing the city. They poured out into the open to welcome her, bearing costly gifts and hailing her as the savior of England.

A writ was at once issued for a meeting of Parliament at Westminster for the purpose of treating with the king, if he were present. In the absence of the king the house was to treat with the queen-consort and the king's son, who was designated as guardian of the realm. Edward, needless to state, was absent, although not of his own wish. He had been taken to Kenilworth Castle, which was owned by his kinsman, Henry of Lancaster. The latter welcomed him kindly and treated him throughout with due respect. Here he was to remain until a decision was reached as to the future occupancy of the throne.

CHAPTER ELEVEN

The Deposition and Death of the King

1

THE deputation sent to see Edward on January 20, 1327, reached Kenilworth after a cold and arduous trip. It was made up of men who did not enjoy rough roads and wintry weather, bishops and judges and a parliamentarian or two. They arrived at the castle with blue noses and heads sunk deep into their hoods and they flailed their arms about them as they waited in the courtyard. Kenilworth was not then the luxurious castle it became a half century later when John of Gaunt built his great hall and graceful quarters surrounding it. It was to Caesar's Tower, with its massive walls, that they were escorted.

Inside the tower there was a warm fire blazing in the room selected for the audience. Orleton was there as the spokesman, a stout ecclesiastic with uneasy eyes and an insensitive jowl. Trussell stood beside him, always ready to jibe at misfortune. None of the great magnates had come, being glad to turn this shabby task over to lesser men.

A door at the end of the apartment opened and Edward entered silently. He was robed in black serge, a cloth regarded in those days as cheap and suitable only for casual use. All the assurance that sits so easily on the shoulders of royalty had left him. His eyes went from one fleshy face to another, seeking an answer. What were they here to do? To pronounce a sentence of death on him? Or to show mercy and propose terms?

He had been told something of the proceedings of Parliament a fortnight before. His bitterest enemy, Orleton (for so the defeated king had come to regard the sharp-tongued churchman, fearing him more than Mortimer), had demanded his deposition, contending that the lives of the queen and the prince would be endangered if he were left in power. The Archbishop of Canterbury,

Reynolds, had agreed with this (he had been in Edward's household when the prince was young and owed his high post to the king), but most of the members had shown disturbed faces, realizing the serious nature of the step proposed. A London mob howled about the building, crying for death or deposition, but some of the bishops had summoned up enough courage to speak for the king. One of them, Rochester, was seized by the mob when he emerged and barely escaped with his life. Accordingly, deposition had been decided upon and the measure duly passed. Then Isabella began to weep, whether in sudden repentance or to conceal her real feelings, no one knew; and the conscience of the young prince began to whisper in his ear. The result was that the prince finally refused the proffered crown unless his father's consent to deposition were first received.

This was the business which had brought a hostile deputation to wait on the king. The latter, knowing himself on trial, turned quickly when Orleton began to speak. He listened for a few moments while the shrill invectives of his enemy assailed his ears, then he was seen to turn pale. His knees began to tremble and then folded under him and he rolled to the floor in a faint.

When he had been raised to his feet by the Earl of Leicester and the Bishop of Winchester, he had to listen to the balance of the unsparing Orleton's diatribe with something of the mien of a schoolboy under the lash of a master's tongue. At the finish he wept again and then spoke in a weak voice.

"I am in your hands. You must do what seems right."

This was what the young prince had demanded, his father's consent. Briskly, then, Sir William Trussell stepped forward as proctor of Parliament to make the customary declaration, managing to inject into it a lack of decency and honorable feeling. Raising a forefinger in the air, he broke the bonds of fealty which bound the members. "I do make this protestation in the name of all those that will not, for the future, be in your fealty or allegiance, nor claim to hold anything of you as king"—his voice raised scornfully—"but account you as a private person, without any manner of royal dignity."

The king, who was no longer king and no greater now than plain Sir Edward of Caernarvon, seemed to shrink inside his shoddy serge. But his humiliation was not yet complete. Sir Thomas Blount, the steward of the royal household, came forward and broke his white staff of office, which was done only on the deposition or death of a royal master.

Edward strove to accept these cruel rites in good spirit, but when he spoke, desiring to do so with dignity, he could frame only the plainest of words. "I am aware," he said, "that for my many sins I am thus punished. Have compassion on me." Then he looked about him with a faint smile, keeping his eyes away, no doubt, from his two chief tormentors, Orleton and Trussell. "Much as I grieve at having incurred the ill will of the people, I am glad they have chosen my oldest son to be their king."

Thus ended his reign. It had been as inglorious as might have been expected in view of his unfitness for the role of king. His back bowed in shame under his threadbare robe, he turned and stumbled from the room, a humble knight, with not a real friend left, not an inch of land he could claim, and not a coin in his purse. His continued existence, he knew, would depend on one thing only: the will of the beautiful wife he now called the she-wolf of France.

2

When the news spread through London that Queen Isabella was leaving the Tower to ride through to Westminster, the worthy guild members donned hats and cloaks and came out to the streets to see, and did not object when their apprentices deserted counter and bench and followed on the heels of their masters. The queen was worth seeing this morning. No longer was she under the necessity of dressing simply in her role of lady in distress. She wore an ermine cloak, white and virginal and costly, and under it her tight sleeves, of the richest silk from the East, were lined with gold buttons. Her skirts had been pleated and flared until they achieved a bouffant extreme. She looked lovely; her eyes sparkled and her cheeks had a high color, and her hair showed not a single traitorous white strand. Not only did she raise her hand in greeting as she passed, she waved to her friends, the Londoners, and smiled and even laughed.

"Our fair lady is happy. She must have made a good notch," said the merchants among themselves. Most of them still used the notched stick as a daybook.

But it was different when Isabella returned as the shades of evening were falling. Already in the streets the heralds were making their proclamation:

When Sir Edward, late king of England, of his own good will and with the common advice and assent of the prelates, earls, barons and other nobles, and all the commonality of the realm, has put himself out of government of the realm, and has granted and willed that the government of the said realm should come to Sir Edward, his oldest son and heir . . .

This should have been a welcome sound in her ears. It was what she had fought for. But there was no smile on her face as she made her way through the crowded streets. The Londoners were out in force and cheering for the young king. They gave her a boisterous welcome, but she did not respond. Occasionally she raised a hand in acknowledgment, but that was all.

A word they had used that morning came again into the comments of the good merchants and the trained band captains, but this time in a quite different sense. "This is out of all scotch and notch," they said, an expression which meant they were completely at sea.

This is what had happened at Westminster: a standing Council of Regency had been appointed, made up of four bishops, four earls, and six barons, it being stipulated that one bishop, one earl, and two barons would be in constant attendance on the king. Henry of Lancaster was named head of the council, the post once held by the late Earl Thomas.

Now Isabella had wanted to be regent. She had fully expected it, and the action of Parliament had been a bitter blow to her.

Why, she asked herself as she rode back to the tower, had she been passed over? Had not Blanche of Castile been made regent of France nearly a century before when her son Louis IX was twelve years old? Although her son had grown up to be the great king called St. Louis, Blanche had maintained her ascendancy over him to the very end. Indeed, Blanche had been so reluctant to have him marry that she had kept the young king on the same floor she occupied in the royal palace and had arranged the bride's rooms on the floor above. Whenever she heard his step on the stairs on the way to pay his young queen a visit, she would be out of the door in a wink, with papers to be signed and other affairs of state which could not wait for a minute.

Did these clods, these assertive bishops and barons, think that she, Isabella of France, could not rule as well as Blanche of Castile? Did they not realize that she had succeeded in ousting Edward from power when they had failed, that the credit for everything which had happened belonged to her?

The stage has now been reached when some attention should be paid to the fifteen-year-old boy who had become the King of England. Edward was a true Plantagenet. He had the fair hair and blue eyes of the family and was perhaps the handsomest of them all. One description which has been handed down is that his face was like an angel's. He would grow to be tall, although he would lack the commanding stature of his grandsire and the massiveness of frame which had contributed so much to Richard Coeur-de-Lion's reputation as a great fighting man.

Behind that angelic countenance a cool and clear mind was already at work. Edward would never be willingly a tool of anyone. He had allowed himself to tag behind his mother's skirts about Flanders and had let her take full command of the invasion which had been so successful; and this raises the question as to why he was willing to aid in his father's undoing. The answer must be that young Edward had already become convinced that the poor weak reign of his father must come to an end for the good of the country. Isabella had not read his mind aright. She undoubtedly thought that his acquiescence was the result of her influence. It never entered her mind that the boy who had agreed to the removal from power and honor of one parent might be prepared later to do the same for the other, if he perceived equally good reasons. She could not see beyond the present and the fact that he was bound to her by bonds of gratitude as well as filial affection.

Edward lacked the noble sense of kingly responsibility which had animated Edward I and which could be traced back to the first great Plantagenet, Henry II, but he was to become such a wise and resourceful monarch that it would be wrong to assume him incapable at fifteen of forming his own conclusions. He was still a rather quiet boy (in fact, he seems to have had nothing in common with his shabbily endowed father), but he was an observant one. It may be taken for granted that he was fully conscious of his mother's relationship with Mortimer and of the evil effect this would have on the country. He must have seen that Isabella's determination to elevate her lover to almost a full partnership with herself was certain in the end to lead to another national upheaval. His opinion of this upstart who had dared to cuckold a king could not have continued favorable for long. Mortimer's silky dark good looks and his masterful ways might be irresistible to a neglected wife, but they did not offer any substitute for sound vision and administrative ability, in both of which the Marcher baron was lacking. Edward III, watching intently and moving slowly, would not be held for long on such leading strings as these.

Isabella decided that she would exercise the duties of a regent, even though the title and recognition had been withheld. Mortimer and Adam of Orleton had been given places on the council and she felt certain that, with their collaboration, she could make the functions of the board purely nominal. The young king, who showed a strain of shrewdness early, must have seen that the council, made up of inert bishops and land-proud barons, would be no more effective than it had been when Cousin Lancaster was head of the Ordainers. He seemed content, at any rate, to let his mother proceed with her theft of authority.

In the unofficial regency that Isabella proceeded to form, she made Mortimer her chief minister and selected Adam of Orleton as her first adviser. That snarling churchman, whose malice seemed always at the boiling point, was as necessary to her as the diabolical Nogaret had been to her father: someone to read the purpose in the royal mind and put it into words for the first time, thereafter acting as the unscrupulous sword arm in carrying it out.

Never had there been such prodigal peculation, such insatiable seizure of honors and lands as when Roger Mortimer, given almost absolute power by his royal mistress, began to gather in the fruit from the medlar trees of Westminster. Here are a few of the benefits he conferred on himself:

Knighthoods for four of his sons the day of the king's coronation.

The return of all of his confiscated estates and those of his uncle of Chirk.

Granted the custody of Thomas Beauchamp, Earl of Warwick, for the term of his minority. (How badly gutted the estates would be when young Thomas came of age!)

Obtained the lands in Glamorgan which had belonged to the wife of the younger Despenser.

Was appointed justiciar of the diocese of Llandaff.

Granted lands worth a thousand pounds a year which had belonged to the elder Despenser, including the castle of Denbigh.

In Ireland given complete palatine rights in the liberty of Trim and in the counties of Meath and Uriel.

Had transferred to him the castle of Montgomery and the Hundred of Chirbury.

Allowed four hundred marks a year in addition to his full fees as justice in Wales.

His barony raised to the earldom of March.

Granted the manor of Church Stretton in Shropshire as a return for his services to Queen Isabella and the young king.

Granted the justiceship of Wales for life.

Two chantry priests were paid ten marks a year to say prayers for him. This was in the nature of a foundation in honor of St. Peter. He had not forgotten that it was on the feast day of St. Peter that he escaped from the Tower of London.

And so it went, lands, honors, wardships, titles, offices. Hardly a week passed that he did not see something his greed craved; and the queen, in the grip of her middle-aged passion for him, could not say him nay. Was it any wonder that soon the wave of enthusiasm with which Isabella had been received began to shrivel into suspicion and resentment? That soon a large part of the people of England would have preferred to have Edward back, with his careless rule, his stupidities and weaknesses, even his favorites?

In the meantime Isabella gave a pension of four hundred marks a year to the faithful Sir John of Hainaut and found means of rewarding the rest of her foreign troops before reembarking them for Flanders. This was just as well, for on Trinity Sunday the queen and her son held a great court at Blackfriars. To start the proceedings the young king knighted fifteen young candidates and the queen gave a splendid dinner for the Netherland nobles. A ball was to follow, but unfortunately it was interrupted by a furious battle that broke out in town between a party of English archers and the grooms of the foreign noblemen. The party broke up before the first minstrel could tootle a note on his horn or the goliards had yet raised their voices in song.

The foreign troops went home after this. They had been in England long enough.

3

In considering the tragic event that followed, it must be borne in mind that a deposed monarch is a menace to constituted authority, a rallying point for all discontent. It was not often possible to deal as leniently with a defeated ruler as in the case of Crassus (the Fat) in Gueldres. In England, as elsewhere, a violent solution had always been found. Henry I kept his older brother Robert in prison until he died and had his eyes burned out with a red-hot iron as an extra precaution. John lost no time in disposing mysteriously of Prince Arthur. There would be other cases later.

Before the coronation of the young prince on January 29, a sermon was preached at Westminster Abbey by the Archbishop of Canterbury, the turncoat Walter Reynolds, who had been foisted on the Church by the hand he now proceeded to bite. He took as his text Vox *populi* vox *Dei*. It soon became apparent, however, that the voice of the people was not being raised as one in favor of the change. There was a growing sympathy for the deposed king throughout the land, a sentiment which could easily be fanned into a great blaze. The desire to be rid of Edward was not confined, therefore, to the queen and her paramour. All who had been actively against him, who had flocked to the standard of Isabella, felt a need to be safe from the ex-king. Remembering the hasty trial of Thomas of Lancaster and the block set up on the hill of St. Thomas, they had no inclination to allow him any chance to regain control. There were many eyes fixed on the not too secure prison provided for him at Kenilworth and many anxious ears pressed to the ground.

The deposed king remained at Kenilworth for the balance of the winter, lapped in luxury and kindly treated by Henry of Lancaster. He complained bitterly in letters to the queen of his separation from his family and received from her in return many gifts, mostly of fine articles of clothing. In one letter she said that she would like to visit him but had been forbidden by Parliament. He is said to have written some verses in Latin which when translated began:

> On my devoted head
> Her bitterest showers,
> All from a wintry cloud,
> Stern fortune pours.

The poor captive had no knowledge of Latin, and the senti-
ments seem quite foreign to what is known of his character. It
seems certain that this was an invention of some later romancer.

While he passed the days as well as he could in Caesar's Tower,
a conspiracy for his release was reaching formidable proportions.
A family named Dunhead possessed considerable property around
Kenilworth. There were two brothers, one a Dominican friar, who
was noted for his eloquence and was held in wide regard for his
sanctity. He had stood so high in the regard of Edward that he
had once been sent on a mission to the Pope at Avignon; having
to do, it was whispered, with the possibility of getting a divorce
from Isabella. The friar was still intensely loyal to the deposed
king and had enlisted the aid of his brother and many of the
neighboring gentry. Henry of Lancaster learned what was afoot
and asked to be relieved of the responsibility for so difficult a
guest.

The decision to send Edward to Berkeley Castle was due, therefore, to the fear of a successful *coup* and not, as has been stated,
because the queen felt he was being pampered. Thomas of Berkeley had been confined to prison by Edward for some political
offense and had been released by Isabella on her return to England. He was married to a daughter of Roger Mortimer, and his
selection as Edward's keeper can be ascribed undoubtedly to that
connection. John de Maltravers, a member of a rich Dorsetshire
family, was chosen as co-keeper, probably because he was married
to Berkeley's sister. A third knight named Edward de Gurney was
then added for good measure. An allowance of five pounds a day
was set for the care of the prisoner, which disposes of the charge
often made that he was removed because of the queen's resentment of the easy living provided for her ex-spouse. It was certain,
of course, that a goodly part of the daily allowance would find its
way into the pockets of Messires Berkeley, Maltravers, and
Gurney.

Edward was removed from Kenilworth at night, before the
plans of the Dunhead brothers had matured, and taken to Berkeley Castle with a numerous escort. The zealous brothers soon discovered where he had been taken and devoted themselves to a
plan to crack open his new prison. At the same time an active
conspiracy in favor of the captive developed in South Wales
under the leadership of a knight named Sir Rhys ap Gruffydd.
This was Mortimer's responsibility, and the deputy he had appointed to keep peace there, William of Shalford, wrote to him

about the scheme, suggesting what he called "a suitable remedy." It is clear that the same thought had been in Mortimer's mind, and many other minds, for some time. Edward alive would always be a menace. The Dunheads might be balked and the activities of Rhys ap Gruffydd might be suppressed, but others would arise to carry on the agitation.

It is of little avail to speculate on the part the queen played in the events which followed. It is reasonable to suppose that she was taken into Mortimer's confidence and that she gave her consent, but no proofs of this exist. It is conceivable, of course, that her paramour thought it unwise to draw her into it in any way. The only piece of direct evidence with any bearing on the point is that after her husband's death she summoned a woman who had embalmed the body and questioned her minutely as to what she had found. The queen's desire to get at this much of the truth does not clear her of complicity by any means, but it does make it certain that she had not been in the full confidence of the instigators of the murder. That much of doubt she must be allowed.

As to Mortimer's share in the plot, there can be no doubt at all. The finger points at him as the one who found "the suitable remedy." He picked out a dependent of his named William Ogle and sent him to Berkeley to act with the others.

Before the remedy could be applied, the council had taken matters into its hands by sending a doctor of law named John Walwayn to Berkeley. He was supposed to direct everything that was done for the safekeeping and the comfort of the king. The activities of the Dunheads came to a peak at this point, and it is now believed that the release of Edward was accomplished. A letter from Walwayn has been resurrected from the records of the day which can be construed as an acknowledgment that he had escaped. If it were so, he was recaptured almost immediately. This may provide proof of another story in the records, that he was removed to Corfe Castle for safer keeping. The sentiment around Corfe was too friendly to the captive, however, and again he was taken back to Berkeley. The time for the "remedy" had come.

In many histories it is asserted that the order for the murder was contained in a line of Latin sent to the circle of keepers by Adam of Orleton. The line ran:

Edwardum occidere nolite timere, bonum est

which, translated, reads, "Edward to kill be unwilling to fear, it is good." The meaning of this ambiguous sentence could be altered by the changing of the comma to appear after the word "unwilling." The keepers of the king took from the first version that they were expected to act and so proceeded with the plan.

This story is not worthy of any credence. In the first place, the bishop was in Avignon at the time on a mission to the Pope, and it is absurd to believe he would put such a damning piece of evidence in writing. It is equally absurd to believe that the rascals to whom it was supposed to be sent would be able to read Latin or to understand the significance of a misplaced comma. It may be taken for granted that any order would have been conveyed by word of mouth so that no incriminating evidence would be left.

4

One day in mid-September, Thomas of Berkeley came to the cell in which the royal prisoner was confined. He had been seeing little of Edward. The trio of keepers appointed by Mortimer— Maltravers, Gurney, and Ogle—had taken things into their own hands. It seems certain that Berkeley had a genuine feeling of sympathy for his unfortunate guest. He said with regret that he must be absent for some time on affairs of his own but would return as soon as possible. Edward's hand clung to that of the owner of the castle as though he realized that his last friend was deserting him.

Life had already become a burden to the prisoner. His clothing was shoddy and always damp. The food served him was sometimes so nauseous that he could not eat it. On at least one occasion he had been brought cold and muddy water from the moat to shave with and his protests had been disregarded.

With Berkeley away, there was no one to temper the grim routine of Edward's days or to stand between him and the other three, particularly the man Ogle, who had made his mysterious appearance a short time before. No one seemed to know exactly why he had come, but Edward had more than a suspicion of the truth and undoubtedly shuddered whenever the man came near him.

As soon as Berkeley departed, the atmosphere of the castle changed. No longer was the lonely prisoner treated with even an outward semblance of respect. Orders were barked at him and rough hands were always ready to enforce them. As a final evidence of hostility, he was removed to a small and dark cell in a wing of the castle devoted to domestic arrangements. It was over the charnelhouse, and the odors which came up from below made it difficult for the new occupant to breathe. The one window looked out on an empty corner of the courtyard, a bleak prospect of damp wall and slimy paving stones. It must have been apparent now that his three grim custodians had one purpose only in mind.

On the night of September 21 the other inmates of the castle were aroused from their slumbers by shrieks coming from the malodorous cell in which the deposed king was confined. Horror and agony were in the sounds. It is said that the outcries of the dying man were so loud that they reached to ears in the village nearby and that people hid their heads under their bedclothing, knowing full well what this meant. Edward of Caernarvon, once Edward of England, was dying a violent death.

In the morning it was given out that he had expired during the night of natural causes. The guards and domestics were allowed to view the body, laid out on a disordered bed in the cell. None failed to notice that the features of the dead man were still contorted with violence and pain.

Many stories were circulated throughout the country as to the manner in which the murder had been committed. One circumstantial account, contained in a chronicle prepared some thirty years after the event, seemed to fit the known facts and was generally believed. It is given for what it is worth, in the absence of any official explanation.

The three assassins waited until their victim was sound asleep and then flung a table over him, which was held down by two of them to prevent him from moving. The third man then proceeded to burn out his inside organs with a red-hot bar of iron. As it was inserted through a horn, no marks of violence were made on the surface of the body.

John Thody, Abbot of Gloucester, claimed the body and took it away in his own chariot. Later there was a burial of much stateliness and pomp in the Abbey of St. Peter's. There was gold leaf on the coffin and lions of pure gold on the hearse; but nothing could be done to remove the imprint of horror on the once handsome features of this weak and unfortunate king, nor to allay the wave of grief and anger which swept over the country.

Book Three
EDWARD THE THIRD

CHAPTER ONE

Hamlet on the Steps of the Throne

1

THE foul deed which brought to a close the days of that poor shadow of a king, Edward II, inaugurated a reign which would touch the peaks. Edward III was the most spectacular of the Plantagenets; fair, of goodly proportions, with a face, so it was said, of a demi-god; a conqueror, brave, vainglorious, extravagant, ostentatious; somewhat shallow of character, lacking, at any rate, the deep sense of kingly responsibility which has kept the memory of his grandfather so green. It must have been a great sight to watch the third Edward riding in a tournament, his lance expert and deadly, his delight in the sport so keen. Or to observe him in his brilliant and gay court, strutting like a peacock in the velvets he loved, the doublepiled new varieties from Lucca and Genoa; his voice richly modulated, his laughter spontaneous, an intimate look in his eye for every pretty lady.

These were the days when chivalry reached its greatest height in England. The armies with which Edward defeated the French and came so close to establishing his claim to the French throne were filled with knights of spirit and repute, knights-errant in the fullest sense of the word, about whom much will be told later. One of the stories of the period which is repeated with the most gusto concerns a beautiful lady of the court who had dressed herself for a ball with such splendor that a line from *Piers Plowman* seems to fit her: "Her array ravished me, such richness saw I never." But the lady's dress had beauties which did not show on the surface, and when she lost a most necessary part of her attire, a delicate thing of rich silk with jewels nestling in its rosebuds, and the king found it, he was inspired (or so runs the story) to form the Order of the Garter, which has been the only rival for the legendary Round Table of Arthurian days. It may be recorded also that only the most perfunctory efforts were made to capture a Frenchwoman of high rank who set herself up as a pirate in and around the Channel. Was she not a lady and beautiful, forsooth?

But the rise of chivalry was no more than the flare-up before its final extinction. The brave knights were certain, no doubt, that they had won Crécy and Poictiers, but a realistic vision would have taught them a different story. Those great battles were won by stout-limbed, brawny-backed, sun-bronzed fellows of low degree who wore lincoln-green jerkins and had a deadly skill with a new weapon called the longbow. The chivalry of France died under the lethal hail of English arrows, without realizing that the fine bloom of chivalry withered with their passing. An insignificant item is found (without foundation) in Froissart. The English, he reports, had something very strange called cannon; long-snouted barrels of bronze which spewed forth shells under the compulsive force of a substance that a very great Englishman named Roger Bacon had discovered a century before, gunpowder. But the longbow and the death-dealing powder would soon revolutionize warfare and change it from the sport of knights to a much deadlier business: the clash of great armies and the use of artillery which would cover battlefields with smoke and cut wide swaths of death in the serried ranks. A form of conflict in which the exquisite rules of chivalry would have no part at all.

The fifty long years of Edward's reign make robust telling after the shambles of his father's rule, although the third Edward took no interest in constitutional matters, granting rights to his subjects with a careless flourish of his pen and then trampling on them with equally careless steel-shod feet. But progress was made under these conditions toward democratic understandings. It was a period also of commercial expansion, a prosaic phase of life in which the king, strangely enough, seemed to take a great deal of interest. Perhaps his consort, Philippa, who came from the Low Countries, where business had become the most important part of life, had influenced him in that direction. His chief interests remained, however, diplomacy and war; and because he was skillful in the one and bold and lucky in the other, he scaled the heights.

Alexandre Dumas, the elder, has asserted that a man reaches the full prime of life between his forty-sixth and forty-eighth years. When Edward III was forty-six he held on St. George's Day at Windsor the most magnificent tournament of the age and competed mightily himself. That Christmas he had among his guests the kings of France and Scotland, both of whom had been taken prisoners in their wars with England and were being held in captivity; and he was entertaining at the moment proposals of peace by which he would have been awarded all of the southeast of France in full sovereignty. This would have restored to him the Angevin empire which had been lost by John and Henry III. The novelist seems to have been right as far as Edward was concerned. When the yule log was dragged into the hall and the three monarchs watched the merrymaking over their goblets of hippocras (a cordial highly spiced and strained through a hippocratian bag of cloth or linen), the English king was at his zenith.

2

For four years the young king was supposed to be under the guidance of the council which had been set up by Parliament, but in reality there was a regency in operation. Queen Isabella had expected to be made regent, and when that honor was denied her she had proceeded coolly to assume all the powers and responsibilities of the post, with Mortimer always at her right hand. The boy seems to have acquiesced. In any event, he did nothing immediately to express disapproval or to interfere with his mother's highhandedness. He even allowed her to appropriate for herself nearly all of the royal funds, two thirds of everything, in fact.

What was the young king thinking as he watched his still beautiful and still popular mother (although the first rumblings of discontent were being heard in the land) assume all the powers of the throne? What were his feelings toward the strutting, arrogant Mortimer, who was proving himself more dangerous and grasping than Gaveston or the Despensers had ever been? Above all else, what did he think of the relationship between them? If he did not know they were living in almost open sin, his were the only eyes in the kingdom which had failed to detect the truth.

Edward, it may be taken for granted, was watching everything and biding his time. A Hamlet in his early teens, he was not in a position to act at once. He knew the fierce temper and the savage methods of Mortimer and he had seen how dilatory and feeble were the men who made up the council. He might be as roughly thrust aside as his father had been. Did he want to share the fate of Arthur of Brittany, who had stood in the way of John of infamous memory? All the qualities he would later display were developing in the young king and would manifest themselves when he felt it safe to make his move. In the meantime he did not mope as Hamlet had done. There was no mooning about the battlements of the White Tower, no soliloquizing at midnight in the ghostly lunar light through the arches of the great hall at Westminster. He was bestirring himself in many ways. And he was watching the men about him, weighing their merits and the courage they had in them, considering, discarding, and finally selecting the few he could take into his confidence.

There were two things he could do while he waited. He could lead an army against the Scots, who had come down in full force and with fire and sword into the northern counties. And he could take the necessary steps to marry his Philippa.

Queen Isabella, who had reason to know the Plantagenet ways, was apprehensive of her son. She wanted to keep him in the background as long as possible, but she saw the need to have him occupied. Accordingly she took his proposed marriage in hand and persuaded the members of the council that a daughter of the house of Hainaut would be the most suitable wife for him. Care was taken not to let the members know that the young king's mind was already made up. It was their business, not his, to find him a wife. The document finally drawn up gave their consent to a match with "a daughter of that nobleman, William, Count of Hainaut, Holland and Zealand and Lord of Friesland." No mention was made of Philippa. Any one of the four daughters apparently would suit the council. The next step was to send a deputation to Count William to lay the proposal before him, and Adam of Orleton was selected to head it.

It will be remembered that when King John sent a deputation to Rome to aid in selecting an Archbishop of Canterbury he told them they could vote for anyone they desired, *provided it was the king's candidate*. Adam of Orleton was given secret instructions of a similar nature. Use your own judgment, Sir Bishop, in selecting one of the four, provided it is Philippa.

The deputation traveled to Valenciennes, where Count William resided with his bevy of pretty daughters, and there was much solemn discussion as to which one was to be selected. It is likely that Philippa did not worry, remembering the long talks she had had with the handsome young prince, their rambles together in the gardens, the vows of fidelity he had sworn. Adam of Orleton finally gave his head an owl-like shake and announced the selection of the fairest, the most apple-cheeked, the somewhat plumper one of the four.

Then the matter of the Pope's sanction came up, for the two mothers were cousins-german and so within the bounds of consanguinity. It was decided to send messengers at once to Avignon to win the papal nod, for an urgency was recognized in getting the matter settled without delay. Edward, after all, was a boy in years and not allowed to make his own decisions. His mother was no longer a suppliant for military aid and she might change her mind in favor of a more important match. And finally there was Mortimer, with daughters of his own and a willingness, possibly, to solidify his position by marrying the prince to one of them. Two Flemish knights and a parcel of clerks were sent off on horseback with instructions to ride fast and long and get the papal consent before London could change its mind.

British poets have been partial to recording the stories of urgent rides. There is the midnight race from Ghent to Aix, the horseback perambulations of John Gilpin, and the mad ride of Tam o' Shanter. Some bard should have selected the journey of the two knights of Hainaut. They had to cover the whole face of France, starting at Valenciennes, traversing the full depth of Burgundy, then through Auvergne, striking sparks from the rocky roads and pausing only long enough to bawl for relays, passing Rheims, Troyes, Dijon, and Lyons, and coming finally to the city of Avignon perched high on the banks of the mighty Rhone; Avignon, once called the windy city because it lay directly in the path of the hot mistral which blew across the Mediterranean, but was now the new home of the popes.

Rome had become almost a ghost city. Her great palaces and cathedrals were empty and silent, for the personnel and machinery of the papacy had been moved to Avignon. Lacking all facilities for accommodating the thousands of priests and clerks and functionaries of all classes, not to mention the acolytes and guards and servants who had come pouring out of Italy at the beck of lordly France, Avignon had become a place of chaos. Pope John XXII was madly busy raising the buildings which would become known as the Palace of the Popes on the rocky Rocher des Doms. He had two thoughts only in mind—speed and solidity—and was not attempting to match the grandeur and solemnity of Rome. The result would be a depressing cluster of gray stone structures where the affairs of the papacy would be conducted for seventy long years. About them miles of square stone ramparts were rising, and in course of time no fewer than thirty-nine massive towers would be added.

When the weary knights from Hainaut came galloping into Avignon, the streets were crowded with priests afoot and on mule-back, there were three albs in every attic, and the church bells were competing with the whine of saws and the screech of winches. Architects and master masons and carpenters were trailing dust through the anterooms of the Pope while clerical deputations sat unnoticed and bit their fingernails in impatience.

Pope John was a tiny man, with hunched shoulders which made him look deformed. He had been born in Cahors, the son of a poor cobbler, and he was still so partial to his old home that seven out of the fifteen cardinals he appointed came from that somewhat insignificant city; an extraordinary thing, surely, for a pope to do. He proceeded now to do something which also seems extraordinary. Instead of letting the Flemish knights wait their turn outside, a matter perhaps of months, he had them in at once. He listened to what they had to tell him, nodded his head, and said "Yes."

3

The Scots had been feeling their oats since Bannockburn. Rome had at last recognized Robert the Bruce as king of the country and there was peace with England, a nominal kind of peace, since the people on both sides of the border paid little attention to it. The succession to the throne had been well established by the arrival of a son who was given the name of David. This Scottish prince was a fine, handsome lad with strong limbs and a will and a fierce temper of his own; all the qualities, in fact, which are looked for in candidates for thrones.

Immediately after the deposition of Edward II, old Robert the Bruce decided it would be a good thing to teach the new king a lesson. He sent his two eager warriors, the Black Douglas and Randolph, Earl of Moray, down into Northumberland to stir up the Sassenach. Things had indeed changed for the Scots. The whole troop was mounted, even the poorest clansman having some sorry sort of Galloway nag of his own. This was the kind of warfare in which they excelled. They had no kitchens, no food supplies, no lumbering wagons to hamper their movements. Each horseman had his bag of oatmeal and, at the worst, he could sustain himself for a long time on that, cooking it on a metal plate. When luck favored them and they picked up English cattle, they would roast or boil the animals in their skins and each man would then carry a haunch over his shoulder. They came and went like the wind and they left behind them the scent of burning homesteads and the wailing of new-made widows and the weeping of children.

The English decided to put a stop to this kind of raiding. A large army was raised, nearly sixty thousand men, and Sir John of Hainaut was brought back with a body of trained Flemish cavalry to help. The young king, eager to win his spurs, rode to Durham and assumed command; a nominal command, since Sir John was there to advise him and all the best English generals, none of whom was very good. It might have seemed to a shrewd observer that the powers behind the throne, the ambitious queen and her constant attendant Mortimer, were content to keep the prince busy at something, even to place him at a disadvantage. They did not want him to emerge victorious from the war like his grandfather and that prince of glowing memory, Richard Coeur-de-Lion. It was farthest from their thoughts to supply the people with a young hero, to the end that they, Isabella and her gentle Mortimer, would be shoved into the background.

He had no chance to win against the Scots. Twenty thousand strong, the horsemen of Douglas and Randolph were never where the English expected to find them. Finally the prince got sound information and caught up with them. He located them in such a strong position back of the Wear River that he dared not attempt a crossing in front of them. After a long wait, hoping the Scots would draw back like chivalrous knights and invite them to come over and fight, the English army waded off through the peat bogs and the marshes to cross at a ford higher up the river. The Scots sidestepped nimbly and were found in a still stronger position at Stanhope Park. By this time the English troops were in a bad way. They had no food and there was no decent forage for their mounts. The great Flanders horses became hopelessly mired whenever they attempted to move. Through it all a persistent and dismal rain continued to fall.

To cap the English misfortunes, the Black Douglas played one of his most daring tricks on the young king. In the middle of night he rode into the English camp with a small body of horsemen, calling "St. George! St. George!" to deceive the sentries. Three hundred Englishmen were killed before the camp stirred to action. The Black Douglas, whose rashness knew no bounds, found the royal tent and cut his way in through the canvas. Ed-

ward wakened to see a tall, grim figure beside his couch. There
was an exultant gleam in the dark Douglas eye, and his drawn
claymore might have put an early end to the reign of the third
Edward if the chaplain had not thrown himself between them,
dying to save his royal master. Edward escaped under the canvas
of the tent and, as the camp was now fully aroused, the daring
Scots took to horse and dashed off into the night, changing their
cries to a triumphant "A Douglas! A Douglas!"

"A little bloodletting," said the Black Douglas carelessly when
he reached his own camp and was questioned by Randolph, his
partner in command.

This was the only bloodletting of the campaign, for the Scots
withdrew immediately after and retired to their side of the border.

Edward, humiliated to the point of tears, took his army back to
Durham and then to York. His first campaign had been a failure.
He had learned some lessons, however, which would stand him in
good stead when later he would face the French on the battlefield
of Crécy. Successful war was not a matter of set procedure like a
tournament. Two well-equipped armies did not march out as
though by appointment to a fair and level field and there fight it
out in bloodthirsty comfort. Instead it was a dirty, tricky business,
a series of feints and stratagems and efforts to totally mislead the
other army. He had seen the Flemish cavalry of John of Hainaut
struggling in the mud. He had seen the Scots come and go like
will-o'-the-wisps, and he had been misled and tricked and made a
mockery of; and he realized, as his grandfather Edward I had after
the royal defeat at Lewes, that his whole conception of war must
be changed. It was a good thing for England that his ideas had altered completely when the time came to fight at Crécy.

In the meantime it was decided to make peace with the Scots
and have an end to all this bootless border marauding. A Parliament was called at Lincoln to open negotiations. The Florentine
bankers, the Bardi, who were now well established in London and
had taken over the financial activities once carried on by the unfortunate Templars, agreed to loan the money needed. Sir John
and his mercenaries were paid off with a lump sum of fourteen
thousand pounds and sent home to Flanders. Edward's first little
war was over.

4

The future Queen of England, all a-flutter as a prospective bride should be, was married at her Flemish home to Edward by procuration. The name of the man who served as proxy for the young king has not been recorded, but of course it was all a matter of legal form. The foolish practice of putting the bride into bed and then admitting the proxy under the covers (with a roomful of witnesses, of course) just long enough for him to touch his bare foot to hers would come into use much later in history. The ceremony, such as it was, served as a legal tie and the bride set out forthwith for England. Her clothes were as wonderful as might have been expected, considering that she came from the land where all the finest textiles were made. Her train was an imposing one. She was escorted by her uncle, Sir John, and among her followers was a youth named Sir Wantelet de Mauny, who was her official carver. It will be well to keep this young man in mind. Under the anglicized name of Sir Walter de Manny, he was to prove himself one of the greatest English fighting men in the Hundred Years' War.

She had been prepared for a rather barren welcome because her young husband was still in the north over the Scottish troubles and both the queen and her devoted Mortimer had also ridden to York to have a hand in the negotiations. On December 23, 1327, she reached London, where a rousing reception was accorded her. The citizens of London seemed to be incurably sentimental where beautiful foreign queens were concerned, and the flaxen-haired Philippa was as wildly acclaimed as Isabella had been. The lord mayor presented her with a service of plate worth three hundred pounds. Leaving at once, escorted by the constable of England, John Bohun, Earl of Hereford, the bridal party made slow progress over snowbound roads. It was not until January 24 that Philippa faced her bridegroom before the altar at York Minster with William de Melton, Archbishop of York, performing the ceremony. Few royal brides were as lovely as Philippa. Edward had grown taller in the interval of their separation and seemed more handsome than ever in her eyes, and so she was also a happy bride. He had passed his fifteenth year and she was a year younger, but no one saw anything amiss in this, for it was an age of early marriages and, unfortunately, of early deaths. Such, how-ever, was not to be the fate of this triply blessed pair. Philippa would live in wedlock with Edward forty-one years and would pre-sent her illustrious Plantagenet mate with twelve children, eight of whom would survive her.

She was the most poorly endowed queen ever wed to an English king, for Isabella had swept the royal cupboard bare. The queen mother had, of course, been in possession of the dower lands which were reserved for each queen during the lifetime of the king, but she was refusing to relinquish them. The young king, on that account, was put to the necessity of making a promissory ar-rangement, that lands to yield an income of fifteen thousand pounds a year would be put in Philippa's hands, including Queen-borough on the Thames. Here, on the Isle of Sheppey, Edward would proceed to build his bride a very special palace, one so handsome and elaborate, in fact, that it took nearly forty years to finish.

The ceremony might have seemed lacking in splendor had it not been for the presence of one hundred noblemen from Scot-land who had come to take part in the negotiations for a perma-nent peace between the two countries. Ordinarily the purses of the gentry of Caledonia were as flat and bare as the moors of that fierce and wild land, but for this occasion they had managed to create a magnificent impression. Their horses were elaborately ac-coutered and the knights themselves, tawny of hair, gray of eye, and rugged of feature, looked handsome in their homespun dou-blets looped with the semiprecious stones mined from their granite hills. Certainly, with their heavy claymores at their belts, they seemed a formidable lot, as indeed they were.

Edward would have liked nothing better than to take his radi-ant young wife over his saddle and disappear with her like the lost bride of Netherby. But this was impossible. The terms of the peace had to be worked out, and this was to prove a far from easy task. There was a determined glint in the eyes of the Scots and a reminder of Bannockburn in the proud set of their backs. It was clear they were going to have peace on their own terms. The treaty finally evolved was nothing short of a surrender of all the claims and pretensions of the English kings. They gave up for all time the claim to a feudal overlordship of Scotland and agreed to restore at once the thirty-five skins of parchment known as the Ragman Rolls, which carried the signatures of the noblemen who had acknowledged the demands of Edward I. All Scottish heirlooms were to be restored, including the Stone of Scone, the royal regalia, and the piece of the cross of Christ called the Black Rood.

For their part, the Scots agreed to a marriage between Prince David, the heir to the throne, and Princess Joan, the second daughter of Edward II. Joan was seven years old and David was five, but it was arranged that the princess would be turned over at once to a board of Scottish commissioners so that she could be raised in the royal household. It was conceded also that the estates in Scotland belonging to Englishmen, which had been confiscated during the wars, were to be restored and that King Robert would pay an indemnity to England of twenty thousand pounds in three annual installments.

Viewed in the light of time, it seems to have been reasonable enough. But the people of England, who had come to regard Scotland as a tributary country, were bitterly resentful. They blamed it on Isabella and Mortimer, believing them to have forced the treaty through Parliament, which had met at York to pass on the terms. It was whispered throughout the country, and universally believed, that the queen put the first installment of the indemnity in her own pocket and that not so much as a Scottish groat (worth no more than threepence at the time) ever reached the treasury at Westminster.

The terms were fulfilled save the one covering the return of the Stone of Scone. When an effort was made to remove it from the abbey, all London rose in wrath to prevent the surrender. The scales had fallen at last from aldermanic eyes, and for the first time the once beloved Isabella was called on the streets "the Frenchwoman." When the apprentices, with cudgels on shoulder, surrounded the abbey, they shouted, "Death to Mortimer!" and even "Down with the queen!" The Stone was left under the coronation chair in spite of the treaty.

The marriage of the young princess, who became known in Scotland as Joan Makepeace, was proceeded with at once. The English court moved north to Berwick in great splendor for the event. Isabella was accompanied by her son, Prince John, her other daughter, Eleanor, and a great train of the nobility. Mortimer stole the show with a train which included one hundred and eighty knights in glittering armor and with gold spurs on their heels. People asked if any of the indemnity money had gone into the rich apparel of the knights, and a rhyme was repeated by the Scottish spectators which ran as follows:

> Longbeards, heartless,
> Gay coats, graceless,
> Painted hoods, witless,
> Maketh England thriftless.

This confirmed the people of England in their newly aroused contempt for the queen and her paramour. Isabella was said to be a heartless mother for sending her little daughter into exile in the barbarous and uncouth land of the Scots.

There was another flaw. The King of England and his bride were not present when the marriage took place between the two infants. Edward had taken Philippa to the royal castle of Woodstock and refused to return for the ceremony. Under the bright gold of his hair the young king had a long head. He was keeping himself clear of any blame for the unpopular peace treaty. The country seems to have been willing to absolve him, believing that the fault lay with Isabella and Mortimer.

CHAPTER TWO

Mother and Son

1

AT this stage in English history a complete lack of evidence is encountered on a point of the first importance, the relationship between the boy king and his mother. Isabella was running things with an imperious hand and Edward was standing to one side and neither doing nor saying anything to indicate his state of mind. He appeared on the surface to have acquiesced in everything she did until the very last moment, when he stepped in and put an abrupt end to it. It is even suggested in some histories that he did not learn of his mother's adulterous conduct with Mortimer until he went to France after his marriage to swear fealty to the French king. This is nothing short of absurd. Only a cretin could have been unaware of it in Edward's place. And this young king, who was to become the most ambitious and one of the ablest of English kings, was a boy of strong character and rare gifts.

It is not hard to understand the course taken by Isabella which was to result in her ultimate downfall. She was unable to submerge Isabella the woman in Isabella the queen, and the faults of the woman undid the queen. In the telling of the story there seems to be a tendency to underestimate the position she won for herself in England after the fall of Edward II, or at least no desire to measure the full extent of her rise. A country thoroughly weary of the rule of an oafish king and bitterly antagonistic to his greedy favorites suddenly saw his estranged queen, the beautiful, captivating, and diverting consort he had treated so badly, emerge with a small army of volunteers and make a successful landing on the eastern coast. The nobility flocked to her, the common people rallied to her banner, the cities were a unit in lending her support. Whether acting on her own judgment or accepting sound advice from those about her, she handled her campaign so well that Edward was captured without striking a blow and the Despensers were taken and executed. A tendency to believe that the country was shocked by her summary treatment of the two favorites is another absurdity. This was a cruel age and the Despensers were so universally hated that anything short of the elder swinging on the gallows in his armor and the younger dying slowly under the knives of the executioners would not have satisfied. That the queen seized the power of a regent from the council of indecisive and unready men selected by Parliament did not seem to disturb the public; no one had much faith in any of the members of that inept and spineless board. The abdication of Edward was the next step, and to the people it was completely logical and acceptable.

At this point Isabella was in a position to turn the whole tide of history in her favor. Blanche of Castile had never enjoyed the personal popularity that Isabella had won. She, Blanche, was made regent in her husband's will and her skillful administration during her son's minority was not of the showy variety. But now the fair Isabella who had done everything spectacularly well began to do everything spectacularly wrong.

If she had been completely her father's daughter she would have succeeded in submerging the woman in the queen. Philip the Fair, that silent and incredible despot, never allowed personal feelings (it is sometimes doubted that he had any) to sway him one inch from his course. Isabella seems to have been willing enough to do anything the Horn-owl of France would have done under the same circumstances, but she lacked the will and the desire to subordinate the woman in her.

The point where she allowed herself to go completely astray was, of course, in the murder of her husband. She undoubtedly was consulted in the decision and did nothing to protect the unfortunate Edward from his fate. It may have been, as history has unhesitatingly believed, that she and Mortimer hatched the plot against him. Aside from the fact that Mortimer did not hesitate to assume the direction of the foul deed, there is nothing to prove how the decision was reached. It must be borne in mind, moreover, that a rule of statecraft had persisted down the ages which taught that deposed kings were always a menace to the peace of the realm. It would continue to be recognized in later ages; and on several occasions, in the cases of Richard II, Henry VI, and the two princes in the Tower, the hand of assassins would be employed to rid the state of the threat they posed. The point is raised to indicate that Isabella and Mortimer were undoubtedly not the only ones in posts of authority who favored the elimination of Edward.

The queen acted throughout with an indifference which is hard to believe. If she had governed herself according to an obvious machiavellian rule she would have been careful to disassociate herself completely from the murder of her husband and then she would have cried aloud for the punishment of the perpetrators. From what is known of her character, she would have done this if her hands had not been tied. Mortimer, that blind and willful upstart, had plotted the death with a carelessness which seems to indicate that he considered himself beyond reach of reprisal or even criticism. He openly planted his confederates about the unhappy ex-king—Maltravers, Gurney, and the man Ogle, the latter an unknown but obviously a killer, perhaps from the dregs of London. There was never any doubt in the minds of the people of England that he had conceived and executed the crime. How did this affect the queen?

If she had been completely her father's daughter in this crisis, she would not have hesitated about throwing Mortimer to the wolves, to use a modern phrase. There could be no doubt whatever of his guilt. The countercharges and recriminations he might have indulged in would not have penetrated beyond the walls of his cell. If his ultimate visit to the Elms of Tyburn had been anticipated by three years, Isabella could have succeeded in washing her hands of any stain. The public, suspicious at first, could have been led in time to condone the favors she had showered on the greedy Marcher baron and to accept him as the sole villain of the piece.

But Isabella the woman was infatuated with her gentle Mortimer. She did not raise her voice after the assassination, either in grief or condemnation. Her questioning of the woman who embalmed the body of Edward may not have been prompted by a desire to get at the truth so much as by a morbid interest in the grisly details. She kept Mortimer at her right hand and took only the most elementary precautions to hide the fact that he was not a stranger to her bed. It was Isabella the woman who held the reins from that time on.

As has been stated earlier, Edward, the son, could not have been unaware of what was happening about him, but he kept himself carefully aloof in every way. He did not even adopt the pose of a Hamlet whose hands were tied. This need not be accepted as a criticism of the young king. His hands *were* tied and he was in no position at first to oppose the imperious will of his mother. He could not have protected his father from physical harm without being completely in control of the administration of justice. That he did not come forward to demand justice for the murderers of his father, no matter where the chips of guilt might fall, was so entirely contrary to the firm character he displayed later as king that only one explanation can be accepted. He stayed his hand to protect his mother, fearing that complicity on her part would be revealed by a searching investigation. He was in a position of unenviable difficulty.

But it goes deeper than that. Young Edward had need of his mother to achieve what had become even at that early stage the great and compelling ambition of his life. They were working together toward an aim which would have made Edward the greatest king of the Middle Ages and would at the same time have placed Isabella higher in historical perspective than the woman she strove to emulate, Blanche of Castile. The throne of France was the prize they hoped to win.

The claim that Edward would soon thereafter make to the throne of France was based on the fact that all three sons of Philip the Fair had succeeded each other as king and had died without legal issue. Isabella was the sole surviving child of Philip, and it seemed to both mother and son that his case had a validity above all other claimants.

Young Edward knew that there would be a great reluctance on the part of the French people to accepting an Englishman as their king, particularly as it would mean the union of the two crowns. That reluctance would be heightened if Isabella's reputation became tarnished in the meantime. They would hesitate to accept the son of a loose woman, even though she had been a daughter of France, the mistress of the man who had connived with her in the murder of her husband. Edward needed the glamorous Isabella of the past, the ill-treated daughter of Philip who was still remembered as beautiful, captivating, and brave. Edward's skill in diplomacy would be one of his strongest assets during his long years as king, and it can be taken for granted that even at this early age he took a realistic view of his position as a claimant to the French throne.

2

While the French dynasty, known as the house of Capet, withered and died on the vine, the whole world began to ask a question: Had the curse pronounced by the Templar Grand Master as he perished in the flames been directed at the family as a whole? Certainly some malignant fate seemed to be pursuing them.

Philip the Fair left four children: Louis, born 1289; Isabella, born 1292; Philip, born 1294; and Charles, born 1294. A healthy and handsome family.

He was succeeded by his oldest son, Louis, called Le Hutin, or the Quarreler. He came to the throne a healthy man of twenty-five and died in two years. His second wife, Clemence (he had quarreled with his first and put her in prison), was with child when the spectral arm of the old Templar beckoned to him. A son was born named John and died in four days. It was believed by many that the second brother, Philip, who was acting as regent, had substituted a dead baby for the real one. Many years later a pretender turned up who claimed to be the real John but did not convince anyone.

Philip V, called the Tall, was a poet and surrounded himself by minstrels and students. He dodged his fate for six years and then died without issue, aged twenty-eight.

Charles IV, called the Fair, reigned another six years and managed to get himself married three times in that period. By leaving daughters only, he became the last of the Capetian line.

Was it any wonder that Isabella and her son watched with mounting interest as the royal brothers died in such rapid succession? When Charles the Fair gave up the struggle against fate, the path seemed to have been cleared. Who had a better right to the throne than Isabella or, if the French persisted in their refusal to allow women on the throne, her son Edward? There was, of course, a document of doubtful application (according to English jurists, at least) called the Salic Law which had been invoked on several occasions to exclude women from the succession. It was a survival from the laws of the Salian Franks and was, in reality, a penal code. Its value consisted of one chapter dealing with private property, in which it was declared that daughters could not inherit land.

Edward was prepared to claim that, even if daughters were excluded from reigning because of this ban on owning property, the prohibition could not be extended to their sons when all other claimants were farther removed in consanguinity. His first step in presenting his claim was to write vigorously to Pope John XXII. He acknowledged that his mother had no right to the throne as "the kingdom of France was too great for a woman to hold by reason of the imbecility of her sex." But he claimed that he was the nearest male in blood to the deceased king, being related in the second degree of consanguinity. Philip of Valois, a nephew of Philip the Fair, who was his only serious rival, was related in the third degree. Pope John, who had been so helpful in the matter of Edward's marriage, does not seem to have done anything about this claim. The issue was laid before the Twelve Barons of France, who decided in favor of Philip of Valois.

The new king promptly sent instructions to Edward to appear before him and swear fealty for the duchy of Guienne and his other holdings in France. No attention was paid to this, and a year later, 1330, a more peremptory summons was sent. Edward was following a rule, even at this early stage, of submitting his problems to Parliament. Accordingly he sought the advice of the next Parliament to meet and was advised to obey the summons. A secret admonition was added that his method of doing homage should not prejudice his claim to the French throne; a proof that the idea of combining the two crowns found general favor in England. On May 26 of that year the young king sailed from Dover, leaving his brother John of Eltham as guardian of the kingdom.

The tendency in some historical records to blame everything indiscriminately on Isabella is noticed in statements that she favored her son's submission because it would be to the advantage of her cousin, Philip VI. This may be termed the third absurdity in dealing with the relations between mother and son. Philip of Valois had been a mere hobbledehoy when she left France to marry Edward II. It is not recorded that she saw anything of him during the time she lived in voluntary exile at the court of her brother Charles, and it is significant that the one member of the French royal family with whom she was on cordial terms was Robert of Artois. Philip VI is depicted as "hard and coarse" and was generally disliked. Why, then, would the queen work in his interests when her own were so clearly bound up in the claims of her son? She believed Edward should obey the summons, but for the same reason as Parliament, the fear that otherwise that hard and coarse king would confiscate all the French possessions.

3

The young king had been carefully coached. He came to Amiens Cathedral, where the act of homage was to be performed, and found that Philip of France had gathered a brilliant company to observe the ceremony, including the kings of Navarre, Bohemia, and Majorca. The choir of the cathedral, in fact, was filled with the nobility of France. The appearance of the young king was the cause of an immediate hush. Some of the spectators had seen him when he was at the court of France with his mother, but they were not prepared for the tall and handsome man who stalked proudly down the aisle. It has already been stated that Edward had an ostentatious side to him and that all his life he was fond of show. This was one occasion when he took every means to appear at his best.

He wore his crown on his head and his sword at his side, and he was garbed in a long robe of the finest crimson velvet, with the leopards of England emblazoned on it in gold. There were gold spurs on his heels. The French king had thought to array himself in what seemed regal state, with his crown and scepter and a robe of blue velvet, but he looked as dark and plain as a native warbler compared to the bird-of-paradise splendor of the young Plantagenet.

The English king proceeded to give his own version of the oath of homage. Reaching his place in front of the throne in the choir where Philip sat, he inclined his body in a bow instead of going down on one knee as was the custom.

"Philip, King of France," he declared in loud and clear tones, "I, Edward, by the grace of God King of England, lord of Ireland, and Duke of Aquitaine, do hereby become thy man, to hold the duchy of Guienne as duke thereof, and the earldom of Ponthieu and Montreuil as my predecessors did homage for the said duchy and earldom to thy predecessors."

Philip had difficulty in suppressing his surprise and dissatisfaction. He whispered to his chancellor, the Vicomte de Melun, to inform the English king that this would not suffice.

"Let my liege man know," he said, "that the only proper manner in which to approach me is to put off the crown and ungird the sword. He must do homage bareheaded and on his knees. His hands must be placed between mine and he must swear fealty to me *as his sovereign lord.*"

Edward's instructions had been precise and clear. He must not acknowledge Philip as his sovereign lord nor place his hands between those of the French monarch. He protested now that he owed simple homage only and not liege homage. On his return to England he would consult the archives and find to what extent his ancestors had bound themselves for their French possessions.

"Cousin," said Philip, "we would not deceive you and what you have now done contenteth us well until you have returned to your own country and seen from the acts of your predecessors what you ought to do."

"Grammercy, Sir King," answered Edward.

The oath was then administered and he responded, *"Voire"* (So be it).

Two years later letters were sent to the French king in which Edward declared that "the homage which he did at Amiens to the King of France in general terms is and must be understood as liege." Thus was the point between them resolved.

CHAPTER THREE

The Cloak of Iniquity

1

THE nation was slow to wrath where Isabella and Mortimer were concerned, but in time the cloak of their iniquity was torn from them. When Mortimer came with an armed retinue to the Parliament at Salisbury on October 24, 1328, and began to display all the airs of a dictator, the Earl of Lancaster refused to attend. He stayed at Winchester with a small force and was joined there by the two royal uncles and many other national leaders. Mortimer demanded an immediate adjournment of Parliament to allow him time to punish the absent barons. He then ravaged the lands of Lancaster, an operation in which the young king joined. The opposition barons met at London and formed an alliance to offer armed resistance to the pretentious favorite.

Mortimer, who seems to have had all the instincts of a modern gangster, decided to strike back boldly, selecting as his victim the mildest of the royal uncles, Edmund of Kent. Ever since the death of Edward II there had been strange rumors circulating in England to the effect that the deposed king had escaped and was still alive. Mortimer used this story to draw the unfortunate Edmund into a trap.

The story current at the time was, briefly, that Edward II had been able to escape from Berkeley through the kindness of the owner of the castle, Lord Berkeley, but that he was still in captivity. Before proceeding with the use made by Mortimer of this rumor, it will be interesting to explain that the story, backed by substantial evidence, came to light again in the nineteenth century. Documents were discovered which stated categorically that the escaped prisoner went first to Corfe Castle, then ventured over to Ireland, and finally reached the continent. He visited Pope John XXII at Avignon and was kindly received and kept as a guest for a fortnight. He then journeyed to Italy, where he remained the rest of his life. The only piece of contributory evidence is the report from Walwayn which was recovered from the records in recent years, as already explained, and which acknowledged that Edward's release had been effected but that he had been recaptured.

An article appeared in the *Fortnightly Review* of December 1, 1913, by Ethel Harter which described evidence she had found on a visit to Acqui in Italy. The castle of Melazzo stands on a hilltop within a short distance of Acqui, and in the entrance hall are two marble tablets on facing walls. The first tablet (translated from the Latin) states that:

Edward II Plantagenet, King of England, deposed from his throne by act of Parliament in MCCCXVII and imprisoned in Berkeley Castle, fled providentially from the knives of the assassins Sir Thomas de Gorney and Simon de Ebersford [clearly Sir Simon de Beresford, Mortimer's friend], hired by his inhuman wife Queen Isabel of France, was afterwards hospitably received in Avignon by Pope John XXII and after many adventurous wanderings remained concealed for two years and a half in this Castle of Melazzo which then belonged to the diocese of Milan.

The second tablet is of later date and contained an explanation of a document discovered in 1877 by the French historian Alexandre Germain in a chartulary among the episcopal archives at Magueloni (which do not carry beyond the year 1368) and which he published in a brochure in 1878. This document purports to be a copy of a letter written by Manuele de Fiesco (or Fieschi) in 1337 to Edward III.

In the name of God. Amen. I have written here with my own hand what I heard in confession from your father and have taken care to make it known to your Lordship. First of all, your father said that finding England raised against him at the instigation of your mother, he fled from his family and repaired to the castle on the sea belonging to the Grand Marshal, the earl of Norfolk, called Chepstow; later, becoming alarmed, he embarked with Hugh le Despenser, with the earl of Arundel and some others and landed at Glamorgan, where he was made a prisoner by Henry of Lancaster, together with the said Hugh and Master Robert de Baldock. He was then shut up in Kenilworth Castle and his followers were bestowed in other places . . . Finally he was removed to Berkeley. There, the servant in whose custody he was, after a time said to your father: "Sir, the officers . . . Gourney and . . . Ebersford are come to kill you. If it please you I will give you my clothing that you may more easily escape." So, at nightfall, thus disguised, your father came out of his prison and arrived without hindrance and without recognition at the outer door, where he found the porter asleep, and killing him took his keys, opened the door and went forth with the custodian.

The officers who had come to kill him, becoming aware of his flight and fearing the Queen's anger, and for their own lives, took counsel together and placed the dead body of the porter in a coffin and after extracting the heart, presented it cunningly, together with the corpse, to the Queen as if it had been your father's body. Thus the porter was buried instead of the King at Gloucester. When he left the prison your father and his companion were received at Corfe Castle by the Governor, Sir Thomas, without the knowledge of his superior, Sir John Maltravers, where he remained concealed for one and a half years. Hearing at length, that the earl of Kent had been beheaded for having asserted that King Edward II was still alive, your father and his companion, by the desire and advice of the aforementioned Thomas, embarked on a ship for Ireland where he remained for nine months. But fearing recognition there, he assumed the dress of a hermit and returned to England, landed at Sandwich, and still disguised, went by sea to Sluys. Thence he went to Normandy and from there through Languedoc to Avignon, where after giving a florin to one of the Pope's servants, he managed to send a note to John XXII who summoned him and entertained him secretly and honorably for over fifteen days. Finally, after considering many projects he took his leave and went to Paris and thence to Brabant and on to Cologne to do homage at the Tomb of the Three Kings; then from Cologne through Germany, he passed on to Milan through Lombardy, and from Milan he went into retreat in a certain Hermitage in the Castle of Melazzo . . . where he remained for two and a half years. Then, as war broke out and reached that Castle, he removed to the Castle of Cecima another Hermitage in the diocese of Pavia in Lombardy, where he remained for another two years in strict seclusion, living a life of penitence and praying to God for us and other sinners.

In testimony of the truth of all I have narrated here etc.

Manuele Fieschi, Papal Notary.

2

The Earl of Kent, who was with Isabella when she landed her army, had been repenting ever since the part he had played. He was a man of limited capacity, fickle and vain and easily led, although of decent instincts in the main. He had not recovered from the shock of the murder of the deposed king, his half brother, and he became interested at once in a story which a mysterious friar told him. The friar came to his house at Kensington and swore the devil had revealed to him in a dream that Edward II was still alive and being held in captivity at Corfe. To check on this strange story, the friar had gone to Corfe and had been shown through the bars of a cell a seated figure which resembled the former king greatly in stature and face.

The earl went at once to Corfe and demanded of the governor that he be allowed to speak with his brother, Edward of Caernarvon. The governor, a party to the conspiracy, did not deny that the deposed king was being held in the castle, but he declared firmly that he could not permit anyone to see him. The thought of his unfortunate brother being in such close confinement aroused in Edmund of Kent a deep desire to do something for him. He sat down and wrote a letter which he requested be handed by the governor to his prisoner.

Edmund then stepped deeper into the net by telling others of his conviction that the ex-king was still alive. He seems to have convinced Archbishop Melton of York and Bishop Gravesend of London among others. He was even imprudent enough to make speeches demanding that something be done in the matter. On March 13, 1330, he was arrested and at an inquest held before Robert Howel, the coroner of the royal household, he acknowledged the authorship of the letter written at Corfe. This confession was taken before Parliament, which was sitting at Windsor, and he was charged with treason. The weak and undoubtedly befuddled earl was led in to hear his sentence, clothed in nothing but his shirt and with a rope around his neck. He made an abject plea for mercy but was declared guilty and sentenced to death. The clerical offenders were released under sureties.

To prevent any measures which might be taken in his behalf, it was decided to carry out the sentence the next day. This decision undoubtedly was made by Isabella and Mortimer. Two explanations are given in various chronicles for the failure of the king to intervene. One is that Isabella kept him so beset with matters of state that he had no time to think of the fate of his uncle, with whom, it should be pointed out, he had always been on affectionate terms. This, of course, is beyond the limits of belief. An impending execution is an event which grips the emotions and cannot be dismissed lightly from the mind, particularly when the condemned one is of royal rank and close in relationship. The second explanation is that the young king was away when this happened. The weakness here is that Parliament was sitting at the time, and duty would have kept Edward at his post. The writ of execution would need the stamp of the Great Seal. Had Edward allowed possession of the Seal to his mother and Mortimer?

There is a bare possibility that he had ridden to Woodstock, where his young consort was expecting the arrival of their first child and that this cruel travesty of justice was put through in his absence. This contingency is not mentioned in any reports of the case. It is the only explanation which would exempt the young king from a share of the odium.

Early the next morning the earl was led out to the block. Word of what was happening had spread and a sense of horror had gripped the immediate countryside. This was even felt by the official headsman, who was not on hand when the white-faced prisoner reached the place of execution in the light of dawn. It was found that the executioner, to avoid any part in this terrible act, had run away. The unfortunate earl was kept beside the block while efforts were made to find someone ready to take the place of the absconding headsman. For long hours no one could be induced to wield the ax, and in the meantime the pallid Edmund, hoping against hope, believing to the very end that his nephew would intervene in his behalf, stood beside the instruments of death. Finally a prisoner under sentence of death was persuaded to perform the act in return for a pardon. It was nearly dusk when the head of Edmund of Kent rolled from the block.

It should be explained that Edmund had never been popular with the people, having some of the qualities of his brother, Edward II. He was of great personal strength and was prone to a display of magnificence in everything he did. The household he maintained was a riotous one, however, and he allowed his officers to plunder the people wherever he went.

Despite the ill feelings which had been engendered in this way, a wave of horror swept the country when the news of his death was heard. Realizing that they had gone too far, Isabella and Mortimer hastened to write the Pope in justification of what they had done and to address explanations to the people of the country. Their attempts at palliation of the deed were coldly received everywhere.

It is certain that this judicial murder convinced the young king that he could no longer delay in assuming full charge of the affairs of the kingdom. If he had needed any further pressure, it was supplied by the birth of his first child on June 15 of that year.

3

The royal manor of Woodstock had always been a favorite hunting lodge for the kings of England. Wychwood Forest stretched east and west from Woodstock to the borders of Gloucestershire, and as far back as the reign of Henry I a large part of it was enclosed to form a royal game preserve. A wall of stone was built around it, so high that the boldest of poachers would have hesitated at scaling it. There were trees of remarkable size within this park, and it is believed that some of the ancient oaks which stand there at the present time spread their majestic arms over glade and path in the days of the Edwards.

Woodstock is best remembered, of course, for the part it played in the romance of Henry II and the Fair Rosamonde. That Henry kept his beautiful mistress in a bower concealed in the garden maze and that she was discovered there by Queen Eleanor and poisoned is a story which has long been discounted. The truth is that the mistress was maintained in a small stone house just outside the stone wall. This became known as Rosamonde's Chamber and it was still standing, although in a state of disrepair, when King Edward took his bride there. Whether or not the young couple believed in the legend of the ball of silk thread which was the only clue to the whereabouts of the bower, they took considerable interest in the House Beyond the Wall and, being so happy themselves, sighed over the sad fate of the fair but ill-fated Rosamonde.

They were so much interested, in fact, that a few years later, in 1334, Edward gave written instructions that the house was to be repaired.

It was at Woodstock that Philippa presented Edward with their first child, a boy, a fine and healthy fellow of great beauty; so it was declared, although it is doubtful if more than a hint of later good looks can ever be discerned in the red and puckered face of a newborn infant. This much was certain: the boy was large and strong and particular stress is laid on the fine texture and solidity of his limbs as he was wrapped in his swaddling clothes. This was taken as an indication that the child would become a great warrior. There was no mistake in that prediction. The lusty child, held so lovingly in the arms of his flaxen-haired mother, was given the name of Edward and would gain great fame in the French wars and would be known forever after as Edward the Black Prince.

Perhaps it should be explained at once that this appellation had nothing to do with the appearance of the prince. He grew up as fair of hair and blue of eye as all the Plantagenets. It grew out of the fact that he wore black armor at the battle of Crécy, supplied by his father. It is not clear whether or not he continued to wear sable mail, but it seems likely that he did. It is true also that he used black in his heraldic devices.

Whatever the reason, the Black Prince he became and by that name he will be remembered as long as the history of England is read.

4

Small credence, either official or popular, was placed at any time in this rumor that Edward II was still alive. The scatteration of the reputed assassins was in itself an admission of guilt.

There was no thought that William of Berkeley had been an accomplice, although there did seem to be a neatness about his being away on affairs of his own at the exact time the foul deed was accomplished. He was summoned to appear before Parliament, where an inquiry was made into the responsibility for the appointment of Gurney and Ogle. Because Berkeley was a son-in-law of Mortimer and a brother-in-law of Maltravers, it was possible to believe that there had been a family compact at work. The selection of Gurney and Ogle was easily traceable to Mortimer, however, and so the inquiry did not uncover anything to the dishonor of the lord of Berkeley. The case was allowed to drag on, perhaps because silence and delay seemed desirable to the king, and at the end of nearly seven years Edward declared himself satisfied of Berkeley's complete innocence.

Edward did not display any great eagerness at any time to track down the guilty trio. This was understandable in the light of his fear that the complicity of his mother would be brought out into the light of day if the murderers were placed on open trial.

Ogle managed to get away at once. This is surprising because it was generally believed that, acting under orders from the others, he had been the perpetrator of the murder. Certainly Ogle would have made a convenient scapegoat. He had no knowledge to divulge of the guilt of higher-ups, his hands were still red with blood figuratively, and the purse of gold under his belt was still heavy. Perhaps he got away ahead of the hue and cry. At any rate, he was believed to have escaped to the continent and to have died there.

A determined effort seems to have been made to apprehend Gurney. Perhaps he had done some indiscreet talking or had placed his hand on an incriminating document. At any rate, they wanted him back. In 1331 he was located in the dominions of the King of Castile and was thrown into prison at the instance of the English king. A member of the royal household was dispatched to fetch him. There were long delays, however, and by the time the officer of the crown arrived, Gurney had made his escape. The following year it was learned that he was in Naples, and Edward sent a Yorkshire knight to bring him to England. Gurney was taken across the Mediterranean to one of the ports of southern France. His jailer decided then to continue the journey by land. Gurney riding chained to his saddle, they got as far as Gascony. Here the prisoner took sick and died.

The story was widely circulated that Gurney was beheaded at sea, but there was no foundation for this. The Yorkshire knight, after the death of his prisoner from natural causes, had the body embalmed and sailed with it from the port of Bordeaux.

No effort was made to bring Maltravers to justice, although his record was far from creditable. He had been an adherent of Mortimer and had been with him during his exile in France. Later he was an instrument in the judicial murder of Edmund, Earl of Kent. He had remained at Berkeley after the killing of the deposed king, ostensibly in charge of the body, until the burial at Gloucester in October of that year, although the other pair, Gurney and Ogle, had vanished in the fear, no doubt, that they would be made the scapegoats. After the death of Mortimer, Maltravers was condemned to death for his share in the killing of the Earl of Kent and no mention was made of his complicity in the death of King Edward. Being an adroit and glib fellow, he had succeeded, it seems, in convincing everyone that Gurney and Ogle had been wholly responsible. Before the sentence could be carried out, he escaped to Flanders, where he had extensive properties and where he proceeded to make himself most useful in maintaining friendly relations between England and the Flemish states. His wife Agnes, a daughter of Sir William Beresford, lived comfortably on her dower lands in Dorset and was even permitted to pay him visits. Maltravers played such a skillful role in international affairs that in 1340 Agnes received the royal permission to stay with her husband as long as she desired.

The Flemish alliances began to crumble and the suave Maltravers found himself in a precarious position, his life as well as his overseas possessions in jeopardy. He obtained an interview with Edward at this time at the port of Sluys and expressed a desire to give himself up and return to England. It must have been a strange interview, the meeting of the king and the man who almost certainly had given the signal for the death plot against the king's father to be carried out. There may have been a tacit understanding that this most tragic page in English history would be left unturned. He received Edward's promise of a safe-conduct to England for trial.

The king seems to have been partial to this controversial figure. In order to facilitate the restitution of his estates, Edward had the properties of Maltravers taken out of the jurisdiction of the Exchequer and reserved for the king's chamber. The settlement of the case was delayed, however, by the errands abroad on which Maltravers was sent. The estates were finally returned to him in 1352, and from that time on he lived in England in comfort, if not exactly in honor, and died in his bed in 1365.

And so nothing was done to make the guilty parties pay for this most terrible murder in all the annals of England.

CHAPTER FOUR

The Royal Hamlet Strikes

1

MORTIMER must have realized that the murder of Kent had been a grievous mistake and that public sentiment was rising against him. But he did not allow the knowledge to check his aggressions or abate his arrogance. Parliament was to meet at Nottingham that autumn, and he rode to attend it with his usual long train of knights and his Welsh mercenaries to strip the country of food as they passed.

What he did not realize at once was that the young king had at last decided to act. Edward had discovered the man he needed, a courageous and compatible friend in the person of William de Montacute, one of the younger barons. He was making his plans in concert with Montacute and a knight in the service of the latter, Sir John de Molines. They had to be very careful, for the king's mother was beginning to sense the danger surrounding her and had been taking minute precautions. It was arranged that Edward was to go into residence with them at Nottingham Castle. Guards were kept about the grounds at all hours of the day and night to prevent anyone from having audience with the king. As a further measure, all the locks on the castle gates and posterns had been changed and each night the keys were taken to Isabella, who slept with them under her pillow. Edward was allowed no more than four attendants. The earls of Lancaster and Hereford, the leading figures in the baronage, had been forbidden to find lodgings in the town and were compelled to seek quarters at some distance in the country. It was almost as though the guilty pair, knowing retribution to be close at hand, were throwing caution to the winds in a willingness to provoke it.

There must have been tension in the castle among the trio. Edward, in addition to evasions and omissions because of the course of action he had decided upon, was anxious to be with his wife and that great fine man child she had presented to him, and so was impatient of delays. Woman's intuition would tell Isabella that there was something on his mind and it would not be hard for her to make an accurate guess. Nothing that is recorded of Mortimer suggests that he had any subtlety about him, but every time his eye rested on Edward he would see the inevitable end to his day of power approaching and he would puff up with resentment and, perhaps, hatred. If the young king could only be trapped and dealt with as he, Mortimer, had disposed of Edmund of Kent! But that was impossible. The rancor in his mind fattened on the inevitability of his fall.

By some means, not disclosed, Edward had succeeded in establishing communication with his two chief aides on the outside. He got word to them of a secret confided to him by the castellan, William Holland. Centuries before, when the danger from Danish invasions was acute, a secret passage had been run underground from the keep to a cave in a woods some distance from the castle, to provide an avenue of. escape. It had not been used for several generations, but it was still open. It was arranged, therefore, that on the night of October 19 Montacute would bring a body of armed men through the passage and join the king at the stair leading up to the keep.

The plan worked perfectly. Edward made a pretense of retiring early but did not undress, and at the appointed time he made his way cautiously down the stone stairway, becoming aware in doing so of loud masculine voices from Mortimer's room. The boudoir-appointed despot was conferring with his immediate assistants and confidants. The young king knew, of course, that his mother occupied the adjoining apartment, and a sense of shame for the imputations to be drawn from this undoubtedly hardened his resolution for what lay ahead.

From below him he heard first a sound of shuffling and a faint murmur of voices. Then he was conscious of lights flashing on and off through the murk of the lower depths. Finally it was apparent that his helpers, torch in hand, were emerging from their crawl through the secret passage. He made out first the intelligent and confident face of Montacute and then the eager dark countenance of John de Molines. He raised a hand to them and then started to lead the way up to the higher stories of the keep.

The king, for reasons of delicacy, did not accompany his friends when they broke into the room where the voice of Mortimer was still to be heard in loud discussion with his officers. There were four men with him, Sir Hugh Turpington, Sir John Neville, Sir Simon de Beresford, and Sir John Deveril. Swords were drawn, but not in time to present any adequate defense. The first-named pair were killed in the brief and bitter scuffle and Mortimer succeeded in mortally wounding one of the king's men. It was a brief encounter and Mortimer was quickly disarmed and his arms bound behind his back.

At this point the queen mother broke into the room from the apartment she occupied. It was clear she had been asleep, for she wore little clothing and her hair was disheveled; and she was in a state of desperate dismay and fear. The young king had remained in the corridor, not through any disinclination to share in the struggle but because he preferred not to witness the plight of his mother. Isabella could not see him but she sensed his presence.

"*Bel filz, bel filz!*" she cried in tones of appeal. "*Ayez pitié de gentil Mortimer!*" (Fair son, fair son, have pity on gentle Mortimer!)

When she saw that no attention was being paid to her appeal, she said to Montacute, "Do no harm to the person of Mortimer, because he is a worthy knight, my dear friend and well-beloved cousin!"

But the days when men would run to do her bidding were over. They stared at her pale face and unruly locks with the curiosity inevitable when a queen, famous for her beauty, is seen in her shift. But they paid no attention to her appeals. Gentle Mortimer was rudely shoved into the corridor, where eager and far from kindly hands fastened upon him. The castle was filled with his adherents, but they seemed to have little sense of loyalty. No effort was made to rescue him. The knights who had ridden so obsequiously in his train outdid each other in their eagerness to forswear his allegiance. The control of the castle passed instantly into the hands of the king and his few followers. The keys were removed from under the pillow of the queen, and Mortimer was ensconced in a deep cell with armed guards outside the door.

Every step had been planned with the care Edward would later display in some aspects of his campaigns in France and had been carried out with boldness and decision. The English Hamlet had now made it clear that he had been biding his time for the right moment. That moment had come and gone, and England was free of the beautiful queen who had gone astray and the lover she had raised to power with her.

Nottingham, called at that time the cave city because of the softness of its sandstone, went mad with joy when Mortimer was led out a prisoner the next morning. It is recorded that a great shout went up in which the nobles joined with the mobs on the street.

The Earl of Lancaster was still the titular head of the baronage. Although a weakness in his eyes had finally resulted in total blindness, he is said to have been consulted by Edward when he arrived at Nottingham, or certainly by the closest adherents of the young king. The approval of the blind peer had been given to the contemplated *coup*, although he could not offer his personal participation. It may have been that he provided some of the men who followed Montacute on his long crawl through the underground passage.

When the earl heard the shouts of the mob in the streets, he had his servants lead him out, and when he learned the reason for the jubilation he joined in by shouting as madly as any tinker's apprentice. He is even said to have gesticulated with his arms to show how deeply he was moved.

History does not tell how Isabella traveled to London. She must have been taken there at once under adequate escort, but it seems highly improbable that she went with the king's party. Edward would spare himself as long as possible the frantic appeals she would address to him on behalf of her partner in usurpation. It may have been that he did not see his mother until the case of Mortimer had been disposed of at Westminster and the penalty exacted.

The prisoner was removed at once by way of Loughborough and Leicester and was lodged in the Tower of London on October 27. Edward must have been with the party, for he issued that same day a statement to the people of England that he had taken the government of the country into his own hands, a proclamation which was received with universal approval. If doubts about him had existed in the minds of people because of his seeming hesitation to assert himself, they were forgotten completely in the acclaim with which his act was received.

Parliament did not meet until November 26, and the first business before it was the disposal of the charges against Mortimer. It is not certain that the prisoner was brought before the house at any time, but this much is known: he was not allowed to make any plea or enter any defense. The peers were asked one by one what they thought should be done with him, and the response seems to have been a unanimous one. Mortimer must be treated the way he had dealt with Hugh le Despenser. He must die the same death *without delay or mercy*.

The charges laid at his door were many and lengthy, the most important being, perhaps, the allegation that he had "falsely and maliciously sowed discord between the father of our lord the king and the queen, his companion. . . . Wherefore, by this cause, and by other subtleties, the said queen remained absent from her lord."

This was the closest approach made to including Isabella in the legal proceedings. Pope John had written to Edward, urging him not "to expose his mother's shame," but this admonition was unnecessary. Edward was in every way striving to respect Isabella's position. This may have been due to filial affection or he may have been influenced by the need to protect her name in France. In any event, Mortimer was to bear the full brunt of the blame; which did not matter very much for there was evidence enough, as was said at the time, to hang a dozen men.

The second charge was the most damaging of all. He had procured the murder of Edward II. This was regarded as definitely proven by the carelessness with which Mortimer placed his creatures around the doomed king. The efforts of two of his companions, who died on the gallows with him, Beresford and Deveril, to disclose the whole story of the assassination were disregarded. It was believed, naturally, that the refusal to hear them was due to fear that Isabella would be involved. It is most unfortunate from every other standpoint that the stories were not taken down.

Other charges were as follows: He had usurped the powers of the council and regency. He had taught the young king to regard Henry of Lancaster as his enemy. He had procured the execution of Edmund of Kent, although that unfortunate member of the royal family had been innocent of any crime. (Mortimer is said to have confessed privately that he knew Kent was innocent.) He had appropriated to his own use the twenty thousand pounds paid by the Scots as one of the peace terms arranged at Northampton. He had assumed the airs and powers of monarchy. He had been guilty of great cruelties in Ireland.

The following day, clad all in black, Mortimer was taken through London to the Elms of Tyburn and was there hanged, drawn, and quartered. It is said that this was the first instance of an execution at Tyburn. That section of London Town would be used so often through later centuries that the name would become synonymous with the exaction of the supreme penalty of the law.

The body of this once haughty and unscrupulous man was allowed to hang on the gallows for two days and nights, for the public to see, although there could not have been much left of the frame after the carrying out of that ferocious and bestial sentence of disemboweling and quartering.

It is recorded that the despair of Isabella, when she realized the fate of her lover, was so intense that she suffered a spell of madness, but there is no official record of this. It may have been no more than a reflection of the inevitable rumors which would spread throughout the country.

CHAPTER FIVE

The Chatelaine of Castle Rising

1

IN the loneliest part of East Anglia stood Castle Rising, where a view could be had of the stolid waters on the south stretch of the Wash. About it were stunted trees and drifting sandhills, with no more than a touch of gorse on the high grounds behind, and over all the stillness of desolation. King William, called Rufus, had given eighteen acres there in fief to his cupbearer, William de Albini. The son of the latter, who was known as William-of-the-Strong-Arm and whose name is generally spelled in history as D'Aubigny, proceeded to make the manor into a castle of considerable strength. He built a massive square keep surrounded by walls three feet thick, with three high towers and the whole enclosed by earthen ramparts. Not content with thus achieving security, he put much fine ornamental work into the gatehouse and the great hall. It had a hint of importance about it which belied the dullness of the marshes and the continuously hostile gray of the skies.

Then William-of-the-Strong-Arm fell in love with the widow of Henry I, Adelicia of Louvain, who had been called the Fair Maid of Brabant, a very great beauty indeed with snow-white complexion and abundant fair hair. Adelicia had been selected as the second wife of Henry in the hope that she would supply an heir to replace the unfortunate Prince Henry who went down in the wreck of *La Blanche Nef.* This she failed to do, but after Henry's death she rewarded the devotion of William d'Aubigny by marrying him. He was an upstanding, honorable, and handsome knight and it is pleasant to record that the stork was kept very busy from that time onward. Adelicia brought seven children into the world in rather rapid succession, four of them sons. The upbringing of this happy brood kept the fair Adelicia so occupied that she seldom stirred from Arundel Castle, the family seat in the south part of Sussex. It was a rare thing for her to find any time for the northern home on which her husband had expended so much effort.

But now Castle Rising was to have a resident chatelaine. The advisers of the young king had convinced him it would be inadvisable to keep his mother at court and that, in fact, she should live thereafter in seclusion. Accordingly it was arranged, with Isabella meekly assenting, that all her dower lands and holdings were to be returned to the crown in return for a steady income, variously estimated at one to three thousand pounds a year. Two years later Edward wrote "that as his dearest mother had simply and spontaneously surrendered her dower into his hands, he had assigned her divers other castles and lands to the amount of two thousand pounds." The dower lands she gave up were mostly in Wales, including the castle of Haverford.

Isabella was thirty-six when she took up her abode at Castle Rising. She still retained some of her beauty, although the turmoil and the stresses of the last years had exacted their toll. It is persistently asserted in the chronicles of the day that she had fits of depression, verging on madness, which began with the events surrounding the execution of Mortimer. There is nothing to prove or disprove this, save that there are no recorded instances of doctors being in attendance or any outlay for drugs or cures. She settled down at once, in fact, to a rather peaceful and certainly a monotonous life. This vital woman who had been active and gay all her days under the admiring gaze of courtiers must have felt a sinking of the heart when she first saw Castle Rising, with no signs of life about it save a gull winging slowly across the Wash with a piteous mew to express the smallness of its hopes. But she accepted her lot with outward equanimity.

It has been stated that she was confined so strictly to the castle that it amounted to a lifelong imprisonment, but this is wrong. As will be shown later, she paid many visits to various parts of the kingdom during the years which followed.

The dowager queen was provided with a household in accordance with her royal rank. She had ladies-in-waiting and a train of knights and squires as well as droves of servants. She had in addition a treasurer, a steward, a seneschal, and grooms, a falcon-bearer, and minstrels to sing during meals and to ease with music the tedious hours. A record in the *Peerage of England* indicates that she had one fault only to find with her household, the appointment as steward of Sir John de Molines, who had been the first to lay hands on Mortimer on the night of the *coup* and who, moreover, had slain one of the attendants. His presence is said to have kept her in constant recollection of that grim occasion and to have contributed to her unsettled state of mind. It seems highly improbable, however, that Molines was there. Edward's gratitude to Montacute and in a lesser degree to Molines was so lively that he found many rewards and honors for both of them. The knight's advancement was so rapid that the post of steward to the queen would have been regarded as far beneath his just deserts. If he did hold the post, it could have been for a very brief space only.

Edward paid regular visits to his mother, some say once a year, others two or three times. From the small fragments of evidence which exist, it is a reasonable assumption that he continued to feel some affection for her. Sons are always proud of beautiful mothers. Edward had been with her continuously in France during his most impressionable years, particularly that exciting period when she went to Flanders to recruit an army and they visited the home of the Count of Hainaut and his four beautiful daughters. He had ridden with her up and down the Low Countries, observing how she won admiration and support and how contagious was her gift of charm. He had been with her on the adventurous landing and the rapid campaign by which the control of the kingdom had been won. None of this could ever be forgotten or forcibly erased from his mind, even during the soul-searing days when he realized his mother and Mortimer had plotted the death of his father, that she and her favorite were not only living together but were making costly mistakes in the administration of the kingdom which would soon be his. It would be impossible for him to forget the days of mortification when the bumptious, black-a-vised Mortimer had expected him to rise when he, Mortimer, came into the room; when he had to permit his mother's favorite to walk beside him evenly, step by step, instead of following behind as a subject was supposed to do; when, most galling of all, he had to submit to the hectoring, the criticism, of Mortimer and the demands made on him by that shortsighted upstart. But in time, as he observed how quietly his mother was accepting her new and humiliating role, it was inevitable that the black entries in the books would cease to affect him as much as the earlier and brighter memories.

Perhaps when he observed the monotony of her life at Castle Rising he regretted the necessity of keeping her there. One thing is certain: he demanded always that she was to be treated with the utmost respect. No mention of her was permitted in his presence unless it was phrased with decorum. She was referred to in official documents as "Madame, the king's mother," or "Our lady, queen Isabella." He was solicitous of her well-being and saw to it that supplies of the best game and fish were sent to her, as well as the delicacies to which she had been accustomed. She had a special liking for sturgeon, and although it was a costly luxury, the records are full of expenditures for barrels to be sent to Castle Rising. A barrel of sturgeon cost something in excess of two pounds.

It is on record that the dowager queen spent some time at Berkhampstead, while Castle Rising was being refitted for her use, that she went to reside at the royal castle of Eltham when she needed a change of air, which happened regularly. She went to Pontefract, and on at least one occasion she spent Christmas at Windsor with her son and his family. In 1344 she celebrated Edward's birthday with him at Norwich. She made numerous pilgrimages to holy shrines, particularly Our Lady of Walsingham.

She was never permitted to take any part in state matters, even when the chancellery or Parliament had knotty points to unravel rising from things she had done while acting as regent. In 1348 the King of France made the suggestion that Isabella and the dowager queen of France be entrusted with the mediation of a peace between the two countries. The suggestion found no favor with Edward. He had conceived a low opinion of his mother's judgment in matters of statecraft. Had he been inclined to the proposal, his advisers would have combated the idea warmly and unanimously.

The slipping of power through hands which have become accustomed to it is one of the hardest things to bear, which is why rulers were so prompt to stamp out anything that bore the faintest scent of treason and to punish with extremes of cruelty anyone who strove to reduce by one iota the royal power. It hardly needs saying, therefore, that Isabella could not have been happy in the seclusion forced upon her. But she does not seem to have complained. If she had loaded her son with reproaches on the occasions of his visits to her, he would soon have fallen into the habit of finding excuses for not going.

She had gambled for high stakes and had lost. That she was willing to pay the price of failure without recriminations is one item, though not a weighty one, to enter on the credit side of the ledger. One other item: she gave no cause for scandal during those last and lonely years of her life.

2

In the last phase of her life the dowager queen's mind turned to religious observance and to doing penance for the wicked deeds of which she had been guilty. She took the vows of the order of Santa Clara and during the final years she wore the traditional garb. The Poor Clares, as the members were called, lived lives of toil and self-sacrifice and poverty, nursing the indigent and tending the lepers and subsisting on charity. They never allowed time to ease their code, as had been done in the Franciscan order from which they sprang. It is certain, therefore, that the queen had been taken into the third order of St. Francis, which was open to lay penitents and did not involve any participation in the arduous duties of those noble ladies, the Poor Clares.

Isabella died at Castle Rising on August 22, 1358, at the age of sixty-three, a ripe age indeed for those days. She had lived in seclusion for twenty-eight years and had done nothing to justify criticism. She had expressed a desire to be buried in the church of the Grey Friars at Newgate in London. With the general willingness to find fault in every particular, some historians have surmised that this was due to the reception there of the mangled remains of Mortimer after his execution. There is doubt whether he was actually taken to Newgate or to a Franciscan church in either Shrewsbury or Coventry. In any event, his widow was permitted to remove the body for permanent interment in the Austin Priory at Wigmore in November 1331, a year after his death. It is highly unlikely, therefore, that this was the reason for Isabella's choice. A better reason is that she would be permitted burial at the Grey Friars in the robes of the order; a precaution against the prying fingers of the devil, whose interest the erring queen had good reason to fear. Queen Marguerite, the second consort of Edward I, was Isabella's aunt and was buried there, as it was through her munificence that the edifice had been raised. This may have been a reason for Isabella's desire.

She had made the request that the heart of the murdered Edward should rest on her breast, and this is accepted as the last evidence of her hypocrisy. Isabella always spoke her mind and did whatever the selfishness or malice in her prompted her to do, but a hypocrite she was not. It seems more reasonable and kindly to assume that after twenty-eight years to think over the past she had a sincere desire to do this much penance.

Edward saw to it that his mother was buried with proper pomp. The streets of London which the funeral procession would cross were thoroughly cleaned. The body was laid in the choir at the Grey Friars and a magnificent tomb of alabaster was raised over it.

It is asserted in some careless records that Isabella's second daughter, Joanna, Queen of Scotland, survived her by a few days only and that they were interred in Newgate on the same day, the two biers being placed side by side at the high altar. A moving picture, surely; but with one flaw. Queen Joanna did not die until 1362, four years after her mother.

There was little mourning for the deceased queen. If Edward or any member of the royal family attended the services, there is no record of it. The interment was quiet, and this was to be expected, for Isabella of France would be called in history the most wicked of English queens. The best tribute that could have been paid her was that she was not wholly bad. Perhaps—who knows?—a witness to this paused beside her bier to drop a tear to her memory: the little Thomeline who had been saved from the sad fate of so many war orphans and had been sent by the fair queen to London to be raised.

CHAPTER SIX

The Embers Rekindled

1

THE peace with Scotland did not last long.

Robert the Bruce had died on June 7, 1329, in his castle at Cardross near Dumbarton. There had been some comfort for him in his last days, although he was not to know that the Pope on June 13 of that year issued a bull confirming his sovereignty in Scotland with the right of anointment at coronation. Cardross was less grim than most Scottish castles. It had brightly painted rooms and glass in the windows and a great tester bed from which the dying monarch could look out at the hills of the country he had fought for for so long.

Before dying Robert laid injunctions of various kinds on his followers. They were to swear fealty to his young son David. Randolph of Moray was to act as regent during the boy's minority. That he chose Randolph and not Douglas as regent was not because of any preference. He had a still more personal and binding duty to lay on the sturdy shoulders of that fine knight whose skill in arms was so great that his face, after a lifetime of cut and slash and come again, carried not so much as a single marring wound. The king had always wanted to go on the Crusades, and this was now impossible. On the Black Douglas, therefore, he laid this sacred duty: he was to go in his king's stead, carrying the heart of the Bruce to be buried by the Holy Sepulcher.

For all the leaders of the Scottish people, he left a set of rules and regulations to be used in the defense of the land which became known in later years as Good King Robert's Testament. These wise directions, which had grown out of all the long struggles by burn and glen, were put into verse by a native bard, the first lines of which ran:

On foot should be all Scottish war,
By hill and moss themselves to ware:
Let woods for walls be; bow and spear
And battle-axe their fighting gear.

It was thus made clear that the lessons of war had been truly learned by the great Scot. The mounted knight, with shining cuirass and jingling spurs, would never win Scotland's battles. It was on the sturdy foot soldier that reliance must be placed.

The Black Douglas set off gladly to carry out his dead leader's injunction. That he was unable to do so was the fault of the times. In all the capitals of Europe there was talk of more crusades, but no effort was being made to fight them. The clock of crusading zeal had finally run down and become silent. Douglas could not undertake a one-man invasion but he decided to do the next best thing, to lend his sword in the wars in Spain against the Moors. His eagerness for a clash with the bronzed warriors who had conquered and held a large share of Spanish territory led him to get too far in advance of his troop. The Moors wheeled about and cut him off.

The Douglas was a great fighting man from the mop of black hair on his brow, which had gained him his name, to the tips of his steel-clad feet. He had, moreover, the fatalistic attitude of most true soldiers. Looking ahead at the jeering, racing horsemen flourishing their curved scimitars in the air, he knew that this was the end. He must go down as befitted the race and the family from which he sprang.

Unclasping from his neck the silver casket in which the heart of Bruce was enclosed, he threw it far ahead of him into the ranks of the eager Moslems. Shouting in his high, lisping voice, "A Douglas! A Douglas! I follow or die!" he urged his steed against the oncoming horsemen.

That he succeeded in cutting his way through the van of the enemy was made clear after the battle was over. Pierced by a multitude of wounds, his body lay on the ground above the silver casket.

Someone has written, "First in the death that men should die, such is the Douglas's right." Not the valiant Sir James himself, however. There was nothing vainglorious about him. He did his fighting in the field and not around the roaring fires where men sat of winter nights to recount their deeds.

The heart of Robert the Bruce was carried back to Scotland by one of the survivors, where it was ultimately buried beneath the altar of Melrose Abbey. The right was granted to the family of Douglas to carry a bleeding heart with a crown on their shields thereafter.

The peace which had seemed so final before Robert the Bruce died was not to stand against the conditions which now developed. Philip, the first of the Valois kings of France, seemed set on bringing about war with England, and the English were not averse to upholding with their arms the claim of Edward to the French throne. Over all of western Europe hung the gathering clouds of the Hundred Years' War. Scotland's treaty obligations with France made it impossible for her to stand aloof; and so it was to start all over again, the marching and countermarching back and forth across the border, the harrying of adjoining lands, while hate mounted again in the people of both races.

2

More fighting with the Scots was inevitable but what set the embers to blazing was the appearance in England of Edward de Baliol, son of the John who had reigned briefly over Scotland and who will be remembered best by his nickname of King Toom Tabard. That ineffective man had been dead for many years, and his son Edward had been living on the estates left him in France. The death of Robert the Bruce seemed to present an opportunity for the Baliol claims to be asserted again, and Lord Beaumont arranged an audience at Westminster between King Edward and the Scottish claimant. Baliol, who was as spineless and as lacking in patriotism as his father, offered to do homage to Edward as his liege lord if he were helped to regain the throne.

Edward was guilty of a skillful example of double-dealing at this point. Openly he rejected the Baliol offer and declared his intention of abiding by the treaty of Northampton. He even went to the extent of ordering that Baliol's adherents should be prevented from crossing the border. Secretly he encouraged Baliol to proceed with his plans. He knew the time was ripe for action. King David was a boy and Randolph of Moray, the valiant regent, had died and his place had been filled by Donald, Earl of Mar, who was known to be an indecisive and rather feeble individual. There was in England the nucleus of an army of invasion, the holders of lands in Scotland who had been awarded their confiscated estates by the treaty but had not yet received them.

With the stealthy connivance, therefore, of the English king, Edward de Baliol got together an army of sorts. As his chief lieutenants he had three brisk noblemen, the aforementioned Henry de Beaumont, the Lord Wake of Liddell, and Gilbert de Umfraville. They recruited a force of something over three thousand men and sailed northward from the mouth of the Humber. Landing in Fife, they surprised the army of the Earl of Mar at Dupplin Moor and gave him a sound drubbing. The victory was so complete that the opposition to the Baliol claims broke up and he was crowned as Edward I of Scotland at Scone on September 24, 1332.

Edward of England had to come out into the open then. He met the new monarch at Roxburgh on November 23 to receive homage as the overlord of the land. Thus young Edward found himself in the same position that his grandfather had occupied on several occasions, the openly acknowledged sovereign lord of Scotland.

But a Baliol was always a weak reed on which to lean. Edward of that ilk allowed himself to be surprised at Annan by a hastily organized army of Scottish patriots under the command of Archibald Douglas, a younger brother of the great Black Douglas. He was the first of that long line of remarkable men who held the title of Earl of Angus down through Scottish history, including Archibald the Grim, that great old Archibald called Bell-the-Cat, another familiarly known as Archibald Greysteel, and finally that handsome fair-haired Archibald who married Margaret Tudor and became a stormy petrel throughout the reign in England of Henry VIII. This particular Archibald was not an astute general, but he succeeded in smashing the Baliol forces and chasing their leader back over the border. The pursuit took the Scots well down into Cumberland.

Edward now realized that he would have to take control himself. Declaring that the Scots had broken the treaty (and writing to that effect to the Pope, because he would have had to pay a fine of twenty thousand pounds to the pontiff if he had been guilty himself), he moved with a large army into Scotland. He came face to face with the bold but overly rash Archibald Douglas at Halidon Hill to the west of the town of Dunse.

The military career of Edward III would seem to consist largely of getting himself into a position of extreme jeopardy, as at Crécy, and then extricating himself by great courage and resolution and the employment of brilliant battle tactics. It was so at Halidon Hill, his first victory of any great importance. He was in peril of being surrounded by the enemy and hemmed in by natural obstacles. East of his army was the sea and Berwick with its Scottish garrison, eager to emerge and join in against him. South of him lay the Tweed, and to the north the army of Douglas, which far outnumbered the English.

Douglas, overconfident, having learned little or nothing from Good King Robert's Testament, led his men down over marshy lands to attack the English. Edward had benefited from experience sufficiently to put his reliance in his archers and foot soldiers. The English army was drawn up in four battles, with the bowmen on the flanks; everyone afoot, even the young king himself, who stood in the van. Flushed with his victory at Annan, the brave Douglas charged across marshy land to strike the English all along the line. The Scots ran into a rain of arrows from the English longbows which decimated their ranks. Their losses were so heavy, in fact, that they fell back in a complete rout. The Scottish nobles had led their clans into the battle. Many of them fell victims of the deadly fruit of the English yew, and it was said afterward that no leader was left to recruit or lead a body of men.

Berwick surrendered at once. Such of the nobility as were still alive gave in their submissions. David, the boy king, had to flee, reaching France ultimately, where he was welcomed by King Philip. In the treaty which resulted all of Scotland south of the Firth of Forth was ceded to England, the counties of Roxburgh, Peebles, Dumfries, and Edinburgh—the whole, in fact, of ancient Lothian. Baliol came back to climb on the throne for the second time.

At the age of twenty-two Edward III had completed the work of his grandfather.

Edward de Baliol must have been the original Humpty-Dumpty, for all the king's horses and all the king's men could not put him back permanently on the throne from which he kept tumbling.

The second disruption of his inglorious reign occurred when Andrew Moray, who had been with Wallace in the first days of Scottish resistance, emerged from semi-retirement and took over command of the northern forces. Moray marched through the Highlands and drove far enough south to raid Cumberland, sweeping the inept Baliol before him. It became so difficult to gather up the pieces, stick them together, and take this puppet king back for seating again on this difficult throne that finally the English king despaired. Baliol then agreed to surrender the kingdom into Edward's hands by delivering to the English monarch a portion of its soil along with the golden crown. In return for this abject betrayal of his country he received a payment of five thousand marks and a pension of two thousand pounds a year for the balance of his life. This weak son of an ineffectual father lived until 1367 on estates granted to him near Wheatly in England. He left no issue, which may be considered a fortunate thing for Scotland, as the old dynastic dispute thus came to an end. It is recorded that he devoted his declining years to the pleasures of hunting.

CHAPTER SEVEN

The Great Emergence

1

THERE was a man in Bristol in these days, a citizen of modest consequence, having no title and no great wealth and no trace whatever of noble blood in his veins, who nevertheless was destined to have his name more widely remembered down the centuries than all the Plantagenets combined, with all their chancellors, statesmen, generals, and bishops thrown in for good measure. This was because his name had been applied to a most useful article that he manufactured. His name was Thomas Blanket.

This circumstance is recalled because it is part of the story of an emergence which was taking place in England and equally in all parts of what was called the civilized world. It was not long, a mere matter of a century or two, since men had shaken off the ignorance and lethargy of the dark ages and had begun to look into their inner selves, to paint, to compose, to sing, to inquire into the first elements of science and to demand political rights, above all else to build; to raise high into the sky the most magnificent of cathedrals with the tall spires which seemed a symbol of their desire to reach the truth. Now this emergence was taking a new form. The ways of living were changing and beginning to bear a traceable resemblance to modern conditions. This had started with an expansion of trade and the acquirement of wealth among those who had never known the meaning of ease, the men of business and their workers.

Some historians are disposed to give much of the credit to Edward III, calling him the father of English commerce. This is allowing him too much praise. Edward, if the truth must be told, took little interest in such menial matters. He was a soldier king, holding fast to feudal rights and feudal wealth, which came from ownership of the land. This new wealth he did not understand,

and approved only so far as it provided him with new sources of crown revenue.

It is possible his marriage to Philippa had something to do with it. It had brought England into closer contact with the lands from which she came, where the stout burghers taught the world a lesson, defending themselves and their walled cities and their weaving machines from the armies, first of France and later of Spain. Edward began to see the need for England to share more fully in the profits of trade; but of real concern for the prosperity of the common people, he had little or none.

Consider first where commerce stood in the first stages of Edward's reign. England's exports were almost exclusively of raw materials and her imports entirely of manufactured goods, which put her in the inferior position of an agricultural nation. Statistics of 1354 place the exports at £2,123 38s 5d and imports at £38,383 16s 10d. Wool represented thirteen fourteenths of the export total, and the share collected by the crown was £818 46s 12d, or nearly 40 per cent. It was no wonder that the term "woolsack" was applied in course of time to the seat occupied by the chancellor in the House of Lords.

It was fortunate for England that she produced so much wool and of such superior quality. Only Spain had anything to offer of a corresponding excellence, and it may have been because of the merino sheep brought to England by Eleanor, the Castilian queen of Edward I, that English sheep now carried such fine wool on their broad backs; that, and the rich grazing lands that the island kingdom had for them. Another reason undoubtedly was the existence of one hundred Cistercian monasteries throughout the country. The Cistercians had broken away from the Benedictines when they saw that the members of the older order were getting lax in their devotions and too hearty at their meals. The Cistercian monk divided his time between his devotions and working in the fields. They were great sheep raisers, and it seems certain that they studied breeding and grading and gradually raised the standards in England. They probably were the first to cross the English breeds with the Spanish merinos. Although they were against the accumulation of property and refused to accept rents or tithes, wealth nevertheless began to reward their industry, as witness the beautiful monasteries they built at Fountains, Rievaulx, Tintern, and Furness. In the larger English monasteries the monks used lay brothers to help in the field work, sometimes as many as three hundred. The lay member was never ordained but lived beside the choir monks, without taking part in the canonical offices.

The earnest and hard-working Cistercians were called the Gray Monks, and wherever they established themselves the hillsides soon became dotted with the backs of cropping sheep. They were allowed few opportunities to speak among themselves, but there must have been evenings after their one meal of the day (a pound of bread apiece, a dish of beans, and sometimes a piece of cheese) when they gathered in the chapter houses and earnestly debated the proper care of the flocks. The records show that in 1280 the Abbey of Meaux alone had 11,000 sheep. The figures fluctuated, of course. A low year was 1310 when Meaux had no more than 5,406.

That so much of the wool thus raised could be sold was due to the needs of the cities of Flanders. The Flemish people manufactured the finest textiles in Europe and they had little wool of their own. They depended almost exclusively on England. At certain periods when English kings experimented with costly changes in trade relations, the Flemish looms would be silent. What would have happened to England if the weavers of Ghent and Bruges had found a substitute for wool? A dire speculation, indeed.

Credit is due Edward III on two counts. He encouraged the bringing over of weavers from Flanders (one detects here the hand of the fair Philippa) to teach the English how to make cloth. Some of them settled around Norwich and some went to points in the west. Master Thomas Blanket started his business in Bristol with a staff of foreign workers. Edward remained rather consistently on the side of the Policy of Plenty, as free trade was called, as against the Policy of Power, or protection.

But this had to do with the purely national side of the subject. The emergence, referred to above, was a matter of world-wide change. It was the result in large part of vast developments in international trade and commerce.

On the exact spot in London where the Cannon Street station stands, there was a very large building with an extensive courtyard and a most handsome hall which was known as the Steelyard. It was a busy spot, tenanted by heavy, sober-eyed men of North German extraction who were acting as representatives of the Hanseatic League. The name of the establishment came from the fact that a steel bar was kept for the weighing of goods. The Hanseatic League was a spectacular development of the theory of union in trade which had begun with the guilds. It was made up of the

trading ports on the Baltic Sea and affiliated cities, including
Lübeck, Hamburg, Rostock, Riga, and Danzig, as well as Thorn
and Kraków in the east, Wisby and Reval in the north, and
Göttingen in the south. Despite the fact that each member city
was within the domain of one of the northern nations, the league
did not recognize national considerations. It had been organized
to control the trade of the Baltic, and this it succeeded in doing
for centuries, in spite of attempts at interference by kings, princes,
and grand dukes. The wealth of the league was enormous, its
power absolute.

2

The feudal system would die hard. Forced upon England by the
Normans, it was so profitable and gratifying to the nobility that
they fought against any change. Although some of the kings
strove to reduce the strength of the baronage, it was not in the interests of the commonality, but to gather more power into their
own hands. To king and noble alike the feudal system was the
bulwark, the unscalable wall about the citadel of privilege.

A few of the kings who would follow this constellation of the
Edwards were brilliant rulers. Many, however, were unable to lead
and too stubborn to follow. Some would be cruel, some sly, some
dull. Even the best of them, with perhaps one exception, were unwilling to relinquish a jot of what they considered their privileges.
A few would even proclaim the divinity of these rights.

But to return to Edward. He was a king of contradictions, consistent only in the grandiose scale of his ambitions. He was more
than extravagant, he was lavish: lavish in his personal life, in his
court; lavish to his friends and his mistresses. Above all else, he
was lavish in the diplomacy with which he sought to gain his
ends. He would go to Flanders and Germany with a bounty
granted by a complaisant Parliament and would spend it all in
reckless subsidies to the rulers of the Low Country states to join
him against France. The diversity of Flemish interests broke up
his first attempts to unite them in a firm alliance. After each
rebuff he would come back to Parliament with empty pockets and
no constructive gains to report. Apparently he was a good advocate, for Parliament would always advance him what he wanted,
generally a tenth of all revenue. Once he asked for a ninth and
got it. This meant a ninth of church revenues, of baronial in-

come, of the stock of merchants; and one horse in nine, one cow, one sheep, and a green bough stuck in one sheaf in nine in every harvest field, which the king's tax collector would come and take away.

Like all strong-willed kings with unenlightened ministers, he often did arbitrary and ill-considered things about the trade of the country. He laid restrictions on the Cistercians which led to a curtailment of their valuable activities. He put restrictions also on trade which had no purpose but to increase the state revenue and which had to be repealed when the disastrous results became apparent. He confiscated to the crown all cloth that his *aulnagers* found to be deficient in measurements. He interfered with the system of fairs, even granting them to towns, which compelled the merchants of London to close their shops and use temporary booths at the seat of activities. If Edward was the father of English commerce, he was an inconsiderate and careless parent.

The subsidies that Parliament granted the lavish king, the untying of the national moneybags, the planting of green boughs in so many sheaves of grain did not suffice for his ambitious schemes. He borrowed money in many quarters and in huge amounts.

If he had paused to reflect, Edward would have been resentful of the thoroughness with which his French grandfather, Philip the Unfair of France, had demolished the order of the Knights Templar. The knights had been sound bankers, and it had been customary for the kings of England to visit the huge headquarters of the order on the banks of the Thames when they needed loans. But now, thanks to Philip, the bearded knights had dropped from sight, the buildings had passed into other hands, the *beauséant* no longer waved in the breeze. So Edward, who never knew the day when he did not need money, had to look elsewhere. He went, of course, to the Italian bankers, the Society of the Bardi of Florence, and the Peruzzi family of the same city, which had opened branches in England to take the place of the Templars. Even with the vast sums they loaned him, he was not content. He borrowed also from the leading figures in trade in England, most of all from a remarkable man of whom much will be told later, one William de la Pole.

The Peruzzi family loaned the king in 1337 the sum of £11,732 for the war with Scotland. This was just the beginning, for in the following year Edward acknowledged an indebtedness to them of £28,000. Later this total was advanced to £35,000, some of which had been advanced "for urgent matters and for the king's secret business beyond the seas."

The Society of the Bardi were perhaps a little more careful and astute. Beginning in 1328 they promised to find him £20 daily for the expenses of the king's household and to give him £16,140 for a period of 807 days, the loan to be protected by a lien on customs receipts. The king continued to go to them when the flatness of the royal purse threatened to thwart him in his magnificent designs. He was loaned £100 for the funeral of his brother, John of Eltham, £300 as a gift for his still dearly beloved Philippa, £97 and some shillings and pence (arrears for nearly three years) for the upkeep of the royal menagerie of lions and leopards in the Tower of London.

But the Italian sources of financial aid were not more helpful to the king than the colossus of the north, this bold, far-seeing, shrewd Yorkshireman, the aforesaid William de la Pole. If there had been a tendency in those days to give extravagant titles in trade as is done in these modern times when we have Napoleons of this and Caesars of that, William de la Pole would undoubtedly have been called the Midas of the Midlands or the Wizard of Wool. This remarkable merchant produced in 1339 the funds which Edward needed for his campaign in France of that year, the colossal sum of £76,180.

These figures are so far above the financial horizons of previous reigns that they serve to demonstrate more vividly than anything else the sudden upsurge in the world. The winds of trade were blowing high and strong and men were beginning to dream wondrous dreams. If Edward had seen fit to employ this strange deep prosperity (deep because it went right down to the roots of society) in strengthening the polity of the state instead of tossing it away on the bloody battlefields of France, his fame would have been everlasting and his place in history higher even than the reputation he was to win at Crécy and Poictiers.

It may have been due to the beginning of this new wealth and the resultant improvement in living conditions that sumptuary laws were introduced at this time. The holders of feudal power and wealth could not tolerate, it seemed, the growth of what might become an aristocracy of trade without an effort to maintain social barriers. Sumptuary laws were intended to check extravagances and the moral decline which grew out of them, also to prevent the sinful adornment of the body in foolish fashions, such

as the toes of shoes which curled so high that they had to be tied
to the ankles. This type of law had originated far back in history,
in the days when paternalism was rampant in Greece. Houses
were not permitted then which required more than the ax and saw
in building, and women were not allowed to adorn their bodies in
expensive clothes, although an exemption was granted to prosti-
tutes.

In the laws which were passed at the stage of history with
which we are dealing there was a tendency to depart from the
original purpose and to impose restrictions solely for the maintenance of class distinctions. In Scotland it was declared by law that
no man under the rank of baron was permitted to have baked
meat and pies. Tasteless stews were deemed good enough for commoners. In England servants of the lower rank were forbidden to
spend more for clothing in the course of a year than three shillings fourpence. No servant was allowed more than one dish of
meat or fish a day. The wives of prosperous citizens were not permitted to wear dresses made of silk.

Fortunately the people of England were not slavish in their
obedience to these irritating laws. The merchant's wife clothed her
plumpness in silk and laughed at the lawmakers. If a maidservant
had spent her yearly allowance on clothes and craved a new rib-
bon for her hair, she bought it. In Scotland many bellies belonging to Scots of low degree were filled with good baked mutton in
spite of King Jamie I, who had passed the law against it. But the
purpose back of these snob decrees stuck in the craws of the good
burghers and their wives. Writing centuries later, Adam Smith
summed it up with the words, "the highest impertinence and
presumption in kings and ministers."

3

The semi-renaissance in England was reflected in a more general desire for education. There had been grammar and chorister
schools long before the Conquest, but these were conducted by
the chancellors of the great churches. The spread of knowledge
among the lower classes was limited largely to portions of the
country within the sound of cathedral bells. It was in the matter
of university training that the fourteenth century demonstrated a
sudden surge of interest.

A degree of antiquity has sometimes been claimed for Oxford

which the facts do not bear out. The town at the junction of the Thames and the Cherwell, nevertheless, had for two centuries been collecting colleges around the administrative center growing out of the activities of one Robert Pullen and was in a position to respond to the sudden desire of the nobility and the wealthy classes to aid in further progress.

Baliol College had been established in 1263 by the one-time King of Scotland. His widow had carried on the design, the original statutes being issued in 1282.

The first practical response to the public desire was given in 1314 when Walter Stapledon, Bishop of Exeter, who has been encountered already in these pages and most creditably, founded Exeter College, providing a foundation for twelve scholars, eight to be drawn from Devonshire and four from Cornwall. The scholars sent up under this arrangement were accommodated at first in Hert Hall, which had been erected around the turn of the century by Elias of Hertford.

Merton College began a little earlier, the estates of Walter de Merton having been turned over in 1264 for its maintenance. The scope of this institution would be enlarged in 1380 by the foundation provided by John Wyllyot, who had served as chancellor of Merton from 1349. Still later, in the last quarter of the century, the Merton library would be built on the gift of William Rede, Bishop of Chichester.

Even Edward II, whose interest in education had never been remarked, founded Oriel College in 1326. The idea originated, it seems, with Adam de Brome, his almoner. The college was dedicated to St. Mary the Virgin and did not receive its final name until twenty years later. A tenement called La Oriela had occupied some of the land which the college finally pre-empted for its own use.

Queen's College, started in 1340 by Queen Philippa's chaplain, Robert de Eglesfield, was always to be associated with royalty. The Black Prince was entered as a student, but there is nothing to indicate that he ever attended a lecture. However, Henry V was at Queen's and it has been the rule for the consorts of English kings to serve as patronesses. Most of the students came from the north of England, and the Eglesfield scholarships were limited to natives of Cumberland and Westmorland.

The same tendency to create colleges where ambitious young men could acquire learning was apparent at Oxford's great competitor, Cambridge on the Cam. Here Peterhouse College was founded in 1284 by Hugh de Balsham. Pembroke College (from which emerged a stream of great graduates) was begun in 1347 by Mary de St. Paul, the widow of Aymer de Valence, who had figured prominently in the Scottish wars. Trinity Hall was founded in 1350 by William Bateman, Bishop of Norwich.

The students who allied themselves with these halls and colleges were undoubtedly outnumbered at this time by those who did not receive nominations to scholarships but went to Oxford or Cambridge with little in their pockets. Generally these poor students found places with one of the many groups who rented small houses under the management of semi-learned officials known as *principilators*. They slept and had their meals in these halls, most of which were given wildly facetious names, at a cost which sometimes did not exceed a penny a week. They enrolled for lectures under men of some recognized worth. The lectures were held generally in the vestibules of churches or in rooms at inns, the students sitting on the reed-strewn floors. For warmth in winter, there being no fires, they would squat close together, knees hunched up to provide a resting place for ink and quill and parchment. Most of them were content with the Trivium, which consisted of grammar, rhetoric, and logic, as well as Latin. Some of the more ambitious of them attempted to scale the heights of the Quadrivium, where arithmetic, geometry, astronomy, and music were also taught.

Classes would begin as early as the hour of prime (six o'clock!), which meant that the students would be up at dawn and indulging in hasty toilets in front of the community *skeel*, a wide wooden bucket. The scholastic labors would continue throughout the day, but the students would have plenty of energy left for frolics in the town after dark, carried on in taverns and on the streets at the expense of the somewhat more sober citizens. There was always an open state of war between Town and Gown.

It will be seen from this that the national conscience was awakening to the need for education, a steady flame which would burn undiminished through all the centuries ahead in which dynastic wars and religious persecution would nearly succeed in plunging the world back into the darkness.

In writing of Oxford, the memory is revived of a very great man who was at the university around the middle of the thirteenth century, Roger Bacon. He occupied a room in a small stone tower at Folly Bridge, and it was there, perhaps, that he had discovered the explosive possibilities in a combination of saltpeter, sulphur, and charcoal, which later was called gunpowder. He did not realize that he had thus uncovered the secret of a weapon which would revolutionize warfare, but others had stumbled on the fact in time to have gunpowder play some part in the wars of Edward III. A writer named John Barbour is responsible for the statement that cannon (called at the time *cracys*) were used by the English king in his 1327 invasion of Scotland. There are records of the existence of small cannon in the Tower of London in 1338, together with a barrel of gunpowder, and that in the same year in Rouen there was an iron funnel called a *pot de feu* which would spray forth metal bolts. That the government of England had been awakened to the potentialities of this new weapon was evidenced in an order issued by Edward in 1346 to buy up all the saltpeter and sulphur in the kingdom. There is nothing in the records, however, to prove that cannon were planted around Edward's windmill at Crécy or concealed in the hedges at Poictiers.

CHAPTER EIGHT

The Merchant Prince

1

Sir William de la Pole, the great Yorkshire magnate, was a man of parts. History deals only with his exploits and has little to say about the man himself. Clearly he was of good address and suavity of manner, for he conducted many missions requiring tact and polish, and he was for a number of years head of the Staple in Antwerp. He came up, however, in the wool trade, where fortunes could be most easily made, and there must have been something bluff and genial about him to stand on good terms with the hard-bitten raisers of sheep. The greatest breeders were the Cistercians, whose lands extended far and wide around their splendid monasteries in the north country, Fountains, Furness and Rievaulx, and it would be necessary for him to stand well with the heads of the order.

Pole's father, also Sir William, and a man of prominence and wealth, is given as of Ravenser Odd and Hull. It was at Ravenser Odd that the son learned the wool business, but all his life he was counted a citizen of Hull.

Hull was called originally Wyke-upon-Hull, standing at the junction of the Hull and Humber rivers. Its importance as a seaport had been augmented mightily since Berwick had become the center of continuous warring and thus was cut off from peacetime activities. It was Edward I who obtained the town from the monks of Meaux and changed the name to Kingston-upon-Hull, although it was never called anything but Hull. It stood on a low plain and needed high dikes all about it. There was a saltiness and an independence about its people, as characteristic as the north country burr on their tongues.

There were two brothers, Richard and William, and they were gaugers of wine for the royal household as well as dealers in wool.

When Queen Isabella had successfully invaded the country and removed her husband from the throne, the brothers advanced her the sum of two thousand pounds to pay off the Flemish mercenaries and at the same time loosened their purse strings to the extent of four thousand pounds to assist in the financing of young Edward's first and unsuccessful campaign against the Scots. This was held against them after Mortimer was executed and Isabella was packed off to Castle Rising. They were deprived of their offices as gaugers of wine and remained under a cloud for several years. Richard moved to London at this point, but William, deciding no doubt to devote himself to what he knew best, remained in Hull and waxed still more prosperous in buying wool and selling it for export.

He built himself a great house on Hull Street, now called the High Street. It may not have been as large and impressive as the one his son raised later, which was called Suffolk Palace, but William had, at any rate, a gatehouse three stories high, with a shield above it with his coat of arms, three leopard faces on an azure fess. To the left of the gatehouse was the great hall, capable of entertaining a king. The inner court was surrounded by many connected buildings, and around it all stood a high wall.

In 1332, when Edward was being drawn into another Scottish adventure by the ineffectual Edward de Baliol, he stopped at Hull on his way north. For a matter of twenty years or more the wealthy citizens had been building themselves fine homes in Hull Street. Among the dozen or more who had elected to congregate together were Sir Robert de Drypol and Sir Gilbert de Alton, and many others who had grown rich in wool. The roof of William de la Pole's home stood high above all the others, and the honor of entertaining the king fell to him. He did it so magnificently that Edward, who enjoyed ostentation as well as any man alive, was both pleased and impressed. By way of return, he knighted his host and changed the chief magistracy of the town to a mayoralty, making Pole the first to hold that office.

The talk over the wine (an official gauger would be certain to have the choicest) must have been stimulating. By the time he took horse for the north, the king had reached a decision. He had seen much of William de la Pole before, of course, but this had been his first opportunity to talk with him man to man, free of ministers of state and the magnates who watched every royal move and gesture with distrustful eyes. Here was a man who knew how to make the money which was always needed so badly at

Westminster. The king said to himself: "This is the one I have been looking for. Not another of these tiresome bishops who mumble in Latin and don't know, I suspect, what a bill of lading is. I shall have now an instrument to my hand, a means of making all the money I am going to require before I am through with my cousin of France."

It is not mere speculation to say that these thoughts were in Edward's mind as he sipped the rich wines and listened intently to the straightaway talk of the practical Yorkshireman. Shortly afterward he put a new policy into effect. When he returned to England after winning a great naval victory, he inveighed, according to John Lord Campbell in his *Lives of the Lord Chancellors*, "against the whole order of the priesthood as unfit for any secular employment and he astonished the kingdom by the bold innovation of appointing a layman as chancellor."

It was not Pole who was selected for this experiment but a soldier named Sir Robert Bourchier. The reason almost certainly was that Edward had reached the conclusion that Pole would be more useful in producing wealth than in handling it after it had been made. He, Edward, could always find a chancellor, but where would he find another servant with the authentic Midas touch? Certainly, however, the long and close connection between monarch and merchant, which was to last for many years, dates back to this meeting under William de la Pole's own roof.

Pole served as mayor of Hull four years. During this time he represented the city in Parliament and he went to Flanders several times to conduct negotiations with the free states as the king's representative; with success, quite clearly, for the king continued to employ him in ambassadorial roles. In 1335 he was appointed to the post of custos to prevent the export of gold and silver and was made receiver of customs at Hull, in return for which he agreed to pay the expense of the royal household at a rate of ten pounds a day. The next year found Edward in desperate straits. His plans were maturing for the great war and his money was flying right and left. In 1338 Pole made two loans, huge ones for a private citizen, the first for eleven thousand pounds and the second for seventy-five hundred pounds. In return for these and still other advances not specified, he received twelve royal manors in the north country, including the lordship of Holderness, and certain houses in Lombard Street, London. Edward promised as well to find husbands among the nobility for Pole's two daughters. Whether it was due to royal matchmaking or because the daughters were fine catches, it is on record that Blanche, the elder of the two, became Lady de Scrope of Bolton and Margaret became Madame Neville of Hornby, Lancashire.

It was soon after this that the ambitious king found himself so involved in debt that he pawned his crown to raise a sum of fifty-four thousand florins from three rich citizens of Mechlin. Needless to state, it was the period of Pole's greatest usefulness to the king, who was turning more and more to the Yorkshireman for assistance. By midsummer 1339 the loans made by Pole had reached the total of £76,180, as already stated.

And this brings us to the time when the wool magnate would learn something about the ways of kings who get themselves involved in financial difficulties.

2

Kings did not make satisfactory debtors in these days. They had too much power. Consider what would happen a hundred years later when Charles VII of France, who as dauphin had failed to go to the assistance of Jeanne d'Arc, found himself deeply in the debt of Jacques Coeur, the fabulous merchant prince of that day. Coeur had financed the final campaign of the Hundred Years' War which resulted in the expulsion of the English. King Charles did not have the money to pay him back and so it occurred to him (or it was whispered in his ear by advisers) that he could get out of the difficulty by having Coeur arrested and charged with various criminal and treasonable offenses. This was done and the fabulous Jacques, owner of departmental stores all over France as well as a fleet of merchant ships, was convicted on the most trumpery and absurd list of indictments ever concocted in that or any other country. Whether this possibility had occurred to Edward is a matter of pure speculation, but tracing the course of the two cases leaves a conviction of the closeness of the pattern. There was this difference: Edward did not pursue Pole with the savagery which Charles of France and the vindictive nobles around him showed to the merchant who had climbed too high. Coeur was sentenced to death, escaped from his prison, and reached Rome, where the Pope of the day appointed him to the command of a fleet against the Turks. He died on the island of Chios before having the chance to offer battle.

None of this is to be found in the sudden breaking off of relations between King Edward and his creditor. This is what happened. Edward returned to London toward the end of 1340 in a mood of sullen resentment. Everything was going wrong. The Flemish allies were still shilly-shallying, the crown officers at Westminster were lax in raising and dispatching the troops and supplies needed on the continent. The money he had been borrowing here, there, and everywhere had melted away as soon as he got his hands on it. He was dissatisfied with everyone.

His first step was to have the constable of the Tower of London arrested on the charge that the place was not guarded with sufficient vigilance. That same night orders were issued "privily" for the arrest of William de la Pole, his brother Richard, Sir John de Pulteney, and a number of others. The blow fell without warning. Pole had gone to bed, believing himself secure in the king's favor, although he had undoubtedly been wondering about the security for the enormous loans he had made the king. He was rudely awakened from his slumbers and told that he was under arrest. On what grounds? The king's pleasure, declared the officers of the law. He was taken to the Fleet prison and consigned to a cell.

In 1337 Pole had been commissioned, together with one Reginald de Conduit, to buy wool and sell it abroad for the king. There had been no indication at the time that Edward had been dissatisfied with the results. Perhaps someone in his train had whispered to him that his two agents had kept too large a share of the profits for themselves. This was made the basis of the charges brought against the Yorkshireman and on which he was convicted in the Exchequer and sent to Devizes Castle in the west. The next year the case was aired in Parliament and the conviction of Pole was annulled. Nevertheless, he was kept in confinement and the year following he was back in the Fleet. Finally on May 16 he was released after being mainperned (a form of medieval parole), to be available to the treasurer and barons of the Exchequer from day to day for a close study of his accounts.

In the meantime King Edward had been riding the high horse of his displeasure with all his official servants. He was using two brothers at the time in the most important offices under the crown. John de Stratford, Archbishop of Canterbury, had also acted at one time as chancellor, but now his brother, Robert, Bishop of Chichester, held the secular office. It was the conduct of the two brothers which evoked the king's angry invective against having priests in secular office. Perhaps they had been lax and easygoing and they had made it clear that they did not favor the king's "secret business," in other words the pending war with France. Robert de Stratford was dismissed from office in favor of Sir John Bourchier, a rough and relatively untutored soldier, and thrown into prison. Stratford decided to get himself out of trouble as soon as possible. Making his submission, he was released and returned to his clerical office.

But the archbishop, John de Stratford, was made of sterner stuff. He was, it became apparent, a strong admirer of one of his predecessors, the sainted Thomas à Becket; so much so that during the closing years of his life he built a chantry in the parish church of his native town to the memory of Becket. When Edward issued a proclamation charging him with malfeasance in office, the archbishop wrote a resounding denial which he sent out to be read in all the churches of the land. When Parliament met at Westminster to act on his conduct in office, he put in an appearance in his pontifical robes, with the cross of Canterbury carried before him and a train of clerical attendants trailing in his wake; a second Becket and just as determined to assert himself. When he was refused admittance, he took up his stand in Palace Yard and refused to leave. Officers of the crown came out and declared him a traitor to the king.

"The curse of Almighty God," cried the archbishop, "and of His blessed Mother and of St. Thomas, and mine also, be on the heads of them that inform the king so. Amen, amen!"

This was a dangerous situation, for St. Thomas was venerated throughout the whole Christian world, and the parallel between the two archbishops was too close for comfort. The case was postponed a year and the charge was then annulled.

But Pole had no clerical immunity to stand behind. Although the charges against him had been annulled by Parliament, it was not until 1344 that his own lands were restored to him; but not those he had received from the king "by gift or purchase." In other words, the king received back the properties he had turned over to the merchant against the loans.

Pole's moments of glory as one of the chief advisers of the king had come to an end. It had been an expensive lesson, but he was not being pursued, at any rate, with the ferocity shown Jacques Coeur when the latter was thrown from office. And up in the hills of England the sheep runs were still thickly tenanted and so there was always the valuable wool which had been the basis of the Pole fortunes. Quietly the Yorkshireman, like the good cobbler, returned to his last.

Later he was taken back, partially at least, into the king's favor; although it is not on record that he advanced any more loans. In July 1345 he was summoned to London to treat with certain "lieges" on "arduous affairs of the realm" and the following year to attend a council "to speak of secret things." His advice, obviously, was still worth having. In 1355, in return for "his great services in lending money to the king," he was made a knight and banneret. In March of that year he surrendered certain manors to the king and in August he executed a release to Edward from all debts up to the preceding November 20. In 1360 Pole and his wife were granted some escheated lands in Yorkshire "in consideration of his great services to the king." Escheated land came from someone who had been found guilty of a state offense; this grant to the Yorkshire merchant, therefore, cost Edward nothing.

3

Sir William de la Pole died in 1366, but in the intervening years he had been quietly and profitably at work. He left four sons and much property to divide among them. His eldest son, Michael, had already begun to carve the great career which would make him richer and more prominent than the father. Michael served through the whole of the French wars, first under the Black Prince and then under the king's second son, who was known as John of Gaunt. He became in time chancellor of England and was made Earl of Suffolk.

This was accounted the main accomplishment of stout Sir William. He was the first merchant prince of England to found one of the great noble families, the earls and later the dukes of Suffolk. He lived long enough to have a glimpse of the honors his descendants would win.

CHAPTER NINE
The Inevitable War

1

THE Hundred Years' War was fought, supposedly, over Edward of England's claim to the throne of France. Actually it was the inevitable outcome of the conditions which existed. It had to be fought sooner or later. Ever since Eleanor of Aquitaine married Henry II and took with her that huge stretch of territory in France, which included nearly all of the western and southern provinces, the French had lived for the day when they could drive the English back over the Channel. They created continuous trouble along the frontiers of the fiefs still held by the kings of England.

A further incentive had arisen through the close trade ties between England and the Low Countries. The French had been looking with covetous eyes at the Flemish wealth and had seen to it that Count Louis of Flanders, sometimes called Louis of Crécy, who exercised a nominal suzerainty over the great cities, was favorable to them. England could not allow the French to become predominant in the best market they had for their wool and had been striving for years to form a firm alliance with the Low Countries.

Finally there was Scotland and the alliance between that country and France.

All that was needed to set the fire ablaze was a pretext, a blow from either side, a bold step, a rash statement. The citizens of London had appointed captains and had set themselves to drill in the expectation of a French fleet landing on the Kentish coast. The Channel Islands were fortified and garrisoned, and new forts were built on the Isle of Wight. King Edward seized the funds which were being held in the cathedrals for a new crusade. Parlia-

ment, in a continual state of flurry, granted the subsidies which
Edward kept demanding.

To make sure of the good will of the Flemish people, Edward
sent a commission headed by the Bishop of Lincoln to discuss
terms. The commission traveled in great state and tossed gold
about in the best tradition of the king. With the bishop were a
number of young English knights who wore red patches over their
eyes and answered questions with cold silence. The explanation of
this singular conduct was that the young men had sworn to wear
the patches and to refrain from giving any information, even on
such trivial matters as the weather, until they had performed some
worthy deed of arms on French soil. The mission made a strong
impression by their liberality but received no promises.

Half of the Low Countries were vassals of the German emperor, Ludwig of Bavaria. Queen Philippa's oldest sister, Margaret, was married to Ludwig and so it was arranged that the two
monarchs should meet. That momentous event occurred at Co-
blenz, where two thrones had been raised on the market place, in
the presence of a vast congregation of the nobility of Europe.
Standing before Ludwig, who was holding his scepter and had a
drawn sword suspended over his head by a mailed knight, Edward
put into words for the first time in public his pretensions to the
throne of France.

Philip of Valois, declared the English monarch, was with-
holding from him the duchy of Normandy and the province of
Anjou. Not only that, he was keeping unjustly *the very crown of
France itself*.

Ludwig was glad enough to have any charges made against
Philip of France, who had refused him homage for the fief of
Provence. He expressed his willingness to make Edward vicar-
general of all imperial holdings on the left bank of the Rhine.
That, of course, was what the English king had been angling for,
as it placed the Flemish cities under his charge.

The two monarchs parted, nevertheless, on bad terms. The emperor had been affronted by Edward's refusal to swear fealty to
him (which would have meant kissing his foot). For his part, the
English king felt he had been treated as an inferior by being asked
to stand before the emperor. The matter of the vicar-generalship
remained a promise and never did reach the signing stage. Edward
returned to England, having spent a fortune in gifts and bribes
and all to no good end.

For a very long and very anxious period of time the rulers of

England and France were like a pair of knights on horseback at opposite ends of a tilting course, lances in rest, waiting tensely for the signal to set their steeds into motion, one against the other.

There were two men who were very important to Edward at this stage. The first, Jacob van Artevelde of Ghent, was honestly convinced that the conflict was inevitable and believed there would be no lasting peace in Europe until after the clash. The second, Robert of Artois, had a grievance against the French king. A suave, soft-spoken, wily knight, he had set himself the task of convincing Edward he could win the French throne for himself.

Jacob van Artevelde belonged to the *poorter* class of Ghent, the burghers who had acquired wealth over several generations and frequently lived in retirement. Over the door of his tall stone house in the Calanderberg, near the Paddenhoeck or Toad's-Corner, there was the family escutcheon, and he was allowed to sign documents with a seal carried on a gold chain. What is more, he had a coat of arms, three hoods *d'or* on a sable shield. He had inherited a cloth-weaving business from his father (Ghent had thousands of looms operating in busy times) and the name derived from the village of Arteveldt and certain *polder* lands reclaimed from the sea. It has been assumed that his wife brought him a flourishing plant where metheglin was brewed, a beer sweetened with honey; and on this account he was sometimes inaccurately called the Brewer of Ghent.

An upstanding man of ample girth, with the strong features and broad brow so often encountered in Flemish portraits, he had done nothing to distinguish himself until he reached his fiftieth year. Then the sorry plight of the Flemish cities, caught between the feudal might of France and the need to cultivate the friendship of England, brought him to the fore. Bands of unemployed weavers were parading the streets of Ghent while their families starved in the houses packed so tightly in the crooked alleys of the town, when the word circulated among them that a citizen of some note saw a way to solve their difficulties and that he would explain the next day at the monastery of Biloke. It was Jacob van Artevelde who rose to address them the following day; and almost from the first moment they listened to him without clamor or dissent, recognizing him at once as the leader they had been waiting for so long.

His plan was simple and logical. None of their great cities was capable of standing alone against the French or the English, but

if they could clear up the petty jealousies and factional differences
which kept the Low Countries broken into small states, their
strength would be multiplied many times over. What was needed
was an alliance between the cities of Flanders and those of Holland, Brabant, and Hainaut. United, they would be strong enough
to defy the French, who wanted to raze their massive walls and
smash their drawbridges and fill up their moats, and at the same
time demand of the English, as the price of their neutrality, a
commercial treaty which would keep them supplied with wool at
all times. Only by a policy of neutrality and the power to enforce
it could the Flemish people continue to exist between the grind-
stones of France and England.

The defensive strength of the city was based on the maintenance of trained bands in each section under the command of a
hooftman and over all a captain-general who was called the
beleeder von der Stad. The good burghers, convinced that Jacob
van Artevelde was the leader they needed, appointed him at once
to the post of *beleeder*. He was to have a bodyguard of twenty-one
men wearing distinctive white hoods. His detractors later declared
this body to be a gang of hired thugs he had organized himself.
The answer was that four assistants were appointed at the same
time and each had a white-hooded escort, ranging down in number from eighteen to fifteen.

The power of France, represented by Count Louis, took steps
immediately to break up this dangerous movement launched in
Ghent. Soon thereafter the sentries placed in the high steeple of
St. Matilda's Church saw bands of horsemen reconnoitering on
the plains outside the walls and wearing the livery of the count.
Immediately a bell called *Roelandt* tolled from the belfry of the
church. A couplet, raised on the rim of this huge bell, explained
its function:

Rolad am I hight [named]; when I call out, there is fire;
When I bellow, there is trouble in the Flanders-land.

Old Roelandt bellowed in real earnest on this occasion and the
citizens hurriedly assembled on the *Cauter*, an open space called
the Place of Arms, in the heart of the city. Van Artevelde, the
cloth merchant turned civic leader, took hold of the situation as
though he had been born a commander of troops. He set the
trained bands in motion and led them out through the gate in the
massive walls. He not only sent the horsemen of Count Louis to

the rightabout, but he marched straight to Biervliet, from which town the hostile cavalry had come, and drove out all the troops of the count.

Great leaders have a way of emerging from obscurity when they are badly needed. Flanders was in need of a Jacob van Artevelde. He had heard the call and he stepped out from the looms where the family fortunes had been made and laid aside the ledgers in his countinghouse. No one disputed his right, not even the nobility of Ghent, most of whom kept a finger in the commercial pie and were classed as *buyten-poorters*. He became so powerful that a plot to assassinate him was hatched on orders direct from Philip of France. That worthy successor to Philip the Fair wrote to Count Louis, "not on any account to let this Jacquemon Darteville act the part of a king or *even live*." The plot was nipped in the bud and the only effect it had on the stout burghers of Ghent was to increase the white-hooded bodyguard of the new *beleeder* to twenty-eight men.

Conscious of the solidarity of the communes behind him, Van Artevelde called a meeting of representatives from the cities of Ghent, Bruges, and Ypres in the monastery of Eeckbout. He had no difficulty in convincing them of the wisdom of armed neutrality. A board, made up of three representatives from each city, was appointed to proceed with the organization of all the Low Countries according to his plan.

Armed neutrality was not what Edward had wanted, but it was the second-best thing. It left him free, at any rate, to deal with France.

The other man, Robert of Artois, might with good reason be called the villain of the piece. He was either that or a victim of the malice of Philip of France. While he was a boy his grandfather was killed at the battle of Courtrai in 1302 and, as Robert's father was already dead, the title and lands were given to his aunt, Mahaut of Burgundy. The decision was the work of Philip the Tall of France, who was married to Jeanne, Mahaut's daughter. Mahaut had produced papers from the Bishop of Arras in which it was asserted that the grandfather had wanted her to succeed in lieu of his grandson. When Mahaut died, leaving the title to her only child, the aforementioned Jeanne, Robert protested bitterly and brought in evidence from a woman named La Division to the effect that a charter from the old count, granting the title to him in the first place, had been stolen by the bishop. There were fifty witnesses to swear that the old man had favored his grandson.

But Philip of Valois, who had succeeded to the throne in the meantime, had a way of dealing with cases of this kind. The woman La Divion was put to the torture until she confessed that the charter was a forgery and then she was burned at the stake. With the key witness thus disposed of, evidence was produced that she had poisoned Mahaut on instructions from Robert. The latter had to fly for his life and crossed the Channel in disguise. He had been a companion of Edward's when they were boys and he went straight to Windsor. The king received him as an old friend.

In the meantime, piling one charge on another, the French king was claiming that Robert and his wife, who was Philip's own sister, had tried to take his life by the oldest trick in the bag of witchcraft, by naming a doll after him and then inserting pins in the frame.

Artois had made many enemies, being proud and quick of tongue, but few people believed the charges brought against him. Certainly Edward did not put any credence in them. He was in a frame of mind to accept anything against the occupant of the French throne, which he was now firmly convinced was his by right. Artois, well entrenched at the English court, took advantage of the opportunity to preach action. "The French throne is yours, take it!" was the advice he poured into the ears of the king. He told Edward of a prediction made by King Robert of Naples, who believed in astrology, that Philip of France would always be defeated in battle if he, Edward of Windsor, led his troops in person against him. "He knows it is true and he trembles!" declared Artois.

This kind of talk served to bolster the resolution of the English king.

2

There does not seem to have been a formal declaration of war. The two countries drifted into hostilities after many starts and stops. In 1335 Philip of France openly declared his intention of helping the Scots, and about the same time he expelled the English seneschals from Agenois. Edward wrote letters to his allies in which he styled himself King of France. The influence of Jacob van Artevelde had resulted in the expulsion of Count Louis from

Flanders. The latter had, however, established his troops at Cadzant under the command of his illegitimate brother Guy. Cadzant was situated between the Zwyn and the mouth of the Scheldt, in a good position to pirate English shipping.

"We will soon settle this," declared Edward, and sent a fleet under the command of Henry of Lancaster (the son of blind Henry Wryneck), with Sir Walter Manny as his chief lieutenant and adviser. Manny will be remembered as the young Hainauter who had come to England in the train of the royal bride and who was known at that time as Sir Wantelet de Mauny. He was a brave and loyal knight and had climbed so high in the service of the English crown that he was now guardian of the Scottish frontier and admiral of the fleet north of the Thames. Edward, who was always generous with those about him, had given the valiant Sir Walter the governorship of Merioneth County and the custody of Harlech Castle. He was still a bachelor knight but later would be permitted to ally himself matrimonially with the royal family, as will be told in due course.

The English ships sailed boldly into the nest of dikes and sandbanks around Cadzant and, after a sharp encounter, succeeded in capturing most of the men of Count Louis, including his brother. This was the first blood drawn in the great war which would last, with many interruptions and truces, for one hundred years.

A truce of two years was then arranged while the two monarchs eyed each other and professed a desire for peace. They were preparing feverishly for war behind their backs. During this breathing spell Edward proceeded to build up his fences in the Low Countries. Jacob van Artevelde had completed his federation and brought all this strength over to the English side. Before doing so, however, he made it clear to Edward that the time for straddling the issue was over. If he intended to fight for the crown of France he must state his purpose unequivocally, and to this Edward agreed during a conference held in Brussels on January 26, 1340. He quartered the lilies of France on his banner with the leopards of England.

It should be made clear at this point that Edward's diplomacy, although cleverly conceived, was involving him in continuous difficulty. He believed in playing one country against another and in trying to take advantage of them all. He pitted the German emperor against the Pope at Avignon because of a feud which had developed between them. He slyly countered Flanders with Brabant. There was civil war in Brittany and he played a crafty game of chess with the rival claimants. No one could ever be entirely sure where Edward stood, and the result was a lack of unanimity and zeal on the part of the allies he was bringing into the field against France.

This was unfortunate, because Van Artevelde had done his work well. The great cities of the Netherlands, including Brussels, Antwerp, Ghent, Bruges, Ypres, Louvain, and many more, had come into the English camp. Their suspicions resulted in a determination to control the initial point of allied strategy.

Philip commanded the Scheldt River with the fortress of Cambrai on the upper branch and Tournai on the lower, thus breaking communications between Flanders and Brabant. The allies, on that account, made it a condition that the war must begin with the capture of Tournai, thus compelling Edward to open the campaign with an attack by water. Anticipating this move, the French king gathered a huge fleet at Sluys. There were one hundred and forty ships of war in the fleet and an enormous number of smaller craft. In command were two Breton buccaneers, Hugues Kiriet and Nicholas Babuchet, and the most noted of sea fighters of the day, the celebrated admiral Barbenoire from Genoa.

The English preparations were made with great care. The Cinque Ports promised twenty-one of their own best ships and the Thames fleet offered twenty-six, to be ready by mid-Lent. The western ports were to furnish seventy ships of one hundred tons and upward. A proclamation was made that any man who had been pardoned for a crime must proceed to the nearest port and volunteer for service, on pain of facing the original charge again. This brought them down in droves, with their packs on their backs and clothed in the rough shirts and drawers which constituted the garb of the sailor. There was equal activity in getting equipment, "espringals, arblasts, actines, blasouns and purkernels." The espringal was a catapult, the arblast the same, the actine something in the way of a clumsy nautical instrument; for the rest, the spelling is suspect.

The fleet was ready by June 10 when the king arrived at Ipswich, accompanied by the queen and a party of ladies who were going to Ghent and would have the escort of the fleet. There was much shaking of heads among the naval authorities over the prospect of meeting the great French armada with such a rag-tag-and-bobtail collection as the English fleet. Sir Robert Morley, who had been made admiral, and John Crabbe, a Scot who shared the responsibility, said they would take the ships out if the king so ordered but that it would mean death for all of them. The king paid no heed to such lugubrious advice. He boarded the cog *Thomas*, a strongly built vessel with rounded bows, capable of taking much punishment, though not comfortable to sail in. Between two hundred and two hundred fifty vessels followed the *Thomas* out to sea, a strange conglomeration indeed. But make no mistake, this was to be one of the memorable moments in English naval history.

About noon on June 22 the English saw behind a projecting ridge the sails of the French fleet. The rigging of the enemy seemed to tower into the sky and the masts were like a deep forest. The English commanders—except the king, who seems to have been an incurable optimist—conceded with glum nods that the odds would be nothing short of desperate. They were still more convinced of this when a reconnoitering party returned from a hasty survey. The French, it was reported, had many ships of gigantic size, and on board they had at least thirty thousand men, mostly Normans, Bretons, Picards, and Genoese bowmen.

The winds were against them, the tide was out; there was nothing the English could do that day. At dawn the next morning they got under way, the *Thomas* well in the van. There would have been more confidence in the attacking ships if they had known of the grievous, the terrible, error the French had made. Brushing aside the advice of the three experienced naval commanders that they break out into the open where they could smother the English with an excess of power, the French had elected to fight the battle as though they had dry land under their feet. With sandbanks on each side of the bay, the fatuous Gauls were convinced their flanks could not be turned, which seemed to them the most important consideration. Accordingly they had drawn up their fleet in four lines of battle across the mouth of the harbor, *linking the ships together with metal chains!* They had filled the watchout turrets with Genoese crossbowmen, believing them the greatest archers in the world.

Most of the English captains were old salts of long experience and they slapped their thighs in delight when they saw the mighty French ships manacled together like galley slaves. "If one takes fire, they will all go up in flames!" was the general opinion. On the decks of the English vessels, and all the way up into the rigging, were Saxon archers equipped with the first longbows the French had seen. Their bronzed faces were covered with confident grins, particularly when they saw from a distance the Genoese attaching their intricate crossbows to the planking under their feet as an aid in winding them up for use. Three gifts from the feather of the gray goose of England would be hurled into the French ships for every arrow that came back.

The English ships sailed in on the starboard tack with the wind behind them. They dropped grappling irons over the sides as soon as contact was made with the enemy; and now the poor Frenchmen found themselves in double bondage, chained to each other and also to the English vessels from which emerged madly shouting islanders with long knives in their teeth. The sound of horn and drum which had greeted the boarders from the Gallic decks died down; nothing now to deaden the vicious *zing* of the English arrows as they swept up and across the crowded French decks. The fighting which ensued was bitter and sanguinary but quite one-sided.

The English admiral, Morley, had singled out the greatest of the enemy craft, the *Christopher*, as his opponent, and soon the English colors, flaunting the lilies as well as the leopards, fluttered from the tall masthead. There were three English ships which the French had captured in their coastal forays—the *Edward*, the *Rose*, and the *Katherine*—and these had been put vaingloriously in the first line of battle. The French must have regretted the gesture, for they were recaptured in rapid sequence, the whole English navy lifting a mighty roar each time the colors dipped.

A large part of the English success was due to the inability of the crossbowmen to compete with the green-jacketed archers from across the Channel. The hail of steel-tipped arrows cleared the decks ahead of the boarders. The first line of French battle crumbled. The crews jumped over the sides or stood in meek clumps with their arms raised in surrender. Babuchet, who had committed atrocities along the English coast, was captured and strung up to a yardarm, which did nothing to repair the sinking French morale. The second and third lines of battle offered little resistance after the destruction of the first.

The fourth line, however, showed a sterner spirit. By some ridiculous error of judgment the fourth line, shut up behind all the rest of the fleet and in danger of grounding on the mudbanks, had been put under the command of Barbenoire, the ablest and most daring of sea fighters. With a fine display of seamanship, the Genoese commander managed to take some of his ships out through the chaos in front of him and into the open water. Here he engaged in a running battle with the English which lasted through the night. He succeeded in getting away with twenty-four of his ships and in capturing two English craft.

Although the fighting seems to have been one-sided, it was actually a bitter and long-drawn-out affair. The French lost twenty-five thousand men in the conflict, the English four thousand. The ships with the ladies aboard had not remained as far back as prudence should have dictated; it is recorded that twelve of them were among the killed. The king's first cousin, Thomas de Monthermer, died. Edward himself was supposedly wounded in the thigh but, if that were true, it must have been a slight matter, for he went ashore on a pilgrimage of thanksgiving soon after. One Nele Loring, a squire, was knighted on the spot for conspicuous bravery and granted a pension of £20 a year. On such an occasion, with death and destruction everywhere and valor the order of the day, young Loring* must have performed some extraordinary feat to be singled out in this way.

Philip of France was inland with his army. When word of the disastrous defeat reached the court, his officers and ministers did not relish the task of telling the king. His temper was like tinder, and no one wanted to be the first to bear the brunt of it. Then someone had the happy thought of sending the court jester in with the news.

The wearer of the cap and bells undertook the task and entered the royal presence in a state of apparent indignation.

"Majesty!" he cried. "These cowards of English! These dastards! These fainthearted sons of sheep!"

"What has come over the fool?" asked the king, looking about him in surprise.

"Majesty!" explained the jester. "They would not jump off their ships into the water as our brave Frenchmen did!"

3

But despite this brilliant victory and the destruction of the French fleet, Edward saw the year end in defeat and humiliation. He could not capture either Cambrai or Tournai and finally he

---

* Readers of *Sir Nigel*, Arthur Conan Doyle's novel of these times, will recall how Nigel Loring, serving as squire under the great John Chandos, heard that bravest of knights tell of the fighting that day at Sluys. The name of the valiant squire no doubt suggested to Sir Arthur Doyle the one he gave his romantic hero.

concluded a truce for one year with the French, to the great dismay and mortification of his Flemish allies.

Philippa came back with him on this occasion, the royal family making the voyage in a small vessel and with very few servants in attendance. With them was an infant son who had been born the day after the great sea victory at Sluys and named John. He would be called John of Ghent, because it was in that city he uttered his first feeble sounds of life, and common usage would in time corrupt this to John of Gaunt. This infant was destined to play a part in history second only to the first-born son, Edward the Black Prince. The homecomers encountered such stormy weather that it was feared for a time the ship would founder and it actually took nine days to cross the narrow neck of sea and come to anchor at Towerwharf in London.

The queen had been in Flanders a considerable time awaiting the arrival of Master John, some say maintaining a court in the city of Ghent, others declare as a guest in the home of Jacob van Artevelde. If she had been a guest of King Edward's "gossip," as Van Artevelde was often called, she would have enjoyed as much comfort as could be found at any royal court. The wealthy residents of the tall cities on the plains had established a high degree of luxury. "Liberty never wore a more unamiable countenance," an English historian would write centuries later, "than among those burghers who abused the strength she had given them by cruelty and violence"; and this was true enough, for the wealthy weavers and goldsmiths and fishmongers were men of dour habit, close-fisted and unscrupulous. But they liked to live well, to sit down at tables groaning with good things to eat, to sleep in the softest of feather beds. The houses of the *poorters* of Ghent were many stories high. The ground level was usually the shop, behind which the apprentices lived and slept. All the floors above were devoted to the most luxurious living. Most of these imposing stone structures had round towers at one corner and, as a measure of safety, the upper story in the tower could be reached only by a ladder. A burgher who desired seclusion could climb the ladder and draw it up after him, and it would be impossible to reach him without demolishing the floors and walls.

The greatest luxury indulged in by these "unamiable" citizens was their handsome, voluptuous women. The air of the Low Countries seemed to supply a freshness of complexion to the ladies they bred and a roundness of contour which made them desirable in all male eyes. On the streets they bundled themselves up in an excess of modesty, but in their luxurious rooms above the shop level they dressed themselves in the finest cloth their husbands produced and in the sheerest of silks from the East. It was at this exact period that they began wearing diaphanous garments to bed instead of slipping under the covers in a state of nature as had been the universal habit. The nightgown may have been conceived in Paris, where most styles originated, but the fragile materials were made in Flanders, and it was the plump ladies of that corner of the world who first made use of them in this way; and so perhaps the credit belongs to Ghent and not to the capital of style on the Seine.

Whether or not Queen Philippa lived in the Van Artevelde household, her fourth son, John, was baptized there. A short time afterward a son, their first, was born to the Arteveldes and the queen acted as godmother, naming him Philip. The Countess of Hainaut, Philippa's mother, was with her during this residence in Ghent, and it was rumored that her interference had something to do with the failure to capture Tournai. She went to the King of France, who was her brother, and beseeched him to agree to a cessation of hostilities. Then she made the same request to her son-in-law.

It is doubtful if this had anything to do with the failure of the campaign. The two armies came face to face before Tournai, but nothing happened. Edward sent a challenge to "Philip of Valois" to meet him in single combat or accompanied by parties of knights numbering no more than one hundred. Philip contended that the letter was not addressed to him. As a result not a blow was struck.

Edward was falling more deeply in debt all the time. Queen Philippa's crown was pawned for twenty-five hundred pounds and all her jewels were put up as security for loans. It was even necessary to leave the Earl of Derby behind as security for the money Edward owed the good burghers.

It proved unfortunate for Jacob van Artevelde and for the Flemish alliance that the partnership had not prospered. The other cities began to complain of the engagement into which they had been drawn by his efforts, and even in Ghent a steady chorus of criticism was heard. It was charged that he had made himself a dictator and that he was putting purely personal interests above the welfare of the states. A rumor spread that he was negotiating with Edward to give the Black Prince the title of Count of

Flanders. Were the great cities of the lowland plains to be absorbed into the realm of England? The stout burghers liked that idea as little as the thought of being absorbed by the French. In thus finding fault with their truly inspired leader, the rank and file were blind to their own interests. They were listening to the nobility and the *buytenpoorters,* who thought their privileges were being infringed, and to the unreasoning voice of the mob. Behind the disaffection could always be found the hand of Count Louis, who believed he had been deprived of his hereditary rights; as indeed he had, and a good thing it was.

History, which at first accepted this view that Jacob van Artevelde was ambitious and dictatorial, has since reversed its decision. It is now realized that his intentions were patriotic and that what he aimed to achieve, an enduring union of the Dutch people, was far-seeing and wise. That he did not seek personal aggrandizement was made clear when he resigned his post at Ghent two years after the naval victory at Sluys. His fellow citizens promptly voted him back into office, to share the responsibility with three of his former colleagues.

Returning from a conference with Edward at Sluys, which had been attended by representatives of most of the leading cities, Jacob van Artevelde found a strained atmosphere in his native city. There was no welcome for him. The citizens stood about in silent groups and stared at him, as though to say, "This is the man who thinks to make himself master of us all." A leader of men is always sensitive to public moods, and the great weaver of Ghent knew what the attitude of his one-time friends meant. He rode at once to his stone house on the Calanderberg and ordered the servants to lock the doors and close the shutters.

Taking his post behind one of the windows, he watched through a small aperture the frightening speed with which a mob was collecting in the street below. It was made up almost entirely of the dregs of the population from the crooked lanes of the slums. No effort was being made to retain control or to restrain the noisy people. His white-hooded guards had not come to escort him through the town, and there was no sign of the other *hooftmen* and their armed bands.

Listening to the cries of the mob, Van Artevelde realized that the burden of their complaint was that he had stolen civic funds. This was a canard which had been handed down by his critics among the nobility, that he had not rendered an accounting of public moneys for seven years but instead had been sending the funds to England. There was not a scrap of truth in it.

Finally he threw open the shutters of one of the windows and leaned out so all could see him. There was a brief second of silence and then the air was split with the loud outcries of the mob. As he looked down into the street, which was now black with angry people, Jacob van Artevelde must have realized that for him this was the end. But his regrets would not be for himself but for the failure of the cause he represented. This bold and clear-sighted man knew that only by joining the crowded checkerboard of little states into one strong union could the democratic Dutch people continue to exist surrounded by feudal and militaristic countries. This meant that the opposing forces had won.

He tried to speak, to protest his innocence of the charges they were making. The belligerent townspeople refused to listen. The air was filled instead with their loud cries while stones began to rattle on the walls of the house. The intrepid leader strove to make them hear, but there was no willingness to grant him the chance. The glint of steel showed above the heads of the mob as the infuriated weavers brandished their daggers and pikes in the air.

Perhaps the delay he needed to rally his own partisans and to achieve an orderly hearing would have been possible had he taken refuge in the top floor of his round tower. He did not make use of it, however. Instead he thought it wiser to escape from the house. He stole out to the stables behind the building with the idea of getting away on horseback. His purpose was immediately detected and the cobbled courtyard filled quickly. One of the hoodlums had a poleax in his hands, and it needed no more than one blow to put an end to the life of the man who had done so much for the Flemish people.

His last words were said to have been: "People! Ghent! Flanders!" which gives a summation in dramatic form of his life and purpose.

Once the deed had been done, the mob melted away, awestruck and repentant. When the streets had cleared, the body was taken to the monastery at Biloke, where he had first preached his doctrine of unity. Later it was removed for burial at the Carthusian monastery at Royghem.

There was a reversal of sentiment almost immediately. Those who had instigated the disorders in the hope of taking power away from him were shocked at the violent reactions of the mob. An expiatory lamp was lighted in the monastery of Biloke and the expense of maintaining it was borne by the top-ranking families, who had always opposed his rise to power: the Westlucs, the De Mays, the Pannebergs, the Pauwels. The lamp was still burning thirty years afterward. But the bloodstained poleax had done more than put an end to the life of the great leader; it had set back for centuries the purpose for which he had worked, the union of the vulnerable Low Countries against aggression.

4

Edward's financial troubles came to a head before he could resume the war with France on a large scale. He found it necessary to repudiate his debts to his Italian bankers.

The Lombardy bankers, as they were called in England, first came into notice in the reign of Henry III. They engaged in business in the island kingdom in order to buy English wool and after a time Henry employed them in making remittances to the popes. They not only transmitted Peter's Pence to Rome each year but also, by a system of bills of exchange, placed in the hands of the pontiffs the large sums that the Church in England paid to the papacy. During the reigns of Edward I and Edward II, the house of Frescobaldi in Florence became the financial agents of the English kings. They grew so powerful that public feeling in the country ran high against them and a member of the family, one Amerigo de Frescobaldi, was banished from the kingdom. Edward II began to distribute his business widely when he came to the throne and discovered that he was saddled with debts amounting to £118,000, partly his own, partly those left by his father. The Frescobaldi assumed a large part of the loan made to the king, but he had business relations also with the Peruzzi family and the Spini, both of Florence. Still another Italian banker, Antonio Pessagno of Genoa, loaned Edward II between the years 1313 and 1316 the sum of £36,985. He stood so high in the king's favor that he acted as buyer for the royal household. It seems also that at one stage he was entrusted with the custody of the king's jewels (perhaps after the forcible closure of the Knights Templar) and was given a gift of three thousand pounds by Edward for his valuable services.

The public did not like so much favor shown to foreigners, particularly as the acumen of Edward II had come seriously into

question by this time. The feeling against the Italians ran so high
that the headquarters of the Bardi in London was burned by a
mob. This episode created an unwillingness among the Lombardy
moneylenders to establish themselves in England, and they gradually closed the shutters over their windows and returned to sun-
nier climes. Of the sixty-nine institutions which had been represented in the time of Edward I, most of them quite small, only
two remained when Edward III came to the throne, the family of
Peruzzi and the Society of the Bardi.

The financial transactions in which the first two Edwards had
been involved were relatively small and even routine in nature
compared with the magnificent scale on which Edward III did
business with the foreign bankers. The third Edward had a full-
scale war on his hands which necessitated the upkeep of armies
and navies and the payment of subsidies to his allies, not to mention the costs of a most brilliant and extravagant court. So much
gold was required that the resources of England were unequal to
the drain and the king inevitably turned to the foreign money-
lenders. He was given loans on such a huge scale that he realized
in 1339 that he could no longer meet his indebtedness. Accordingly on May 6 of that year he issued an edict suspending all payments on his debts, "including that owing to his well-beloved
Bardis and Peruzzis." He owed the two houses the stupendous
sum of 900,000 florins. To add to the difficulties of the two banking houses, another monarch was deep in their books, the King of
Sicily, who owed each the sum of 100,000 florins.

The city of Florence went into a slump. The financial world of
Europe was shaken to the core. The Flemish cities which had entered into alliance with Edward and had loaned him money were
so disturbed that they lost faith in the leadership of Ghent's Jacob
van Artevelde, which led to his assassination. Philip of France,
with a vulpine smile no doubt, proceeded to make capital of the
situation after the manner of Philip the Fair. He accused the Italian bankers in France of usury and extorted large sums from them
by way of fines. Believing that this form of bankruptcy meant the
end of English pretensions, he was said to have begun plans for
turning the tables by invading England. In Florence riots broke
out between the *grandi* and the *popolo*. The Bardi and the
Peruzzi had been the financial backbone of the republic, so the
news that both houses were in difficulties had the impact of an
earthquake. They had been called "the mercantile pillars of Chris-

tendom" and it seemed impossible that they had been reduced so close to failure by the bad faith of one king.

One of the heads of the Peruzzi family, Bonifazio di Tommaso Peruzzi, set out at once for London to discuss the situation with the English ministry. It is evident from brief records in the Peruzzi archives that he failed to obtain any satisfaction. It is not certain that he reached the ear of Edward, who was deep in his international relationships and the preparation of the navy for the invasion of France. The unhappy banker remained in England for over a year and finally died there in October 1340, unquestionably of grief and worry. There had been a brief period when the brilliant victory at Sluys raised expectations. Surely, thought the sad and aging Bonifazio as he pursued his unending peregrinations between the headquarters of the company in the city and the chancellery at Westminster, the king will now be in a position to reopen the question of his indebtedness. Edward did not return to England until the head of the Peruzzi family had died, but it was reported at the time that he was willing to resume the obligations. Parliament, seeing no way out of the morass of debt in which the lavishness of the king had involved the nation, took a negative view. No promises could be obtained from the legislative body of a willingness to pay in the future.

In January 1345 both banking houses gave up the struggle and went into bankruptcy, dragging down with them more banking concerns and many mercantile houses. The Bardi paid seventy per cent to their debtors, but the house of Peruzzi did not do nearly so well. All properties of the two houses were turned over to the creditors, but two years later a settlement was reached. The period precipitated by this great smash has been called the darkest in the annals of that great city.

The banking proclivities of the men of Florence could not be extinguished by one great misfortune. More than a century later the family of the Medici arose to outdo the records of the earlier days and place Florence on a much higher pinnacle.

CHAPTER TEN

The Great Victory

1

IN reaching this stage of Edward's brilliant and reckless reign, it has become apparent that optimism was one of his most marked characteristics. None but a great optimist would have thought of winning the crown of France by force of arms. None would have assumed such an appalling burden of debts unless certain that success would provide the means to pay them off. None but a believer in a personal star would have turned at Crécy to face an army perhaps four times greater than his own.

Optimism had involved the sanguine and lavish king in very great difficulties and perplexities. The curtain had fallen on the last act of the Baliol pretensions to the throne of Scotland, and so the Scottish problem, as viewed from Westminster, remained unsolved. Young David Bruce, Edward's brother-in-law, had returned in 1341 from his long absence in France, where he and his English wife Joan had occupied Château Gaillard, the great stone fortress on the Seine built by Richard Coeur-de-Lion. Crossing in a ship provided by the French king, David landed at Inverbervie near Montrose. As he and his English wife were a handsome and attractive pair, the people rallied to their cause and David assumed the government for the second time. It became apparent at once, however, that the new hand on the reins was a weak one. No effort was made to control the arrogant nobility, who fought openly among themselves. Edward saw that the weaknesses of David would provide a good pretext for interference but that he would have to wait until the matter of the French succession had been settled.

In the same year that David landed in Scotland, the Duke of Brittany died and two claimants came forward for the post, Charles de Blois and Jean de Montfort. Philip of France threw his support to Charles. Edward declared for Montfort and sent an army over to help the Montfort faction, with Sir Walter Manny in command. Sir Walter thus had his chance to begin the career which won him a place among the great knights of history. He performed many extraordinary deeds. But in a very short time the whole nature of the struggle changed; the English and the French were fighting it out between themselves and the Bretons had retired to the sidelines, where they watched their land being devastated, their towns ravished, their castles burned. All this was costing Edward dearly in men and money.

The situation at Avignon had also taken a turn for the worse. The new Pope was striving to bring about peace, but Edward was viewing his proposals with a suspicious eye; as well he might, for Avignon was more certainly under French dictation than it had been since the first days of the Babylonish captivity.

John XXII had died in 1334 and an inventory of his estate had revealed a most astonishing hoard. There were eighteen million gold florins in specie and seven million in plate and jewels. When the cardinals went into conclave to appoint a successor, there was no difficulty in agreeing on the Bishop of Porto save that the honest bishop refused to accept with the understanding that he must keep the papacy at Avignon. "I had sooner yield up the cardinalate," he declared, "than accept the popedom on such conditions." The cardinals, a large majority of whom were French, turned against him and demanded another vote. It happened that they had not provided themselves with a substitute, so it was agreed that they would not try for any decision on the next ballot. Each man would throw his vote away by putting down any name that appealed to him. By an extraordinary coincidence they all thought of the same man.

"My friends," said the nominee when the result was announced, "you have chosen an ass."

His name was James Fournier, a Cistercian abbot, and he was, in reality, a man of much piety and resolution. Taking the title of Benedict XII, he proceeded to spend much of the fabulous wealth left by John in enlarging and beautifying the Pope's Palace at Avignon. Dying in 1342, he was succeeded by Cardinal Roger, Archbishop of Rouen, who assumed the name of Clement VI. The new pontiff was completely French in his leanings, and it was soon clear to Edward of England that nothing was to be gained through pontifical action. The king was so certain of this that he made an unusual suggestion, one which caused Avignon to overflow with wrath. He was willing to have the Pope act as mediator only if he would do so as a private citizen and not as Pope.

Philip now proceeded to bring things to a head. He sent his son, John of Normandy, with a large army to invade the English provinces of Guienne and Gascony. This was open war. Edward countered by dispatching reinforcements to Gascony under the Earl of Derby. To be sure that there would be good leadership, he detached Sir Walter Manny from his post in Brittany and sent him with Derby as second-in-command. Manny performed there with his usual boldness and intrepidity, but the French forces were too powerful to be held back. It became apparent that, unless drastic steps were taken, the Aquitanian possessions of the English crown would be swallowed up.

Edward gathered an army to go to Gascony under his personal command and they sailed on July 11. The new army was made up of twenty-four hundred horsemen and twelve thousand foot soldiers, mostly archers, as well as small divisions, including a force of Welsh foot soldiers, a thousand hobilars (mounted spearmen), and the king's personal guard. These figures are more or less arbitrary because many estimates can be found, some as low as eight thousand. All are in agreement, however, that Edward had made one tactical decision. In battle they would fight on foot. He had not forgotten the lessons of Bannockburn and Halidon Hill.

A French knight named Godfrey de Harcourt, who bore the nickname of Le Boiteux (The Cripple), had escaped from France after an altercation with the Bishop of Bayeux. He was the seigneur of St.-Saveur-Bayeux and belonged to one of the oldest families in Normandy, founded before the time of Rollo by Bernard the Dane. To escape punishment, he retired to Brabant, where he had estates, but three friends who had helped him to escape were seized by the king, put to the torture, and then executed; good King Philip having a furious way with him when things went contrary to his royal will. Harcourt was condemned by default and his estates confiscated.

He came to England and offered his services to Edward. This, as it developed, was the greatest possible stroke of good fortune. Harcourt hobbled noticeably, but on a horse he was as good a fighting man as any. More than that, he was a shrewd soldier with a sense of strategy which Edward seems to have lacked. He had, moreover, a keen eye for troop dispositions and a capacity for judging the ground over which cavalry might have to advance, the dips in the land, the advantages and disadvantages of hillsides, the exact danger from soft moss land along small creeks. Edward seems to have appreciated his value at once, being optimistic in his choice of men. The French fugitive rode close to the royal shoulder throughout the campaign, and his advice was acted upon in matters of first importance. He was even given the rank of marshal, which was most unusual. Men attained that honor usually because of being born the son of a son of a marshal.

It was Harcourt who suggested a change in the English strategy. Edward's idea was the simple and obvious one of going direct to the aid of his hard-pressed troops in the south. Harcourt pointed out many disadvantages in this plan. It involved a long and slow sea voyage with heavy losses in men and ships. The most they could hope to accomplish that way was to check the French advance as long as the army remained there. The force that Edward was taking out was not large enough to make a decisive victory possible in Gascony and any advantage which might be gained would be transitory. On the other hand, if the army landed on the coast of Normandy, which the French had left undefended, they would compel the enemy to withdraw some of their strength from the south to meet this new threat; thus accomplishing all they could hope to do by landing in Gascony. The rest of the plan seems to have been to march swiftly across the face of northern France, ravaging the country as they went and collecting enough in spoils to pay the cost of the whole operation. Finally they would join the Flemish armies before Bouvines, which might lead to a decisive result. This realistic plan had one other advantage. Edward's army would never be far from the home base and could recross the Channel quickly if the French attacked in force.

Edward saw at once the advantages to be gained by this strategy. Instead of taking his transports on the long and dangerous trip across the Bay of Biscay, he landed on the Cotentin at La Hogue St. Vast. It was apparent at once that Harcourt had been right. An attack had not been expected here and all of Normandy seemed bare of French troops. The English, moving fast at first, swept down on Barfleur, took everything of value in the town, and then pushed on, capturing Valongnes, Carentan, and St. Lô (a thousand tuns of wine being found in the last-named town, to the great delight of the thirsty troops) and reaching the important city of Caen. Here a small army under the constable of France offered some resistance. It was at Caen, which had played such a part in the life of William the Conqueror, that Edward got his hands on a plan drawn up by the Normans for a second invasion of England. It was a detailed scheme, showing how England would be divided among the victors. Edward was so infuriated that he announced his intention of putting the whole population of Caen to the sword the following day. It was Godfrey de Harcourt who persuaded him to give up this act of revenge, pointing out that the success of the campaign depended on speed.

Harcourt's plan, as has been said, was to sweep the northern coast of France before the French could organize any effective opposition. This was a thoroughly sound strategic conception, but they had not figured on such weak resistance and such chances for loot. The wagon train was already filled with chairs, beds, statues, suits of armor, and tapestries. Each man in the ranks had his own booty—gold and silver flagons, crucifixes, silver candlesticks— which he suspended around his neck. Many of them had feather beds strapped on their backs. It was not strange that twenty-eight days were consumed from the landing until they came in sight of Poissy and knew that Paris lay only twelve miles ahead. Even though they knew that French forces were now gathering everywhere, there was an intense desire to push on. Reports were received that, behind the gates of Paris, Philip had fallen into a panic and was preparing the city to stand siege, tearing down all buildings which touched the walls. Later word reached them that Philip was also gathering a huge army on the plain of St. Denis, and this led to a wiser decision. A small force was sent on to threaten Paris while the main body set to work to build a pontoon bridge across the Seine. This was accomplished in three days and the English leader sighed with relief to have this serious obstacle behind him.

Now the safety of the English army depended on the fleetness of their heels. Only desperate haste could undo the damage of that slow processional through Normandy and the Isle-de-France, with everyone searching for loot. Edward was thoroughly sensitive to the danger and in four days he drove his heavily laden troops at top speed, covering nearly sixty miles through the Vexin of Normandy. All the roads behind them were black with French troops. Clouds of dust raised by cavalry seemed to fill the horizon. The most serious obstacle had still to be surmounted, the broad Somme which rolled sluggishly through peat bogs on both banks. Edward, in something approaching a panic, sent his two marshals, Warwick and Harcourt, to secure a crossing ahead. They found all the bridges down and the fords guarded by Picardy troops. Four attempts to seize fords were unsuccessful. To add to the jeopardy

of the invaders, the French king now had a huge army in movement and was marching parallel to the English. French horsemen
were already in Amiens, which meant that Edward was being
shoved into a triangle formed by the seemingly impassable
Somme, the waters of the Channel (where there would be no
ships yet to take them off), and the French army. The French
were so close on the English heels that at Airnes they found meat
simmering on the spits. Edward's men had left their dinner behind them in their haste.

The English king now found it necessary to change his plans. It
was no longer possible to join forces with the allied troops from
Flanders. Instead he must by some means get across the Somme
into his own province of Ponthieu and maintain himself there
until the fleet could arrive to get the army back to English soil.
Edward summoned all his prisoners before him and offered liberty
to anyone who would lead the way to a navigable spot, together
with the release of twenty other prisoners. A peasant named
Gobin Agace finally came forward and said he knew of a ford
called the Blanche Taque close to the mouth of the Somme where
it was possible to cross at low tide.

Darkness had fallen, but the order to march was given and by
midnight the vanguard reached Blanche Taque. The tide was in
and this necessitated a delay of several hours. The prospect
seemed a grim one, for on the other side of the water was a body
of two thousand Picards under the command of a resourceful
knight named Godemar de Fay.

It was to prove as close a thing as the crossing of the Red Sea
by the children of Israel. After several hours of tense waiting, the
dawn began to break and the tidal waters receded. While the
English bowmen drove the men of Picardy back with a storm of
arrows, the army tramped waist-deep over the solid white stones of
the Blanche Taque and reached the far shore just as the van of
the pursuing horsemen appeared through the morning mists. The
French got their hands on a few of the English wagons but that
was all. In a mood of intense relief Edward ordered that not only
should Gobin Agace be set at liberty but that he was to have a
horse and one hundred crowns in gold.

From the ford the English marched to the village of Crécy,
which lay some miles north and east and within a very few miles
of the sea. It was August 25, with a prospect of rain in the skies. It
did not seem likely that the French would be able to cross in time

to offer battle that day. The possibility of a rest was welcome to the foot-weary English.

Crécy: an inconspicuous village, the home of a few dusty peasants, a miller, a faithful priest; it boasted one church, a manor house, one smithy. It lay between two small streams, the Maye and the Authie. This was a country of gently rolling downs and at an equal distance of two miles, forming an irregular square, were three other villages. Between one of the three, Wadicourt, and that which would give its name to the battle, there was a ridge of no great height, sparsely wooded but susceptible of defense against attack from the plain below. Back of this ridge was a windmill, its arms almost still in the humid air.

There is a legend that Edward placed some small cannon or *cracys* around this mill, but there is no proof of this. Certainly no effective use was made of gunpowder in the battle which followed. The French knights, who came tilting like so many Don Quixotes against this unattainable windmill, would encounter only the usual hazards and would not be subjected to a first taste of the powder which was to revolutionize warfare.

South of the Maye stretched the forest of Crécy, a thick and almost impenetrable wood which covered the landscape for ten miles. This natural barrier lay between Edward's army and the city of Abbeville, where Philip was making his headquarters. To reach Crécy from Abbeville, it was necessary to take either one of two roads leading around the forest, a matter of eighteen miles. Through the heart of the forest, however, ran a narrow path leading north to the sea, and this was the route the English would take if a final retreat became necessary.

A quiet and sleepy country, this, each village rather solemn in a setting of orchards and scattered elm trees. The inhabitants had realized what lay ahead as soon as the English vanguard came tramping through their fields at midday. Already, in crude carts and on muleback, these innocent bystanders and their families were fleeing as fast as creaking wheels would take them.

The English king raised his standard close to the windmill, in front of his azure and gold silk pavilion. It may not seem necessary to say again that the always ostentatious Edward did everything with a splendid gesture and that his pavilion was of grand dimensions, large enough, in fact, for scores of guests to sit down to a meal and for minstrels to play as the flagons were drained.

Back of the pavilion, on a stretch of land which leveled off, were the wagons and the camp followers. The campfires were being lighted and trenches dug for the roasting of meat.

As the day wore on, word reached the king that Philip of France was at Abbeville and had occupied the bridge across the Somme. His army was said to be one hundred thousand strong and it was further said that the Oriflamme had been hoisted above his headquarters. This meant they would neither give nor accept quarter. Allowing for exaggeration, it was still certain that the French would outnumber the English at least four to one. Could they face such desperate odds?

There was a deep frown on the brow of the Frenchman, Harcourt, whose advice had brought Edward to this pass. He kept his eyes on the dark path in the forest of Crécy as though he now favored a retreat to the coast, where a last stand could be made, an opinion in which most of the others concurred. But not Edward. Only a great man faces such danger as this without fear, and there was no hint of uncertainty in the king's eye as he glanced across the treetops beyond which the French might already be advancing with their blood-red flag.

"This is land of my lady mother's," he said, motioning about him. "We will wait for them here."

2

That night the French king supped in the monastery of St. Peter's at Abbeville with a large and distinguished company. The rain still threatened and there was a damp wind which beat about the windows with a mournful insistence. The company was rather subdued, for they would be in mortal conflict the next day and there was much on the minds of all of them. The king, who was in a particularly dark mood, had many violent sins on his conscience and for that reason, perhaps, had little to say.

The company about Philip included the blind King of Bohemia, who had no reason to be there save a love of war which he could scent from afar and which had brought him to the French banner with a division of German knights and mercenaries. There were also the king's son, Charles of Luxemburg, King Jayme of Majorca, the Duke of Lorraine, the Count of Flanders. Between the lot of them they commanded at least eighty thousand men from all parts of the continent, so it was little wonder that the town was packed to the eaves and that grumbling men-at-arms were sleeping in the markets and the churchyards and under the porches of houses.

Perhaps Philip sensed the dangers in such a situation as this: so many proud and jealous leaders, so many quarrelsome men of all races. It is recorded that he spoke seriously of his fear of disunion. He begged his allies to be friends and eschew all jealousy and to be courteous one to another. It was a sound observation, for even as he spoke, frowning over his flagon of wine, they could hear loud altercations in French and German and Wendish, and the shrill complaints of the Genoese that they were soaked to the skin and had no way of keeping the strings of their intricate crossbows from getting wet.

Edward dined in his pavilion, surrounded by his barons and captains. Most of them showed concern for what the morrow held, but it is said that the king himself wore an air of confidence. After the meal he rose and went out through the curtain which screened off a corner of the space for an oratory. Here he remained alone until midnight.

Edward might be weak as a strategist, but as a tactician he was above reproach. Soon after dawn he and his oldest son, the latter wearing the black chain mail which would fasten on him the sobriquet of the Black Prince for all time, emerged from the royal pavilion. They made a survey of the field, the king riding on a white palfrey and carrying a wand in his hand. He went slowly up and down the line. The green-jacketed archers, he perceived, still had their bows in the cases provided to keep them dry, and there was nothing but a jaunty assurance on the bronzed faces; they knew their power, these yeomen. The forest of Crécy guarded the flank of the English right, and here Edward stationed the prince with many of the best English knights, including the two marshals and a very brave and honorable warrior named Sir John Chandos, of whom much will be told later. This division consisted of eight hundred men-at-arms, at least two thousand archers, and half as many lightly armed Welshmen. A second battalion of equal strength covered the rest of the hilly crest as far as Wadicourt. Because there was some danger of being outflanked beyond Wadicourt, the king had seen to it that a formidable barricade of wagons and tree trunks had been raised where the enemy would have to penetrate. A third brigade of equal strength was being held as a reserve under the command of the king himself. For the time being they were stationed in front of the windmill and could be dispatched swiftly to any part of the field where a need for them might arise. The horses had been taken back to where the wagons were placed. For on this day, in accordance with a new conception of warfare, all Englishmen would fight afoot.

Nothing was amiss. The king was keenly aware that the thick forest of Crécy provided him with his greatest advantage. The French, approaching from Abbeville, had to follow a winding road around the forest which would bring them abruptly to the battlefield. There would be neither time nor space for them to form a proper array before finding themselves involved in conflict. The larger the French force, the greater this difficulty would become.

The rain began to fall early and continued intermittently through the morning and the early part of the afternoon. It was about three o'clock when the scouts placed on the Abbeville road brought word to Edward that the French were coming. Half an hour later the first of them appeared around the end of the forest and began to debouch in the direction of Etrees, the most southerly of the four villages enclosing the Crécy plain.

"Bowmen!" cried the men about Edward. This was a surprise, for it was known that Philip of France had nothing but scorn for new ideas and regarded archers as a necessary evil. The reason was soon clear: the crossbowmen would cover the arrival of the knights and permit the latter to form in proper battle array.

The Genoese archers were weary, having marched eighteen miles over muddy roads, carrying their heavy equipment. Their reluctance to begin the battle had no weight with the French high command. The Count d'Alençon, who was a very chivalrous gentleman, cried scornfully, "This comes of making use of scurvy cowards!" The Italian archers were literally forced across the wet field by the weight of horsemen behind them, until they came within range of the English bows. At this moment the rain stopped, the dark clouds parted, and the sun came out. It shone on the backs of the English and on the faces of the attackers.

A new kind of battle began. The bowmen of England with their outlandishly long weapons, according to the French, had been placed on the flanks of each division so ingeniously that they could face in any direction. When the tired Genoese halted to wind up their crossbows, the air was filled suddenly with English arrows. It was, witnesses declared later, as though a snowstorm had come to take the place of the rain, for the arrows which filled the sky were feathered with white. They were propelled with such violent power that the breastplates of the Genoese offered no protection. In a matter of minutes their ranks were decimated and the survivors, screaming with terror, were trying to force their way through the armed knights behind them.

King Philip, aware that something was seriously amiss, rode out on the field. When he saw what was happening he cried, "Kill me these cowardly rogues!" The cavalry, nothing loath, spurred their horses forward and rode the archers down, at the same time cutting at the Genoese with their swords. Never had war produced a more ghastly spectacle, the brave knights destroying their own men with no mercy or concern.

Philip had been of two minds before, being partly convinced it would be wiser to delay the battle another day. But having ventured within sight of the English lines and thus having a glimpse of the banner of his enemy stamped with the lilies of France, he fell into such a black rage that nothing could suit him but an immediate start. And so began a battle which has never been equaled for sheer disorder and lack of discipline. As fast as the French horsemen could swing onto the plain, they rode up the slightly sloping ground, which was already choked with the bodies of men and horses and slippery with blood, to meet in their turn that frightening rain of steel-tipped arrows against which the strongest of armor offered no defense.

It did not seem possible for the French marshals to check this madness; or perhaps, being of the old school, they did not try very hard. If the chivalry of France could have been kept in hand long enough to form a battle line and then attack the full English position at once, there might have been a different story to write. But the frenzy continued unabated, and at no time was the French strength fully engaged. Ill-supported companies were striking in hit-and-miss fashion without plan or sequence and were being wiped out; not death from knightly sword or chivalrous mace, but a mean ending with vulgar arrows in their throats.

The blind King of Bohemia came riding onto the field between two devoted companions, and this same madness seized him. "Sirs," cried the veteran, "do me this much favor! Lead me where I may strike one clean blow!" The two knights tied their bridles to his and the three of them rode up the hill together. All three were killed.

It seems that once only did the furiously attacking French get through the line of archers. Against the English right they managed a temporary break and came to grips with the men-at-arms stationed around the Prince of Wales. The danger was so great that Sir Thomas Norwich was dispatched to ask aid from the reserve. King Edward, bareheaded, was standing at his windmill. He seemed in no hurry to comply.

"Is my son dead?" he asked.

"No, Sire."

"Is he wounded?"

Sir Thomas shook his head. "No, Sire. But he is full hardly matched."

"Then go back and tell those that sent you hither not to send again as long as my son is alive. Tell them my son must have the chance to win his spurs."

The danger was over when the messenger returned to the confusion and turmoil on the right flank. The prince had been wounded, not seriously, and one of the Welsh light troops had thrown the dragon standard of Wales over him as he lay on the ground. With the resilience of youth (he was only sixteen at the time) Edward got quickly to his feet and continued to take his part in the struggle for the rest of the day.

History is like a slate, and there is generally something to be written on each side. This story of the seeming nonchalance of the king and his willingness to let the heir to the throne take his full share of risks is something to be entered to the credit of chivalry.

The confusion on the field grew worse as the few hours of daylight wore away. The French army continued to arrive piecemeal; never any break in the ranks of the knights who rode on to the field, singly, two abreast, never more than three at a time, for the road was as narrow as the ramp to a slaughterhouse; always a fluttering of pennons and a blasting of trumpets and the monotonous cry of *Montjoye St. Denis!* They came, they charged, they died. The king shouted orders which no one heard, for his marshals had fallen. The sun disappeared and the clouds were too heavy again to let a single star shine through. The Welsh and Cornish foot soldiers did not hesitate to venture out into the French lines. They even crept into the path of the oncoming knights and did great execution with their long knives. The French royal standard-bearer went down and another Frenchman ripped the Oriflamme from its staff and carried it off the field. It would be raised on many occasions thereafter, but never with such dire results.

Philip watched the carnage with grim intentness but finally was persuaded to leave the field. "You have lost this battle," said one of the knights who left with him. "You will win the next." But there was to be no next for the first king of the Valois dynasty. His fleet had been destroyed at Sluys and now his army had been vanquished. No monarch had ever before been so humiliated.

Philip rode first to the castle of Broye and was admitted when he hailed the watch from the outer gate. "Open!" he cried. "This is the fortune of France." A curious employment of terms. There was no fortune for France that day, nor for a long time thereafter. Philip died in 1350 before anything had been done to brighten the prospects of the kingdom.

The night after Crécy the small English army remained in their lines along the crest. No effort had been made to pursue the broken enemy. When the scouts brought assurance that the French army had dissolved, the victorious English lighted campfires on the field. The king came down from his post at the mill and sought Prince Edward. He did not recognize his heir at once, for the fine apparel of the prince had suffered in the melee. His crimson and gold surcoat was ripped to shreds and blackened with mud. He was indeed a black prince in every sense of the word.

"Sweet son," said the king, "you have acquitted yourself well this day."

A prayer was said, with every fighting man on his knees, before any sounds of jubilation were allowed. The feasting did not begin until it was certain that not a single straggling French knight was left on the weary road from Abbeville.

The next day, which was Sunday, a party made up of several of the nobility and a staff of heralds and secretaries examined the dead on the bloodstained field and brought back a report which the victors found hard to believe. One king lay dead in his armor, the blind John of Bohemia, still strapped to the bodies of the two knights who had led him into the fray. Ten princes had died. The body of Alençon was found among the Genoese bowmen for whom he had expressed such contempt. The Count of Flanders, who had deserted the English alliance, had paid the penalty for his change of coat. The Earl of Blois, nephew of the king, and the Duke of Lorraine, his brother-in-law, were among the slain. A brother of Sir Godfrey de Harcourt was found on the slope of the hill. More than a thousand knights in all had died during those few sanguinary hours and as many as thirty thousand common soldiers. Eighty banners had been captured.

The English losses were negligible. A few hundred only had fallen.

The Abbot of St. Denys had seen the French as they rolled by his walls in all their pride and glory. "God has punished us for our sins!" he cried when he was told that this mighty host had been destroyed in a few hours of fighting. He could think of no other explanation.

But there were two reasons for the French defeat. The command of that mighty army had been hopelessly bungled, and the English had made supreme use of a great new weapon.

3

Crécy is not counted among the decisive victories of history. It did not bring the war to an end, certainly; but it had a significance far in excess of the importance attached to the fall of a curtain on any clash of national interests. It was the end of an epoch.

The princes who commanded at Crécy did not realize this fully. King Edward had so disposed his forces that all the fighting fell on the shoulders of the bowmen, but when he returned to England he devoted himself to establishing the Order of the Garter, a glorification of chivalry. The Black Prince would continue to win fame by his adherence to the code. But the men who fought on that bloody field had no doubts. These yeomen of England, with their clear sight and their bronzed cheeks, who dipped with such coolness into the endless stock of lethal bolts and then sent them flying among the French with the velocity of death, these men in green knew that they were fighting, and winning, the battle. They knew that the day of the knight would soon be over.

CHAPTER ELEVEN

The Aftermath of the Victory

1

EDWARD made no effort to capture Paris, although some of his advisers clamored for action to that end. The French powers of resistance had been so shaken at Crécy that he could have won the city, but it would have been no more than a temporary triumph. Instead he made the wise decision to establish a bridgehead on French soil for use in future operations and, for that purpose, marched to the siege of Calais.

In the meantime French aggression in Gascony had come to a standstill, thus vindicating the judgment of the Frenchman Godfrey de Harcourt. As soon as Edward landed on the Cotentin, Philip sent word to his son, John of Normandy, to come to his assistance. Six days before the battle of Crécy was fought the French forces in the south began their march north. They arrived to find the great French army destroyed and Philip himself at Amiens in a state of bitterness and gloom. So deep was the beaten monarch's dudgeon that no one cared to go near him and no plans could be discussed with him for the relief of Calais. John did not hesitate to beard the defeated lion because he had a grievance to air. Before leaving for the north he had given a safe-conduct to Sir Walter Manny, who wanted to make an overland march to join the English royal forces. Philip had refused to honor his son's promise. Manny and his party had been laid by the heels at Orleans and were still being held in rigorous confinement.

The prince gave his bitterly depressed father an ultimatum. If Manny was not released at once, he himself would not strike another blow in the French cause. Philip, still in a state of intense irritation, was reluctant to give in; but he finally yielded and even gave Sir Walter some jewelry to the value of a thousand florins for the ill treatment he had received. The English knight accepted on condition that his own king approved. As soon as he reached the English camp before Calais, Sir Walter informed the king of what had happened.

"Send them back!" commanded the English monarch. "You have no right to keep them. We have enough, the Lord be praised, for you and for ourselves."

There was no exaggeration in this. The English camp was filled with the loot of northern France. For a long time thereafter the English people would luxuriate in the spoils which were carried home. Every mother or wife of a soldier who fought at Crécy had a bracelet on her arm or a silver cup for her table. Many of them had feather beds, which were regarded as among the very choicest of all the spoils of war. The castles of the nobility were filled with rare things and there were blooded horses in all their stables.

The siege of Calais took a long time. It was a strong position and could be reduced only by starvation. Edward built a town of small wooden huts around it and, to make his men comfortable, had a market place in the center which was open three days a week for the sale of food and clothing from England. Philip of France got an army together from what was left after Crécy and came up behind the English with the intention of compelling them to raise the siege. But back of the English camps were wide marshlands, and the phlegmatic and unimaginative Philip could not find any way to get across. He squatted down with his men beyond the marshlands and, no doubt, spent his time bemoaning the defeat at Crécy. Finally the townspeople, having eaten all the horses and dogs and every rat they could catch in the city, reached the stage where they must yield or starve to death. They had been watching the campfires of Philip's army at night and hoping against hope that he would do something to help them.

There were only two ready-made approaches to the beleaguered city, and the French king did not propose to try either one. The first was a road along the coast where his troops would be under arrow fire from the English fleet (and they did not want any more of that violent medicine), and the other was a bridge across the marshes called Neuillet, and this was strongly guarded by the English. William the Conqueror had found ways of taking his army across the fens at Ely, a much more difficult feat, but there was no such resourcefulness in Philip. He sulked a little longer while his people in Calais starved, and then broke up camp and returned with all his troops to Amiens.

The governor of the besieged city, Sir Jean de Vienne, had to ask for terms. Edward would listen to nothing at first but unconditional surrender. Calais had been a hotbed of piracy in the past and had sent out ships to prey on English commerce. Now the citizens had cost the English monarch much in time and lives by the stubbornness of their defense. They must, he declared, be punished as befitted their crimes.

The king's advisers were against too much severity and Edward finally compromised by demanding that six of the most notable men of Calais come out to him in their shirts and bare feet and with ropes around their necks. They must bring the keys of the town and castle and place them in his hands.

"On them," he declared, "I shall work my will. The rest I will receive to my mercy."

Six of the most highly respected and richest burghers volunteered to be the victims, and they were sent out in their shirts as stipulated, all of them so weak from famine that they could barely walk. They were brought into the presence of the king, who had surrounded himself with the queen and her ladies and all of his captains and best soldiers. There the six old men knelt down before him.

"We bring you the keys," said one of them, "and put ourselves at your mercy to save the rest of the people who have suffered so hardly."

The king, whose handsome face was suffused with anger, had his headsman ready. He motioned to him to begin.

Up to this point the story is a familiar one. Many kings in different countries and at divers times had butchered the common people of cities which had resisted too bravely and too long. Edward I had ordered the killing of all the men of Berwick, and the work of extermination was well under way before he relented. Casting ahead some years, Edward the Black Prince would provide a classic example of this kind of savage behavior. He would put all the common people of a captured town to the sword but would pardon the knights. The story of Calais is, therefore, one of many such. It would not have been selected for particular remembrance if all the people around the angry king had not urged that he show mercy, Sir Walter Manny acting as spokesman. The latter did not prevail over the vicious Plantagenet temper, and it remained for Queen Philippa to add her voice. Although she was close to her time with a tenth child, she went down on her knees before Edward and begged earnestly that he show mercy.

The king took a long time to make up his mind and once at least he raised his hand as though signaling to the headsman. Finally, however, and with obvious reluctance, he granted the queen's request and allowed the hostages to go free.

That this became one of the favorite stories of the period was due, in all likelihood, to the intimate picture of the queen which emerges. Following so soon after the beautiful Eleanor of Castile, to whose memory the costly Eleanor Crosses dotted the great northern road as proof of the undying love of Edward I, and the spectacular and passionate Isabella of France, who was still living in seclusion at Castle Rising and of whom men in the taverns spoke in whispers as "the she-wolf of France," Queen Philippa had seemed rather colorless. She was pretty, sweet, and domestic, a typical Dutch girl. But at Calais she showed herself to be brave as well as understanding and compassionate (it took courage to beard Edward in one of his Plantagenet tempers), and the people of England rolled the story over their tongues and kept it green in their memories.

Must a sequel be told, even if it takes much of the gloss from this picture of the fair (and rapidly becoming buxom) queen and shows that she had other qualities common to the hardheaded burghers of the Flanders cities? Edward, with a careless gesture, had given her the six old men to deal with as she pleased. This included their properties as well as their bodies, and she did not scruple to take advantage of the chance thus offered. It is on record that she took over the houses of one of the six, John Daire. As he chose not to become an English citizen and had to leave the city as a result, it is highly improbable that he ever got the property back.

2

The saga of the border warfare became in this reign a story of the struggle between the strong son of a weak father and the weak son of a strong father. David the Bruce had inherited little of the great quality of his father, Robert. He proceeded, however, to carry out Scotland's treaty obligation to France when the word spread that Edward III had led an army of invasion into France. He got together a force of fifteen thousand men and led them across the Tyne above Newcastle and down into Durham. The northern barons, under the leadership of the Archbishop of York, assembled in force to meet him and on October 17, 1346, they came face to face at Neville's Cross. It proved a repetition of a now familiar story. The English archers cut the charging Scots to pieces and scored a complete victory. Many of the nobles of Scotland were killed in the battle and David himself was made a prisoner by an English north-country squire by the name of John Copland.

Following the lead of Froissart, the historian of the Middle Ages, there has been a tendency to give the credit of this victory to Queen Philippa. Circumstantial stories are told of her bravery and coolness; how she rode out on a white charger and inspired the troops with a rousing speech, and how she returned to the battlefield afterward on the same charger. Hearing the story of David's capture, she is supposed to have demanded of Copland that the royal prisoner be turned over to her. Copland refused and rode forthwith to Calais to explain himself to King Edward. "I hold my land of *you* and not of *her*," he declared. The king is said to have told him to return to England forthwith and deliver the royal prisoner into the hands of the queen. With this command went a promise of lands to the value of five hundred pounds a year for the great service rendered the crown.

The reliability of this story has always been questioned because no mention is made of it in the English chronicles; and a gentle queen riding to battle on a white horse is not an episode that any monkish chronicler would overlook, or any kind of historian, in fact. It must be taken into consideration also that the battle of Neville's Cross was fought on October 17 and that Edward did not land at Sandwich with his queen and family until October 12. The queen could not have been at Durham in time for the fighting.

The captive king was brought to London and paraded through the streets on a handsome black war horse and was then lodged in the Tower of London. He spent the next eleven years as a prisoner in England.

He was not kept in close confinement all the time. His wife, who was Edward's sister, Joanna (Little Joan Makepeace), was allowed to join him. They lived in various places close to London, always under guard, of course, and at Odiham in Hampshire. As negotiations over the amount of the ransom took an endless time, he was permitted on one occasion to return to Scotland to talk the estates into agreement. All this time there were secret under-standings between the two kings about which the estates knew nothing, although they suspected much. David, in fact, was will-ing to sacrifice Scotland as a condition to his release, and several of the Scottish leaders were partners with him in what was called "the business." Finally, on July 13, 1354, the ransom was fixed at ninety thousand marks, to be paid in nine yearly installments. Now Scotland was not a rich country and ten thousand marks was a great deal of money to be raised and paid out each year, particu-larly for a king who was not regarded highly. David ruled for four-teen years after his return and was in debt all the time, sometimes paying nothing, sometimes as little as four thousand marks. Fi-nally he and Edward reached an understanding by which the bal-ance of the ransom could be liquidated without further payments. David was to agree to the transfer of the Scottish crown at his death to an English prince, the one chosen being Edward's very tall son, Lionel. The Scottish Parliament refused to accept this ar-rangement, so the two royal conspirators put their heads together on a still more drastic agreement. David promised to settle the succession on Edward himself, with certain precautionary provi-sions to maintain the independence of Scotland. In consideration of this the balance of the ransom was written off, although David continued to keep up a desultory correspondence with the English chancellery in order to conceal the truth from the dour Scottish parliamentarians, who would have raised the roof of Edinburgh Castle in their wrath had they known.

In the meantime David's gentle English queen had died. He married a second time rather promptly, choosing the fascinating widow of a knight of comparatively low degree. Her name was Margaret Logie, and the estates were as little pleased with this choice as they would have been about the secret pact between the two kings. The new queen caused considerable trouble by persuad-ing the king to put her relatives in important posts, and it did not take long for the coterie about the king to get rid of her. They found some basis for a divorce and snipped the marriage bond with legal scissors.

David died in Edinburgh Castle on February 22, 1370, leaving no children.

The secret transaction between the two kings did not play any part in the succession. The Scottish estates promptly chose Robert the Steward, a man of mature years, who was the son of David's sister, Marjorie. The new king had shown rare promise as a youth and had been widely popular. He was described as "beautiful beyond the sons of men," in spite of having red eyes (the color of sandalwood, according to Froissart) owing to a caesarian birth after his mother's death from the fall of a horse; or such was the accepted explanation.

Robert II did not have much chance to display great powers during the nineteen years of his reign. He is chiefly remembered as the founder of the Stuart dynasty which reigned in Scotland for centuries.

David II was forty-seven years old when he died and had been king for forty-one of them; in name, at least.

3

Edward came back to England after his triumphs at Crécy and Calais in a jubilant mood and was welcomed enthusiastically by the people. Thinking himself entitled, perhaps, to some recreation after the years of strain and struggle, and convinced no doubt that in no other way could his reputation be more widely and permanently enhanced, he proceeded to turn a pet dream into an actuality. He established the Order of the Garter.

On the first day of January in 1344, and in advance of the great venture of the landing in France, Edward had announced a series of tournaments at Windsor Castle to which knights from all parts of Europe were to be invited. In order to provide proper facilities for these spectacular events, he planned some building developments at Windsor, a meeting place to be called the Round Table. As early as February of that year carpenters and masons were at work at Windsor and vehicles were bringing in loads of stone and timber from adjoining points. When the international pot began to boil and Edward found it necessary at last to take decisive steps in France, the work at the royal castle had to be suspended.

Then the king and the Black Prince returned to England to the thunderous applause of the whole populace. Their heads were now filled with plans for this great and somewhat mysterious order which was to be a successor to Arthur's Round Table. The exact date when the first steps were taken cannot be established. The official register of the Order of the Garter, which is called the Black Book because it is bound in black velvet, was not compiled until the latter part of the reign of Henry VIII. It is vague as to the facts and clearly has drawn on hearsay.

This much is now accepted as more nearly correct than any other theory: that Edward on returning announced his intention of establishing the order, which was to be called the Knights of the Blue Garter, a title once used by Richard Coeur-de-Lion. Froissart says that all the original members were at the feast where this statement was made, forty in number, and that all of the king's sons were included. It is now accepted that the original enrollment was twenty-five and that of the king's sons only the Black Prince was there.

A wider vision began to occupy the royal mind. Windsor consisted of the Round Tower and some small and not too substantial dwellings which Henry I and Henry III had erected. This far from imposing residence must now be converted into one worthy of a great king and suitable for this universal order.

This brings to the fore a man known as William of Wykeham, who was later to play a quite remarkable part in the history of the day, chiefly as a builder of castles and the founder of Winchester College. He was a clerk on the staff of Nicholas Uvedale, governor of Winchester. There was a rumor current at the time that this promising young man was in reality a son of Queen Isabella and her paramour Mortimer. Ever since the execution of Mortimer and the placing of the queen in seclusion, the rumor had persisted that a son had been born as a result of their illicit relationship; but why Master Wykeham should have been selected for this doubtful honor has never been traced.

He was, in plain fact, of very plain parentage, born in 1323 in the village of Wickham in Hampshire. His father was John Long (or perhaps Long John), a carpenter and a freeman, and his mother was Sybil Bowate, of gentle birth. There is no hint of mystery about his birth and there was nothing in his personality to suggest a parental link with the two principals in that great scandal.

While still quite young he became private secretary to his patron, and it is said he occupied a room in one of the high turrets of Winchester Castle, from which he could look down at all the magnificent buildings about and so acquired a burning admiration for Gothic architecture. He studied the structure of cathedrals and castles in all parts of the country. This hobby, for it could have been nothing else at this stage of his career, was noticed by Uvedale, who mentioned it to King Edward. The king sent for the young clerk and was much impressed with his manners and his well-expressed enthusiasm for fine buildings. The result was

Wykeham's early appointment as clerk of the royal manors of Henle and Yelhampstead and later as surveyor of the king's works in the castle and park of Windsor. The king's readiness to employ him in such a post, when he had no education and no actual knowledge of building, may have roused suspicions which in turn led to the rumors about the young clerk's parentage.

William of Wykeham was in the royal service for many years, during which time the bald and forbidding walls of Windsor were converted into a place of graciousness as well as strength. It was assumed at the time that he had designed the plans and was entitled to the credit for the splendid changes which were wrought. Later and more careful consideration of the available facts has resulted in limiting his part to the administrative control. The architectural inspiration at Windsor was supplied by a highly skilled worker named William of Wynford. It is certain, at any rate, that Wynford was always with him as the "appareller," which meant the master mason, among other things. He was with Wykeham at Wells, at Abingdon Abbey, at Winchester Cathedral, and Winchester College. The royal accounts do not indicate, however, that this man of genius was well paid for his labors. At Wells he received forty shillings a year and sixpence a day. For the work he did at Abingdon he received a yearly wage of three pounds six shillings and threepence and a fur robe. Wykeham received a shilling a day in addition to the yearly salary which went with the post.

The once humble clerk did not underestimate his own part in these quite monumental efforts. He wanted to be remembered and so had the words *This Made Wicham* carved over a small tower in the middle bailey. He was discreet enough to want this piece of self-glorification to go unnoticed at the time, for the words were inscribed in small letters. Not small enough, however; immediately jealous sharp eyes detected what he had done and the story was carried to the king. Edward visited the tower in a fine rage and would have dealt summarily with Master Wykeham if the latter had not been quick to explain that the words were meant to convey a quite different meaning. It did not mean, explained Wykeham, that he had made the building but that the building had made him. The king accepted this somewhat flimsy excuse, but the slab seems to have disappeared at once. It was copied later when the first tower was remodeled and named Winchester Tower.

Wykeham became later one of the greatest "pluralists" of English history. That term was applied to anyone in any stage of holy orders who managed, through favor in high places, to have various benefices conferred on him, canonries here, prebendaries there, livings everywhere. Such benefices did not entail any work or responsibilities on the holder. A grubby curate or a half-starved clerk could always be found to do the work and to accept a small, an exceedingly small, part of the stipend. The greatest pluralist of all time, perhaps, was John Mansel, jack-of-all-trades and Man Friday to Henry III. He fell into the habit of putting his own name on most of the appointment papers which passed across the long marble table at the upper end of the Cage Chamber in the palace at Westminster, where all official documents were signed and sealed. The offices he held were variously estimated at between three hundred and seven hundred and he was called "the richest clerk in the world." The famous Cardinal Wolsey was ranked second in this competition in simony and Wykeham third.

The latter moved up rapidly in the royal service and finally became chancellor. After taking holy orders in 1366 he was appointed Bishop of Winchester. This was one of the richest plums in the kingdom. Refusing to become Archbishop of Canterbury, he was said to have remarked that *the rack of Canterbury was higher but the manger of Winchester was larger*. William of Wykeham did very well indeed there. In addition to the many profitable appointments made for him by the king, he found the Black Death a great aid in his march to preferment and wealth. The plague was no respecter of persons, and fat-waisted churchmen seemed particularly vulnerable. Wykeham was an assiduous gleaner on the very heels of the Grim Reaper, making himself the successor to all the ecclesiastical victims.

He was different from the other great simonical beneficiaries, however, in that he did not keep the benefits to himself. He was one of the most charitable of men, which may have been one of the reasons for the wide popularity he enjoyed.

There are many explanations given for the selection of the name of the new order, the most favored being the story of the Countess of Salisbury and the king. She was the wife of his great friend and early companion, Montacute, whose part in the capture of Mortimer will be remembered. The daughter of a handsome Burgundian knight and Sibyl, the heiress of Tregose, Katherine de Grandison had inherited wealth from her mother and beauty from her father. When David of Scotland laid siege to

Wark Castle, the seat of the family, it happened that her husband was a prisoner in France and so the conduct of the defense had fallen on her slender shoulders. The fair Katherine showed a rare fighting spirit and held the invaders at bay with a small garrison consisting of the constable, a few knights, and not more than twoscore archers and servants.

However, the wail of the pipes around the walls day and night had begun to weigh on her, together with the frequent sound in the distance of *Hey, Tuttie Tatie* which meant that more of the wild Scots were arriving. When she saw an English army approaching with the royal standard carried in the lead, she was delighted beyond measure. It is quite understandable that she lost no time in discarding the chain-mail jacket and the steel helmet in which she had subsisted for so long and arraying herself in her very best raiment to welcome the king.

The fashion in clothes for ladies of rank had been changing, at the dictate of France. No longer were they content to appear in the loose flowing robes which afforded such slim chances of displaying their charms. When she went down to the drawbridge to greet the king, the fair Katherine wore a tight inner jacket of a tawny shade, buttoned straight down in front, and over this a very gay surcoat of lustrous brown and gold, with the hanging sleeves which were the very latest thing in feminine attire, and a very fetching device indeed. The surcoat was elaborately embroidered with the heraldic quarterings of the family and with a great many garters in a variety of shades. To borrow a modern word, there had been a "run" on the garter as a symbol for decoration. It was used for the men quite as much as for the ladies, and the royal accounts refer to a blue taffeta bedcover "powdered" with garters for the king himself. Another item is found of a jupon "for the king's body," with garters and buckles and pendants of silver gilt.

The king had a roving eye and a plausible tongue, but he was silent as he followed the chatelaine to the best chamber in the castle. Wark was one of the very earliest Norman castles and so was little more than an empty shell, the great hall extending clear to the beamed roof and the personal apartments being mere cubicles along the outer walls. The king was to have the lady's own chamber, which was little larger than any of the others but warmly furnished, no doubt, with rugs and hangings. It was reached by a steep and dark staircase opening off from the entrance.

The story runs that when they reached the entrance to the tiny room the king seemed disposed to take advantage of her husband's absence. Much to his surprise, he was rebuffed, gently but firmly.

She returned sometime later to summon him to the evening meal, which was spread out on the long table in full view below, and was somewhat disconcerted to find that he had not arrayed himself in his full finery but apparently had spent the interval in thought. He paused in the doorway and regarded her with somber eyes. She began to regret then that she had gone to such pains with her own attire, fearing that he had misconstrued her motives.

"I pray you will think well of what I have said," stated the king, "and so have the kindness to give me a different answer."

"I hoped, gracious liege," she replied, "that the good Lord in heaven would drive from your noble heart such villainous designs." Then she paused before going on. "I am, and ever shall be, ready to serve you, but only in what is consistent with my honor, and with yours."

The king was silent all through the meal and he left at an early hour the next morning. He had quite apparently given the situation much earnest thought and had arrived at a decision in line with the principles of the new order. The first thing he did on reaching his camp was to give instructions that the Earl of Salisbury, her husband, was to be ransomed and brought home at once.

This was how things stood between the king and the virtuous lady of Salisbury, if the story is to be believed, when a great ball was held at Windsor Castle to inaugurate the order. The earl had been brought back in the meantime and Edward, according to Froissart, "expressly ordered the Earl of Salisbury to bring the lady, his wife. . . . All the ladies and damsels who assisted at this first convocation of the Order of the Garter came superbly dressed, excepting the Countess of Salisbury, who attended the festival dressed as plainly as possible." It may be taken for granted that she was, nonetheless, one of the most beautiful in all that brilliant company.

It happened that the good lady had the misfortune to lose a garter during the dancing. This was quite a common occurrence, for elastic materials were still a matter of the distant future. Although she was plainly attired on the surface, the fair Katherine had seen to it that the accessories she wore were of the best. The garter certainly was a handsome little trifle, of fine silk and most neatly jeweled. Knowing to whom it belonged and being "in full knowledge of their lord's feeling," everyone smiled when he paused to survey it as it lay on the floor at his feet. Observing this, he stooped and picked it up and then fitted it on his own sleeve.

"*Honi soit qui mal y pense* [Evil to him who evil thinks]," said the king in the hearing of all.

The best that historians have to say for this legend is that the title and motto of the order may have been acquired in some such way but that the lady in question could not have been the fair Katherine, wife of William de Montacute, Earl of Salisbury. The chief evidence against it is the fact that the king's old friend and confederate died in 1344—before the idea for the order had entered the royal head—from injuries incurred in a hastilude at Windsor, a form of tournament in which the contestants used spears. It is significant also that Froissart, who delights in all such tales and had moreover a great gift for inventing them, tells the story of Edward's passion for the virtuous chatelaine of Wark but makes no allusion at all to the incident of the garter. It came into circulation at least a century later and was the work of one Polydore Vergil.

Other writers accepted the incident but disagreed as to the identity of the lady. Some said it was Queen Philippa who lost the garter, which obviously was wrong, for the king would not have made his classic remark if it had been her property; no one could think ill of a husband who wore his wife's garter on his sleeve. Still others contended that the lady of the story was none other than the Fair Maid of Kent, who later married the Black Prince. This theory seems to be based on slightly better ground. The Fair Maid, a great beauty but a far from amiable lady, was first contracted to marry the second Earl of Salisbury, the son of the fair Katherine, but allowed herself to be swept into a marriage with Lord Holland. This reigning beauty would most certainly be at the ball and, from what is known of her character, she might even have been capable of loosening her garter to attract the king's attention. Edward may not have been in love with the wife of his old friend (the fact that Froissart tells that story in such detail inclines one to believe there was some degree of truth in it), but there does not seem to be any doubt at all that the king entertained a secret liking for his beautiful madcap niece; secret only in the sense that it was never openly avowed even though it was the cause of much sly gossip about the court.

There is no way of getting closer to the truth, so it seems safe enough to assume that there was a lady who lost her garter and so provoked a much-whispered-about anecdote and led in due course to the finding of a title for the king's order. No other explanation has been provided, at any rate, for the appearance of the words *Honi soit qui mal y pense* on the regalia of the order.

It is impossible to find the exact date when the order was finally established. The chapel of St. George was finished, as far as Edward was to continue with it, on August 22, 1348. It was even at that stage one of the finest examples of Perpendicular architecture in England. It was built, said the letters of patent, "for motives of piety, to the honor of God, the Virgin Mary, St. George and St. Edward the Confessor." There is no mention of the order. Nevertheless, it must have been in the king's mind. There is an item in the accounts, "For making three harnesses for the king, two of white velvet worked with blue garters and diapered throughout the field with wild men." There was in September 1351 a mention of mantles to be delivered to the knights, a receipt of payment for twenty-four robes covered with garters.

The original Companions of the order were: two princes of the blood, Edward and the Earl of Lancaster; the earls of Warwick and Salisbury; five barons, Stafford, Mortimer, Lisle, Grey, Mohun; fifteen knights, all of whom had served at Crécy, and one among them whose name stands out for valor and knightly achievement, Sir John Chandos; and the Captal de Buch, a Gascon nobleman of great intrepidity and stainless reputation.

It is more interesting and significant to note those who were not included. No relatives of the queen had been invited, none of the younger princes nor the Earl of Kent, a first cousin. Men of inferior station had been preferred to such powerful members of the aristocracy as the Bohuns, Clintons, and De Veres, the earls of Hereford, Essex, and Northampton, the lords Cobham, Bourchier, and Dogworth, and Sir Walter Manny. The exclusion of so many of the aristocracy may have been due to their lack of military reputation and as such is to be commended, for if the order was to have any excuse for existence it was to pay honor to valor and chivalry. The exclusion of Sir Walter Manny is hard to understand, for no knight had been performing with greater bravery, and he had, moreover, been in charge of the siege of Calais. He was included in the second list of members.

The selection of the first Companions seems to point to a purpose on the king's part to link the order with the victory at Crécy, for none of the leaders at Neville's Cross were included.

CHAPTER TWELVE

The Royal Household

1

AN incident which occurred many years after the founding of the Order of the Garter gives the best possible picture of the royal household, and so it may be inserted at this point.

The second great battle of the Hundred Years' War, Poictiers, was fought and won in 1356 by the Black Prince. Philip had died and had been succeeded by his son John. The new king was unfortunate enough to be unhorsed and taken prisoner. He was carried to England and taken on a great white horse through the streets of London to the Tower. With the defeated king was his fourth son, Philip, a boy of fourteen, who had fought beside his father and had been almost as hard to subdue as the king himself. The fierceness of the boy's temper was demonstrated the first day of their arrival in London.

The evening meal in the Tower was an event of considerable magnificence. The captive King of Scotland was there and all the leading nobility of the island kingdom. Candlesticks of gold and silver lighted the hall, and the tables were covered with standing cups and flagons and ewers of extraordinary size and beauty. The English king, in fact, had been determined to dazzle the eyes of his fellow king and involuntary guest. The French monarch was seated between Edward and Queen Philippa and the boy was a short distance away.

The young prince was in a mood of smoldering resentment and for the most part kept his eyes on the table in front of him, having little or nothing to say and taking small interest in the rich food served.

It was an evidence of Edward's pride that he kept one of the best tables in Europe; and, incidentally, it was one of the reasons why he was always so deeply in debt. It cost a pretty fortune to supply the food which the lavish king demanded, particularly for occasions such as this. Much of the supplies had to be brought from foreign countries. All the spices of the East were to be found at the royal board: marjoram, galingal, thyme, basil, coriander, fennel, cloves, and cinnamon. In France the quince had been cultivated to the point where it was regarded as the best of all delicacies, and the state had adopted the practice of giving boxes of the best varieties (some came from Portugal, some from Orleans) to all visitors of note at the point of entry into the country. Edward had often been the beneficiary of this clever custom and had acquired such a taste for the fruit that he had arranged to have boxes sent across the Channel regularly for his use. There they were, in flat silver dishes, quite close to the hand of the melancholy young prince if he desired to indulge in them.

In addition there were apricots from Armenia, plums from Syria, cherries from Cerasus, nuts from the Hellespont, and all the fine fruits of the Far East: pomegranates, figs, and dates.

It is possible also that the thistle was served, for it had become one of the choicest of vegetables; not, however, the common thistle but a rare variety which later was further cultivated and became the artichoke. The bread was French, the white bread of Chailly which Edward had been served on his sojournings in France and which he liked so much that now he used it exclusively. Much to the chagrin, it may be said, of the bakers of London; who, stubborn fellows, believed that the kind they made was at least as good.

This, then, was a meal which would appeal to the palate of even the most fastidious of guests. But the son of the captive king had no appetite. As already stated, he sat in an unhappy silence and refused the dishes offered to him. Suddenly, however, he jumped up from his chair and soundly cuffed the official cupbearer of King Edward, a member of the English aristocracy.

"Knave!" cried the boy. "You have served wine to the King of England before the King of France!"

An uneasy silence fell over the large company at table. This was indeed a contretemps, not covered by any known law of etiquette. Someone seems to have remarked that this was England, where the King of England was supreme; that the King of France was there in the capacity of prisoner and guest.

"It is true that my father, the King of France," declared the boy, "is a prisoner. He has been unfortunate. But he is still the

King of France and the liege lord of the King of England, who has sworn fealty to him!"

King Edward handled the situation with good humor and diplomacy. He smiled at the boy and said that indeed his father had been the victim of misfortune, for he had fought bravely and well. But, pursued Edward, it had to be recognized that they were in a somewhat unusual position. What did the recognized laws of etiquette have to say about it? The last question was addressed to Queen Philippa, who regarded the boy kindly before answering that this was indeed a matter which would have to be studied. The young prince returned to his seat and a hum of relieved conversation rose from the crowded tables. It was felt, quite properly, that the royal couple had shown much tact in their attitude.

It required quite as much tact always to handle this fiery French princeling. He did not get along very well with the Black Prince and once engaged in a bitter dispute with him over a game of chess. Again the king and queen acted as mediators and declared in favor of the visitor.

This self-willed young man became regent of France years later. As regent he ruled vigorously and well; he was undoubtedly of the stuff of kings.

2

The inference might be drawn from the above that the royal couple were amiable and prepared to go to great lengths to set a guest at ease. Another lesson to be drawn from the incident is the extravagance of the court and the lavish scale on which everything was done.

The sun was warm and the sky was clear over the royal palace at Woodstock many years before this, on June 16, 1332, to be exact. When the word was carried to the young king that his wife had been delivered of a second child, a girl, he was so delighted that he indulged in an extravaganza of spending. The child showed every indication of great beauty and he gave her the name of Isabella, after his own mother, who had been for a very brief time in seclusion at Castle Rising. Then he proceeded to make sure that the small Isabella would start in life on a scale fitting her rank and potential beauty. One cradle was not enough for her, she must have one for daily use and one for state occasions. The state cradle cost sixteen pounds, being elaborately gilded and decorated with the escutcheons of England and Hainaut. This did not include the coverlet, which was made of nearly a thousand skins.

The child was placed in the care of William St. Maur and his lady, who already had the Black Prince in their charge. Their pension was raised to twenty-five pounds a year, a truly stupendous salary. Even a little maidservant, whose name seems to have been Joanna Gaunbun and who was appointed as official rocker of the said cradles, was allotted the sum of ten pounds a year. To understand the absurd liberality of these arrangements, it is only necessary to point out that twelve years later that genius in stone design named William of Wynford was creating the dignified beauty of St. George's Chapel at Windsor on a yearly stipend in the neighborhood of two pounds a year.

Edward's exuberance could not be controlled. He decided that the *relevaille* of the queen, her first appearance after the birth of the child, was to be notable. Philippa welcomed the members of the court in a state bed with a coverlet of green velvet and wearing a purple velvet robe embroidered with pearls. New costumes in keeping with that of the queen had been provided for her ladies-in-waiting, and even the humblest of her household servants were wearing new livery. When it is revealed that the queen's household had grown to a total of one hundred and sixty, it will be realized that the quiet little Dutch bride had at that early stage begun to fall in with the ostentatious habits of her royal spouse.

The child was no more than a month old when the king appointed a tailor named John Bromley to engage exclusively in making her clothes. The idea that children should be provided with clothing especially suited to their needs had not yet occurred to anyone and would not for a very long time; with the result that the poor little creatures were subjected to all the discomforts that their elders inflicted on themselves, being trussed up tightly, and belted in, and put to the inconvenience of "points." For the occasion of the queen's "uprising," Master Bromley had the infant looking like a miniature of the queen in a silk dress with garnitures and trimmings of costly fur.

The next year a second daughter was born in the Tower and named Joanna, and again the lavish hand of the king was evident in the steps taken for her care and upbringing. The child was placed in the hands of the Countess of Pembroke, who received for her services the manor of Strode in Kent. An elaborate household was maintained for the two small children, including two chaplains, squires, clerks of this and that, a chief cook, a valet of the larder and kitchen, a valet of hall and chamber, a water carrier, a candlemaker, a porter, and numerous attendants of low degree known as sub-damsels.

In spite of all the things in Edward's favor—his good looks, his ability, his energy (he was such an early riser that he might have been called the wakecock king), and later his great successes—he was not a popular ruler. It began with his extravagance and the freedom he allowed his people on royal processionals to raid the countryside. Later his continuous demands on Parliament for a fifteenth, a tenth, a fifth of national revenue embittered even the dullest yokel without a farthing to his name. The population grew very tired of the ever-rising cost of his victories and his defeats.

As the years rolled on and the size of the royal family increased, the court became increasingly ostentatious. The lavish habits of Edward reached their highest point when he indulged in his greatest luxury, the formation of the Order of the Garter. The tournaments attracted contestants from all parts of Europe, all of whom had to be received as guests and made the recipients of costly gifts. Things became even worse toward the later part of the reign when ladies were admitted and costly robes of furred cloth with ermine trimmings had to be provided for them.

Edward was a generous giver, which is commendable in itself but not when carried to such extremes. Princess Isabella grew up to be quite as carefree a spender as her father. She had been given a handsome income, but it never sufficed. She would run into debt and then have to get loans, giving her jewelry or her wardrobe as security. For want of money she always owed wages to her servants and even borrowed from them. Once she pledged her jewels to the royal treasurer and the chamberlain of the Exchequer. Either they told the king or he noticed she was not wearing them. It is said that on this occasion he rebuked her severely.

Nothing did any good. The lovely and generous princess, like her handsome and outgiving father, always spent a great deal more than she had. To give her more only increased her difficulties.

3

Edward had no success in making brilliant matches for his daughters. This was regarded as very strange, for the star of England was in the ascendant and the girls were beautiful, gay, and pleasant of disposition. The fault probably lay in Edward's method. In diplomacy he was devious, and the reigning heads of Europe had come to know that he could not be trusted. If he sought a husband for one of his lovely daughters in Spain, it could be taken for granted that he was also negotiating in other quarters.

Isabella was first affianced to Louis, the son of the Count of Flanders, to cement the alliance with the Low Countries. She was jilted by the young man, whose sympathies lay entirely with France, particularly as he had seen his father slain on the field of Crécy. He ran away to the French court and later was married to Margaret of Brabant. Isabella did not seem at all disturbed because she had in the meantime conceived a liking for one Bernard Ezi, son of the Lord of Albret in Gascony. She was even ready to go to Gascony for the ceremony and had a wedding gown prepared of rich India silk, trimmed with ermine and embroidered with seven ounces of gold thread. Perhaps some quarrel developed between the young couple before the time came for the ships to leave; at any rate, the match was broken off, at the solicitation of the bride. The poor bridegroom-elect was so stricken with grief that he relinquished all his property rights to his younger brother and retired into a monastery. He had been sincerely in love with the gay princess.

Finally, when the charming but capricious Isabella had reached the age of thirty-three, she fell deeply, completely, irrevocably in love with a handsome French nobleman of twenty-four, Ingelram de Coucy, who was in England as a hostage. Although he belonged to the lesser Gallic nobility, the young man regarded himself as of the first importance, a trait which had persisted in his family for generations. The motto of the family, in fact, was an open demonstration of their pride:

> King, duke, prince nor earl am I;
> I am the Lord of Coucy.

Fortunately, or unfortunately as things turned out for the fair Isabella, the young man was as much in love with her as she was with him; and with much persistence they succeeded in winning the consent of the royal parents. They were married at Windsor Castle and the king, characteristically, gave his daughter as brilliant a marriage as though she were wedding the most exalted monarch in the world. On the morning of the ceremony Isabella was presented with jewelry to the value of £2,370. At the wedding feast her father assembled all the best minstrels he could summon and with a lordly gesture paid them a truly colossal figure for their services, one hundred pounds.

Isabella was pleased to find that the lords of Coucy lived in a feudal state quite in keeping with their inordinate pride. The castle of Coucy had a grand staircase twenty-two feet in width, which led to many galleries where the family had their living apartments. There were double walls about the structure with ten ramparts and four bastions, and a donjon tower 176 feet high and 305 feet in circumference. They lived with all the pomp of kings.

The marriage was a success at first. Isabella, who had retained most of her good looks and slender proportions, presented her youthful bridegroom with two daughters, Mary and Philippa. In course of time, however, the pride of the lord of Coucy, who had been given the title of Count of Bedford in England and very extensive estates, rebelled at serving a foreign monarch. As a substitute measure he thought of joining the great Hawkwood in Italy, but this did not accomplish his purpose. The couple parted, to enable him to renew his homage to the King of France. Isabella returned to England and died, it was believed, of a broken heart. Extravagant to the end, she left debts which had to be paid by the crown.

When the second daughter, Joanna, was two years old, Edward arranged to marry her to Frederick, the eldest son of Duke Otho of Austria, and at the age of five she was taken to the Austrian court to be raised.

The poor little princess was caught in a difficult position at the Austrian court, for Duke Otho died and his brother, Albert, who became guardian, was favorably disposed to France. The child, who was now six years old, had the good sense and courage to send secret messages to her father, telling him that she was practically a prisoner. Edward had to make three formal demands before the child was returned to her own family. A journey of fifty days brought her to Ghent, where her mother was staying, and she arrived just in time to help celebrate the arrival of another son in the family. The boy was named John and became the famous and controversial John of Gaunt.

Joanna was thirteen when it was finally decided that she was to marry Pedro, the heir to the throne of Castile. A Spanish ambassador was sent to England to see her and decide whether she would make a suitable bride for the Castilian heir. The princess had her full share of the Plantagenet beauty and was, moreover, the favorite of the royal parents, so the report was affirmative. On January 9, 1348, a time of rough weather and stormy seas, the nuptial party set sail. When they reached Gascony, the Black Death was raging there and the princess was hurriedly removed to the small village of Loremo, where it was believed she would be safe from contagion. The plague spread, however, and the princess was the first victim.

She was deeply mourned by her parents, but it may have been that her early death saved her much grief and suffering. The prince she was to have married developed into the most depraved of men and won for himself the name in history of Pedro the Cruel.

The young claimant to the dukedom of Brittany, John de Montfort, was raised at the English court while the struggle over the succession raged in his homeland. It was understood from the beginning that he was to marry Mary, the fourth English princess (the third, Blanche, had died in infancy), and fortunately they became sincerely attached. Edward was trying a new policy with his family at this stage, one of austerity, and the little Mary was allowed no more than twenty marks a year as her allowance. This did not disturb her at all, for she was a quiet and gentle child and did not like to travel around as her older sisters had done.

John de Montfort was a handsome and vigorous fellow and in due course became duke, but not in time for Mary to share the honor with him. They were married at Woodstock before the issue of the succession was settled, and after seven happy months the bride died of a form of sleeping sickness.

The fifth daughter, Margaret, was married to a commoner, John, the son and heir of Lawrence Hastings, Earl of Pembroke. It was a love match and she was very happy for the brief time it lasted. The princess died after two years of married life at the English court.

CHAPTER THIRTEEN

The Black Death

1

It was not called the Black Death at the time but it was feared as the worst scourge ever to visit the earth. The symptoms mentioned in the scanty records make it clear that it was the bubonic plague or a very close variation. To the terror-stricken people who heard of its appearance, vaguely at first, it was a visitation of God, perhaps even the first manifestation of the end of the world. Men in those days lived in dread of many things, but it was the fear of the second coming which gripped them most firmly; a state of mind which was intensified by the paintings on the walls of so many churches depicting the tortures of the damned.

Rumors reached England first from the Far East. It was said that it started in India and that the visitation had been heralded by strange occurrences on three successive days. On the first day there was a rain of frogs, serpents, and lizards. The second brought thunder and lightning and sheets of fire from the heavens. On the third day there was more fire and a great cloud of heavy, stinking smoke which moved across the earth and blotted out everything. On the fourth day came the plague.

From that time on the people of Europe talked of little else, although there was not as yet any fear that it would reach them. It was conjectured that the terrible visitation was due to an earthquake which opened up graves and filled the air with infection from the uncovered corpses. The tales which white-faced men exchanged in the taverns were all of natural catastrophies. Great winds straight from heaven or hell were sweeping over Asia and carrying the disease with them. There were floods which converted lowlands into swamps from which noxious odors arose.

Then the conjectures, which had been casual before, turned

into panic. The plague had come to Europe. Could anything stop it? Would it loose all its wild terrors on country after country?

It first appeared at a port called Caffa on the Black Sea in 1346. This was a busy shipping center and the vessels there hurriedly spread their sails to escape from this terrible visitation which filled the inns and the crowded houses with bodies carrying the black sign. They spread the disease to every port on the Mediterranean. It manifested itself in an earthquake of unexampled fury which shook Greece and Italy. The air became so heavy and noxious that wine spoiled in tight casks, becoming sour and undrinkable. Then the "thick, stinking mist," which had been described before, advanced over the land and sea and mountain, obscuring everything—the sun, the moon, and the stars. It spread over Italy and the crops wilted and died and the fruit rotted on the trees. There was no food for the poor until in Florence large bake ovens were built from which as many as ninety-four thousand loaves of bread were distributed daily to the starving people.

All of western Europe waited and trembled while this supernatural visitor came closer and closer. A pillar of fire appeared for an hour at sunset over the Palace of the Popes at Avignon. Large meteors were seen in the skies in many countries. A ball of fire was seen over Paris one August evening.

When the plague reached France, the people of England became aware for the first time that it was universal. Word of strange and fearful things came over the water to the island. At Avignon the churchyards could not hold the dead and the Pope consecrated the Rhone so that bodies might be committed to the waters. The French people were said to be adopting strange methods to escape the contagion. Some were wearing small lions carved out of gold. The gates of Paris were erupting with people seeking escape. Only in houses with windows opening to the north could there be safety. The doctors, who were completely in the dark, were advising people to avoid the sun and warm winds. Stay inside, they were saying, and fill the air with the scent of burning juniper and ash and young oak.

But even with France in the grip of this monstrous visitor from the East, the people of England lived in hope. At its narrowest point, the Channel was twenty miles wide, filled with fast and turbulent water and bringing winds which swept strongly westward. How could the contagion spread over this natural barrier, this clean rampart of wind and water?

2

But not the fast-flowing waves of the Channel nor the winds which swept all before them could prevail in the end. There was no cessation of shipping between the island and the mainland, because there was no hint of the strange truth: that there were always rats in the holds of ships and that on the bodies of the rats were black fleas which carried the contagion. It might have been a reasonable precaution for the government to stop all shipping from the mainland, and this might have saved England from the Black Death. But of course nothing of the kind was done.

The first indication of trouble came from the port of Melcombe on the Dorsetshire coast in August 1348. A sailor died there after three days of intense suffering, pitching and moaning in a high fever and spitting blood. People who had been near him came down with the disease at once, the foul symptoms repeating themselves and their faces wearing a black mask of death. Sometimes the agony was prolonged to five days, with tumors appearing outwardly on the groin and under the armpits.

There could be no doubt about it. This was the plague. The people of Melcombe began to die by the hundreds. The terror spread with amazing speed, sweeping over Dorset, Devon, and Somerset, reaching Bristol by the middle of the month. Efforts were made to cut the great western port off from adjoining districts, but nothing could check a wave of death carried, seemingly, on the wind. It spread quickly to Oxford. On All Saints' Day it reached London.

London, of course, was ripe for it. The sanitary conditions there could not have been worse, with people jammed together in little wooden tenements, the streets rank with offal, and swine roaming about at will. The death list mounted so fast that the victims died untended. Those who could get away did so with a haste which filled the roads with galloping horses, and women on couches swung from saddle to saddle. The poor tramped with furious haste, their belongings on their backs. Even members of the priesthood were fleeing, for every report had spoken of the mortality among the clergy. Master Gaddesden, the royal physician, got away with the king's family to the cool seclusion of Eltham Castle. He would not have remained in London at any cost, for this disease was the most disagreeable of all and the one which could profit a man of medicine nothing. A meeting of Parliament had been set for the summer, but the officials at Westminster, prior to packing up themselves, issued a hasty notice of prorogation.

Before leaving London it became the custom to visit Westminster and go to the south transept, where a painting of St. Christopher, the kindly patron saint of travelers, occupied one wall. Here they would pause and study a promise printed under the painting, *Non Morte mala Morietur.* With this assurance of immunity from an evil death they would then depart in a less agitated frame of mind. The greatest dread inspired by the plague was the threat of a death so sudden that the last rites could not be administered.

The toll in London grew so high there was soon no space left in cemeteries. A *toft* of land was obtained near East Smithfield and enclosed with a high wall of stone, and most of the bodies were buried there. Sir Walter Manny, who seems to have been more charitably disposed than most military leaders, bought thirteen acres next to no man's land, called Spittle Croft. Some reports have it that fifty thousand bodies were buried here in the first year of the plague, but this obviously is an exaggeration. Authorities place the population of London at the time very little above that figure.

The Black Death followed close on the heels of England's greatest period of prosperity and success. The victory at Crécy had put national prestige on the highest level, the country was rich and the harvests ample. When faced with the likelihood of death, men looked at one another with wonder as well as fear. "What have we done that this punishment is visited on us?" they asked. "Have we allowed ourselves to become so proud that the wrath of God has been aroused?"

The archers had returned after Crécy with their bows on their backs and ropes of flowers around their necks. Proudly they carried the spoils of victory. They knew full well that they had won the great battle and they proclaimed the fact long and loud. So sure had they become of themselves that if Robin Hood were alive (it has never been established that he actually lived) he would have had hundreds of challenges from these new champions of the longbow, and undoubtedly would have lost some of them.

It seemed impossible that the bowmen of Crécy could die like ordinary men. They enjoyed some immunity, in addition, by living in the small villages where the plague was less likely to strike. But this loathsome disease, produced in the reeking slums of the Far East, was no respecter of locale. The stout yeomen living on the edges of cool green glades and by the clear water of streams caught the infection as quickly as other men and the loss among them ran as high as one in two.

In the larger cities, such as Bristol, Oxford, Norwich, and of course London, the victims were buried in layers in deep pits. In Yarmouth the total stood at 7,052. English statistics seem small, nevertheless, when compared with the records in continental cities. In Florence the death total ran as high as 60,000, Venice 100,000, Paris 50,000. In Marseilles 16,000 people died in one month.

The Black Death reached its peak in England in August of the following year. It subsided then but returned with somewhat lessened fury in 1361 and 1368.

There was no escape possible, even by the method of seclusion made famous by Boccaccio. To go to sea seemed the surest way to invite fate, for the contagion spread more quickly aboard ships than anywhere else. It was not uncommon to see along the southern shores of England ships under full sail being driven by the waters of the Channel, tossing about aimlessly and making it clear that all on board had died. They would vanish finally beyond the horizon into the rough embrace of the Atlantic.

3

One of the most astonishing phases of what has been called the Great Emergence (the trend toward modern conditions of living) came about as a result of the Black Death. England, for the first time, began to have labor troubles.

It happened because the population of the island had been cut almost in half. Most of the great landowners had survived, by immuring themselves behind the thick stone walls of their castles, but after 1349 there were not enough laborers to go around. Much of the land remained untilled and crops were not harvested, while untended flocks and herds ran wild. It followed naturally that a competition developed for the services of the yeomen. Wages went higher and higher, but the laborers, finding such things sweet on the tongue, showed little tendency to work at the beck of the once omnipotent landlord. Labor had gained the upper hand, an extraordinary thing to happen in a country which was still feudal by instinct.

This could not continue beyond a brief, a very brief, period. The land magnates were stirred to fury, and in the cities the prominent merchants swore they could not pay such wages as were demanded. They overlooked the fact that whatever advantage the poorer classes had gained was swallowed up in the increased cost of living. Not being organized, the people could not make themselves heard at Westminster.

The solution reached by the government made it very clear that the tendency toward better conditions had not touched the minds of the ruling classes. A royal proclamation was issued making it incumbent on all unemployed to accept work at the wages which had prevailed before the plague. When this failed to have the desired effect, a Statute of Laborers was passed by Parliament which read:

Every man or woman, of whatsoever condition, free or bond, able of body, and within the age of threescore years—and not having of his own whereof he may live, nor land of his own about the tillage of which he may occupy himself, and not serving any other, shall be bound to serve the employer who shall require him to do so, and shall take only the wages which were accustomed to be taken . . .

This meant that the laborer was in a worse position than he had been for a century at least. While his pay went back to the low levels of previous years, the costs of living remained at the highest peak. The sorriest aspect, however, was that again the agrarian laborer was *bound to the land.* It was specifically forbidden him to quit the parish where he lived in search of better employment. If he disobeyed, he was regarded as a fugitive and was subject to imprisonment. Later the punishment was raised to branding on the forehead with a hot iron. The free men of England had been reduced again to slavery.

If they had been organized sufficiently to hold meetings of protest in all quarters of the kingdom, they might have compelled some amelioration of this great injustice; but the day of labor unions and parties was far in the future. They lived in smoldering discontent under the conditions which had been forced upon them, growing unhappier with each passing year. This led inevitably to trouble, to the Peasants' Revolt which occurred in the reign following that of Edward. It was a sanguinary failure from the standpoint of the leaders who died on the gallows. But it opened the way to later reforms.

It is probably incorrect to say that the laboring classes lacked all organization. Delving into the records of the day, one is likely to stumble over certain odd circumstances which suggest that there were stirrings continuously under the surface. These seem to trace back to one man, a friar named John Ball, who had the habit of assembling the people in the market place after they had heard mass, and haranguing them about their wrongs. He was called the Mad Priest by Froissart, but instead he was a man of a fine and high courage and with such an eloquent tongue that no one could hear him without being persuaded to believe. Twice he was thrown into Canterbury Prison by the archbishop, but word of him got about through all the shires by a system of whispers. "The angel of the Lord will open the prison as he did for Peter" and "Be of good cheer for soon the bell will be rungen by John Ball." It was clear that the men of the soil waited for a signal which was to come from the wandering priest, and this was known and planned for whenever the plowmen got together in secret.

The signal came in time, but that is a story in the future and does not belong here.

The Black Death brought many changes in conditions, mostly for the worse. Farm laborers who refused to accept the hard laws imposed on them formed themselves into bands and lived by waylaying those who passed on the highways. So many priests had died that many churches were closed and people fell easily into immoral ways. The ownership of lands became so involved by death that the number of lawyers increased by leaps and bounds. In one district the number of wills for probate rose from 22 to 222 in a single year.

One circumstance is cited as a great boon. Fecundity in women became most pronounced, and the birth rate began to increase as soon as the Black Death had passed. Twins and even triplets became almost commonplace. Thus, according to medical authorities who had shown a complete ignorance about everything else, did nature find a remedy for the evils of the plague.

CHAPTER FOURTEEN

The Battle of Poictiers and the Peace of Bretigny

1

THROUGH all these years of strife the king had one aide on whom he could always depend, his cousin, Henry of Lancaster. This nobleman was not only a fine soldier but a man of great courage, honesty, and tolerance; a scholar of sorts, moreover, and deeply religious. Having raised him to the rank of duke, Edward sent this cousin on a mission to Avignon in 1353 to discuss with Pope Innocent VI the possibility of a lasting peace between England and France.

The duke had two hundred men-at-arms in his party, and when he arrived on Christmas Eve he was met by such a host of churchmen and soldiers, not to mention curious townspeople, that it was difficult to cross the bridge into the papal city. Lancaster had seen the need to make friends and, with a prodigality worthy of Edward himself, had ordered that one hundred casks of wine be ready in the building he was to make his headquarters. After seven weeks of fruitless discussion, there was nothing left in any of them but a hollow sound.

The first impression gained of Avignon by this urbane ambassador was that the term "Babylonish captivity" was a complete misnomer. It should have been called the "French captivity," for the papal court at Avignon was overrun with Frenchmen. There were French cardinals everywhere he turned, favoring him with sharp looks out of the corners of their eyes and questioning him to find what he proposed to say to the pontiff. French officials of all kinds were doing the same with the members of his train. Outside there were French architects, French builders, French sculptors, French merchants of Eastern goods, all trying to get their share of the enormous wealth which had been left by John XXII, so much of which had already been spent on the Palace of the Popes.

"Peace?" said Innocent VI. "That will depend on the terms you bring me."

Innocent was a man of impartial and judicial mind, although he had been born Étienne Aubert at Mons in Limousin. He wanted above everything to stop the war, but he knew the temper of French royalty too well to see any chance when he heard the terms that Edward was proposing: to give up his claim to the throne of France in return for having his possessions in that country confirmed to him in full sovereignty. The wise Pope knew this would not be acceptable, so it was clear from the start that the mission would not succeed.

The popes at Avignon had all been Frenchmen, and all of them, even the present incumbent with his real desire to be impartial, had found it necessary to favor the French cause. The miraculous victories won by the English had begun to suggest to quizzical and irreverent minds that the Lord on high was not in accord with His vicar on earth. The court at Avignon, where rumor and tattle were always rife, had fallen into the habit of discussing this in sly whispers. Even bits of doggerel were coined and passed from ear to ear. One of these was current when Lancaster paid his visit. A translation into English runs as follows:

> The Pope is on the Frenchmen's side,
> With England Jesus doth abide;
> 'Twill soon be seen who'll now prevail,
> For Jesus, or the Pope, must fail.

The only result was that at Avignon Lancaster met Charles, the King of Navarre. The Navarrese king was young but he had already earned the name of Charles the Bad. It was well deserved, for Charles of Navarre was crafty, unscrupulous, cruel, and notoriously unfaithful in affairs of the heart. Although he was married to Joan, a daughter of the King of France, he was on the worst of terms with that monarch. His royal cousin, he informed Lancaster, meaning his father-in-law, had an eye on his possessions in Normandy which were strategically important. He proposed to the English ambassador an alliance between England and Navarre, with a promise on his part to join any army of invasion they sent into France. This alliance was confirmed later.

In the meantime King Philip had died, with no one to lament his passing. He had not been a success as a king; a glum, proud, and bitterly suspicious figure, whose defeat at Crécy had left

France prostrate. He had been succeeded by his son John, who is known in history as John the Good for no visible reason except perhaps his personal bravery in battle. Otherwise he was credulous, vain, and cruel, and with all the incapacity to rule wisely which his father had displayed. One of his first acts was to behead the constable of France, a brave and loyal man named Raoul, Count of Eu. The new king showed Raoul a letter and demanded to know if he had ever seen it before. When the constable protested he knew nothing about it, the king cried, "Ha, wicked traitor, you have well deserved death!" So the constable went to the block without the formality of a trial and not knowing what the letter had contained.

John, it seems, liked only one man in his train, a naturalized Castilian called Charles of Spain. When he gave to this favorite some of the Norman properties of Charles of Navarre, the latter had the Castilian murdered in his bed. This led at once to hostilities.

Edward was not anxious for war at this stage. He had sent his chamberlain to ask Parliament if they would favor the making of a permanent peace, and the members had responded with loud cries of "Yes! Yes!" England, clearly, had no more stomach for war. Still, there was the obligation to support Charles the Bad.

An army was raised and sent across the Channel under the command of the Duke of Lancaster, and word was sent to the Black Prince at Bordeaux to support the move by advancing against the French flank. The prince had just completed a drive up the Garonne River for the purpose of paying his troops (being completely out of funds) with the spoils of that rich and quiet country. It was said that after the sacking of Carcassonne and Norbonne the horses of his army were so heavily laden they could hardly move. As Charles the Bad in the meantime had made his peace with France and left the English in the lurch, the Black Prince now found it necessary to march again to aid the hard-pressed army of Lancaster. He was slow in getting under way and did not reach the Loire country until much later than had been planned. In the meantime the duke had been forced back to Cherbourg and seemed about to suffer a major reverse. Word of the movements of the Black Prince came just in time, and the French king, who was eager to wipe the score of Crécy off the slate, moved his troops south to meet the heir to the English throne.

The Prince of Wales dallied along the Loire in an attack on

Romorantin. A favorite squire was killed by a stone from the battlements, and Edward swore to avenge him by burning the place to the ground. This was accomplished by the use of Greek fire but not before the French army crossed the Loire south of him. When he became fully aware of their movements, the French had swung around him and were across his line of retreat to Bordeaux.

Prince Edward's army was a small one. He had in all about ten thousand men, including two thousand cavalry and four thousand bowmen. It was certain that the French were out in force, and the situation looked desperate for the English. Falling back toward Poictiers, the prince sent out a party to reconnoiter. When they returned after a brush with a party of French horse, he dispatched the Captal de Buch with a strong force and with instructions to get as close as he could to the French lines. The Captal, who was a brave and resourceful soldier, gained a position on a high hill, from which he saw the royal banners of France waving over Poictiers. The whole countryside was covered with troops. Realizing that they had the full strength of France against them (some prisoners placed John's army at sixty thousand), the Gascon rode back with his information.

"God help us!" said the Black Prince. But he spoke in reverent terms and not in fear.

2

The prince resembled his father in his tendency to loose planning, but he also had the king's great tactical skill in ordering a battle and in fighting it through. He placed his meager forces as skillfully as Edward had done at Crécy. He took up his position on the field of Maupertuis on the crest of a slope so thickly covered with grapevines that the presence of the English was hard to detect. The ground here was unfit for cavalry and only a narrow lane gave access to the crest where the tiny English army waited. The bowmen were placed behind the hedges and in the thick vineyards, with the rest of the troops on foot behind them. The prince lacked one advantage that his father had enjoyed at Crécy: he had no protection on either flank, for the wood and abbey of Nouaille on his right offered no effective cover, and a ravine on the left might delay but not halt an attack. All that John of France had to do, in fact, was to divide his forces and push divisions of his men around both English flanks until the Black Prince would have only two courses: to retreat, which would be to invite complete disaster, or to surrender.

Fortunately for the English, the French king had no more sense of generalship than his father. He does not seem to have thought of the obvious and certain way of beating a small army with a large one, that of surrounding it. At the same time he did not like the look of the field at Maupertuis. It was not a fair and open field where knighthood could perform to advantage. He decided, on that account, to propose terms and sent the Cardinal Talleyrand de Périgord to discuss the matter with the English.

Edward had no illusions about the danger which faced him and he agreed to give up what he had won during the campaign. In addition he promised not to fight against the French for a period of seven years. John scoffed at these terms.

"First," he cried, "he must surrender himself to me with one hundred of his best knights. Then we shall talk of other conditions."

It was Edward's turn to laugh. Had the French king forgotten Crécy that he allowed himself to entertain such a degree of confidence? He, Edward, would never give himself up.

Back and forth all day rode the Cardinal Talleyrand, striving to reconcile the two viewpoints and making no progress whatever. In the meantime the Black Prince had his men hard at work digging ditches and erecting ramparts of earth back of the encompassing vines. He even had time to do something about his vulnerable flanks in case a flash of military intelligence might come to the French king or his overconfident knightly advisers.

It was a Sunday, September 18, 1356, a bright and cheerful day. The French, sitting in their tents, were a happy and rather noisy lot. The late King Philip had created a brotherhood called Our Lady of the Noble House in opposition to the English Order of the Garter. The membership was limited to five hundred knights who had sworn never to retreat in battle but, if necessary, to die on the field. There was some rigmarole as well about never yielding more than four acres of land under any circumstances. They were all on hand, these five hundred bold knights, and it did not enter the head of anyone that on the morrow things would happen to make a mockery of their oaths. All they could see was that the English were trapped and must come to terms or be crushed.

The English remained stubborn and the bright sun sank in the west with no advance in the negotiations.

The battle began early next morning. The Black Prince stationed himself on the level ground above, where he could command a view of the narrow path winding crookedly up the hill. Sir
John Chandos stood beside him as usual. This English knight, the
finest the wars had produced, was tall, clean-shaven, with a nose
like the beak of an eagle, and a disfiguration caused by the loss of
an eye in battle. He was the ablest lieutenant of them all and his
advice was always good.

As they stood together waiting for the French to advance, a
scout brought word that the French king had donned black armor
with a white plume in his helmet. A shout of laughter arose when
it was reported soon after that nineteen French knights were also
wearing black armor and with the same kind of plume in their
head guards in order to protect the king from identification during
the battle.

The talk between the prince and John Chandos was directed to
one point. How much had the French learned from the battle of
Crécy? Had they become convinced of the futility of sending
knights against English archers before making an effort to rout
the men of the longbow?

It soon became apparent that John of France had learned nothing. On a field covered with thick hedges and screened by vines,
the stubborn king ordered an attack by his knights. He sent them
up the narrow path, four abreast, and the English bowmen, shooting from cover, cut them down as fast as they appeared. The
French army had been divided into three divisions. The king commanded one, his three oldest sons shared the leadership of the second, and his brother, the Duke of Orleans, led the third: five
Bourbons who had forgotten nothing and learned nothing.

When the attack was broadened, the English archers shot down
the horses of the charging knights, throwing the line into complete confusion. The English foot troops could now creep forward
through the thick vines and with their long knives dispatch the
knights before they could get themselves disentangled. It was
Crécy all over again, but with the English in a still firmer command of the field. The division led by the three princes was
thrown into such a turmoil that the marshals, who were actually
in charge, saw nothing to be done but to get the royal sons off the
field. The result was that the one division fell back on the next
and the sanguinary chaos of Crécy was re-enacted.

It remained for the Captal de Buch to complete the wreckage

of French morale. Charging from ambush with a small force of mounted men, he drove headlong into the flank of the second French division. Forgetting their oaths and perhaps confused as to how much land constituted four acres, the knights of the Noble House took to flight, prepared to yield not only four acres but the whole of France.

"Sir Prince!" said John Chandos quietly. "Push forward: the day is yours. God has given it into your hands."

Mounting their horses, the English knights charged down the slope after the prince, crying, "St. George, for Guienne!" The retreat of the French became general, and one body of eight hundred lancers galloped off the field without having struck a blow. Soon there was nothing left of that huge and confident army but the troops under the direct charge of the king. These were still capable of winning the battle, being double the size of the whole English army, but for some reason they had no thought but to escape or to sell their lives as dearly as possible. King John cried out to his men to alight and then dismounted himself. His youngest son, Philip (who would survive to cuff a cup-bearer at the English court), was beside him and behaving with great coolness for a lad of fourteen.

The king finally yielded himself a prisoner to a French knight who had been fighting on the English side, having been banished earlier. There had been excited rumors in the English lines during the battle about the nineteen French knights in black armor, and many of them had been captured or killed. The mystery as to the identity of the king was now solved. The king removed his helmet.

"Where is my cousin, the Prince Edward?" he asked. Then to the English men-at-arms, who were scuffling to get possession of his person, recognizing the value of the prize, he said: "I pray you take me peaceably to my cousin. I am great enough to enrich you all."

The Black Prince had seen to it that his standard was brought down from the crest to serve as a new rallying point. His silk pavilion was raised and here a supper was served to the captive king, the prince waiting on him personally and doing everything possible to set him at ease. During the meal a survey was made of the field and it was learned that the French had left eleven thousand dead, over two thousand of them men of knightly rank. The English loss was low in the hundreds.

A curious anecdote of the battle has survived. A Welsh soldier named Howell y Twyell had performed so bravely that the Black Prince knighted him on the field and endowed him with a pension. As a further honor, the battle-ax of the Welshman was taken to the Tower of London and every day a full meal was placed beside it for the owner if he should appear. As soon as it was certain that Sir Howell would not come, the food would be distributed to the poor, with instructions to pray for the soul of the rightful partaker. This custom was followed for over two hundred years and was ended with the Reformation.

3

A truce for two years was arranged and the captive king was taken to Bordeaux. Here the winter was spent in tournaments and recreation of all kinds. John hoped he would not be removed from the country, but early in the spring orders were received from King Edward that he was to be brought to England. The prince set sail with his prisoner in April and they landed at Sandwich eleven days later. Desiring to meet the unfortunate John on an informal basis, the English king rode out from London with a hunting party.

"Sweet Cousin, you are welcome," he said when the two parties met.

The citizens of London outdid themselves in their welcome a few days later. Tapestries were hung from all the windows and the twelve prettiest girls in the town were suspended above the streets in cages so they could shower flowers on the victorious Edward and the French king as they passed. John was on a splendid white charger, but Prince Edward contented himself with a black pony. King Edward received them at Westminster Palace and later presided at a great feast. A luxurious river-front palace, called the Savoy, was given to the royal prisoner for his residence. Here he was to remain in great comfort for a very long time.

There was no comfort for anyone in France. As the fighting was over temporarily, the soldiers who had been engaged in it formed themselves into bands called Free Companies and proceeded to prey on the people, robbing and burning and laying the country bare. Wherever one looked, the fields were black and desolate. The houses were piles of rubble and the fences had given up and were allowing the wild growths of nature to take back their own.

Even the sun seemed to have caught the infection and shone with a wan light. Never did one hear, even at dawn when farmyards came alive, the cheerful lowing of cows or the confident cackle of chickens.

The French soldiers were as active in this freebooting as the English and the mercenaries from other countries. While the land was thus being bled white, the need to raise ransoms for the captured nobility led to new taxes and exactions laid on the overburdened backs of the people.

The hardships they suffered were so great that finally the peasantry rose in rebellion. Armed with scythes and clubs, the maddened peasants attacked and captured many castles and murdered all the occupants, irrespective of age or sex. This insurrection, which was called the *Jacquerie* from the name Jacques Bonhomme applied to the tiller of the soil, was suppressed in a thorough and bloody manner in time to prevent it from spreading and attaining the proportions of a civil war. The *Jacquerie* set off even more significant troubles. The eldest son of the king, Prince Charles, had been made regent in his father's enforced absence and had taken the title of the dauphin, because the land of Dauphiné had recently been ceded to France. He resorted to many unpopular measures to raise money, including the debasing of the coinage. The people of Paris rose indignantly under the leadership of Stephen Marcel, their provost, and put such pressure behind the States-General (the equivalent of the English Parliament) that radical measures were taken to make the government of the country more democratic. Marcel, who was a combination of patriot and demagogue, went too far, however, and his following fell away from him and in the end he was killed in a riot on the streets of Paris.

In spite of the dire conditions in France, the people rallied back of the young regent to reject a treaty which had been negotiated in England between the English king and the captive French monarch. The terms included the cession to England of Maine, Touraine, and Poitou in the south and Normandy, Ponthieu, and Calais in the north, which thus established again the Plantagenet empire of the days of Henry II and went a vast step beyond, because the ceded territories would belong to the English king in full sovereignty.

This rejection in 1360 forced Edward to cross the Channel with another army in an effort to bring the French to terms. Knowing that he could not expect his army to live off a country which had been stripped so thoroughly, he took a long provision train with him, including equipment such as ovens, forges, and mills. The train following the army was six miles in length.

He met with no resistance in the open but was unable to capture Rheims, his first objective, and so pushed his forces down the Seine with the idea of attacking Paris. The mettlesome Parisians organized to defend themselves and succeeded so well that it soon became apparent to Edward that his supplies would be exhausted before he could expect to see his leopards floating above the Louvre. Accordingly he moved down into the fatter lands of the Loire and here he met envoys from the Duke of Normandy with proposals for peace. The dauphin had given in sufficiently to seek better terms, and in May a treaty was finally drawn up and concluded at Bretigny, a small town in the neighborhood of Chartres.

Although there was some disappointment in England because Edward agreed to abandon his claims to the throne of France, the Treaty of Bretigny was a triumph for the English king. He was confirmed in his possession in full sovereignty of Gascony, Guienne, Poitou, Saintonge, Limousin, Anjoumois, Périgord, Bigorre, Rouerque, Ponthieu, Guisnes, and Calais. The French king agreed to pay a ransom of three millions of gold crowns in six years, and a first payment of six hundred thousand florins was guaranteed by John Galeas Visconti, Duke of Milan, as the price of his marriage with Isabel of France, John's daughter.

All this was humiliating to the French people, but they had suffered so much in the wars that they welcomed the peace with much ringing of bells and dancing in the streets.

Edward returned to England, believing the war to be at an end and the victory his.

CHAPTER FIFTEEN

The Black Prince

1

THE Black Prince caught the fancy of the English people almost from the day of his birth. He became a national hero, and nothing he did, not even the extreme savagery he displayed on several occasions nor the financial disorder of his official as well as his private life, disturbed or diminished the admiration the public had conceived for him. When he came home to die at the age of forty-six, with the dreams of conquest shattered and the star of England in the descent, he was still the idol of the commonality.

Little is known about him. It is almost impossible to see and understand the man back of that imposing façade. He was brave to a fault. He had certain fixed ideals which nothing could shake or change. He was courteous to those about him and generous to his friends, but there seems to have been little actual warmth in either his courtesy or generosity. Money meant nothing to him and he was always deep in debt. To gratify his generous impulses ("a war-horse called Bayard Bishop to William Montacute," "a hobby called Dun Crump to a German knight"), he had to permit his stewards to extract every penny they could from his tenants. The peasants on his lands in Cheshire broke out in revolt in 1353 because of the burdens laid upon them. His managers in the stannaries continued to get out tin in large quantities without any record being kept or any payments being made. It was said that in the face of an almost universal admiration his tenants had nothing but detestation for him.

As a boy he was handsome, strong, and manly. The kind of gossip circulated about the rowdy household of the young Edward II, which got into the chronicles of the day, was never told or believed about this prince, who was so obviously destined for great things. To the people he seemed like a wonderful and flawless painting in oil glimpsed high up in a cathedral gloom. The story of his bravery at Crécy swept over England. The whole nation went mad with joy when he defeated John of France at Poictiers with a handful of men, even though his opponent knew as little of warfare as, say, that fanatical lover of chivalry, Don Quixote himself.

There are few anecdotes told about him, none which help to a real understanding of the man himself. Had he a sense of humor? He smiled gravely and courteously, but did he ever laugh out loud? Did he enjoy the wine which flowed so freely after the evening meal? Did trivial emotions ever ruffle that stern and handsome countenance? Did his luminous eyes, as blue as the skies of Gascony but as fixed as those of an eagle, ever soften at the sight of a beautiful woman?

Although he did not marry until he was thirty years of age, it was known that he had two illegitimate sons, Sir John Sounder and Sir Roger Clarendon, and that a hint of a third was conveyed in a household record in 1349 about "a horse called Lyard Hobyn to his own little son Edward."

Less is known of a daughter of the Black Prince. Historians have ignored her existence. But there are records which prove her to have been married to one Waleran de Luxemburg, Count of Ligny and St. Pol. In a written challenge issued by the count to King Henry IV he identifies himself as having had as his bride the sister of the "high and powerful Prince Richard, King of England." The countess's Christian name, her personality, whether or not she inherited the blond Plantagenet beauty, the royal grace and temper, are lost to the pages of history.

The possession of illegitimate children was not regarded as a sign of weakness or of dissolute living. It was merely a proof that a small streak of frailty existed after all in that perfect statue of a man.

He was as extravagant and lavish as his father, but his largess was dispensed with a more regal hand. Because he never seemed to step down from his pedestal, he maintained a higher degree of dignity than his splendid father. Even his closest and most devoted friends, including John Chandos, always had to look up. It may have been that he felt the eyes of posterity on him; or it may have been that he lacked the small common weaknesses. Whatever faults he had were great ones; but it is clear that he did not recognize them as faults.

As he was handsome in his person and kingly in air and carriage, and most particularly as he always seemed to be riding high in the clouds like a mythological god, he grew rapidly into a legend, a symbol of everything right and fine. He attached men to him with a fanatical devotion but perhaps not with the warm ties of affection which can exist between close friends.

His father, the king, was said to have a preference for his son John above the other royal princes, even the brilliant first-born. John of Gaunt was a fine knight in his way, tall, handsome, and deeply ambitious, but he was of baser metal. The people of England were more observant and acute in their judgment of the pair. They worshiped the Black Prince to the day of his death, but at the first opportunity they burned to the ground John's magnificent palace on the Thames, the Savoy.

2

Almost from the day of his birth at Woodstock there had been talk of a suitable marriage for the heir to the throne. At first it was felt that only a French princess would serve, and some preliminary steps were taken to arrange for his union with a daughter of Philip of Valois. Then the inevitability of war between the two nations became apparent and that plan was dropped. There was talk later of marrying him to Margaret, daughter of the Duke of Brabant, or to a daughter of the Count of Flanders. After that the possibility of a match with a princess of the Portuguese royal family was explored, even though the advantages were remote. Some obstacle always developed. Perhaps the well-known tendency of the king to be overdemanding and something less than open and aboveboard in his methods had this effect. Certainly the prince himself was never co-operative. This may have been due to his complete absorption in matters military. He loved horses and dogs, and the fine blade of a sword seemed brighter than a lady's eyes. Or it may have been due to an early preference he had felt for a cousin, Joan of Kent.

Joan, who has been mentioned before, was the youngest daughter of Edmund, the half brother of Edward II, who had stood all those grim hours beside the block waiting for Mortimer to find someone base enough to wield the ax. When Mortimer's turn came to die and Queen Isabella was bundled off to Castle Rising, the girl had been taken in hand by Queen Philippa and raised at court. The prince had not been much at court before that, having a preference for hunting and military exercises which he could indulge in his household at Berkhampstead. As he grew up, however, he became increasingly aware of this fair second cousin, who was two years older than he was and who fluttered about the court in the most beautiful robes of shimmering silk, with bodices embroidered in ermine and the costliest of furs. She was not only very winsome but very gay, and he found her loquacity and easy laughter quite entrancing; although, being silent as well as strong, he did not often share in her gaiety. He began to see less of the hunting fields at Berkhampstead and more of his large stone house on Fish Street in London, which gave him opportunities of appearing at court. It was clear to him, of course, that he could never marry Joan. Even if his parents could be persuaded to such a course, which was highly unlikely, the leaders in Parliament would have frowned on it.

This is one explanation of the undefined and rather vague relationship which existed between them. There is another, which has found more general acceptance: that Edward had no more than a cousinly affection for the golden-haired hoyden but that Joan's eye had been on him from the start and that she was very unhappy because she knew she would never be allowed to marry him, even if she could break down his seeming indifference to her. Whichever is the true one, the time came when Joan had to think seriously of marriage. There was still no evidence of a willingness on the part of the king and queen to permit a match with the heir to the throne. Two contestants had come forward for her hand, the young Earl of Salisbury (the son of the king's fair Katherine) and Sir John Holland, the steward of the royal household. Both were so madly in love with "the little Jeanette," as Prince Edward called her, that their struggle for her favor had to be carried finally to Avignon. Holland had gained the upper hand by getting a contract of marriage, but he was summoned to France on the outburst of war before the ceremony could be performed. The Earl of Salisbury took advantage of his absence to enter into a marriage contract with her, and when Holland came back there was a pretty problem to solve. It was referred to Pope Clement VI, who finally gave judgment for Holland. With many regretful glances over her shoulder in the direction of the unattainable Edward, the Fair Maid of Kent allowed the masterful Holland to carry her off.

That was in 1349. In 1360 Holland died in Normandy, leaving his widow with three children, a son and two daughters. Joan was beautiful enough to be called still the Fair Maid, although she was no longer as slender as she had been and the gold of her hair might have shown some of the tarnish of time had her maids been less zealous in the care of it. She was, after all, only thirty-two years of age and of much physical vitality.

As a widow she was, of course, a great catch. Her only brother had died and she had become Countess of Kent and Lady Wake of Liddell in her own right. She had wide possessions and a handsome pension from the crown for her lifetime.

And now the story of the romance has arrived at a point where all the chronicles agree. There were many suitors for the hand of this most desirable widow, and some of them came to the Black Prince to beg his kind offices in their behalf. That determined bachelor (he was now thirty years of age and it was generally believed he would never marry) listened to all of them with due attention but had little to say.

He was in England at the time and maintaining a rather lively household in his stone habitation on Fish Street. But he was far from content with what life was doing for him. It was clear to him that he had reached the peak of his military reputation in winning the battle of Poictiers. For years he had been acclaimed as the perfect exponent of chivalry, the peerless paladin of the civilized world. What more could life offer him now? He was feeling the sense of futility which comes to all men who have achieved in their youth what they had hoped to win in a long full life. And now, as a further reason for discontent, there was this clamorous bidding for the hand of the fair widow, the lively Jeanette he had always admired. He began to show little interest in anything, to sit at the head of his board with an air of preoccupation, failing to share in the laughter of his companions, leaving the wine untouched in his jeweled flagon.

Finally a suitor came asking for his help who could not be put off with a courteous word and an indifferent shrug. It was Sir Bernard de Brocas, a member of a Gascon family which for generations had suffered many hardships in the service of the English. He had been with Edward at Poictiers and was one of the first to cry "St. George for Guienne!" and go charging behind the prince through the vineyards. Frowning unhappily, the prince listened to the fervent protestations of his friend. He could do no less than inform the Lady Joan of this offer.

So the Black Prince carried to the Fair Maid of Kent the word that the young, brave, and handsome Sir Bernard de Brocas was in love with her and would be most unhappy if she could not be persuaded to smile on his suit. History does not tell where the meeting took place between them, but it is safe enough to assume that it was either Westminster or Windsor. Knowing that the question of her future would soon be settled, the Countess of Kent (who was as shrewd as she was fair) would be at court to get her own way.

It has already been said that she had retained most of her beauty. The slight tendency to matronliness in her figure would have no other effect on the prince than to enhance her attractiveness in his eyes. She looked intently at the heir to the throne, the man she had always wanted, while he explained his errand.

"Fair Cousin," she said, "I shall never marry again."

The prince protested that she was too young and too lovely to retreat from life. "Why do you refuse to marry any of my friends?" he asked. "You may have your choice of them."

Joan began to weep, being, as one chronicle says, a lady of great subtility and wisdom. "I desire none of them," she declared.

The prince began to find it hard at this point to retain the air of judicial calm which he showed at all times. He said in tense tones, "There is no lady under heaven that I hold so dear as you!"

As she continued to weep, but not copiously enough to make her very lovely eyes red, he took her in his arms and kissed her.

"Do you not know," he forced himself to explain, "that the one I have spoken of to you is a chivalrous knight? That he is the most honorable of men?"

The fair Joan knew that at last the chance to win him over to her had come. She whispered, with her head held down: "Ah, sir, before God, do not talk to me thus. For I have already given myself to the most chivalrous knight under heaven. Because of my love for him, I will never marry again as long as I live." After a moment she added, "It is impossible that I should have him to my husband, and so my love for him parts me from all men."

The prince demanded with sudden fierceness the name of the man she loved. His fair and clever cousin would do no more than shake her head and profess her inability to answer.

Edward protested then that he would make it his concern to find who the favored man was and that he would consider him a mortal enemy.

The time had come to reveal the truth. The Lady Joan said, still screening her eyes with her hands: "My dear and indomitable lord, it is you! It is for love of you that I will never have any other knight by my side."

Edward was quite amazed at this admission and fell at once into a fervent protestation of his love.

"My lady," he declared, "I vow to God that as long as you live never will I have another woman save you to my wife!"

And so it came about that after all the years which had passed the faithful prince won his fair lady. The prince became a devoted husband, and yet it is hard to escape the impression that if it had been left entirely to him he might have been willing to go on living in solitary state as before; that, in fact, he had been the victim of a woman's tears glistening on lowered lashes, by the sweet curve of her cheek reviving memories of her girlish charms, by the enticement of a very fine figure bent before him in womanly supplication.

Be that as it may, the happy couple proceeded then to lay their plans most carefully. They knew that the king and queen would be strongly and even bitterly opposed. Queen Philippa had loved the Fair Maid when as a small girl she had fluttered about the court like a butterfly, but as the years passed she had come to assess the Lady Joan at her proper worth. The prince and his bride-to-be on that account made all their preparations quietly for the ceremony before allowing a word of their plans to get out. When the prince finally announced his purpose, he made it clear to his royal father and mother that he would allow nothing to stand in the way of his happiness. Discomfited and sorely disappointed, they nevertheless knew their son well enough to be sure he meant what he said. Reluctantly they gave in and the marriage was celebrated with great pomp and circumstance at Westminster. All the royal family were present, and all the nobility of England, to see the national hero lead his lady love to the altar.

It was clear to all concerned, however, that there was a rift in the once happy family. King Edward was wise enough to realize the possible consequences and he planned to make his son the lord of Guienne and Gascony and to vest him with all power of government in the French provinces. It was settled that the Black Prince was to have a yearly grant of sixty thousand crowns from the money still being paid on the ransom of the French king. This should have been enough for even as lavish a spender as the heir to the throne, but of course it failed to meet his needs, and he was in debt almost from the first days of his rule.

The prince agreed eagerly to his father's plan, for he loved the south and was always happiest at Bordeaux. He and his bride left

England in February 1363 and did not return until many strange and tragic things had come to pass.

3

The ruler in Spain at this time was Pedro V, who had been given the nickname of "The Cruel" and most richly deserved it. It will be recalled that little Princess Joanna of England was on her way to marry this unnatural creature when she died in Gascony of the Black Death; and in view of the record he had since established, it may be accepted that the unfortunate child had escaped a much worse fate. Pedro had married Blanche of Bourbon and had thrown her into prison (and later had seen to it that she died), but he had remained faithful to a mistress, Maria de Padilla, and had given it out that they were married. Two daughters, Constance and Isabella, had been born of this union, and their father had demanded that they be accepted as legitimate.

This bloodthirsty despot kept about him a Moslem guard whose leaders he confided in, and he had felt safe in committing a long series of judicial murders which kept his subjects trembling.

A revolutionary party had formed in the country under the leadership of a bastard brother of the king, Henry of Trastamara. Charles V of France had conceived a way of ridding his country of the Free Companies by seeing that they were offered inducements to join the Spanish revolutionaries. Several thousand of them had accepted this bribe, including many of the best English captains. Pedro was a weak leader and he found himself powerless against an opposition bolstered by such capable fighting men. He abandoned his throne, after executing two innocent churchmen, the Archbishop of Santiago and his dean, and came whining to the Black Prince for help.

There was no good reason for Edward to listen to this savage despot. His reputation as a great knight and leader was assured. His court was recognized as the most brilliant in Europe. He was happily married and had one son who bore his name. He enjoyed his life at Bordeaux, in a palace which was broad and spacious and opened out graciously to admit the warm sun and the sea breezes.

Pedro whispered slyly in the ear of the prince that he had left treasure behind him in Castile, so cleverly and securely hidden that no one would ever lay hands on any of it. This he was prepared to divide among the men who would restore him to his throne. Further, he intended to divide his dominions and would give the crown of Galicia to the little Edward, the prince's very much loved son. These were tempting bribes, but the Black Prince was little concerned with such material considerations. What weighed with him was that a lawful king, the son of a king, anointed with the holy oil, had been ejected by an uprising of his subjects. His deeply rooted feudal sense rebelled at such a thing. What security would there be for other kings if this outrage were permitted to go unrectified?

After convincing himself that it was his duty to support the cause of the predatory Pedro, the prince summoned his council and laid the case before them. He was surprised, and secretly much annoyed, that they did not agree with him. It was Sir John Chandos, the true knight, whose loyalty was so deep that he could give no advice save what he believed himself to be right, who acted as spokesman for the council. Sir John spoke of the cruelty of the deposed king, the sacrilegious acts of which he had been guilty, of the sufferings of the people under him. Why should they undertake war on behalf of such a man?

"Chandos, Chandos!" cried the prince, his handsome face suffused with emotion. "I've seen the time when you would have given me the other advice. Whether the cause was right or wrong."

Chandos shook his head. "No, liege lord," he declared. "Not when the cause was wrong."

After several more meetings, with the schism between the prince and his council becoming wider all the time, Edward decided to act. He issued a proclamation, reading in part:

My lords, I take it for granted and believe that you give me the best advice you are able. I must, however, inform you that I am perfectly acquainted with the life and conduct of Don Pedro, and well know that he has committed faults without number, for which at present he suffers; but I will tell you the reasons which at this moment urge and embolden me to give him assistance. I do not think it either decent or proper that a bastard should possess a kingdom as an inheritance, nor drive out of his realm his own brother, heir to the throne by lawful marriage; and no king or king's son ought ever to suffer it, as being of the greatest prejudice to royalty. Add to this, that my father and this Don Pedro have for a long time been allies, much connected together, by which we are bound to aid and assist him.

An embassy was sent to England to get the opinion of King Edward and his royal council. The verdict was quickly returned in favor of the prince. Word was conveyed to him, moreover, that his brother, John of Gaunt, who had been made the Duke of Lancaster, would be sent with a force from England to assist in the military operations. A potent argument in favor of intervention had been a prophecy of Merlin, that "the leopards and their company should speed themselves to Spain." That great fraud had left many senseless prophecies behind him and they seemed to crop up always at the very worst moments, to bolster false causes, to raise unwarranted hopes, to justify the worst of decisions. None had been more harmful than this particular absurdity was to prove.

Quite apart from the acknowledged principle that an outside nation had no right to interfere in the internal troubles of another country, there were good reasons why the prince should have turned a deaf ear to the blandishments of the false Pedro. The French provinces under English rule were seething with discontent. Edward was not a good administrator and he was following his old method of leaving things in the hands of stewards and deputies. A lack of method had developed which was resented by the people, who had a strong predilection to system and order. It was even more damning that looseness and lack of honesty in the law courts made justice hard to obtain. The revenues were falling off. The prince himself was deeply involved in debt and not at all particular in the ways he employed to meet his obligations; or to evade them, as the case might be. Even the ruling classes of Bordeaux and the wine-growing localities, who favored the English connection because of the easy market it provided for their wine, were growing restive and concerned.

The prince should have realized that his fences needed mending in all parts of the land which had come to England by the Treaty of Bretigny. To absent himself at such a time was to invite trouble. He did not seem to care. His adventurous spirit had taken fire again. Across the Pyrenees lay chances for more glory. Was he to be bound instead to the boredom of law courts and the monotony of administrative detail? Such were for the starling and the sparrow; the eagle must spread his wings and soar. Even a sick eagle; for Edward was not well at all.

The pass of Roncesvalles across the Pyrenees had always been a difficult one, as the great Roland had learned. The English forces marched through boldly but with strict attention to the possibilities of attack. Roncesvalles was in the domain of Navarre and, although Charles the Bad had been paid handsomely for the right of passage, no one put any stock in his promises. As it turned out, however, they got through without seeing a single plume above the rocky crags or hearing a cry of defiance.

Three days before the march began, Edward had been presented with a second son, who had been named Richard. He departed, therefore, in high spirits. This mood did not desert him when his army debouched on the other side of the gloomy mountain heights, which had greeted them with sullen rains and blasts of wind sweeping through the declivities. Even when he found that the forces of Henry of Trastamara under French command consisted of sixty thousand men while his own, after the reinforcements under John of Gaunt had been added, were about half that number, his feeling of confidence did not leave him. He marched through the rains to the flat country around Vittoria and came face to face with the enemy forces near Navarrete.

The story of Navarrete did not differ much from the now familiar pattern. The Black Prince rode through the lines and prayed aloud: "God of Truth, Father of our Lord, who hast made and fashioned me, condescend through Thy benign grace that the success of the battle today may be for me and mine. Advance banners in the name of heaven and St. George!"

When the division which the prince commanded himself struck the forces led by Sancho the Stammerer, a brother of Henry, the Spaniards turned in terror and fled so precipitously that Edward suspected a ruse and did not pursue. There was no serious opposition offered except by the Free Companies under Bertrand du Guesclin. The latter fought like a demon, with Pedro shouting furiously from the safety of the English lines that none were to be spared. When his shrill cries of "Kill! Kill!" attracted the attention of the great Frenchman, Du Guesclin plunged out from his own array and attacked Pedro with such concentrated power and fury that the deposed king fell in a faint. Before he could be revived, the prince had persuaded Du Guesclin to surrender and had placed him in the custody of the Captal de Buch, thereby turning the tables between those two gallant paladins, as will be explained later.

The conduct of Pedro the Cruel, exhilarated by the victory his English allies had won for him, was so disturbing that all the Saxon leaders under the prince found it hard to contain themselves. The next morning Pedro came to the tent of his benefactor and offered to pay him the full weight of Du Guesclin in silver if the brave Frenchman were turned over to him. When this was refused, he begged to have his half brother delivered into his hands as well as all Spanish prisoners of high rank, his avowed purpose being to cut off their heads. The prince refused brusquely and demanded of Pedro a promise that he would pardon all his opponents. The leniency of the English robbed the revengeful monarch of much of the pleasure he had anticipated from his restoration.

The English army remained on the bleak plains for several months, waiting for the payment promised by Pedro to cover the expenses of the campaign. No word came from him. Not a single coin was received. As for the fabulous secret treasure, its hiding place was never revealed; probably it had no actual existence. The offer of a crown to Edward's son was withdrawn. When the prince sent three knights to demand satisfaction, they brought back nothing but a letter; a furtive and muddled communication which gave no satisfaction.

The English losses in the battle had been small, four knights and a few hundred soldiers. But after the unhealthy camp conditions and the rigors of the return march, only one fifth of them were alive when they reached France.

As the Black Prince led his hungry and disappointed troops back over the dangerous defile of Roncesvalles, he had much time for reflection. It is doubtful, however, if the treachery of the Spanish king had caused him to change his mind. He had certain fixed beliefs and ideals, and these he held to in spite of everything. It was as clear to him as ever that kings should never be deposed, no matter how villainously they had behaved. Pedro was almost a homicidal maniac. He was treacherous and as much to be feared as a poisonous snake under a rock. But he was the legitimate king and it had been to Edward a sacred duty to go to his assistance. What would his thoughts have been had he known the fate reserved for the little three-day-old son he had left with his wife in Bordeaux?

The aftermath of the situation created by Edward in thus adhering to his unshakable belief in monarchy can best be told by a brief mention of certain unusual occurrences. The Princess of Wales, out of admiration for the bravery of Du Guesclin, contributed ten thousand florins to his ransom. John Chandos, that fine old warrior, offered to loan him the same amount. In spite of his youth and comparatively humble antecedents, the King of France appointed Du Guesclin constable of France. The two younger brothers of the Black Prince, John of Gaunt and Edmund of Cambridge, married the two daughters of Pedro a few years later. John of Gaunt strove for eleven years to make himself King of Castile because his spouse, Constance, was the eldest child of Pedro.

Hurrying back to Spain, Du Guesclin joined forces again with Henry of Trastamara and surrounded the restored ruler in the castle of Montiel. Pedro, trying to escape under cover of darkness, was detected and in a scuffle with his brother was stabbed to the heart. So Henry the illegitimate became king after all.

Prince Edward had made no effort to assist the ungrateful Pedro a second time. He had been a sick man when he started on his march through the mountains to Navarrete. On the return he found it hard to retain his seat in the saddle. His face was as gray as the wind-swept plains along the Ebro, and he moved with the greatest difficulty. The nature of the disease which had fastened upon him was never diagnosed accurately, but no one needed more than a glance to realize that the days of the prince who had been the idol of England all his life were numbered.

4

The prince was guilty of two great errors during his term as suzerain of Aquitaine and Gascony. The first was getting himself involved in the Castilian adventure. This left him in such financial straits that his second great mistake followed quickly. He imposed a *fouage*, a hearth tax, on the people. The taxes were already so high that there was bitter discontent, and this new exaction caused the resentment of the people to boil over. It happened when all France was in a turmoil and a renewal of the war with England seemed certain.

No one alone can be blamed for the troubles which followed the peace of Bretigny. It was impossible to cut a great country in two and turn one large part of it over to a foreign power with any

expectation of making it permanent. The English were blamed for
the horrors of Free Company depredations, particularly after Edward ordered them out of Aquitaine, thus driving them over into
the Loire country. The terms of the treaty, moreover, had not
been fulfilled by either side. When the captive King John returned to his throne and found his people unwilling to live up to
their part of the agreement, he went back voluntarily to England
and took up again the role of royal prisoner. Some regarded this
act as a shining example of chivalry at its best. Others, more realistic about it, considered that he had crowned a career notable for
its folly with a final and supremely idiotic gesture. Some believe
that he knew the end was near and by arranging to die in England
he made it unnecessary for France to continue paying his ransom.
Perhaps it is only fair to assume that this was back of his action.
When John died in the luxury of the Savoy Palace in 1364, his
oldest son succeeded him as Charles V and, for a change, the
country found it had a practical and vigorous king. The new ruler
brought to the throne one fixed resolve, to break the treaty and
drive the English out of France.

To break the treaty was not hard, for neither country had lived
up to the most important clauses. To make the agreement binding, both sides had to give up certain fortresses and to exchange
official letters. Some of the fortresses had not been given up and
the letters had not been exchanged. The French seemingly could
not bring themselves to give away the western and southern provinces and Edward found himself unable to forswear formally and
finally his right to the throne of France. When things became
tense later, he maintained that he had not abandoned his rights.

Charles V took the first overt step by sending an embassy of
two members to wait on the prince at Bordeaux. When they appeared at the Abbey of St. Andrew, where the prince held court,
there was astonishment and indignation over the French king's
choice of representatives, a mere knight and a lawyer. The lawyer,
who acted as spokesman, insisted on reading aloud the communication he carried, which was a command to Edward to appear before the French king and answer for his oppression of the
people of Aquitaine. "Let there be no delay in obeying this summons," Charles had written, "but set out as speedily as possible
after hearing this order read."

The indignation of the prince was so great that at first he could
not utter a word. Finally he said in ominously low tones, "We
shall willingly attend on the appointed day at Paris, since the

King of France sends for us; but it will be with our helmet on our head and accompanied by sixty thousand men."

When the two ambassadors had withdrawn (they were later arrested for having left without obtaining passports), the prince had at first nothing to say. The scene had drawn heavily on his small store of strength. Finally he remarked to those about him, "By my faith, the French must think me dead already."

It was clear to his people that his days for action were numbered. The prince managed to retain his hold on life for six years after the malady first settled upon him, but there was never any doubt of the ultimate result. Some medical men held it to be a fever, others declared it a serious attack of dysentery. It was almost certainly one of the slow degenerative diseases, perhaps of a cancerous nature, about which the doctors of the day knew absolutely nothing.

After this step the French king moved swiftly to prepare the way for war. Offers were made to the Free Companies to join the service of France at high pay, and some accepted. The Low Countries were won away from their English alliance. Scotland and Aragon were notified to be ready to act. To mask his intentions, however, he sent an embassy to London to discuss the situation and to present the English king with fifty pipes of wine. On one day three things happened: the French plenipotentiaries departed from Dover, Edward returned the fifty pipes of wine, and a scullion of the French king arrived with a formal declaration of war. The French king seemed to take a bitter satisfaction in thus belittling his opponents.

The Black Prince now found that he had need of all the help he could get. His first move was to summon back Sir John Chandos, who had left when his advice against the hearth tax had been unceremoniously brushed aside. Appointed seneschal of Poitou, Chandos found it impossible to accomplish much. Another force under the Earl of Pembroke, who was an aristocrat to the tips of his steel gloves, being married to a daughter of the king, and who probably knew little about war (he succeeded in losing the whole English navy in an engagement with the Spanish), refused to co-operate with Chandos because he was only a knight bachelor. Chandos, with a tiny force, was killed at the bridge of Lussac. A third English force under Sir Simon Burley was defeated at Lusignan. The war was going so wrong and the condition of the Black Prince was so obviously bad that King Edward sent out John of Gaunt to take control. When the brothers met at Cognac, where the Black Prince arrived in a litter and in a sinking condition, the transfer was effected without any hard feelings.

But when the Bishop of Limoges handed that city over to the French, the sick warrior roused himself to a final act of retaliation; and in doing so left a blot on his reputation that nothing could erase. Still in his litter, he led an army against Limoges, breathing defiance. After a siege of a month, a mine was sprung under the French walls which opened a great breach in the masonry. The prince was borne through the breach, crying out orders for the city to be sacked.

The order was carried out. Even Froissart was startled out of his partiality in reporting what followed. The innocent people of the city were brutally murdered in the streets while the prince, his wasted face convulsed with rage, refused to allow mercy. The heritage of Tortulf and Fulk, his Angevin ancestors who were noted for their savagery, had him in its grip. Still, he responded to the teachings of chivalry when he saw three French knights defending themselves with great courage in the streets. He cried out that they were to be spared, and later he pardoned the bishop who had been responsible for the whole thing. But, according to Froissart, three thousand common people were slain in cold blood.

Soon thereafter the prince returned to England to die, leaving his brother to carry on the almost hopeless task of holding back the French. John of Gaunt, a rather indifferent leader at best, was not able to accomplish much.

CHAPTER SIXTEEN

These Great Fighters

1

THE peace of Bretigny did not end the war in France. It left the soldiers who had been engaged in it without any gainful occupation. The Frenchmen as well as the English and the Gascons proceeded to form themselves into large bodies known as Free Companies for the purpose of indiscriminate looting of the French countryside. Never before had an unfortunate land suffered as much as France in the long black years that the Free Companies were at large.

Two outstanding Englishmen who turned themselves into brigands were Sir John Hawkwood and Sir Robert Knollys. Hawkwood played a short part in the saga of French despair before taking his famous organization, known as the White Company, to Italy, where they sold their swords and their longbows to the warring cities on the Lombardy plain. Knollys, who had risen from the ranks, stands second in prestige to stout John Hawkwood. All France feared him, and he did his work so thoroughly that he returned to a peaceful manor in Norfolk with a large fortune and died at a ripe old age.

King Edward did not openly countenance the activities of the Free Companies, but he did not hesitate to share in their illgotten gains. He sent ships with supplies to Knollys—fresh bows and arrows, and armor, and gunpowder—and received back cargoes of loot and French wines, a businesslike arrangement which enabled Knollys to continue his depredations and at the same time filled the pockets of both men. It was fortunate for the English king that such an opportunity arose to supplement his income. After Bretigny, he again stood on the threshold of bankruptcy.

There were other men among the Free Companies who played bold and aggressive parts. The best of them, after the remarkable pair already mentioned, was quite clearly Sir Hugh Calveley. He had fought well all through the wars. He had the head of a giant, with a strong jaw and a receding forehead (the face, in fact, of a born fighting man), with red hair and long teeth like tusks. It was said of Sir Hugh that he could eat as much as four men and drink as much as ten. Calveley was a full partner with Knollys in many spectacular exploits and was always noted for a fearless impetuosity which made him irresistible in the field. He lacked, however, the cool judgment of a good general and so during the campaigns he was never entrusted with an independent command. In the years of the Free Companies, he deferred to the wisdom of Knollys.

Other names which are sprinkled throughout the records of these grim days are Sir James Pipe, Sir Nicholas Dagworth, Sir William Elmham, and a picturesque knight from the Poitevin country named Sir Perducas d'Albret. None of them quite achieved a position with the leaders.

Then there was that loyal and brave Gascon who would not descend to loot and who comes continuously into the history of that time, the Captal de Buch. Jean de Grailly was the perfect knight-errant, particularly in his undeviating adherence to the oath of allegiance he had sworn to the English overlords of Gascony. The Captal was a confidant and invariable companion of the Black Prince and had fought in most of the battles of the long war. It will be recalled that he played a great part in the victory at Poictiers by his bold charge into the French flank with a mere handful of mounted men.

The title of Captal originated in Gascony, where it had a rather loose application, used only by men of the highest rank but referring to degree rather than position. In other words, it meant a great count or an illustrious viscount; a perfect application, therefore, for a man as courageous and fine as Jean de Grailly.

The Captal de Buch wielded a deadly battle-ax in conflict but was unfortunate in his one chance to direct an independent force. It came about this way. He was in command of a considerable body of Gascons and at Cocherel he encountered the redoubtable French constable, Bertrand du Guesclin. The constable was a shrewd leader. After studying the battlefield with a keen eye, he raised his mailed fist and pointed at the open space in front of the Captal de Buch, where the dreaded battle-ax of the mighty Gascon had caused the French to draw back.

"Sirs," he cried, "there stands the Captal, as gallant a knight as can be found today on all the earth. Set we then a-horseback thirty of ours, the most skillful and the boldest. They shall give heed to nothing but to make straight to the Captal, so they may carry him off amongst them and lead him some whither in safety and hold him till the end of the battle. If he can be taken, the day is ours!"

The plan succeeded. Thirty armed men suddenly broke through the ranks about the Captal. His mighty battle-ax could not prevail against such odds and he was carried off a prisoner. The mighty Du Guesclin proceeded then to shatter his leaderless forces.

This proved to be a great blow to the pride of the gallant Captal. There was not an Englishman with him and he had hoped to demonstrate the greatness of the Gascons.

He was ransomed and had his revenge at the battle of Navarrete, where Du Guesclin was captured and placed in his custody. Years later he was taken by the French and because he refused to break his oath of allegiance to the English prince he was held in a French prison until he died.

Jean de Grailly was chivalrous in every respect and so deserves to be classed with the two English knights who stand at the head of the paladins of that period, neither of whom had taken any part in the peacetime marauding of the Free Companies, Sir John Chandos and Sir Walter Manny.

2

The True Knight

One of the few intimate glimpses that history affords of Sir John Chandos was early in his career. A Spanish fleet had been ravaging the English coast. They were an arrogant lot, the Spaniards, fully convinced they could sweep the seas of any English fleet which might venture out against them. Nevertheless, the ships of the royal navy had come out, with King Edward himself and many of his leading people on the cog *Thomas*. Having disposed of the French navy at Sluys, the English were not too apprehensive; and yet there was some doubt, for a tradition of invincibility surrounded the Iberian fleet and at close range their ships seemed monstrous and most amazingly equipped. There was tension, a tendency to stiff lips and clenched fists, among the group about the king.

Beside the king stood Sir John Chandos, a tall lath of a man with an extraordinary face; completely clean-shaven, with a hawk-like quality and an eye puckered in blindness from a battle wound (not covered with a patch, for there was no hint of vanity in Sir John); an air about him of austerity and a hint of deep spirituality. A band of minstrels had been brought aboard, perhaps to raise the spirits of the crew, and they were pounding out a light tune which Chandos himself had brought back from Germany.

An idea occurred to the king. It would please him much, he said, if Chandos would sing the song with the minstrels. The knight nodded and climbed to the poop deck (or whatever equivalent they had at the time), where he lined up with the musicians. Like a great cavalry leader of a much later date, the Confederate general Jeb Stuart, Chandos was quite an accomplished minstrel himself, with a high, clear voice. He threw himself into the song with complete nonchalance, as though there was not a Spanish sail on the skyline. He could be heard all over the ship and on some of the other vessels of war, for fleets were disposed to sail in close formation. The musicians set themselves to their work, feet began to tap to the tune all over the cog *Thomas*, and, when the knight had finished, any tendency to tension had vanished.

The brave tars settled to their work with complete confidence and gave the Spaniards a thorough drubbing.

Sir John Chandos was a true knight. He would have been chivalrous if the code had never been invented. It was born in him; but it went much deeper with him because it not only committed him to extremes of bravery but filled his soul with compassion for people in all ranks of life and gave him the inner courage to stand by his beliefs.

Some of his career has already been covered through the preceding narrative, particularly the historic moment when he and the Black Prince mounted their horses and led the drive to victory down the vine-clad slopes of Poictiers. He was probably the closest friend the prince possessed and he was consulted on most matters. Sometimes the heir to the throne listened to the candid advice of Chandos, but on two occasions he did not; and both times it soon became apparent that the austere knight was right.

When the peace of Bretigny had been signed, King Edward rewarded Chandos with the St. Sauvier estates in Normandy and the latter settled down there, believing the wars to be over. He had also been appointed, however, as lieutenant and regent of

King Edward in France. This soon involved him in more fighting and, incidentally, led to the greatest achievement of his life.

The succession in Brittany was still unsettled. Charles of Blois, who was not a soldier by choice, had an ambitious and arrogant wife. The latter would not agree to any compromise which did not bring Brittany undivided to her and her heirs. "Either you shall be duchess or I will die in the cause," declared her husband. So he brought a French force to the castle of Auray which was being besieged by the Montfort adherents under the command of Sir John Chandos. The Blois forces included a remarkable knight, Sir Bertrand du Guesclin, who was destined to become constable of France and the best-remembered figure in French medieval history. A great day, then, in the annals of warfare, England's true knight and France's future constable, facing each other for the first time at this little and not too important castle!

Sir John, who had become accustomed to the bad generalship of the French, was astonished to discover at once that this young Du Guesclin knew what war was about. The French lines were vigorously directed, but in the end Chandos prevailed. Charles of Blois, absurdly conspicuous in a white ermine cloak, was killed and his men fell into a panic. Bertrand du Guesclin, armed with a huge iron hammer, continued the fight almost singlehanded until Chandos, finding his way through the melee, cried to him: "Messire Bertrand, the day is against you. Yield to me."

Later Du Guesclin was asked to set the amount of his own ransom. To the astonishment of everyone, he named the enormous sum of one hundred thousand crowns. It was not pride which caused him to agree on this figure. "I know a hundred knights in my native land who would mortage their last acre rather than Du Guesclin should languish in captivity or *be rated below his value.*" This may have been true, but it is said that Queen Philippa, when informed of what had happened, cut the figure in half; and he was brought out of captivity for fifty thousand crowns. Another lady had figured in the story of the battle of Auray, Du Guesclin's beautiful but fay wife, Typhaine, who tried to prevent the clash because her tablets of the stars said it would be a bad day for him. Chandos had no wife to play any part in this, his greatest military achievement. He remained single all his life because he had no time for matrimony and perhaps also because of an admiration for the fair sex so general that he could not find one to exclude all others from his mind.

It was three years after the victory at Auray that the Black

Prince involved himself in the dynastic struggles in Castile. Pedro the Cruel, a beast in human guise, had so alienated his subjects that they rose in rebellion, as already told, under Henry of Trastamara. Thrown off the throne, Pedro appealed to the Black Prince. Edward was not in the best of health and his life might have been prolonged had he remained peacefully at Bordeaux, the home he loved above all others. But it was not hard to convince him that it was his duty to support a rightful king against his rebellious subjects. This was the first occasion when the fervent arguments of Chandos were disregarded. He had good company in opposition, for the one-time Fair Maid of Kent, now the Princess of Wales, was also against any interference; even though Pedro, to win her over, presented her with a table of gold so large that it had to be carried on the shoulders of four men.

Chandos was Edward's man, however, so he went along in command of one division of the army which the Black Prince led across the Pyrenees and he had his part in the defeat of the army of Henry of Trastamara at the battle of Navarrete.

The second occasion for disagreement between them arose soon after. Chandos realized how unpopular the hearth tax would be and begged the prince to change his mind. Sick and disappointed, the latter would not relinquish his plan and asserted his intention so sharply that Chandos left the palace at Bordeaux and returned to his estates in Normandy.

Chandos had been right. The nobility of Aquitaine took such umbrage over the tax that they carried the case to the King of France. War broke out again, and the Black Prince thought immediately of his faithful friend. Appointed seneschal of Poitou, Chandos encased his aching limbs in armor once more and came back into service. He was badly outnumbered in a skirmish at the bridge of Lussac. Tripping on the hem of a long white traveling cloak he was wearing, not expecting to meet the French, he fell on the planking of the bridge and one of the French soldiers stabbed him through the eye. The true knight passed away the next morning. He was the first to die of that remarkable galaxy of Englishmen.

If the prince had listened to his wise and honest lieutenant, they would both have been allowed a longer span of life.

3
The Complete Knight-Errant

The young Hainauter known as Sir Wantelot de Mauny but later as Sir Walter de Manny was of the class of chivalrous knights who excited Don Quixote to his frenzies of admiration. He abided most rigorously by all the rules of the code. Before a campaign he would wear a red patch over one eye and not remove it until he had performed a suitably brave deed. He was always ready to take the most desperate chances. A lost cause drew him like iron filings to a magnet. A resourceful leader as well as a rash participant, he could be described best, perhaps, as a combination of Launcelot and Galahad.

He came to England as a squire in the train of Queen Philippa in 1326 and was knighted soon thereafter, having served with distinction in the current Scottish campaign. As soon as the wars with France began he was completely in his element, as has already been made clear. In 1338 he went to Flanders after taking the Oath of the Heron, swearing to capture a town or castle. This vow he fulfilled in quick order. Taking only forty lances with him, he rode through Brabant and Hainaut and right on into French territory. Coming to a strong castle called Thun l'Evêque, he captured it with a surprise attack. It was one of those bold and strategically useless feats in which the good knights of the day delighted. Tearing off his red patch, the well-pleased Sir Walter rode back to the English lines.

He was with King Edward at the great naval victory at Sluys and was among the first to follow the grappling irons over the side and board the chained French ships.

The bold Sir Walter is seen at his best in his entry into the wars in Brittany. It will be recalled that there were two contestants for the title of duke and that England was backing Jean de Montfort while France espoused the cause of Charles of Blois. Jean de Montfort was taken prisoner, but his wife, who came of the ruling family in Flanders and was known in Brittany as Jannedik Flamm, was courageous enough to assume his place. She threw herself into Hennebonne and withstood a siege by a large French force. She hung on grimly but was compelled finally to promise the garrison she would give in if the help promised from

England did not arrive in three days. The third day was nearly over, and the besieging force had come up to the gates in expectation of a surrender. The courageous Jannedik had gone up to the highest turret of the castle and was keeping a still hopeful eye on the waters of the Channel. Suddenly she sprang to her feet, uttering cries of joy. The harbor below had filled with ships carrying English pennons.

Sir Walter Manny was in charge of the English troops. He came ashore without a red patch but with a burning desire to accomplish something spectacular. The happy countess had a splendid meal ready for him and his officers, but they had barely taken their places at the table when a loud noise was heard. A large rock had come sailing over the top of the wall and had landed in the town. A mangonel clearly was at work in the enemy lines.

Manny's face lighted up. "I think, madame," he said, "that we must take some action about this at once."

Leaving the meat to grow cold on the table, he collected a few of his knights and some archers, all volunteers, and made a sudden sally from the nearest gate. The French troops operating the siege machine were scattered easily and the huge mangonel was destroyed, as well as several smaller ones which were not in use. Before the party could get back behind the town walls, a large force of French knights came clattering up, breathing fire.

"My vows compel me," cried Manny, "to unhorse at least one of these good fellows before I return to the hospitality of our kind lady."

Laying his lance in rest, he rode headlong into the ranks of the oncoming French. It is possible that Don Quixote had this episode in mind when he charged, lance down, at the windmill; but the outcome was more useful for the records of chivalry. The tip of Manny's lance caught one French knight squarely on the shield and sent him down under the hoofs of the galloping horses. Swinging about, he realized that some of his own men had followed his example and that a brisk encounter was under way. The English were badly outnumbered, but the sheer audacity of their attack so startled the French that they turned about and rode away even faster than they had approached.

This incident is perhaps more typical of Sir Walter Manny than anything else that happened in all the years of the French wars. There was, of course, his determination to reach Edward's army in time for the battle of Crécy, which led him to ride through the heart of hostile France and to fall into the hands of the French king. His most successful display of leadership was evident in 1345 when he shared the command of an army with the Earl of Derby and captured nearly sixty castles and towns on the outer edges of Gascony in rapid succession.

The great regret of his life was that he missed both Crécy and Poictiers. He was engaged in the relief of Berwick when the Black Prince marched to the Loire and came face to face with the huge French army of King John. Having accomplished the relief of the city on the Scottish border, Manny reached Westminster just in time to hear of the amazing victory of the prince. However, he accompanied the army of Edward to France after the repudiation by the French dauphin of the treaty arranged with John in his English captivity. He led the scouting party which came closest to the gates of Paris. Never before had mad desire tugged so insistently at his heart strings as on this occasion. Rising in his stirrups, he gazed under a cupped hand at the high walls of the great city. If he had been free to act, he undoubtedly would have tried some rash enterprise, such, perhaps, as scaling the outer wall and hoisting the leopards of England over the gate, if only for an hour. But he was there on strict orders from the king which precluded any foolhardiness of this kind. Regretfully he turned back and rejoined the royal army.

It was on this expedition that he was given the honor he desired above all others. Lord Grey of Rothersfield had died and his place in the Order of the Garter was given to Manny, who had not been included among the original members.

Manny married into the royal family, becoming the husband of Margaret, daughter and heiress of Thomas of Brotherton, the oldest son of Edward I by his second wife, Marguerite of France. It must have been a love match, for Margaret had succeeded to the honors of her father (she would later be created Duchess of Norfolk) and was one of the great catches of the kingdom. Manny himself had been given much property, but he was relatively a poor man. The picture of him that emerges from the brief references in the chronicles of the day is that of a soldier of unusual qualities, friendly and likable, and of much lighter spirits than most of his countrymen. He was a generous man and spent a fortune in the formation of the Charterhouse in London, beginning with the donation of land for a cemetery during the Black Death.

It was characteristic of him that in his will he stipulated that a penny was to be paid to every poor person who had attended his funeral.

4
The Knight with the Iron Fist

When things were blackest for the French and the freebooters were ravaging the countryside, the English soldiers had a saying, "Sir Robert Knollys all France controls." Sir Robert seems to have had a good opinion of himself, as well, for he carried on his device of a ram's horn the words:

Qui Robert Canolle prendera
Cent Mille moutons gagnera.

Which can be translated as follows:

Who captures Robert Knollys most surely gains
A hundred thousand muttons for his pains.

This stocky soldier of low degree, with his lowering brow and split upper lip, became to the French what the Black Douglas had been to the English, a figure of dread. And yet he was in no sense bloodthirsty as some of the freebooters seem to have been. He did not kill for the sake of killing, although he burned and ravaged the country when it suited his purpose. But inside his steel glove there was a fist of iron.

Stout John Hawkwood with his White Company had departed from France and was on his way to the Lombardy plains before Knollys and his close friend, Sir Hugh Calveley, started what they called the Great Company. It was made up of all the best Englishmen left and a fair sprinkling of Gascons. They established themselves in the valley of the Loire, calling that province their "chambre," and in a very short time they had forty castles in their hands, and the personal share of Knollys in this colossal accumulation of booty was said to be a hundred thousand crowns, a constable's ransom. It was at this time that the two daring leaders threw Avignon into a panic by announcing their intention to burn the papal city. Calveley, who was a man of mad impulses, would perhaps have undertaken this feat, but Knollys saw no profit in it; so they did not go nearer than thirty miles and contented themselves later with burning the suburbs of the great city of Orleans. These depredations were so thorough that soon the naked gables of burned houses became known as the "mitres of Knollys."

He had married early and his wife, Constantia, was reported to have been "a woman of a dissolute living before marriage." She was of good birth, however, and had a crest of her own, a fess dancette between three pards' faces sable. From this, heraldic authorities concluded she belonged to the family of Beverly in Yorkshire. She was, at any rate, a woman of spirit and was a perfect mate for a soldier of fortune. At one stage, when he needed recruits, she got together three shiploads of men of an adventurous turn and took them over to Brittany personally.

Knollys and Calveley, who run through the freebooting saga like twin brothers, were at the battle of Auray and were given credit in some accounts for the capture of Bertrand du Guesclin. Early in 1364 Calveley was holding the castle of Le Pont d'Onne against a besieging force led by the great Bertrand. Several assaults had been repulsed and then the marshal decided to try a mining operation. His purpose was discovered by the defenders when a flagon of water, left on a parapet, was upset. Every member of the garrison swore not to have touched it and so it was filled a second time. Soon after it was found on the ground again. This made it clear that tremors in the masonry had been the cause. Calveley put his ear to the ground and heard sounds deep in the earth which he identified as digging.

A bold defense was decided upon. The defense ran out a mine of their own and destroyed the shaft of the attacking force. Du Guesclin found it advisable then to raise the siege.

Knollys had his great chance in 1370 when he was summoned to Windsor and given command of one of two armies which were being sent across the Channel to forestall a French attempt at landing a force in Wales. With an army of fifty-five hundred men, mostly archers but with a certain number of knights among them, Knollys proceeded to cut quite a swath. Landing at Calais, he marched so close to Paris that the watch over the city gates could see the smoke of burning villages. The French king was in Paris at the time but he would not allow any attempt to offer battle. Knollys waited long enough to become convinced that Fabian tactics were prevailing in the councils of the king and then marched westward. The booty secured on this bold foray was almost incalculable. Sir Robert was not having an easy time in his command, however. The knights serving under him disliked taking orders from a man who had risen from the ranks. They called him "the old brigand." Finally a party of them took things into their own hands and set off with a considerable part of the force. Meeting with a French troop, they took a good shaking up and were glad to get on board their transports for home. Here the ringleader laid charges against Knollys, but at the court-martial which resulted the leader was exonerated. The accuser was arrested later and executed as a traitor.

It is on record, nonetheless, that the king had to be placated by a personal gift of a very large sum of money.

For ten more years Knollys was in the middle of things, sometimes in an official capacity, sometimes on personal ventures, and always doing well. Once the Duke of Anjou, a brother of the French king, was trying to capture Knollys' own castle of Derval and executed some English hostages. The old brigand retaliated by chopping off the heads of an equal number of Frenchmen and throwing them out over the walls.

He retired in 1383, after more than thirty years of continuous fighting and a consistent record of success. Settling down at his manor house at Sculthorpe in Norfolk, he devoted himself to charitable work. He had wide estates and so much wealth that he built a chantry at Rochester and a hospital at Pontefract, large enough for a master, six priests, and thirteen people of the poor. This became known as Knollys' Almshouse and it continued in existence until the Reformation.

In 1389 he went to Rome on a pilgrimage and met Hawkwood there. Between them they established an English hospital at Rome. What a meeting that must have been between the two most successful freebooters produced by a country with a remarkable record in that direction: the once black-a-vised but now grizzled Knollys, who was still called in France *le véritable demon de guerre*, and old John Hawkwood, who had just retired after leading the armies of Florence to a conclusive victory over Milan! Brigands they were, but they were more than that: they both had been supremely able leaders. Abstemious in their habits (for no drunkard could keep control of a freebooting company) and not much given to talk, their tongues must have wagged nevertheless with tales of this and that, of the new cannon and the deadly longbow, of comrades dead and gone, and in general of the futility of war, a lesson which must have been very plain to them.

Hawkwood was to have no more than four years of peaceful retirement, but the burly Knollys outlived him by thirteen years, dying finally in his bed at Sculthorpe at an age in the proximity of ninety years. His wife died a few days later and they were buried side by side, the once dissolute lady and the always realistic gleaner of the spoils of war. He had not received the supreme honor of membership in the Order of the Garter.

5

The Finest General of Them All

Sir John de Hawkwood differed in two respects from all the other great military leaders on the English side. First, there was not a chivalrous bone in his body. He did not fight for the sheer love of conflict, for the admiration of fellow knights, for the love of a beautiful lady; he fought for wealth and power, and he became the greatest condottiere of his time, perhaps of all time. Second, he did not treat common people with scorn or unnecessary cruelty. In fact, he preferred when possible to levy on the nobility and the clergy.

Students of his campaigns declare him to be the first general of the modern type and, further, that he has never been equaled at his kind of warfare.

Some say he began life as a tailor in London, and one Italian historian calls him *Granni della Ginglia* (John of the Needle). The truth is that he was the second son of Gilbert de Hawkwood, a holder of land and a tanner at Hedingham Sibil in Essex.

Entering the army under John de Vere, the Earl of Oxford, he came to the attention of the Black Prince and was knighted. When the truce had been made after the capture of the French king at Poictiers, Hawkwood turned his eye to personal gain and became the leader of a body of Free Companions. France was the sorriest land in all Christendom, for even the French soldiers turned to freebooting and the rape of their own home. Hawkwood seems to have been the most successful of all, even though he often acted on the principles imputed to Robin Hood. Certainly he was the first to see that France had been bled white and that the return of the plague, which was beginning again, would complete the work the Free Companies had begun.

He was a handsome man, above the average in height, with the shoulders of a woodsman and the deep chest of a runner. His eye was that of a born leader, keen, luminous, firm. Because of the confidence he inspired among Englishmen who were at loose ends in France, he got the very best of them. He could pick and choose, and his picking and choosing were so expert that he gradually gathered about him a band of superlative strength known as the White Company. Some writers think the name arose from the splendor of equipment they used, but there must have been some more tangible reason. They may have worn cloaks of white, or at least of light gray, or perhaps they had white cockades in their riding hats. It might even have been that the baldrics they wore crosswise on their chests were of that color. Whatever the reason, the White Company, or the *Compagnia Bianca* as it was called in Italy, became the most talked about and the most feared of the Free Companies.

Hawkwood trained his men with a thoroughness equal to that of Oliver Cromwell in a later century and in accordance with his own theories. The company consisted of a thousand lances, a misleading count which came of considering three mounted men as one lance; a thoroughly trained man-at-arms, a squire, and a page, the latter having to be content with riding a palfrey. Both the man-at-arms and the squire rode heavily armed. Their chief weapon was a long lance of such weight that it took two men to handle it. The lance, however, was only for use when fighting on foot, when the stout companions would form themselves into a square or circle and receive the enemy on the lance points. For use in the saddle, they had heavy swords and daggers. Five lances constituted a company, five companies a troop.

With the thousand lances were two thousand foot soldiers, or perhaps it would be more accurate to call them bowmen. Most of them had carried a longbow on the fields of Crécy and Poictiers and they were supremely expert with it. In fact, they had learned a better way of handling that deadly weapon. They would place one end in the ground, which kept the bow firmer and made a steadier aim possible. It may be taken for granted that Hawkwood placed his greatest reliance on his bowmen; having nothing of the Bourbon in him and being quick to learn. These strong-limbed sons of Albion could make twenty miles a day and would be in camp before the weary horses, with their heavy loads, hobbled in on stiff limbs.

Well, here was a France as bare as a bone on a dust heap. And here was the White Company, fit to battle any force in Christendom and avid for spoils. And here was John Hawkwood, the best leader in all the armies. What to do?

Hawkwood knew what to do.

Over the mountainous barrier between France and Italy lay the Lombardy plains, bounteous and fertile and dotted with cities fairly bursting with wealth; all of them fighting with bitter jealousy among themselves. In Lombardy, moreover, was the great family of the Visconti, the dukes and absolute rulers of Milan. The present head of this great family was the ambitious Bernabò Visconti, who was determined to get all of the plain under his rule and to oust the Avignon popes at the same time. Hawkwood decided that the White Company would have a fine future in this warm and luscious land. After capturing the city of Pau as a final gesture (and robbing only the clergy), he made an arrangement with another band of freebooters under the command of Bernard de Salle by which the newcomers enrolled themselves in the company.

Hawkwood spent the rest of his life in Italy, thirty years of almost continuous fighting. To tell the whole story of those sanguinary years while the White Company marched and countermarched across the rich plains would fill a long volume. Hawkwood, whose word was law, changed sides often, sometimes fighting for the Visconti, sometimes against them, at intervals in the employ of the Pope, as often against him. Once he received 180,000 florins as ransom for the Count of Savoy. The city of Pisa paid the company as high as 25,000 florins a month. Sometimes he lost a battle (when pitted against heavy odds), but generally he was the victor. The warring cities bid against each other for his services. When the second son of Edward of England, Prince Lionel, the handsome young giant who stood nearly seven feet in his harlots (as the pointed dress shoes of the period were called), arrived to marry a daughter of Bernabò's, Hawkwood took his band back into the Milanese service and was rewarded by being made, by the left hand, a brother-in-law of the English prince. At least Bernabò gave him in marriage the handsome Donnina, one of his illegitimate daughters. It is not known if the Englishman made this a condition of his services, but it is certain that it was a love match. Bernabò was at war at this particular moment with

Pope Urban V, who had braved the wrath of the French cardinals by taking the papal court back to Rome. Perhaps the pontiff began to show signs of weakening and thus stirred the ire of the Milanese ruler. Whatever the cause, the Englishman found himself chasing the Pope out of Montefiascone and all the way to Viterbo.

The largest amount Hawkwood was ever paid was 220,000 gold florins from a combination of five of the richest cities to leave them alone for five years. Once, when fighting for Rome, the name of the band was changed to the Holy Company, a misnomer which the realistic leader accepted with a wry smile.

The fame of this truly remarkable man as a general rests largely on the campaign he fought on the side of Florence against the almost overpowering strength of Milan. By this time his original company had changed in personnel. Thirty years of continuous fighting had thinned out the Englishmen in the ranks, although a few of the original members were still in harness; the toughest and bravest of the lot, bronzed beyond recognition and still capable of shooting off the finial on a stone gate at a distance of a hundred yards. The armies of Milan, under the command of the Count of Virtue (so called because he was a most villainous fellow), a nephew who had murdered Bernabò, were large and powerful. As commander-in-chief of the forces of Florence, the Englishman won an initial victory. When a second Florentine army, which was supposed to attack Milan from the west, failed to move, Hawkwood found himself alone against the Visconti might. He had less faith in his band now, having no archers save crossbowmen (what a step down from the longbowmen of Crécy!), and he had to stage a quick retreat. The Florentine historian Bracciolini calls his generalship in this extremity the equal of anything in the annals of Roman history. He crossed the Oglio and the Mincio and then had to get his troops across an inundated area caused by the breaking of the ditches on the Adige, a feat of the utmost daring. In the meantime the second Florentine army had been soundly beaten and Hawkwood found himself alone to face the strength of the Visconti.

By the use of brilliant hit-and-run strategy he kept the Milanese armies from uniting and finally succeeded in hammering their main force so resoundingly that they all turned back and sought sanctuary in Liguria. Milan was happy to make an honorable peace with Florence on the strength of this.

During the rest of his life, four brief years, Hawkwood lived in peace in Florence in a fine house called Polverosa in the suburb of San Donato de Torre. He was regarded as the savior of the city and was cheered whenever he appeared on the streets. Knowing that he had little time left, he transferred all his castles and holdings to the government of Florence for sums of money, intending to return to England. His beloved Donnina was still alive and his three daughters were married to high-ranking captains in the Florentine armies; but he longed for the cool breezes and the green fields of his native land. Death forestalled him and the grateful republic did honor to his memory with a magnificent funeral.

The one anecdote about him which seems to have survived is that he encountered one day at Montecchio two wandering friars and was accorded the customary greeting of "God give you peace." The leader of the White Company stared at them in silence for a moment before responding, "May God take your alms away!" The poor friars stammered in surprise and had nothing more to say. "You come to me," declared Hawkwood, "and pray that God will make me die of hunger. Do you not know that I live by war and that peace would undo me?"

He had indeed lived by war, but the brief peace which came to him in his final years did not undo him. He left a comfortable fortune to his family when the grateful republic laid his body in a splendid tomb in the choir of the Duomo. His one son had returned to England and later saw to it that the bones of the old warrior were brought home and buried at Hedingham Sibil in a chantry which friends had raised to his memory.

CHAPTER SEVENTEEN

Some Incidental Achievements in the
Course of a Long Reign

1

THE reign of Edward III can be divided into two periods, the days of national glory and the days of decline. Most of the incidental achievements, which may now be briefly mentioned, came in the second period, when the gray goose no longer flew high in the sky. They had no bearing on military matters and so provide a welcome change.

It was at this time that English became the accepted language of the nation, ushering in what may reasonably be termed the birth of English literature. Edward III either initiated the movement or at least gave it his sanction. One of the many churchmen who served for brief periods as chancellor during the reign, William de Edington, introduced into Parliament the famous statute which provided that all proceedings before the courts of Westminster, the judgments as well as the pleadings, must be expressed in English. The statute went further and stipulated that schoolmasters must teach their pupils to construe in the English tongue. This was a radical measure, for Norman-French had been the official language since the days of the Conquest. It took a long time for the enactment to be fully accepted.

Edward had been fortunate in his tutor, a learned and witty churchman named Richard de Bury, who later became Bishop of Durham. It was in his last years that he wrote his famous book *Philobiblon*, which was in a sense an autobiography although it was devoted largely to books and book lovers, a rare class, it must be agreed, in those days. It was written in bad Latin, say scholars, but when translated into English was found to be most beguiling and witty. He was perhaps the first, and most certainly the most active, of book collectors in England, rummaging in the dust heaps of abbey and cathedral archives and rescuing the volumes which made his personal library larger than those of all other bishops combined.

This period produced five rather remarkable writers of widely different gifts. The first, of course, was Geoffrey Chaucer. Born in 1340, he did not achieve any prominence in letters until near the close of the reign. His youth was spent in the Vintry, where his somewhat wealthy citizen father had a house of two cellars, a hall, a parlor, a solar bedroom with a chimney and a privy, a kitchen and larder and chambers in the garret. From this substantial home could be heard very distinctly the deep bass notes of the bells of St. Martin-le-Grand tolling the curfew. Here an observant eye could see enough of life to prepare him for the writing of the wonderful tales he later produced in the native tongue. The productive period of the poet coincided with the closing of the deep shadows about the senile king.

John Gower, called the prince of poets, was born in 1325 but did not produce his serious work until he had reached his mature years. One of his major works, *Confessio Amantis*, was written in the English tongue and was a monumental effort of thirty thousand rhymed lines.

Little is known about Will Langland except that his long narrative poem, *Piers Plowman*, was the most noteworthy single effort in the native tongue at this period. In this passionate picture of the life of the common people, he not only displayed intense feeling and power but won himself recognition later as the spokesman of the lower classes.

Jean Froissart came to England bearing letters of commendation to Queen Philippa. He served for a time as secretary to the queen and was given every opportunity to observe and set down the things which transpired. He was born for the life of courts, having a fanatical enthusiasm for knights who lived by the code and who spent their days in the pleasing occupation of snipping, slashing, shearing, mutilating, and disemboweling each other. If he had been content to remain permanently in England on the fat pension that the lavish Edward would have provided for him, he would undoubtedly have produced a great mass of biased but readable and useful history in his *Chronicles*. Many incidents which are no more than a scratch on a page of history would have come to life in some form or other if Messire Jean had been on hand to track them down and present them in his pleasant but irresponsible prose. What stories he might have told! Of the great

John Hawkwood who formed the White Company; of the Lady
Joan de Clisson whose bitter grief over the unjust execution of her
husband by the French king led her into piracy in the English
Channel; of the long and silent conspiracy of the villeins of England which culminated when John Ball had "rungen their bell";
of the real story of Dick Whittington with his cat and the voices
he heard in the bells!

But Froissart went later to France and transferred his enthusiasm to the exploits of French knights.

The most important of this first school of writers from one
standpoint was a strange young character who became known as
the Hermit of Hampole. His name was Richard Rolle. Feeling the
desire to live a detached life, he took two kirtles of his sister's, one
white and one gray, and a rain hood of his father's, and in this
patched-up costume lived in the woods near his home in solitary
contemplation. Later he went farther afield and first attracted wide
attention when he entered a church at Dalton, put on a surplice,
and delivered a sermon of passionate fervor. The rest of his life
was spent in a cave at Hampole near the Cistercian nunnery of St.
Mary and was devoted to writing messages on spiritual and inspi-
rational questions in the vigorous but little-known dialect of
Northumberland. He preached a gospel of hope and joy in a period given over to gloom and despair. The nuns aided him by pre-
serving copies of his work in his own hand in their choir bonds.
He was carried off in 1349 by the Black Death, which seemingly
could penetrate into dense forests and the deepest caves.

Richard Rolle has been called the father of English prose because he was the first to give written form to what had only been
spoken before, an amalgam of Old English, Norman-French, and
Latin, the basis of the present tongue. His fame did not penetrate
the closed circle known as the court, however, except perhaps as
an amusing anecdote about an unhinged recluse.

2

The one branch of the arts in which it may reasonably be
claimed for Edward that he led the way was architecture and
building; and in this field his contribution was largely administrative.

The last quarter of the century saw the change from the Curvilinear style to the glories of the Perpendicular. This was, in a

sense, a revolt from the great elaboration of the Curvilinear period, when beauty in tracery was eagerly sought and other elements were sometimes neglected. The Perpendicular was manifested in a preference for straight lines rather than flowing, a demand for the sterner and more dignified aspects of simplicity.

Edward was wise enough, and sufficiently discerning in taste, to accept the change and put all his power behind it. A Royal School was founded with headquarters at Westminster in the great administrative building over against the abbey. Here the many ventures in renovation and addition were discussed and planned. It is doubtful that Edward took an active part in the purely technical discussions as his ancestor, Henry III, undoubtedly had done. He was always too busy for that, and his departures from the kingdom were so frequent and so prolonged that he had no time left for such lesser labors. It is certain, however, that he always knew in a general way what the master masons were going to do. The costs were tremendous and so the great Plantagenet king, who was always shivering on the brink of bankruptcy, would have to know what his responsibility would be.

Edward's activities in building centered at Windsor and Westminster, but his lead was being followed elsewhere. Richard of Farleigh was at work in the west, his chief contribution being the truly beautiful steeple of Salisbury Cathedral. The erection of Salisbury had been a major triumph for England a century before; a rarely fine building, designed, planned, and raised by Englishmen in the record-breaking space of forty years instead of the centuries which more leisurely races allowed. It had always presented one lack, a suitable main tower. Richard of Farleigh proceeded to supply this.

After completing their work at Windsor, William of Wykeham and his right-hand man, William of Wynford, moved on to Winchester and began their memorable contribution there. William Joy transformed Wells Cathedral and John Clyve designed the chastely lovely tower of Worcester. In addition to these major accomplishments, there were native artists, unsung geniuses of the chisel and the mallet, at work on churches throughout the country. It is in the rare artistry of her small churches that England has always excelled.

The spearheading of this change in architectural design in England is said in some quarters to have been the contribution of Robert de Bury, the wise and witty Bishop of Durham. He was above all others the one who might have felt the need for change, but the evidence available is not tangible or convincing. He went, on one of the many continental missions which were entrusted to him because of his suavity and culture, to visit Pope John XXII, who also has had his place in these pages. John was more concerned in the practical and administrative aspects of the papacy but at the same time he was deep in the evolution of the Palace of the Popes at Avignon. This brought many great architect-masons to the spot, and it is conceivable that the urbane Richard would be a welcome visitor in all cultivated circles and that he would come to know in what direction the thought of the great continental leaders was trending.

This much is certain, that the author of *Philobiblon* met Petrarch at the city where the winds blowing so insistently from the south were no hotter than the controversies raging about the new papal domain. The Italian poet is said to have questioned the English prelate about his island home, which with poetic license he called "the distant north."

In spite of these interesting speculations, De Bury remains a figure on the outside and far removed from the dust of the building sheds, the screech of winches, and the toil on the ramps. On the inside there was a figure whose contribution can be weighed in more concrete terms, Henry Yvele, and at his shoulder a brother, Robert. Of the birth and early life of Henry Yvele, nothing is known, and the record begins with his work in London in the year 1355. This year belongs in the final stages of the first of the plagues, called the Black Death. The plague had turned this teeming capital from a busy, cheerful, confident city into a center of gloom and fear and new-made graves, where one man was left of two and the dread of the unknown hung over all. Men no longer congregated in noisy crowds for fear of contagion. Their thoughts had turned to the life after death, and those who could afford a chantry were sinking their funds in the building of them; a chantry being a small chapel dedicated to the chanting of masses for the soul of one lowly mortal. This was the kind of thing in which Yvele excelled, and he was kept busy in the planning of royal tombs and, later, the breath-taking naves of Westminster and Canterbury. His success was so quick that in 1356 he was made director of the royal work at Westminster. In 1369 this post was granted him for the duration of his life.

There was also a man who must have been a superb craftsman, although his period antedates the swing to the Perpendicular, William de Ramsaye. He was first heard of in 1326, when he was employed under Thomas of Canterbury on the work being done at Westminster. Ten years later he was engaged in the needed repairs and additions to the Tower of London, where he became the chief mason of the king. In 1344 he was engaged on Edward's Round Table, the circular hall which was planned for Windsor. The war with France did not stop all architectural activities, but it did lead to the suspension of this major venture. It was never resumed, although in 1365 the king paid the sum of fifty pounds to one John Lindsey for a table to be used in St. George's Chapel.

How unfortunate it is that little is known of these men. The past yields up so much about the figures of royalty, about the fighting men killing each other with so much zest, even about the dull, rule-ridden, sniveling, and acquisitive creatures in the chancelleries. Although scientists have been known to claim that with one bone the complete body of any long-extinct animal can be recreated, it is impossible to conjure up a flesh-and-blood man of this supreme age of building from a date and an obscure reference in moldy state documents about "our well beloved servant" of such-and-such a name. History pays no heed to the unspectacular citizen who worked hard all day and walked at night to a humble home with dust on his tunic and his flat cap. But in the end the builders have had the better of it. The miracles they accomplished in stone are still standing and still beautiful, even with the disintegration of so many centuries on them, but the battlefields where great warriors died are so encroached upon by modern villas and so befouled by the rotting remains of motorcars and the staves of oil barrels that they do not always repay a visit.

CHAPTER EIGHTEEN

The Days of Decline

1

THE year 1369 marked the beginning of the English decline in power and prestige. First came the visit of the French king's scullion to declare the resumption of hostilities, at a time when the island kingdom was not prepared to wage successful war. In the same year occurred an event which can be considered as of almost equal consequence. Queen Philippa had been suffering for two years from a dropsy and as a result of the disease had become very heavy of body and so lacking in strength that she could not move from her couch. On August 14 the good queen knew that her time was at hand and sent for her royal husband, begging him to come to her at Windsor Castle. When the king arrived, she extended to him an arm from underneath the covers, having still too much pride to want him to observe how gross she had become, and placed her hand in his. The only other member of the family present was their youngest son, Thomas of Woodstock, in many ways the least admirable of them all, being full of pride and truculence, and his good looks (for of course all Plantagenets were handsome) differing from the rest in being darkly smoldering.

Philippa must have been unhappy that her other sons could not be with her; her beloved first-born who was, she knew to her sorrow, very likely to follow her soon into the shades; her amiable, huge-framed Lionel for whom she had felt a protective love and who had died abroad three years earlier after his brilliant marriage to the daughter of Bernabò Visconti; the suave and clever John of Gaunt.

"My husband," whispered the queen, "we have enjoyed our long union in happiness, peace, and prosperity."

Edward, whose affection had never faltered, even though he had not been blind to the charms of others, nodded in silent grief.

"I entreat," she went on, "before I depart and we are forever separated in this world, that you will grant me three requests."

Edward, his eyes brimming with tears, responded: "Dear lady, name them. They shall be granted."

The requests seemed of small moment: the payment of her lawful debts, the fulfillment of the legacies in her will, and her wish that he be buried beside her in the cloisters of Westminster when his time came.

"All this shall be done," declared Edward.

Very soon after this she made the sign of the cross and died. With her passing a serious change came about in the king. His deterioration in body, in mind, in spirit was very marked; and these changes were contributing factors to the final collapse of what he had striven so hard to achieve. There had been signs of it before, a loss of energy, an increasing moodiness, a tendency to debauchery. His tall and proudly straight back developed a stoop, his nose seemed to grow longer and thinner, and his freshness of color gave way to a tallowy gray, his eyes lacked their one-time fire. He still strutted a little and he dressed as usual in the expensive black velvet cloaks and tunics he had always affected, although a carelessness in the matter of food stains could not be overlooked. Even the inevitable cock's feather in his velvet hat seemed to have lost its jauntiness.

He no longer came into the offices at Westminster like a blustering north wind, full of plans, bursting with confidence and pride, keen to be about the affairs of the nation. Instead he was likely to sit in long ruminative silences at his place beside the long marble table, while documents piled up around him and his ministers found it increasingly difficult to get decisions from him. His arrogance, his self-confidence, his ostentation showed only in flashes. He had ceased to be the conquering king and had become, to his subjects as well as to those close about him, old Edward of Windsor, who drank too much and who allowed a haughty, round-hipped hussy named Alice Perrers to lead him about publicly by the nose.

Alice Perrers had been one of the ladies of Queen Philippa's household, and the king had made little effort to conceal his interest in her while his wife was still alive. He had given her a valuable manor house the year before and soon after the demise of Philippa he granted her several other pieces of property. It was generally believed that the girl had already presented Edward with two daughters and that these grants were to provide for them.

The queen must have been fully aware of what was happening, for in her will she left pensions to all the damsels of her bedchamber, naming each (including Philippa the Pycard, who became the wife of Geoffrey Chaucer); with one exception, Alice Perrers. Edward proceeded to compensate his mistress for this omission, issuing an order in the following terms: "Know all, that we give and concede to our beloved Alicia Perrers, late damsel of the chamber to our dearest consort Philippa deceased, and to her heirs and executors, all the jewels, goods and chattels that the said queen left in the hands of Euphemia, who was wife to Walter de Heselaston knight; and the said Euphemia is to deliver them to the said Alicia, on receipt of this our order."

It is clear that there was a story back of this grant. As already stated, the sick and world-weary queen was fully aware that the one damsel for whom she had the least liking, the bold and buxom Alice, had won the favor of the king. She did not want any of her own prized possessions falling into the greedy hands of the interloper and undoubtedly made arrangements to prevent it. All her personal possessions were confided into the care of the reliable Euphemia, in the hope that they could be kept safely until such time as they might be distributed to those for whom the queen had intended them.

But courts are hotbeds of gossip and tittle-tattle. It was impossible for such a plan to be made without some word of it getting out. It came to the ears of Alice Perrers, who probably had anticipated some such action. The mistress of a king always has many enemies, but it is also true that there are invariably other members of the court sycophantic enough to hitch themselves to the rising star. The word of what the dying queen had done was whispered into the alert ear of the favorite and she lost no time, once the queen was dead, in going to Edward. There may have been quite a scene between them, but in the end the mistress won. She received the jewels and other possessions, and the story of what had happened went into quick circulation outside the palace.

All England soon learned the shoddy step into which the king had been cajoled by his favorite. Indignation was felt everywhere and the pride of the people in their once magnificent king began to wane.

2

After the death of the queen, Edward tossed shame aside and had Alice Perrers constantly with him. He held a great tournament at Smithfield and selected her in advance as Queen of Beauty. They rode in a colorful procession through the Chepe Ward from the Tower, with the beauteous Alice in the lead and wearing a costume which won her the description of Queen of the Sun: a rich yellow gown, covered with gold and precious jewels, and a flaring headpiece of the same color, all of which accented her lively brown eyes and long dark hair. In her train rode a number of ladies, some of the court, some of much less lofty degree, but all of them more wantonly attired than the favorite because they had donned men's attire, with parti-colored tunics and tight hose and gold and silver girdles. All of them were very gay and noisy, ogling the knights who rode with them knee to knee. This was at best the fringe of the court, of course, none of the women being of good birth or standing; perhaps it might have been the medieval equivalent of what is now called "the younger set."

The whole nation was shocked, the clergy indulged in pulpit tirades; but the tournaments went on, and the people turned out in dense crowds to gawk at the brazen hussies. The king seemed to be enjoying himself immensely.

His relationship with Alice Perrers took on a more dangerous aspect when she began to play the part of a medieval Madame Maintenon, sitting beside him at meetings of the council and actually ensconcing herself on the bench at Westminster and advising the judges as to what their verdicts should be. She lacked the finesse of the French dictatress, and her methods of interference became so open at last that a parliament called the Good took a step which had never been dared before. It publicly chided a king's mistress by name and ordered her expelled from court. How the Henrys and John and Edward I and Edward III himself in his prime would have raged and roared and sharpened the ax and called loudly for the execution of all of them for this invasion of royal privilege! But poor old Edward of Windsor had outlived his fighting days. He took the reprimand like a schoolboy and actually did keep the indignant Alice away until a new parliament, called the Bad, came into existence and restored her to favor.

Not much is known about this lady who flaunted the preference of the aging king more openly than any of the bevy of mistresses of Charles II would ever do. Efforts have been made to prove that she was a woman of common birth, even a domestic drudge. This, however, seems absurd, because no one who had handled a broom or wielded a scrub brush would have been raised to the circle of the queen's ladies-in-waiting. It is reasonably certain that she was of the family of Perrers in Hertfordshire, the daughter or perhaps the niece of the Sir Richard Perrers who had been sitting in Parliament earlier. Edward, becoming credulous in his old age, assumed that she was unmarried. He refused to believe she had a husband when the fact was brought out publicly, basing his stand on the grant to her of the manor of Oxeye (which involved her in furious altercation with the monks of St. Albans), in which she was described as a spinster. It soon became apparent, however, that she was married to one William de Windsor, who was willing to play the role of wittol.

In spite of this her power over the ruler grew steadily and she began to interfere in both royal and bench decisions. Not content with thus displaying her power over a king who had fallen into his dotage, the ambitious Alice went still farther afield. She entered into some kind of secret alliance with John of Gaunt, who was prepared to take advantage of the disorder which had descended on the kingdom. She undoubtedly had some part in the political chicanery which first kept the king from summoning a new parliament and later led to the calling of the well-packed body known as the Bad Parliament. Things had reached a sorry pass in England by this time; with the king behaving like a senile pantaloon, the Black Prince dying, and John of Gaunt, who had an instinct for mischief-making but lacked the courage to come out into the open, hovering about and pulling strings. It was a situation which gave boundless opportunities to a woman like Alice Perrers, and she seems to have taken full advantage of it.

So much for the fair Alice up to this point in the sorry tale of the last years of Edward. It has been assumed that she was fair, although the chronicles of the day are not specific about her appearance. One even goes to the length of calling her plain and asserting that she succeeded by "blandishment of her tongue." She undoubtedly had a tongue skilled in the tattle of the court, but that would hardly have been enough. It might help to hold the aging philanderer, but she would have needed a pair of sparkling eyes and a trimness of figure to win him in the first place. The point is not important; whatever her weapons, she had caught him, and she seemed capable of holding him in spite of everything.

3

Merlin had predicted that one day an eagle would fly out of Brittany to rescue France, and the truth of this was eagerly accepted when Bertrand du Guesclin came into prominence in the middle years of the long war. He had been born in a quiet valley called Glay Hakim, the ugly-duckling son of a beautiful mother. He had a squat figure and a face somewhat on the order of a gargoyle, but he had enormous strength in his misshapen body, and inside him there burned a greatness of spirit such as nature creates only once in many centuries. His merits as a leader were so manifest after the Castilian campaign that the new King of France, Charles V, had the great good sense to appoint him constable of France instead of selecting one of the titled nonentities of his court. Du Guesclin himself protested that a poor knight-bachelor without fortune was not fit to lead the lords of France. The king, who had suffered enough from the incompetence of the lords of France, insisted.

The appearance of Bertrand du Guesclin as leader of the French changed the whole course of the Hundred Years' War.

There was a bad moment at the very start, however, when the new constable found that the army he was to command consisted at that precise moment of five hundred men-at-arms. Now he had been fighting the English long enough to know that to win battles from them he would need trained archers using bows as powerful as the dread longbow; this, above all else.

"Sire!" he cried. "These are but a breakfast! What am I to do with them?"

"You understand war," declared Charles. "But I understand peace. I will not risk a battle."

This was the policy that the new king, remembering Crécy, Poictiers, Auray, and Navarrete, had decided upon. He would not throw great armies against the English on open fields. Nobles and knights he had by the thousand, but they had proven their inability to win battles. And where in France were there archers to equal the green-jerkined bowmen of England? No, the new plan was to wear the invaders out from behind castle walls and by forcing them into continuous marching and countermarching.

With the Black Prince close to death's door, the old king had to leave the command of his armies to John of Gaunt, who had some military capacity but who most certainly lacked the genius of his father and his older brother. Encountering a defense in keeping with the new French plan of campaign, the English armies which were sent across the Channel had to wander about in pursuit of forces which seemed to dissolve like marsh mists. Whenever the English paused to attack a castle, they found the story a different one. The French fought furiously behind their tall stone walls, and it was seldom that anything could be accomplished by siege operations. The English caught glimpses on the horizon of Paris and Rheims and Orleans, but there was little satisfaction in that. With a much larger army than any that the king himself or the Black Prince had ever led, John of Gaunt marched from Brittany to Gascony and saw nothing of Bertrand du Guesclin during the whole of that laborious progress through the heart of France. When he arrived at Bordeaux, his great army had been reduced to a shadow by disease and fatigue. He left the remnants there and hurried home.

The French king had been right. Wars could be won by not fighting battles.

Further proof of this came in every day. The French forces, not meeting any opposition, soon overran the province of Ponthieu, capturing Abbeville, St. Valery, and Crotoy in one week. This was especially galling for Edward of England. It meant that the field of Crécy, where he had won so much glory that the whole world had wondered, went back into his rival's hands. This seemed the most bitter blow that could be dealt him, for Crécy had ceased on that eventful day to be a village in France and had become a great page in English history.

But Charles of France did not have anything like the same respect for the historic battleground. The blame for that shattering defeat rested on the memory of his grandfather, and in the royal family there was no great regard for that bitter and unsuccessful man. Charles had his eyes fixed on a spot farther north, the ancient city of Calais, washed by the waters of the Channel on one side and ringed by marshes on the other, the key to France which that same Philip had allowed the English to take while he sat far back with his futile army. Calais was much more than a piece of hillside where a defeat had been suffered. It was the bridgehead which the English needed so much, an arrow pointed straight at the heart of France.

The French king was so concerned about Calais that he kept relays of mounted couriers riding day and night between Paris and the north, bringing him news of everything that happened, hoping that someday there would be a hint of a development he could use. As he walked up and down in his map-hung room in Paris, he kept his head turned in order that his eyes might always be fixed on that important corner of France which remained captive.

When John of Gaunt sailed for England, Bertrand du Guesclin came out in force and proceeded to storm or to starve into subjection castle after castle and town after town, until he became master of all Saintonge and Angoumois. It was not long before the English possessions had been reduced to Bayonne and Bordeaux and the handful of land around Calais.

By this time the objective of the English had changed. They were no longer thinking in terms of a conquest of France or even the retention of a large part of their holdings. They were realizing that the best they could hope for now was to retain the important points of entry—Calais, Brest, and Bordeaux.

If England could retain the mastery of the seas won at the naval battle of Sluys, it would be relatively easy to maintain bridgeheads on the continent. When the French laid siege to the port of La Rochelle and the Spaniards sent a large fleet to attack that city from the sea, Edward saw that he must act at once. He assembled a great fleet to go to the relief of La Rochelle. It cost nearly a million crowns to secure and equip the ships of war, the largest sum yet expended in carrying on this costly war. Everyone knew the importance of the stake, and the hopes of the nation went with the sails of the great armada when it put to sea under the command of the Earl of Pembroke.

The Spanish fleet proved to be much more powerful than had been expected. As it happened also, the advantage of the wind was with the Castilians when battle was joined. The English commander seemed unable to overcome the handicaps he faced, although he continued to fight grimly for two days. In the end every English ship was either captured or sunk and every Englishman was killed or made prisoner. Pembroke himself was held in rigorous confinement for several years before the French king would consent to having him ransomed.

It should be understood that although the term "navy" has been used in dealing with the war at sea, there was no such thing as a navy in England. The way a fleet was put together was an example of the ruthless methods employed at the time to organize national defense. There were two admirals acting for the king in much the manner that a marshal had charge of land operations. The admirals were always soldiers of some experience and high in the echelons of the aristocracy but with little or no knowledge of the sea. One was in charge of operations in the North Sea and the other had for his share the English Channel. When a fleet was needed, the admirals would be notified to begin, and the first step was to impound every ship that sailed the seas, from the largest cog to the smallest shallop; all of them privately owned, of course. No ship would be allowed to leave any port until the admiral and his aides had selected those which seemed best suited to war service. Not until this had been done and the ships for use had been manned by methods similar to the "press gangs" of later centuries (by which armed parties would come ashore and seize for duty every able-bodied man they could find loose) were the rest of the vessels allowed to proceed with their regular function, the carrying of goods to and from England.

The admirals were in general notoriously unfitted for the work. They would prove so slow that for long periods all the merchant ships of England would be tied up in port, their hulls accumulating barnacles, their sails rotting, while the blue-blooded incompetents boggled about the task of getting the fleet equipped and ready. It happened thus that during these times of incompetent preparation the English flag would be off the seas. Piracy would spring up, with no way of checking it, and the fleets of other nations could ravish the coasts of England.

Edward III had always recognized the extreme importance of commanding the sea but he took no steps to create a national navy. When the need arose, it would be possible to get together a fleet by this time-honored incompetence. When the Good Parliament was sitting at Westminster, the French and Spanish ships were sweeping the seas and burning English ports and fishing villages. The Speaker, bold and outspoken Peter de la Mare, brought the situation up during the attacks made on the disorganization at Westminster. "There used to be more ships in one port," he exclaimed, "than can be found today in the whole kingdom!"

When the Earl of Pembroke sailed for the relief of La Rochelle with the fleet which had been gathered at such monumental expense, every able-bodied seaman from the ports and creeks of Cornwall was aboard, many of them having been "pressed" into the service. This meant that the coasts were left unprotected and French vessels swarmed across the Channel to burn the towns and steal everything they could get their hands on. None of the Cornishmen came back from that ill-fated venture.

4

At this black juncture in what had been such an exciting and brilliant reign, with the king in his dotage, the Black Prince close to death's door, and the war which had been won being now as surely lost, a strange story gained circulation in England. It was told in whispers, for it was treasonable stuff and a man might hang on the nearest gallows for the repeating of it.

On her deathbed, so ran the story, Queen Philippa had made a confession to William of Wykeham, Bishop of Winchester: that Duke John of Gaunt was not her son, nor the son of Edward III. The child she had brought into the world at Ghent had been a girl and through some carelessness had been suffocated. Fearful of the ire of the king, they had persuaded a porter in Ghent, whose wife had given birth to a son at the very same hour, to let them pass his child as the son of the queen. This story the queen swore to with almost her last breath and, moreover, she had laid an injunction on the bishop "that if ever it chanced this son of the Flemish porter affecteth the kingdom, he will make his stock and lineage known to the world lest a false heir should inherit the throne of England."

It was pure invention, of course. John of Gaunt resembled his father more nearly than any of the others. He was of the identical commanding height and he had the same long profile, the same straight nose, and the same eye, restless, intelligent, and vibrant. This may have been one of the reasons why the king had a preference for Duke John over the others. The Black Prince was courteous but austere and reserved; Lionel was an amiable giant; Edmund of Cambridge was of shallow character; Thomas of Woodstock was quarrelsome, intolerant, and fiercely opinionated. On the other hand, Duke John was a brilliant talker, a fine raconteur, an urbane companion. He and his father could talk far into the night over their wine.

The true key to the character of *John of Gaunt, time-honored*

Lancaster, has never been found. He was in his day, and still is, a mystery. Intensely ambitious, he never involved himself, in spite of many opportunities, in any definite move to seize power. It was not a lack of courage which held him back, for the valor of all the brothers was apparent. Perhaps it was a scrupulous reserve which came to the fore when he found himself facing desperate measures. The people of England sensed in him these inward desires for a larger part in the affairs of England than his position on the family tree warranted, and they based their estimate of him on that score, not allowing him any credit for not putting the thought into action.

He is charged with playing an evil part in the last years of his father's life. There is a rather strong case against him and yet there are circumstances which make it hard to accept the verdict of history which depicts him as a rather low kind of criminal, a combination of pander and thief.

A small and ignoble coterie in the offices at Westminster had seized the reins which had fallen from the fumbling hands of the prematurely old king. Some were members of the Royal Council, two belonging to the second order of nobility, the third a wealthy merchant of London. Around this group had gathered a motley crew of hangers-on—thieves, smugglers, and swindlers; and between the lot of them, they were stripping the royal cupboard bare.

The chief villain seems to have been the London merchant, Richard Lyons by name, wealthy, unscrupulous, and able. He provided the funds. The other leader was William, fourth Baron Latimer.

The opportunities for corruption were unusually favorable, owing to the absence of a watchful eye from the throne. All goods exported to the continent were routed through Calais, where the government tax was collected. The members of the "ring" began to sell the right to unscrupulous merchants to export through other ports where the tax would not be collected. Richard Lyons was appointed farmer of the customs at Calais and took advantage of the chance to assess a higher duty than the government had set and to pocket the difference.

The most glaring activity of the inner circle was in connection with the debts of the king. For thirty years Edward III had been spreading his "paper" about, on the continent as well as in England, in the form of promises to pay for money advanced him on loan. Few of these notes had ever been redeemed, and the unfortunate holders, denied the right of suing the king, had long since despaired of getting their money back. Lyons and his aristocratic crew now went to the king's debtors and bought the notes at a staggering discount, paying no more than ten, or even five, per cent of the amount due. They then took the redeemed notes to the Exchequer and had them paid for *at face value*, using their control of the Royal Council to compel payment by the crown officers. The profits in this highly shady business were nothing short of enormous and, as the loss was being sustained by the government, the guilt of the participants was of the blackest variety.

Finally they were guilty of "cornering" the market in commodities for public use. When certain goods were imported from the continent, these honorable gentlemen would buy up all available supplies and charge the public at a much-enhanced figure, claiming that the reason was a shortage in supply. Sometimes, for better measure, they would devise means of bringing the goods in free of duty in the first place, before proceeding to "squeeze" the poor public.

It was claimed that Duke John was the "boss" of this circle of unscrupulous rascals and that it was because of his power over the king that they were able to operate safely. His guilt was accepted pretty generally at the time, and he became so unpopular throughout the country, and particularly in London, that people clamored for his head. Through the ages historians have been inclined to believe in his guilt without much question, although it has been impossible to produce any form of positive evidence to prove his participation in the thievery.

It is hard to believe that a man of his intelligence and ambition would have been so shortsighted as to involve himself in this plundering of the public funds. There was something so mean and repulsive in the operations of the graft-ridden council that one of the duke's background and training would have turned from it with disgust. Because of his first marriage to the Lancaster heiress he was the wealthiest man in England, holding more land and more titles than any of the other princes and peers. Would he stoop to such low practices as the shaving of his father's notes and the juggling of customs duties to increase his fortunes? For him to take the lead in the knavery of graft-ridden Westminster would be proof of bad judgment amounting almost to idiocy.

There are still surer grounds for refusing to believe that John of Gaunt was as venal and stupid as he has been made out. His great ambition was to become a king; of England first or, failing that, of Castile. This is not based on surmise. When the Parliament was summoned in 1376, which was to become known as the Good Parliament, he was very active in a move to introduce the Salic Law into English acceptance. His reason was this: the first son of the Black Prince, the little Edward who had occupied such a warm place in the heart of that great warrior, had died before the health of the prince compelled him to return to England, and this meant that his second son, Richard, was now heir to the throne. Young princes had often been passed over or put out of the way. But if anything happened to little Richard, the next in line for the crown would be Philippa, the daughter of Prince Lionel, the second son, who had died in Italy. Philippa had married Edmund Mortimer, Earl of March, and her claim to the throne could not be brushed aside in favor of John of Gaunt, save by the application of the Salic Law. Duke John was so anxious to clear this obstacle from his path that he conducted a busy campaign of buttonholing (buttons did exist in those days but not in large quantities) among the members of Parliament, but without winning many adherents. The point arises now: If circumstances removed the obstacles from his path, would John, who was openly a candidate for the throne, allow his reputation to become besmirched by participation in the looting of the government funds and in the lowest forms of fraud and thievery? Would he throw away his chance for the insignificant fruits of dirty politics?

John of Gaunt was a man of extreme elegance and sophistication as well as the possessor of a quick intelligence. He could not conceivably have been guilty of such shortsightedness. His course later, which is generally advanced as proof of his complicity, will be shown to have been dictated solely by his deep desire to feel the crown of England on his brow.

It should be explained at this point that Duke John's marriage with Constance of Castile was not proving a happy one. He had fallen in love with a beautiful woman, Catherine, the daughter of a knight of Hainaut, Payne Roelt, and the widow of Hugh Swynford. The fair Catherine, whose sister was the wife of Geoffrey Chaucer, had been given charge of the duke's children after the death of his first wife, and she had fallen in love with her handsome and fascinating employer. She had become his mistress very soon thereafter but, being of fine character and a gentle susceptibility, she had insisted on a careful screening of her compliance.

Now, with his second marriage proving a failure, John allowed his infatuation for the beautiful widow to show.

The populace, always willing to believe the worst of him, took a hostile view of the affair. Bishop Brunton of Rochester, a man of passionate convictions as well as eloquence, attacked the duke from the pulpit, calling him "the adulterer and pursuer of luxury." The duke's love for Catherine, which later led to his marriage with her and the legitimatizing of their children, was linked in the public mind with the shoddy affair of the old king with Alice Perrers. It was charged that the duke stood by his father in the matter of the brazen Alice in order to keep the king from interfering in his own tangled affairs.

5

The Exchequer was empty. There was nothing new about this, because the extravagances of the king and his family had kept the government on the verge of bankruptcy ever since Edward had come to the throne. At this particular moment, however, the emptiness of the national "till" was accentuated by the activities of Messires Latimer, Lyons, et al. It was decided, reluctantly, to summon Parliament and ask for a vote of supplies.

The Parliament which came to Westminster in the late spring of 1376 was made up, fortunately, of men with a serious regard for the public weal and a stoutness of courage to stand out for reform in high places. The members were acquainted with the corruption in the Royal Council and they were determined to do a thorough piece of house cleaning before agreeing to vote supplies.

At no other time in the reign of Edward had there been such a tense atmosphere in advance of a session of the House. The country was in a bad way, the royal family had broken into two sections, the king was soon to die, and the succession had become almost a fighting issue. The Black Prince had watched things from a sickbed in his castle at Berkhampstead with so much apprehension that he now forced himself to rise and be driven to London. He realized that he would have to fight for the succession of his son and that in doing so he would find himself in opposition to the king.

The division of the two houses had not been accomplished then, although the knights from the shires and the citizens from the towns had fallen automatically into one body, while the barons and bishops formed an upper house. The lower house elected a speaker whose duties were not merely to preside and pass on points of procedure. He was the leader, the voice of the commons. It happened that in this crisis there was a bold and convincing voice ready to hand, Peter de la Mare, one of the two knights sent up to represent Hereford. He had been filling the post of seneschal in the household of the Earl of March, which placed him among the opponents of John of Gaunt.

The history of the Commons is a record of great men; fearless, honest, able leaders who risked their lives and sometimes forfeited them to protect the rights of the people. No bolder figure ever arose in a moment of stress than Peter de la Mare.

After the usual request from Chancellor Knyvet for a grant of taxes, the Commons retired to the chapter house of the abbey, taking with them a number of the strong men among the magnates to aid in their deliberations. The decision was arrived at that no taxes would be granted until there had been a systematic house cleaning at Westminster. Mare, elected Speaker, had the task of announcing in full Parliament what had been decided. He spoke with so much authority that the houses drew together as a unit behind him. The demand was made that the men guilty of the Westminster frauds should be impeached.

Richard Lyons, the wealthy London merchant, who was a poor specimen indeed to have arisen in that company of forceful men, appeared next day and proved himself a weak witness, conceding so much that the case of what was called the King's Party fell to pieces. He even acknowledged holding back for himself the receipts paid in at Calais, on the ground that the king had been agreeable. It was whispered about through the house that, in the hope of providing a cushion for himself, Lyons had sent a large sum of money to the king (which Edward did not refuse, saying it was his money anyway) and that a barrel filled with gold was sent across the Thames to the Black Prince, who had taken up his quarters in the royal palace of Kennington. The prince rejected the bribe with indignation. His note to the sender of the gold read in part: "sending back all that the said Richard had presented him with, and bidding him to reap the fruits of his urges, and drink as he had brewed." This did Lyons no manner of good. He was dealt with summarily, being removed from the council, fined heavily, and committed to prison "at the king's pleasure."

Before Latimer appeared in his own behalf, he had Lord Neville speak to the house. This proved a highly injudicious move.

Neville spoke in a bombastic mood which succeeded in raising the hackles of the members. "It was intolerable," he declared, "that a peer of the realm should be attacked by such as they." After that it was not to be expected that Latimer would be treated with soft gloves. His share in the peculations and in the swindles arising out of the king's debts was established; and he was deprived of all his offices and perquisites, including his place in the Royal Council. Sent at first to prison, he was later released on bail.

With the two major figures thus disposed of, the house handled the lesser defendants with equal severity. Lord Neville was removed from the council. Sir Richard Stury was dismissed from office and three prominent London merchants who had been allowed to dip their fingers in the rich pie—Elys, Peachy, and Bury —were forced to relinquish their profits.

After the lords and gentlemen of the council had been disposed of, the house turned to Alice Perrers. She was called before the Lords and was dismissed from her post at court. If she should voluntarily emerge from the seclusion to which she had been condemned, her lands were to be confiscated and a sentence of banishment pronounced against her.

John of Gaunt took little part in the proceedings. He had made no move to defend the members of the "ring," who were supposed to be under his orders. On the morning before Lyons was brought in for questioning, the duke appeared in the house and expressed his desire to have an end made to the abuses at Westminster. He seemed appalled at the nature of the charges brought against the members of the council, which reflected directly on himself. If he had intended to fight the impeachments, he quietly drew in his horns. He had always been a temporizer. Whatever fighting he would do would come later; and in the meantime he openly broached the matter of introducing the Salic Law to govern the succession. He found the house adamant in its opposition on this point. Nothing would be done to lend aid to any ambitions he might be nursing for the throne.

6

The Black Prince had found his old stone house on Fish Street too dark and damp and had moved to the other shore, to Kennington. Here the grounds were open and there were no close walls to keep the sun from the windows. For several weeks he lay there in great agony of body and an equal anguish of the spirit. He knew that everything was going wrong in England. The war was being lost and the administration reeked of incompetence and corruption. It would be a poor heritage that would pass into the hands of his little son, provided the boy were permitted to ascend the throne. There was no certainty that his rights would be observed.

William of Wykeham, who had been discharged from all his posts by the King's Party and forced to relinquish every piece of property he possessed, became the chief adviser of the prince. The passing of the years had brought wisdom and a mellowness of vision to the bishop-builder and, if the prince had been able to rise again from his couch, they would have been a strong team to oppose the connivings of the duke.

But for the prince to take any active part in the warring parties was now impossible. The disease had fastened on him with such violence that he existed in torment. The vital force ebbed, day by day. Finally, knowing that he had few hours left, the victor of Poictiers had the doors thrown open so that all who cared could pass through and see him for the last time. His servants were allowed to come first and he bade them farewell separately. At the end he asked to see his father and brother. They arrived together, knowing what the great prince would have to say to them.

The king's time was rapidly running out, but he was still capable physically of walking and riding. His deterioration had been more of the spirit than the body. His face was crisscrossed with the tiny lines of age, his hands trembled, and his voice, when he spoke, was high and inclined to become shrill; but it was in what he said that the change in him was most to be observed. His once keen mind no longer functioned.

The duke was in a wary mood at first when he entered the room, but the condition of the older brother he had once loved and admired had its effect on him. His face softened as he listened to the halting speech of the dying man.

The Black Prince had his wife and son summoned to the room. Richard was an extremely handsome boy of nine years, a Plantagenet to his fingertips; golden-haired, blue-eyed, as straight as the small sword he carried on his thigh. Although slender, he was beautifully proportioned and there was grace in all his movements. He looked about him mutely, showing the dread that the young have of death.

The Princess Joan, no longer called the Fair Maid but a handsome matron nonetheless, was very much on her guard. She kept her eyes on Lancaster, knowing his ambitions and fearing him for them.

"I recommend to you my wife and son," said the prince in a weak voice. "I love them greatly. Give them your aid."

The Book was produced, and neither the senile king nor the vigorous younger brother showed any hesitation in swearing upon it to maintain the rights of the young prince. It was an affecting scene and brought much relief of spirit to the dying Edward.

Lancaster may have had inner reservations. His course made it clear that, at any rate, they returned to him later. In justice to him it must be said that, when the time came, he remembered his oath. He made no positive move to deprive the boy of his inheritance.

After the king and Duke John had left, the members of the nobility came and swore, each one in turn, to support the boy in his rights. When the last of them laid down the Book, the Black Prince gave them "a hundred thanks."

Prince Edward lived for one more day. "My doors must be shut to none, not to the least boy," he had ordered; and so he lay on his couch while a seemingly endless line of people filed through the room and saw him in his last moments. The agony of death was upon him, but he repressed all signs of suffering. Only when Sir Richard Stury passed him in the line did he express any feeling. Stury was one of the knaves who had profited in the Westminster corruption; he had already been before the house and had been declared guilty and forced to disgorge. The prince had nothing but contempt for him. It was perhaps in the man's mind to make his peace, but the sight of him brought back a flare of anger in the dying man.

"Ha, Richard!" he said, his voice showing the reediness of near dissolution. "Come and look on what you have long desired to see."

The knight tried to protest his loyalty, but the prince demanded his silence. "Leave me!" he managed to say. "Leave me, and let me see your face no more."

It was apparent almost immediately thereafter that this incident had robbed the weak body of its last store of life. The prince sank back on his couch and closed his eyes. The Bishop of Bangor approached the couch and adjured him to ask forgiveness for all his own sins and to cleanse his mind of any feeling against those who had offended him.

"I will," said the prince; but his tone lacked what the worthy bishop desired to hear.

The churchman moved about the room, sprinkling it with holy water, in the fear that some hint of evil spirit remained in the heart of the prince. In a few moments the eyes opened again and there was no trace in them of any hostile feeling.

"I give thanks, O God, for all Thy benefits," he managed to say. "I humbly beseech Thy mercy for all my sins and for those who have sinned against me."

It was on Trinity Sunday, June 8, 1376, that the great prince closed his eyes for the last time.

All England went into a deep mourning that was not only one of form but of the spirit. The dead man had become to them more a symbol of the greatness of the nation than his father, whose faults had always been understood and whose unfortunate last years were robbing him of the respect of the people. The prince had had his faults also, rising from racial traits, but there had never been anything small or selfish about him. It was always clear where he stood. Although he often took his stand against the wishes of the people, it had been on points of principle. While the old king doddered along on his pitiable approach to the grave and while Duke John, filled with undivulged desires and ambitions, made himself feared and disliked, the first-born of the family had died as bravely as he had lived, his spirit never faltering.

7

The course followed by John of Gaunt after the death of his brother made many things clear. He may have been sincere in the abandonment of any idea of brushing young Richard aside, but certainly he was going to make sure that no other obstacle remained in his path. There were possible ways in which this could be done.

First, there was the support of the king. Despite the pitiful condition into which Edward III had fallen, his word might still count if he came out definitely and asserted his desire to be succeeded by his son John. If this happened, he, John of Gaunt, would be absolved from his promise to the father of Richard. In any event, however, it would make him second in the line of succession. The daughter of Lionel and her place-seeking husband, the Earl of March, for whom Lancaster had nothing but hatred and contempt, would be out of the running. Accordingly Duke John did everything he could to strengthen his position with the king; and by doing so made clear certain things about his policy which had been mystifying before, particularly his attitude toward Alice Perrers.

The duke had no illusions about the feeling the people had for him. He knew they disliked him intensely. Why, he could not tell. It had never seemed to matter before; let the stinking rabble clamor against him! But at the same time he was realistic enough to know that popular support might be sufficient to win for him if the old king could not be persuaded to name him, or if the royal wish did not prove sufficient. How could the support of the people be won?

There were two courses open. He could come out strongly against the great nobles and landholders, whose power was becoming more and more obnoxious to the downtrodden people on the land. By the influence he now exercised over the old king he could take steps to break the feudal hold of the barons. The people who had felt no liking for him in the past would turn to him if he obtained for them some relief from the shackles which had been forced on them since the shortage developed in labor after the Black Death.

The second course was to stand out against the exactions of Rome and even to attack the strength of the English bishops. It was with no sense of irreverence that the people objected to the way the best land was falling more and more into the hands of the Church. There was in the Church itself a tendency to think along national lines and to fight against the continuous drain of church revenues to the treasury of Rome. Lollardism, it was called; and there were many Lollard priests preaching to the people against the old order. Among them, and already acknowledged as the leader of the movement for church reform, was a little man at Oxford whose frame was frail but whose spirit was stout and who was deeply learned and eloquent. His name was John Wycliffe.

What if he, John of Gaunt, made himself the advocate and protector of John Wycliffe? Could the acclaim of the populace be won in this way?

The Good Parliament accomplished two forward steps before it was dissolved on July 9. It demanded that the boy Richard be brought to the house and acknowledged as heir to the throne, and it appointed a council of leading men of the kingdom, all antagonistic to John of Gaunt, who were to act with the king on matters of policy. Among the new councilors were the Earl of March, Courtenay, Bishop of London, and William of Wykeham.

As soon as the members had returned home, John of Gaunt began to work openly on his two objectives. He saw the king constantly and made sure that the new councilors were barred from admission to him. Almost overnight he succeeded in undoing everything the Good Parliament had accomplished. Sir Peter de la Mare was thrown into prison at Nottingham Castle and kept there without trial. The council appointed by Parliament was summarily dismissed. Latimer was recalled as a member. The late Parliament was declared to have been unconstitutional and all its acts were removed from the statute books. Finally, Alice Perrers was restored to the favor of the king.

To a man as fastidious as Duke John, the old king's relationship with this brazen woman must have been obnoxious. That he recalled her was evidence of his willingness to go to any lengths to hold the full favor of the king. He still hoped, perhaps, that the senile monarch would select him openly as successor to the throne. As things fell out, there would not be enough time to pave the way for any move as drastic as that.

A new Parliament was summoned the following year, and the duke saw that it was thoroughly hand-picked. Few of the members of the Good Parliament were returned. Sir Peter de la Mare was still in his dungeon at Nottingham and the duke's seneschal, Sir Thomas Hungerford, was selected as Speaker. The only evidence of revolt against the juggernaut methods of the new dictator was among the bishops, who demanded the presence of William of Wykeham. Simon of Sudbury, the Archbishop of Canterbury, who had been playing a somewhat subservient part, was pressed into summoning him to attend. Except for this minor repulse, the duke had things all his own way. Because of the weakness it displayed, this ignoble assemblage of legislators would go down in history as the Bad Parliament.

The duke made one tactical blunder. He attempted to put a harness of his own devising on the citizens of London. His proposal was to substitute a captain for the lord mayor and to put the city under the jurisdiction of the marshal of England, a post filled at that time by Lord Percy, the duke's closest supporter. The men of London, who always played a stormy and independent part in the making of English history, controlled their own courts, and they were not going to let the king's son slip manacles on their wrists.

The night after this proposed step had been introduced in the house, angry mobs filled the streets of London. Thousands of determined men swarmed down the river road to the Savoy. If the duke had been there, his career would have come to a violent end. But he was not there. He was, in fact, having supper peaceably in the city with a wealthy merchant named John of Ypres. A messenger, breathless from the speed with which he had come, arrived as they were settling down to the first course, which happened to be a dish of oysters. The duke, declared the messenger, must fly for his life. Lancaster got so hastily to his feet that he injured a knee and spilled the oysters over his handsome doublet and his well-fitting hose. He betook himself across the river in a very great hurry and found refuge for the night in the one place where the mob would be least likely to seek him, the palace of Kennington, where the widow of the Black Prince lived with her son, Richard. She received him graciously.

Duke John made many mistakes in his life, but never a more serious one than this effort to take away the established rights of London Town. The citizens never forgave him.

CHAPTER NINETEEN

John Wycliffe

1

ALL through the reign of Edward III, with its periods of high achievement, even of glory, its moments of depression, its excitements, its reckless use of life and wealth in the pursuit of impossible goals, there had been among the people a movement toward something greater than military success and more lasting than conquest.

This was not based on new teachings. John Wycliffe, the father of Lollardism in England, was not the first to preach and write of the need of reform in the Church. His beliefs stemmed from the inspired work of Francis of Assisi, who had sent his followers out among the people, to earn their bread by manual labor and the begging bowl, and to devote themselves unreservedly to the service of the poor, the sick, and the downtrodden. The rise of the Franciscans and the other mendicant orders—the Dominicans, the Beghards in the Low Countries, the Fratricelli—had been a widespread one. In England the coming of the brown friars had been welcomed and, although the orders had not continued in their first rigid beliefs and observances, the support of the people had not been lost.

But if John Wycliffe was not the first to favor a Christian church of poverty and service to the great institution of power and wealth, under the leadership of men who were so often able statesmen rather than spiritual teachers, into which the Church had inevitably grown, he was the first to approach the problem from what might be called a practical standpoint. He perceived clearly, and preached openly, that a change of direction could not be expected to come about from within. The strength and wealth of the Church had grown on endowments; the tendency of individuals to leave their property, in part at least, to the Church, in

the expectation of forgiveness and absolution from sin. How could
the great men who fought their way to the top in this immensely
rich and powerful organization be expected to see disendowment
as anything but a mad dream of fanatics and troublemakers?
Wycliffe said openly that the ever-increasing wealth of the
Church could be touched only by lay action; in other words, that
the state must step in.

This was not heresy, but it was an opinion of such tinderlike
quality that it might set fires to blazing all over the Christian
world. The orders which had grown out of the teachings of St.
Francis and St. Dominic had been contained within the Church
and had gradually been moderated and controlled. But this little
man Wycliffe from the scholastic calm of Baliol College at Oxford, where he was master, was proposing an attack from the outside, an assault on the high, mysterious walls of the church edifice
with a weapon as powerful as the gunpowder which an English
Franciscan, Roger Bacon, had invented a century earlier.

If opinion in England had not been so ready to welcome a
weapon of the kind, it would not have been hard to silence the
scribbling pen of this insignificant pedant. But in the island
kingdom there had been a growing discontent, dating back per-
ceptibly to the reign of John, over the gold which left the country
every year, in part as direct payment to the Vatican, but largely in
the form of stipends to absentee holders of English benefices.

The name Lollard, which was given to the "poor preachers"
who went out to preach the beliefs of Wycliffe, came probably
from the word *lullen*, to sing softly. Wycliffe had a stout enough
heart under his plain scholastic gown, but it was not his purpose to
preach passionately and fiercely against the power which existed
behind those high, mysterious walls. He believed that in England,
at least, the reforms he saw as essential could be accomplished
without religious war and the blazing of inquisitional bonfires;
and so the name Lollard was a good one for the earnest men who
embraced his ideas.

The crusade, beginning in the scholastic walls of Baliol and
being transferred later to the rectory at Lutterworth, a quiet parish on the River Speed near Oxford, where Wycliffe spent his last
years, did not come into much notice until the late years of the
reign of Edward III. It was not a matter of much state concern
until succeeding reigns. If the harvest he was sowing so indus-
triously had produced a sudden crop of general discontent, he
would undoubtedly have faced the issue with courage, even if it

meant a martyr's death. As it happened, he died peacefully in his bed at Lutterworth. It was forty-four years after he breathed his last that the hand of ecclesiastical retribution reached out. His bones were exhumed from the grave and burned. The ashes were committed to the waters of the Swift; but by that time the tinder had caught fire and had started flames in many parts of Europe.

It would verge on the absurd to say that John of Gaunt was attracted by the teachings of this eloquent but retiring scholar and priest. But the duke was a keen politician and he was searching eagerly for issues he could use to bring himself support and to counteract the unpopularity he had achieved among the people by his arrogance and disregard of established rights. He saw possibilities in what Wycliffe was preaching and extended a protecting hand. What a curious combination they made: the unscrupulous son of the once great king, who was always ready to trample opposition under his steelshod feet; and the gentle little man whose aim at this point was to see the Church become again purified and strengthened by poverty!

By this time the duke and Lord Percy, the marshal of England, were working closely together. They were as one in seeing in Wycliffe a man supremely able in the art of debate. They proceeded to make it easier for him to get the audiences he desired. He began to preach in London, and it is said he found ready listeners among the court nobility. What many laymen and some leaders in the Church had been thinking was now being spoken boldly and publicly.

Bishop Courtenay of London became incensed at these attacks on the Church. His father was the Earl of Devon and he was a great-grandson of Edward I and, with such connections, he did not hesitate to place himself in opposition to the powerful duke. "He would not," he declared, "hear himself and his order attacked in his own diocese by this unauthorized priest from Oxford!" It was not an easy matter, however, for even as aggressive a churchman as Courtenay to get his fellow bishops to agree on any line of action, particularly Archbishop Sudbury, who was generally assumed to belong to the duke's party. The bishops, it should be pointed out, were strongly averse to the continuous demands made by the popes on their revenues. This feeling had grown since the papacy had been moved to Avignon, where the influence of France was paramount. A few years before, the bishops had met a demand from the king for a subsidy by declaring themselves no longer able to meet the calls made on them by the crown and the papacy. They had said then that they could help the king only "if the intolerable yoke of the pope were taken from their necks." Men who had expressed such feelings could not be expected to find too much fault with a churchman who was repeating what they had said and doing it with a high degree of eloquence and persuasive logic.

Courtenay, however, was not an easy man to withstand once his mind was made up. He brushed aside the contentions of Simon of Sudbury and summoned John Wycliffe to appear before the bishops at St. Paul's.

2

It was on February 19, 1377, while the Bad Parliament was still in session, that the bishops assembled solemnly in the Lady Chapel of St. Paul's. The chapel, which was situated behind the high altar, had been chosen because it was not large, there being no desire on their part to have the hearing before a noisy assemblage. They had not reckoned on the curiosity of the citizenry of London. It was a proud claim of the church that the main aisle of the cathedral was the longest in the world; but when the time came for the hearing, every inch of space was filled with eager townspeople. Even that long aisle itself was packed tight. The issue, quite clearly, was too important in the public mind to allow an airing *en camera*.

John Wycliffe came through the main entrance and found his way completely blocked. He was accompanied by four friars, one from each of the main mendicant orders (who over the years had become anathema to the bishops), as volunteers to aid in his defense, if necessary, as well as to demonstrate their belief in him. That was of small consequence compared to the significance of two others who arrived at the same time. The marshal of England, Lord Percy, strode in front and the duke himself walked beside the Oxford divine.

Percy was a man of imperious temper (and of many other faults) and, when he found the main aisle so packed with humanity that there seemed no way of getting through, he plunged vigorously into the mass, shouting loud demands to the people to stand aside, to remove their vulgar carcasses, in fact, no matter how it had to be done. Bishop Courtenay had remained near the entrance to keep an eye on things, and he now cried out angrily that he would not have his people mistreated.

"Like it or not!" retorted Percy. "We'll allow none of them to stand in our way!"

The assembled multitude seems to have behaved with unusual docility. Ordinarily the touch of the hand of authority on the shoulder of the merest apprentice was enough to set off a riot in the city. The explanation was, perhaps, that the curiosity of the people was great enough to hold their natural combativeness in check. Walking calmly beside the much-execrated duke was the man who had so boldly set the honorable bishops of England by the ears. Some of them had heard him preach, but to most of them he was a stranger.

John Wycliffe walked slowly up the aisle as a path was cleared for him; a small man, and almost emaciated of frame, but with the stamp of greatness on him, the broad brow, the keenness of deep-set eye, the resolute line of mouth, the long white beard of a lifetime of scholarship. To an observant eye, the fine proportions of his forehead gave an indication of the insight and power needed for what was to be the great labor of his life, the translation he was making of the Bible into the English tongue. It was completed, fortunately, before his death, in such seclusion as was allowed him from the clamor of persecution, in the quiet of his rectory at Lutterworth.

He seemed completely at ease, in spite of the ordeal which lay ahead of him, and a silence fell on the swaying, jostling people as he came within their range. It was a good thing that the men of London did not allow their mounting hatred of the duke to influence their feeling for this frail churchman; for this was their chance to see one of the greatest of Englishmen as he faced what might prove his most severe test.

The storm broke when John Wycliffe and his guard of honor reached the Lady Chapel. The bishops were seated about the archbishop in a suitable gravity. The duke and Lord Percy promptly took chairs and the latter motioned to the defendant to seat himself.

"You have much to reply," he said. "You will need the softer seat."

This aroused the Bishop of London, whose stormy temperament stemmed perhaps from his share of Plantagenet blood, to an emphatic protest.

"This is impertinence!" he charged. "The accused must stand to give his answers!"

It was the right of the archbishop to settle the point, but Courtenay did not wait for the complaisant Sudbury to speak. He refused point-blank to permit Wycliffe to be seated during the hearing. The examination might conceivably take several days and it was clear to all, except perhaps to my lord Courtenay, that the frail scholar lacked the strength to remain on his feet for such an extended time. Accordingly the duke declared loudly his intention not to accept the dictation of the Bishop of London. He even hinted in an undertone that if necessary he would drag the bishop out of the cathedral by the hair of his head.

The loud voices from the Lady Chapel had reached the crowds assembled in the cathedral. The Londoners tried to break into the inner room, uttering loud threats. They were held back by the pikes of the duke's guards, and for a time it seemed certain that there would be much bloodshed before peace could be restored.

Throughout the confusion Wycliffe remained standing and did not lose any of his composure. Perhaps he was regretting that he had agreed to an escort. Perhaps, on the other hand, he was realizing for the first time the depth of the feeling he was stirring up in the country.

The final outcome was that the defendant was permitted to leave by another door and the cathedral was cleared as rapidly as possible. No effort was made at the time to hold a delayed hearing, which may have meant that Courtenay had lost some of his influence over his fellow bishops.

The old king, living in his castle of Shene, was entering his final stage of life while this furious controversy shook the capital. In the few months left to him, there was too much else in the way of state problems to be done for the bishops to continue in their determination to try Wycliffe. Probably he returned to Oxford, to the council of his friends and followers. It may have been that he sought instead the quiet of Lutterworth, realizing that little time might be allowed him for the great work which lay ahead. John Wycliffe was no longer content to deal only with the wealth of the Church. Other questions, some of them treading over the borders of heresy, were occupying his mind and in time would command the services of his pen. And there was the translation of the Bible to be completed, the labor which, perhaps, lay closest to his heart.

CHAPTER TWENTY

The Death of the King

1

THE old king liked his palace at Shene (which later became Richmond) so well that he spent his last days there. It must have been a pleasant spot, for his successor, Richard II, used it as a summer palace. The young king made many additions and alterations and is said to have entertained thousands of people there. The life of Richard's court was so elaborate that a combined staff of six hundred people had been needed by his queen and himself.

The views were enticing and the air soft. Edward found it ideal for the weak condition into which he had lapsed. He dozed a great deal and made no pretense of attending to business, although his mistress, who was with him continuously now, kept calling certain matters to his attention, always having to do with favors for someone or other. There was, for instance, the bishop who had been so much disliked by his son John, that busybody who had built some parts of Windsor. She kept talking about him and urging that he be restored to his posts. Well, he might as well sign the paper she kept shoving before him and have done with the fellow.

Alice Perrers had not taken the action of the Good Parliament seriously, for she had come back in spite of all of them. Edward had been pleased to see her because she went to the pains of maintaining a fiction for his benefit. He was getting better, she assured him, and would soon be able to resume all his old activities. He was tired of seeing the doctors shake their heads over him, and what she told him relieved his mind mightily. He did not want to die yet.

He depended entirely on his son John now and, if he had lived long enough, it is certain that many changes would have been made in the interests of the duke. The course of history might have been changed.

It is not likely that Edward gave much time to memories of his long reign. He talked continuously about hunting and hawking and his mind did not wander much from these engrossing interests. When he did think of the past, it was unquestionably with a sense of satisfaction. His had been a remarkable reign. England had become the most powerful nation in Europe, the most feared certainly. If it had not been for the Black Death which had cut the population in half and so reduced the fighting strength of the nation, the leopards might still be waving over the fairest provinces of France and flying in the breeze on a conquered sea. Chivalry had been brilliantly revived and the English court had been talked about as far away as the lands where the Mongols were supreme.

There had been other things that the dull fellows at the chancellery and in the universities had considered important. He did not remember much about such matters. There were the looms which his Philippa had persuaded him to bring over from Hainaut. Now they were making cloth in the country and did not have to buy so much from abroad. Then there had been the change made about the use of English in the law courts and the schools. He recalled that he had been interested in this at the time.

The end came suddenly. His sight had not been good for a long time and then, on June 21, his voice deserted him entirely. He was too weak to do more than raise a feeble hand to indicate his wants. Soon even that effort proved too much and he sank into a condition almost of coma. None of his children were with him, not even the duke who had made a point of attending him closely. The household officials, having been convinced long before of the imminence of death and seeing nothing to be gained now, were paying small attention. Alice Perrers remained in the room and a small knot of household servants and courtiers kept watchful eyes on her. She had never thought it necessary to win the favor of the staff and had been repaid by a general suspicion and dislike.

The king's confessor was in the room, hovering tensely over the royal couch. When the dying monarch recovered enough strength to mutter the words *Jesu miserere*, the priest placed a crucifix in his hands. The royal lips were pressed to the cross. The breathing became less and less perceptible and finally ceased.

Thus died the most brilliant and colorful of English kings. He had lived to the ripe age of sixty-five years and had been king for fifty of them.

The last scene, before the curtain fell finally on that long and spectacular reign, concerns the disreputable favorite of the deceased monarch. Alice Perrers remained in the room until everyone else had left, even the saddened confessor. Then she moved stealthily to the royal couch.

The poor old king had continued through the years of his senility as ostentatious as ever. The rings on his thin fingers were costly and brightly shining with precious stones. The gold chain around his neck was massive and formed many loops. With nervous glances over her shoulder the woman stripped the fingers of the rings and then succeeded in removing the chain. These valuables she made into a bundle which she hid under her gown. Then she stole away on noiseless feet.

Index

J 15